Wm Constable

A

HISTORY

OF

LEWIS COUNTY,

IN THE

STATE OF NEW YORK,

FROM THE

BEGINNING OF ITS SETTLEMENT TO THE PRESENT TIME.

BY

FRANKLIN B. HOUGH,

AUTHOR OF THE HISTORIES OF ST. LAWRENCE, FRANKLIN, AND JEFFERSON COUNTIES, AND CORRESPONDING MEMBER OF THE NEW YORK, CONNECTICUT, VERMONT, PENNSYLVANIA, MARYLAND, WISCONSIN, MINNESOTA AND IOWA HISTORICAL SOCIETIES.

ALBANY:
MUNSELL & ROWLAND, 78 STATE STREET.
1860.

PREFACE.

An interior county, with no antiquities older than some of its inhabitants and no traditionary legends, or incidents of border life, beyond the ordinary privations of a new settlement, appears to offer but slender materials for history. Still there are certain duties which the Present owes to the Future, to transmit in a permanent form the record of the Past, that the memory of the olden time, and the names of those who have aided in the formation of society fall not into oblivion ; and although our annals may be quite void of those dramatic events which have too often filled the historic page, it is believed the quiet origin and growth of our community, have presented facts that will interest the present, and instruct a future age.

In tracing out and connecting the historical items of his native county, the author has been actuated by an earnest wish to do full and equal justice to the memory of the pioneers and founders of the several towns, and any omission or imperfection of statement is due to absence or error of information. All those interested in preserving facts worthy of record, were invited by public notice to communicate with the author, and due industry and care have been bestowed in the verification of our narrative, which may, notwithstanding, contain faults that it would have been desirable to avoid. The indulgence of the public is solicited toward these, and we shall ever consider it a kindness to have them indicated, with the view to future correction, should opportunities occur. To those who have aided by imparting materials for use in these pages, we wish to return thus publicly our acknowldgements, and especially to the following persons :—To Vincent Le Ray of Paris, P. Somerville Stewart of Carthage, Henry E. Pierrepont of Brooklyn, and Charles King of New York for facts relating to land titles. To James L. Leonard, Stephen Leonard, Joseph A. Willard, W. Hudson Stephens, Charles Dayan, A. G. Dayan, Leonard C. Davenport, N. B. Sylvester, Andrew W. Doig, Edward A. Brown, Wm. L. Easton, Henry E. Turner, and W. Root Adams, of Lowville ; Apollos Stephens of Denmark ; David T. Martin, Wm. King, Jas. H. Sheldon and Diodate Pease, of Martinsburgh ; S. P. Sears of Montague ; Charles G. Riggs, Emory B. Holden, Dr. C. D. Budd, Orrin Woolworth, Henry Ragan, Elisha Crofoot, and Walter D. Yale, of Turin; Seth Miller, Jonathan C. Collins, James Crofoot and Homer Collins, of West Turin; Ela Merriam, Ezra Miller, Thomas Baker and W. J. Hall, of Leyden; R. T. Hough of Lewis; Seymour Green of Osceola; Lyman R. Lyon, Francis Seger, Caleb Lyon of Lyonsdale, and Cyrus W. Pratt, of Greig; Nelson J. Beach and Jehiel R. Wetmore of Watson; Josiah Dewey of Delta; Clinton L. Merriam of New York; Wm. Collins of Cleveland, O.; Baron S. Doty of Portage city, and M. J. Stow of Fond du Lac, Wisconsin, and D. P. Mayhew of Ypsilanti, Michigan, for written materials and facts derived from documents. To Daniel S. Bailey, late editor of the Lewis County Republican, Henry A. Phillips of the Northern Journal (now Journal and Republican), Henry Algoever of the Lewis County Banner, and the editors of the New York Reformer at Watertown, for friendly notices of the enterprise while in course of preparation, we also wish to return our thanks. The late Alson Clark of West Turin began publishing, a few years since, a series of historical articles in the newspaper of that town, all of which we have examined, and from several of which we have derived facts. His useful researches were interrupted by an early death. Lewis being the fourth county which the author has attempted to embody the details of local history, an opportunity has been offered of learning from dear bought experience, at least some of the difficulties attending this class of researches. With what success this labor has been performed on this occasion, the following pages are an impartial evidence. The steel plates chiefly by J. C. Buttre, of New York, and the lithographs drawn by C. G. Crehen of New York, and B. F. Smith, Jr., of Albany, and printed by A. J. Hoffman & Co. of the latter place, are mostly faithful likenesses, and creditable as works of art. It would have been gratifying to extend this already unusual amount of illustrations, but of many worthy pioneers and incumbents of public office, no portraits have been preserved.

FRANKLIN B. HOUGH.

Albany, April 16, 1860.

Engraved by J. C. Buttre.

Franklin B. Hough

HISTORY OF LEWIS COUNTY.

CHAPTER I.

ORGANIZATION OF THE COUNTY.

First County Seal.

The rapid settlement of Oneida county on its northern and western borders, had within a few years after its formation rendered attendance upon its courts and the transaction of public business burdensome and expensive.[1] This led to the discussion of plans for division, in which the future location of county buildings became a leading motive with many of those who were most active in preparing the way for changes which must soon necessarily be made.

Redfield, Champion, Lowville, Martinsburgh, Watertown, and Brownville, were each regarded by their inhabitants as entitled to the honor of a court house, and active partizans were engaged in pressing the claims of each. The hopes of Champion depended upon the erection of but one county from Oneida, and in anticipation of this result, several young and talented lawyers had settled there in their professions.[2] Silas Stow of Lowville, and Walter Martin of Martinsburgh, were largely interested in newly settled lands that would be enhanced in value by the location of a county seat near them, and each of the places named had its

1 This region of country, originally embraced in Albany county, was included in Tryon, March 12, 1772, changed to Montgomery, April 2, 1784, included in Herkimer, February 16, 1791, and in Oneida, March 15, 1798.

2 Moss Kent (a brother of Chancellor Kent), Henry R. Storrs, and Egbert Ten Eyck, then resided in Champion.

active advocates of relative and prospective importance. The old settled parts of Oneida county, were far from being united in their approval of the selection of Rome as a county seat, and in the sharp personal discussion which occurred between Jonas Platt on the one hand, and Thomas R. Gold on the other, each had appealed to the public. Active efforts were being made to secure a change, and as the county was ripening for a division, the bearing of every measure tending to this end was watched with interest, and favored or opposed as it affected the prospects of the several parties.

Jacob Brown, then a young and enterprising land agent, surveyor and settler at Brownville, and afterwards major general, had as early as 1797 passed through the Black river valley to Whitestown, and then and subsequently had associated with Jonathan Collins of Turin, Walter Martin of Martinsburgh, and other prominent settlers, with whom he continued a friendly acquaintance, and between whom the plan of two counties from the north part of Oneida was discussed and agreed upon, if sufficient influence could be secured to attain it. Brown's manifest object in conciliating the southern interest, was to so arrange the boundaries that the centre of one of the new counties would fall within his reach; but other influences were at work near each of these parties, equally intent upon two counties, and quite as eager to seize upon the prize. It is not probable that Turin expected to gain the county seat, and it naturally favored the nearest party, but in Lowville, Stow and others were confidently relying upon their ability to prove that the balance of wealth and population centred upon them. The citizens of Watertown were equally active, and the result proved that they were a match for Brown in intrigue or influence if not in both. The northwestern settlers of Oneida county, under the lead of Nathan Sage of Redfield, were indifferent to these schemes except so far as they interfered with their favorite plan of a county, having as its natural boundaries the gulf of Sandy creek on the north, and the east lines of townships 3, 8 and 13 of the Boylston tract on the east.

Mr. James Constable, one of the executors of the estate of his brother William, travelled through Macomb's purchase in 1803, 4, 5 and 6, and has left in his diary under date of Sept. 20, 1804, a notice of these plans:[1]

[1] This diary is written out with great care from observations made upon the spot, and abounds in interesting historical details; we shall have frequent occasion to quote from its pages.

* * * "Finding that Mr. Shaler was from home, and not knowing what situation his people were in, we went to Squire [Jonathan] Collins, who although he has left off keeping tavern, received and entertained us kindly from a very heavy rain. He gives us some information of the local proceedings about roads, the division of the county and other intrigues, and with what I have heard from other quarters it appears that Stow and Martin had made themselves very obnoxious and they will differ about the division of the county on their side of it. Each will be supported by opposite interests, and they will both be defeated by the management of the proprietors of Redfield or that of Jacob Brown of Brownville.

Each of the gentlemen requires a court house near to himself, and if they are all to be gratified, Oneida must be divided into five; but there will be opposition to their wishes and perhaps to any division of the county, which would be for the interest of the land owners as the extra expense would be saved. There will be a contest for the clerkship as Mr. Martin, Mr. Stow and Mr. Kelley, brother-in-law to Stow are all candidates. Mr. Stow has declared publicly he will have it in spite of all opposition, but the people are most in favor of Mr. Kelley.[1]"

To give definite form to these movements a convention of delegates, mostly chosen at special town meetings was called to assemble in Denmark village to unite in an application to the legislature for a division of the county. One of these delegates[2] has assured us that the majority of those sent, were instructed to vote for but one new county. The result of their deliberations is best shown by the record of their secretary which is as follows:

"At a meeting of three delegates from each of the towns of Brownville, Watertown, Adams, Ellisburgh, Malta,[3] Harrison,[4] Rutland, Champion, Harrisburgh, Lowville, Martinsburgh and Turin, convened at the house of Freedom Wright in Harrisburgh,[5] on Tuesday, the 20th day of November, 1804, Jonathan Collins in the chair; Egbert Ten Eyck, secretary:

On examination it appeared that the following persons were regularly chosen to represent their respective towns at this meeting.

Jacob Brown, John W. Collins, Benjamin Cole, for *Brownville;* Tilley Richardson, Henry Coffeen, Solomon Robbins, Joshua Beals for *Adams;* Lyman Ellis, Matthew Boomer, jr., John

1 It will be noticed elsewhere that Richard Coxe was appointed.

2 William Coffeen, then of Rutland. 3 Now Lorraine. 4 Now Rodman.

5 The present town of Denmark was then included in Harrisburgh.

Thomas, for *Ellisburgh;* Asa Brown, Clark Allen, William Hunter, for *Malta;* William Rice, Cyrus Stone, Simeon Hunt, for *Harrison;* Cliff French, Abel Sherman, William Coffeen, for *Rutland;* John Durkee, Olney Pearce, Egbert Ten Eyck, for *Champion;* Moss Kent, Lewis Graves, Charles Wright, jr., for *Harrisburgh;* Silas Stow, Jonathan Rogers, Charles Davenport, for *Lowville;* Asa Brayton, Clark McCarty, Chillus Doty, for *Martinsburgh;* and Jonathan Collins, John Ives, Elijah Wadsworth, for *Turin.*[5]

The above names being called by the secretary, respectively answered and took their seats. It was now moved and seconded that the sense of this meeting be taken whether all the members mentioned in the above list be admitted to act in this meeting. Carried in the affirmative, 30 to 6.

Moved and seconded that all questions arising in this meeting excepting questions of order, be taken by ayes and nays. Carried unanimously in the affirmative.

Moved and seconded that this county be set off from the county of Oneida. Carried in the affirmative, 27 to 9.

Moved and seconded that this meeting will adjourn for half an hour. Carried unanimously, adjourned accordingly.

Met pursuant to adjournment. It was now moved and seconded that a petition be presented to the legislature of this state to appoint a disinterested committee to affix our limits for a new county, and to decide whether we ought to have a whole or a half shire on the Black river, and affix the spot or spots as sites for the court house. Carried in the negative, 25 to 11.

Moved and seconded that the southern boundary of the counties to be established in the Black river country, begin on lake Ontario, at the south west corner of Ellisburgh; thence along the south line of Ellisburgh to the south east corner of said town; thence along the eastern boundary of Ellisburgh to the corner of No. 1 and 6 on said boundary; thence along the line between 1 and 6, 2 and 7, to the corner of 3 and 8; thence along the line between 7 and 8, 12 and 13 to the line between Macomb's and Scriba's patent; thence along said bounds to the county of Herkimer; thence along the western boundaries of Herkimer and St. Lawrence to the river St. Lawrence; thence up along said river St. Lawrence to lake Ontario; thence along the margin of said lake to the place of beginning. Carried in the affirmative, 20 to 16.

Moved and seconded that so much of the above resolution as

---

5 Leyden appears not to have been represented at this meeting, although on two previous occasions special meetings had been called and delegates chosen for this purpose. At one of these held December 15, 1803, Stephen Butler, Moses Ostrander and Joel Jinks had been appointed, and at the other held February 3, 1804, Stephen Butler, Samuel Snow and Richard Cox were chosen to represent this town, at a convention to be held at Champion, on the first Tuesday of February, of that year.

respects the south bounds of the town of Leyden be amended in such a way as to leave it optional with the inhabitants of that town to remain with the county of Oneida or come into the new county. On this amendment the vote was 18 to 18. It was then moved and seconded that so much of the above resolution as respects the south bounds of Leyden be reconsidered, vote stood 18 to 18. It was now moved and seconded that all the country included within the boundaries as agreed to by the above resolution be divided into two counties. The division line between the two and the sites for the same to be established by a disinterested committee, to be appointed by the governor and the council of this state. The men to be appointed, to live out of, and have no interest in the western district; and that during five years no expense to be paid by the counties to be organized as aforesaid, for the erection of public buildings. Carried in the affirmative, 20 to 16.

Motioned and seconded that a committee be appointed to draft a petition to the legislature of this state according to the resolutions of this meeting, and to carry the same into effect with the proceedings of this meeting. Said committee to consist of five and to be chosen from amongst the members attending as delegates, and be chosen by ballot.

The meeting was then adjourned for fifteen minutes in order that the members might prepare their ballots, on counting which it appeared that Jonathan Collins, Jacob Brown, Henry Coffeen, Cliff French and Joseph Beals were chosen. Ordered that the secretary supply each of the members of the committee with a copy of the proceedings of this meeting. There being no further business, ordered that the meeting be dissolved.

JONATHAN COLLINS, Chairman.

EGBERT TEN EYCK, Secretary."

During the winter of 1804–5, numerous petitions and remonstrances were presented to the legislature, having in view the division of Oneida county, and of several of its towns. These were referred to the delegation from that county, then consisting of George Brayton, Joseph Jennings, Joseph Kirkland and Benjamin Wright, the latter of whom, from his intimate knowledge of the county, and especially of the part embraced in Macomb's purchase, was eminently fitted for the duty assigned him. He accordingly on the 4th of March introduced a bill for the erection of *Jefferson and Lewis counties.* Seven days after, it was discussed in a committee of the whole, amended, the blanks filled and clauses added, chiefly relating to the location of the county seats and the division of the public moneys. On the 12th it passed the house, and on the 22d the senate receiving from the latter a few amendments which were concurred in by the house. The vote upon its passage is not preserved in the journals of either house, nor are the amendments of the senate a subject of record. The bill received the governor's signature on the 28th of March. As the motives presented to the legislature to induce the passage of this act, possess permanent interest, we here insert the petition circulated extensively throughout the district set off from Oneida. Many copies of it were taken for use in the several towns, and although its authorship is not stated, it bears within itself the evidence that it emanated from the pen of Jacob Brown.

To the Honorable the Legislature of the State of New York, in Senate and Assembly convened:

We your petitioners, inhabitants of the Black river country, beg leave to represent, that we humbly apprehend that the time has arrived when our true interest and the prosperity of the country in which we are situated, requires a division of the county of Oneida. On this subject there appears but one sentiment in our county, and we flatter ourselves that it will be superfluous to multiply arguments to the legislature, to show the propriety of a division. We believe that your honorable body will be led to inquire why we have not presented a request at an earlier period, for we believe that no instance can be produced of so numerous a body of people, spread over such an extensive and highly productive country, so remote from the old settled parts of the county and seat of justice to which they are attached, without praying for and obtaining relief. Relying therefore upon our former experience in the justice and wisdom of your honorable body, we pray the legislature to divide the county of Oneida by a line * * * [the same as that which now includes Jefferson and Lewis,] and we pray the Legislature to divide all the country within the aforesaid boundaries into two counties, the division line between the two counties and site in each for the seat of justice in the same, to be established by a disinterested committee to be appointed by the governor and council of this state, the men so appointed to live out of, and to have no interest in the western district. Having appointed a committee to wait upon the legislature with this petition, and to make such further representations to the government as they may deem best calculated to promote the interest of this county and the welfare of the state, we shall not go into a detail of our reasons on the subject of this petition, but refer your honorable body to this committee. One subject, however, being of primary magnitude, and involving as we apprehend the best interest of this country, we cannot pass in silence. That we are not ignorant of the opposition that is premeditated to the town of Ellisburgh and Malta being connected with the lower county on the Black river, and that the opposition to this connection is powerful and respectable, but we humbly presume that we are not mistaken in believing that the prime mover and first cause of this opposition[1] is not fully acquainted with the true interests and make of this county, and that when he is rightly informed on this subject he will act consistent with himself, and not pursue measures so injurious to a respectable portion of his fellow citizens. The town of Ellisburgh and Malta are separated from the Redfield and Camden country by the strong and intelligent hand of Nature, and our duty constrains us to say that they can not be thrown into that county (if one should be organized there) without violating these natural right and sacrificing the best interest. With the Black river country they are strongly cemented by natural boundaries and natural interests, and we flatter ourselves that the legislature will resist every exertion and influence so deeply injurious to the peace and prosperity, and so unfriendly to the interest of the state as the separation of the towns of Ellisburgh and Malta from the Black river country, in any arrangement that may be contemplated for the organization of new counties. Situated on the confines of the dominions of a powerful empire, we flatter ourselves that our country is viewed with an eye of particular solicitude by the government, and fondly cherish the hope that it will with pleasure pursue such measures as are best calculated to increase its strength, and advance its prosperity.

We therefore conclude by renewing our solicitation that your honorable body will at your present session cause two counties to be organized on the Black river and establish their southern boundary agreeable to our request, and your petitioners as in duty bound will ever pray.[2]

Black River, Dec. 1804.

---

1 Referring to Nathan Sage of Redfield.

2 The opposing petition referred to in the above was as follows:

"The petition of the inhabitants of the western part of the county of Oneida respectfully sheweth, that whereas, a convention of delegates from the towns on the Black River has been held and the members of that convention recommended a division of the county of Oneida, and appointed a committee to carry their resolutions into effect, and this committee having drawn a petition directed to the legislature of this state setting forth their reasons for and praying such division. We beg leave to suggest the propriety of a general division for we humbly apprehend that the recent controversy in this county respecting a site in it for a seat of justice will appear to you a sufficient argument to show the propriety of a general and early division.

We therefore pray the legislature at their present session to divide the county of Oneida by a line to commence on Lake Ontario, at the northeast corner of Ellisburgh, and run along the north line of Constable's 13 towns to the corner of 3 and 4 on said line, thence south between 3 and 4, 8 and 9, to the north line of No. 13, from thence southeast until the line intersects the main branch of Fish creek, thence down Fish creek to the Oneida lake, thence along the lake and Oswego river to lake Ontario, thence along said

The act erecting the two counties applied to them the names of the executive heads of the national and state governments respectively at the time of its passage and read as follows:

AN ACT *to erect part of the County of Oneida into two separate Counties by the names of Jefferson and Lewis, and for other purposes*

Paſſed March 28, 1805.

I. BE *it enacted by the People of the State of New York, represented in Senate and Assembly,* That all that part of the county of Oneida, contained within the following bounds, to wit: Beginning at the ſouthweſt corner of the town of Elliſburgh, on the eaſterly shore of Lake-Ontario, and running along the ſoutherly line of ſaid town; thence along the eaſterly line thereof to the ſouthwest corner of the town of Malta; thence along the ſoutherly line of the ſaid town of Malta, and continuing the ſame course to the corner of townſhips number two, three, ſeven and eight; thence north, along the eaſt line of the town of Malta aforeſaid, to the northeaſt corner thereof; thence in a direct line to the corner of the towns of Rutland and Champion; thence along the line between the ſaid town of Champion and the town of Harriſburgh to Black-river; thence in a direct line to the bounds of the county of St. Lawrence, to interſect the ſame at the corner of townſhips numbers ſeven and eleven, in great tract number three of Macomb's purchaſe; thence along the weſterly bounds of the ſaid county of St. Lawrence to the north bounds of this ſtate; thence weſterly and southerly, along said bounds, including all the islands in the river St. Lawrence and in Lake-Ontario in front thereof and within this ſtate, to the place of beginning, ſhall be and hereby is erected into a ſeparate county, and ſhall be called and known by the name of Jefferſon.

II. *And be it further enacted,* That all that part of the ſaid county of

---

lake to the place of beginning. And we pray that all the tract of country lying within these boundaries may be established and organized into a separate county, and a site within the same appointed for a seat of justice at such place as you in your wisdom may deem best situated to promote the interests of the people and advance their prosperity. It appears totally superfluous to make use of many arguments to show the rectitude of the division lines proposed, for excepting the line between Ellisburgh and the 6th town in the Black river country it may with propriety be termed a natural boundary—between Malta and Adams the line is within a short distance of the south branch of Sandy creek whose course is marked by an impassable gulf for many miles in length; on the east side of this county and between it and Black river the line is also marked by a continued chain of swamps, morasses and gulfs, and should the division line be established within 8 or 10 miles of those natural boundaries on either side it will require the aid of the legislature at a future period to give that relief to the inhabitants that justice would demand. We therefore beg leave to refer you to a map of this county and rest fully assured that you will resist any arguments that may be adduced to effect a separation of any part of the aforesaid country where the interests of the people are so essentially connected. We conclude by renewing our request that your honorable body will take our case into consideration and grant us our prayer, and your petitioners as in duty bound will ever pray."

Oneida, contained within the following bounds, to wit: Beginning at the ſoutheaſt corner of the county of Jefferſon aforeſaid, thence ſoutherly on the weſterly line of the town of Turin, to the ſouthweſt corner thereof; thence eaſterly, along the ſouth line of ſaid town, to the ſoutheaſt corner thereof; thence north ſixty-two degrees eaſt, along the ſoutherly line of the tract of land known by the name of Macomb's purchaſe, to the line of the county of Herkimer; thence north, along the ſaid laſt mentioned line, to the bounds of the county of St. Lawrence; thence along the ſouthweſterly line of the ſaid laſt mentioned county to the line of the ſaid county of Jefferſon, and thence along the ſoutherly and eaſterly bounds thereof to the place of beginning, ſhall be and hereby is erected into a ſeparate county by the name of Lewis.

III. *And be it further enacted*, That all that part of townſhip number nine, which is compriſed within the bounds of the ſaid county of Jefferſon, ſhall be annexed to and become a part of the town of Harriſon, in ſaid county; and that all that part of the ſaid townſhip number nine, compriſed within the bounds of the ſaid county of Lewis, shall be annexed to and become a part of the town of Harriſburgh in ſaid county.

IV. *And be it further enacted*, That there ſhall be held in and for the ſaid counties of Jefferſon and Lewis, reſpectively, a court of common pleas and general ſeſſions of the peace, and that there ſhall be two terms of the ſaid courts in each of the counties reſpectively in every year, to commence and end as follows, that is to ſay: The firſt term of the ſaid court in the ſaid county of Jefferſon, ſhall begin on the ſecond Tueſday of June in every year, and may continue to be held until the Saturday following incluſive; and the ſecond term of the ſaid court in the ſaid county of Jefferſon, ſhall begin on the ſecond Tueſday of December, in every year, and may continue to be held until the Saturday following incluſive; And that the firſt term of the ſaid court in the county of Lewis, ſhall begin on the ſaid firſt Tueſday of June in every year, and may continue to be held until the Saturday following incluſive, and the ſecond term of the ſaid court in the ſaid county of Lewis, ſhall begin on the firſt Tueſday of December, and may continue to be held until the Saturday following incluſive; and the ſaid courts of common pleas and general ſeſſions of the peace shall have the ſame juriſdiction, powers and authorities in the ſame counties reſpectively, as the courts of common pleas and general ſeſſions of the peace in the other counties of this ſtate have in their reſpective counties; *Provided always*, That nothing in this act contained, ſhall be conſtrued to affect any ſuit or action already commenced or that ſhall be commenced before the firſt terms to be held in the reſpective counties of Jefferſon and Lewis, ſo as to work a wrong or prejudice to any of the parties therein, or to affect any criminal or other proceedings on the part of the people of this ſtate, but all ſuch civil and criminal proceedings ſhall and may be proſecuted to trial, judgment and execution as if this act had not been paſſed: *And provided further*, That the firſt of the ſaid courts in each of the ſaid counties, ſhall be held on the ſecond Tueſday of December next.

V. *And be it further enacted*, That three Commiſſioners ſhall be appointed by the council of appointment, who ſhall not be reſident in the weftern diftrict of this ftate, or interefted in either of the faid counties of Jefferfon and Lewis, for the purpofe of defignating the fcites for the court houfes and gaols of the faid counties refpectively, and to that end the faid commiffioners, fhall as foon as may be, previous to the firft day of October next, repair to the faid counties refpectively, and after exploring the fame afcertain and defignate a fit and proper place in each of the faid counties for erecting the faid buildings; and that until fuch buildings fhall be erected and further legiflative provifion be made in the premifes, the faid courts of common pleas and general feffions of the peace fhall be held at fuch place in each of the faid counties neareft and moft contiguous to the places defignated as the fcites for faid buildings, as the faid commiffioners or any two of them fhall determine and fix on; and the faid commiffioners or any two of them are hereby required as foon as they have defignated the places for erecting the faid buildings, and determined on the places for holding the faid courts, to make out and fign a certificate certifying the places defignated for erecting the buildings, and the places fixed on for holding the courts in each of the faid counties, and to tranfmit one of the faid certificates to each of the clerks of the refpective counties who are required to receive and file the fame in their refpective offices; and that the faid commiffioners fhall be entitled to receive each the fum of four dollars per day, for the time they may be neceffarily employed in executing the trufts repofed in them by this act, the one moiety thereof to be paid by each of the faid counties.

VI. *And be it further enacted,* That the freeholders and inhabitants of the faid counties refpectively, fhall have and enjoy within the fame all and every the fame rights, powers and privileges as the freeholders and inhabitants of any other county in this ftate are by law entitled to have and enjoy.

VII. *And be it further enacted,* That it fhall and may be lawful for all courts and officers of the faid counties of Jefferfon and Lewis refpectively, in all cafes civil and criminal to confine their prifoners in the gaol or gaols of the county of Oneida until gaols fhall be provided in the fame counties refpectively, the said counties paying each the charges of their own prifoners.

VIII. *And be it further enacted,* That the diftribution of reprefentation in the affembly of this ftate, shall be three members in the county of Oneida, and one in the counties of Jefferfon and Lewis and St. Lawrence, any law to the contrary notwithftanding.

IX. *And be it further enacted,* That no circuit court, or courts of oyer and terminer and general gaol delivery, fhall be held in either of the faid counties of Jefferfon and Lewis, until the fame fhall, in the opinion of the juftices of the fupreme court, become neceffary.

X. *And be it further enacted,* That the faid counties of Jefferfon and Lewis fhall be confidered as part of the weftern diftrict of this ftate, and alfo as part of the fifteenth congreffional diftrict, and that as it refpects all proceedings under the act, entitled "An act relative to diftrict attornies, the faid counties fhall be annexed to and become part of the diftrict now compofed of the counties of Herkimer, Otfego, Oneida and Chenango.

XI. *And be it further enacted,* That as ſoon as may be after the firſt Monday of April, in the year one thouſand eight hundred and ſix, the ſupervifors of the ſaid counties of Oneida, Jefferſon and Lewis, on notice being firſt given by the ſupervifors of the ſaid counties of Jefferſon and Lewis, or either of them for that purpoſe, ſhall meet together by themſelves, or by committees appointed by their reſpective boards, and divide the money unappropriated belonging to the ſaid county of Oneida, previous to the diviſion thereof, agreeable to the laſt county tax liſt.

XII. *And be it further enacted,* That the votes taken at the election in the ſaid counties of Jefferſon, Lewis and St. Lawrence ſhall be returned to the clerk of the county of Jefferſon, to be by him eſtimated and diſpoſed of as is directed by the ſtatute regulating elections.

XIII. *And be it further enacted,* That all that part of the town of Leyden remaining in the county of Oneida, ſhall be and remain a ſeparate town by the name of Boonſville, and the firſt town meeting ſhall be held at the houſe of Joſeph Denning, and all the remaining part of the town of Leyden, which is compriſed within the bounds of the county of Lewis, ſhall be and remain a town by the name of Leyden, and the firſt town meeting ſhall be held at the dwelling houſe of Hezekiah Talcott.

XIV. *And be it further enacted,* That as ſoon as may be after the firſt town meeting in each of ſaid towns, the ſupervifors and overſeers of the poor of the ſaid towns of Leyden and Boonſville, ſhall by notice to be given for that purpoſe by the ſupervifors thereof, meet together and apportion the money and poor of ſaid town of Leyden, previous to the diviſion thereof according to the laſt tax liſt, and that each of ſaid towns ſhall thereafter reſpectively maintain their own poor.

It will be noticed, that as originally bounded, the town of Pinckney was divided by a line running from the northwest corner of Montague, to the west angle of Denmark, and that east of the river the line was direct from the corners of Champion and Denmark, to St. Lawrence county, passing just south of Carthage, and including more than a quarter of the present town of Wilna. The town of Pinckney was brought entirely within this county upon its organization in 1808, and the line east of the river has since been twice amended, as stated in our history of Diana.

A concise notice of the man from whom the county derives its name, may interest its citizens.

MORGAN LEWIS, of Welch ancestry, a son of Francis Lewis, one of the signers of the Declaration of Independence, was born in New York city, Oct. 16, 1754, graduated at Princeton College in 1773, and entered the law office of John Jay. In June, 1775, he joined the army before Boston as a volunteer, in a rifle company of which he was chosen captain in August. In November he was appointed major of the 2d regiment of which John Jay was colonel, but as public duties withdrew the latter from the command it fell upon Lewis. In June, 1776, he accompanied Gen. Gates into Canada as chief of his staff, and was soon after appointed quarter-master-general for the northern department with the rank of colonel. In 1777 he was appointed to receive the British troops, surrendered by Burgoyne, and in 1778 he was sent with Gen. Clinton on an expedition up the Mohawk against a body of partizan troops under Sir John Johnson. In 1780 he accompanied Clinton to Crown Point to intercept the enemy who had made an incursion upon that frontier. At the close of the war he was appointed colonel-commandant of a volunteer corps, and had the honor of escorting Gen. Washington at his first inauguration as President.

In 1790 and 1792 he was elected to the assembly, in 1791 appointed attorney-general, and in 1804 elected governor for a term of three years. In 1810 he was chosen to the state senate by a larger majority than had ever before been given, and served four years. He was appointed quarter-master-general of the army of the United States April 3, 1812, and on the 2d of March, 1813, he was promoted to the rank of major-general.

The descent on Niagara in April, 1813, was planned and conducted solely by General Lewis, as Gen. Dearborn the senior officer was confined to his tent by indisposition. After the evacuation of Fort George, Gen. Lewis set off in pursuit, but when just arrived within sight he was recalled by a peremptory order from Dearborn. The next morning the latter ordered Generals Chandler and Winder to pursue the enemy, but upon coming up with them the latter considering their situation desperate, turned upon their pursuers. In the darkness, both of these officers fell into the hands of the enemy, and the American troops returned to Fort George. Late in the fall of 1813, Gen. Lewis accompanied Gen. Wilkinson's inglorious expedition down the St. Lawrence. He continued in the service until disbanded in June, 1815, when he resumed the practice of his profession. While on the Canada frontier he advanced large sums from his private means to pay the expenses of exchanged prisoners, at a time when drafts upon the government would not be received. His indulgence towards such of his tenants as had served during the war either as militia or in the regular army is especially worthy of record. The following is a copy of an order sent to his agent for this purpose:

"Every tenant who has himself, or whose son living with and working for his father, has served in the course of the last war, either in the regular army or militia, is to have a year's rent remitted for every campaign they have so served either personally or by substitute. A regular discharge during a campaign on account of sickness to be considered as serving a campaign."

A second order directed three years' rent to be remitted to every family who had a near relative killed or maimed during the war. Gen. Lewis married in 1777 Gertrude, fourth daughter of Judge Robert Livingston of Clermont, Manor of Livingston. This union lasted fifty-four years. He was a member of the New York Society of the Cincinnati, and at the time of his death, which occurred in New York city April 7, 1844, he was president of that body. The general order issued upon this occasion, after enumerating the prominent events of his life, closes as follows:

"His last appearance in public life was on the 22d of February, 1832, when at the request of the corporation of this city he delivered an oration in honor of General Washington at the celebration of the centennial anniversary of his nativity. * * * His pure life and patriotic disinterestedness are worthy of all imitation and a bright example to those who follow him. He has gone down to his grave in a good old age and the fullness of his honors, and his memory will ever be cherished and honored as one of the chosen band who were prompt to respond to the call of their country in the "time that tried men's souls," and as one of the chivalrous spirits who were found ready to endure the privations and dangers of the field in our second war of independence. In all the relations of life he discharged his duties with fidelity and honor. He was a gallant soldier, an accomplished statesman, a kind parent, a benevolent man, and a good citizen."

The commissioners appointed under the fifth section of the act organizing the county, were *Matthew Dorr* of Chatham, Columbia county, *David Rodgers* of Washington county and *John Van Benthuysen* of Dutchess Co. The names of the council of appointment were at that time, John Schenck, Joshua H. Brett, Stephen Thorn and Jedediah Peck, of whom Thorn was an intimate personal friend of Walter Martin, through whose influence the appointments are said to have been arranged. It has been reported upon very reliable authority, that the driver of the coach, in which the commissioners came in from Utica, overheard from their conversation that the location of the seat of Lewis county was already decided upon, and that he made an affidavit to that effect.

Whether the formation of the 26th brigade which immediately followed the division of the county, or the appointment of Martin as brigadier-general, or the election of Stow to the twelfth congress, had any connection with the division of the county, we may not perhaps decide; popular tradition has associated these events, but no written evidence is known to exist. In 1805–6 the sum of $74 was paid to Dorr, a like amount to Rogers, and $82 to Van Benthuysen as compensation for their services in locating the county seat. The county drew $293.54, from Oneida in 1806.

CHAPTER II.

COUNTY BUILDINGS.

The act erecting the county, made no provision for a court house and jail, beyond the designation of their site, and the expense of these was left at the request of the Denmark convention till the end of five years. Mr. Martin had as early as 1803, began to grub up the stumps for the site of a court house, but upon being assured of the decision of the commissioners the measure was not pressed for some years. At Lowville, active efforts were at once made to secure if possible the location, and a wooden building was erected, with the design of offering it to the county for a court house, but failing in their enterprise, the citizens of that place converted the edifice into an academy.

The first session of the court of common pleas, was held at the inn of Chillus Doty in Martinsburgh, Dec. 8, 1805; present, Daniel Kelley, Jonathan Collins and Judah Barnes, *judges*, and Asa Brayton, *assistant justice.* This court adopted as the county seal, the design figured at the head of the first chapter in this volume, proceeded to draft a system of rules for the regulation of its business, and established the jail liberties of the county.

The jail liberties, although not peculiar in their day, or essentially different from those of other counties, will doubtless be considered by many as a curious illustration of the absurd legal form and usages of the olden time, and as belonging to a barbarous period in the history of our penal code. The *limits* comprised the site of the court house, a path two feet wide across the street to the store opposite, a path eight feet wide along the west side of the street to the premises of Chillus Doty, afterwards a brick tavern (including the store, the house, garden and front yard of Gen. Martin, and the house, garden, barn and shed of Doty): a path eight feet wide from the middle of Doty's shed across to the premises of David Waters, with the house of Mr. Waters and a space eight feet wide in front and at the ends, and twenty feet wide in the rear, and a path eight feet wide northward to, and including the house of John Waters. These were subsequently extended to other houses, and finally included nearly every building in or near the village, from Foot's tannery on the north, to the inn then kept by John Atwater on the south, with narrow paths between, and crossing places at distant intervals. These liberties were duly surveyed and recorded, and the unlucky debtor who might find himself upon them, would need a sober head and steady eye to keep himself within the right angles which the court had so precisely marked out for his footsteps. An obstacle in the path might stop his course, or an inadvertent step subject his bail to prosecution and himself to close confinement. In 1814 the jail liberties were extended from A. Foot's tannery to John Smith's hat shop, with a breadth of twenty-five rods, and since about 1822, they have embraced a square area of 500 acres around the court house. The boundaries where they crossed the public roads were designated by posts painted red, but these have long since rotted down and nothing indicates their locality. The county courts were held during nine terms at the house of Chillus Doty, and during the succeeding eight, at the house of Ehud Stephens. One term of the court of oyer and terminer was held by Judge Ambrose Spencer at the Lowville academy, previous to the erection of the court house.

In 1809 Gen. Martin undertook to raise means for the erection of a court house by subscription among his townsmen and those living south, leading off on the list with a liberal sum himself. The Lowville people were not indifferent to the movement and procured the signature of nearly every taxable inhabitant north of Martinsburgh, to a petition against the final location of the courts on the site already designated.[1]

The petitioners indirectly charged the commissioners with having acted upon slight and superficial examination, appealed to the map, for proof that Lowville village was

[1] A package of these papers has 682 names *for* and 474 *against* a change of site.

nearer the centre of the county, and to tax lists,[1] military returns, and opinions of gentlemen who had travelled through the county and were acquainted with it, as evidence that more than two-thirds of the population lay north of the court house site. They stated the want of accommodation in the little village where the site had been located as compared with the larger village of Lowville, and ask the legislature to fix by direct act, or appointment of sound and candid commissioners the county seat in what shall appear to be the centre of population; closing their memorial with the sentiment, "that however misrepresentation may succeed, for a time justice and discernment may ultimately be expected of the legislature."

The remonstrants claimed by the map, that the centre of the county lay a mile south of the site, and showed by the tax list, that over $200,000 more of taxable property lay south of the court house.[2] They denied the assertion that the southern portion of the county was incapable of tillage, and proved by affidavits that one principal cause of non-settlement was because the lands had not been opened for sale. They stated that nearly $2,000 had been subscribed in good faith for the erection of a court house as located by law, and claimed that justice entitled them to a continuance of the site. These memorials led to the introduction of a bill entitled " an act relative to the establishment of a scite for the courthouse and gaol in the county of Lewis," which failed to reach a third reading in the house. It was introduced by Dr. S. L. Mitchill of New York, as chairman of the committee to whom the subject was referred.

On the 30th of October, 1810, Gen. Martin engaged for $1500 to complete the court room like that of Jefferson county, and the jail like that of Salem, Washington county, and on the 1st of March, 1811, an act was passed for raising $1200 by tax in one or two years, and $300 by loan, to complete the building. The commissioners for building were Benjamin Van Vleck, Daniel Kelley and Jonathan Collins; and the sheriff was directed to give public notice by proclamation when the work was finished and accepted. The first county courts were held in the new building Jan. 7, 1812, and prisoners who had previously been sent to Rome, were thenceforth lodged in the new county jail.

---

[1] The assessment rolls of 1809 gave Leyden 137, Turin 167, Martinsburgh 126, Lowville 206, Denmark 169, Harrisburgh 82, and Pinckney 63 taxable inhabitants. Of these 630 were claimed north of the court house.

[2] The valuation of 1809 was, Leyden $188,700; Turin $297,715.25; Martinsburgh $70,921; Lowville $90,257; Denmark $83,556; Harrisburgh $29,405; and Pinckney $27,077.

These premises were nearly the same as those now in use, consisting of a large wooden building, with a court room and two jury rooms above, and three prison rooms, the sheriff's office and rooms for the jailor's family on the first floor. The front jail room has since been fitted up for the office of the county judge and surrogate, but otherwise there has been but little change. On account of the exposed situation of the St. Lawrence county jail on the frontiers at Ogdensburgh, an act was passed April 6, 1814, authorizing the prisoners of that county to be confined in this. We are not aware that any were sent hither under this act.

In the fall of 1852, public notice was given of application for the removal of the county seat to Lowville or New Bremen, and, in the hope of effecting this change, the citizens of Lowville proceeded to erect an elegant brick building for this purpose. The effort failed, and the structure is now used as a town hall. No serious expectation was perhaps entertained with regard to the New Bremen application.

The Clerk's office was kept in the house of Richard Coxe, the clerk, until the act of 1811, which required it to be kept within a mile of the court house, after the first day of October following. The office was kept in the dwelling of the clerk or his deputy for the time being, somewhere in the village of Martinsburgh, until 1822, when Martin erected a fire proof brick office and rented a part to the county. In 1824 an act was passed requiring the erection of a clerk's office, but this was not done. In 1847 an association was formed in Martinsburgh for the purpose of building a clerk's office, which was finished and leased to the county free of rent. It has since been in use as the clerk's office.

Pauperism.—For many of the earlier years, the several towns of this county supported their own poor by an annual tax, and paupers were generally kept by those who would bid the lowest sum for their support. Persons becoming a public charge before they had gained a residence, were sent back to the town where they had last resided, or if they could not be removed were supported at the expense of such town. In 1817, a committee was appointed in Lowville to confer with one from Martinsburgh, upon the subject of a poor house, but nothing resulted. In 1824, the secretary of state, under a resolution of the preceding session, reported such statistics of pauperism as could be obtained, and upon his recommendation an act was passed in 1824, under which the supervisors resolved to erect a poor house in Lewis county. At that period this county ranked the 46th in the scale of pauperism and the 51st in taxation, as compared with the rest of the state. Paupers formed one-fifth of one per cent. of the population, and the poor tax was a fraction over one cent per $100 of valuation. Several of the towns had acquired a surplus poor fund.

In the fall of 1825, Jonathan Collins, Charles D. Morse and Stephen Hart were appointed to purchase a site and take preliminary steps for the erection of a poor house. The farm of Maj. David Cobb, a mile west of Lowville village, was bought for $1,650, and the premises were fitted up for the county use. The first county superintendents of the poor, appointed in 1826, were Nathaniel Merriam, Philo Rockwell, Stephen Leonard, Paul Abbott and Samuel Allen.

The distinction between town and county poor under the act of 1824, was abolished in 1834, restored in 1842, abolished in 1845, and finally restored in 1851. Several towns have, upon each of these occasions, passed resolutions at their annual meetings with reference to this measure. The premises originally fitted up continued in use until it became necessary, in 1845, to call public attention to their condition, and to take measures for securing either an extension of accommodation or the erection of a new building. In 1845, several of the towns passed resolutions instructing their supervisors to give their attention to the subject; and a representation of the facts to the legislature procured an act passed March 26, 1846, directing a tax of $1,500 to be levied upon the county for the repair and extension of the poor house. Miss D. L. Dix (whose earnest efforts in behalf of the poor and insane have earned her the appellation of the "crazy angel"), visited our county poor house in the spring of 1844, and her conversation is said to have had an influence in calling attention to the necessity of reform.

A new stone building, forty by sixty feet, and two stories high, was erected in 1846, and has since been in use, affording comfortable accommodation to such as are reduced to that dependence which it is designed to relieve. The farm attached contains 59 $\frac{41}{100}$ acres, valued, with the buildings, at $3,500, and partly cultivated by the labor of paupers. The statistics of the institution showed, in 1858, that 30 per cent. were foreigners, and that 54 per cent. were reduced to poverty by intemperance. The expense of weekly support was 76 cents, and had, in early years, been half less.

Under an act of April 20, 1818, male felons, convicted in Lewis county, were sent to the state prison at Auburn. Since the erection of the Clinton prison, convicts have usually been sent thither from this county.

Statistics of Pauperism as reported annually on the first day of December, since 1829.

Years.	Number Relieved.		Annual Expense.		In Poor House at end of year.			Changes in Poor House.					
	County.	Town.	Poor House.	Total.	Males.	Females.	Total.	Received.	Born.	Died.	Bound out.	Discharged.	Absconded.
1830	19	20	.....	$388	8	11	19	39	4	4	1	15	..
1831	37	29	.....	1467	8	9	17	31	1	2	1	26	1
1832	33	15	.....	891	9	8	17	32	2	2	2	25	2
1833	20	30	.....	1287	10	8	18	30	3	1	1	26	5
1834	15	55	.....	1615	11	8	19	11	..	3	1	4	2
1835	67	...	.....	1119	19	17	36	50	3	3	3	13	1
1836	86	...	.....	1421	8	15	23	37	..	..	1	35	..
1837	82	...	.....	1955	13	13	26	39	2	6	1	43	3
1838	87	...	$1290	1633	12	12	24	27	1	3	4	16	4
1839	76	...	1905	2281	16	20	36	76	4	6	..	36	2
1840	93	...	2030	2742	14	23	37	93	3	3	1	49	..
1841	96	...	1919	2366	23	13	36	96	1	6	1	53	..
1842	89	...	1861	2288	17	15	32	89	2	3	2	50	..
1843	52	38	1594	1958	22	22	44	90	5	4	..	41	1
1844	51	26	1261	1433	18	16	34	30	2	4	..	33	4
1845	192	...	1285	1758	23	19	42	35	..	3	1	14	4
1846	84	122	1762	2632	26	26	52	38	1	6	4	16	6
1847	181	...	2385	2904	35	30	65	35	1	8	..	12	1
1848	205	...	2197	2865	32	31	63	40	2	5	5	29	5
1849	210	...	2002	2692	40	24	64	68	2	4	1	34	9
1850	213	...	2461	3228	31	29	60	49	2	2	1	42	9
1851	94	96	1782	2503	27	29	56	35	1	4	2	30	4
1852	62	51	2461	3351	27	43	70	56	2	6	5	31	6
1853	220	62	3534	4218	42	33	75	68	6	8	1	25	8
1854	175	128	3907	5354	37	53	90	153	1	7	..	32	6
1855	120	46	5012	11187	49	45	94	61	2	10	..	34	4
1856	198	52	1478	2297	31	38	69	43	1	3	3	56	7
1857	125	53	4615	5067	24	26	50	46	2	7	2	49	9
1858	126	48	3564	4126	20	23	43	35	2	6	2	25	..
1859	152	28	3816	4531	20	26	46	80	..	5	1	38	..

A classification made in 1837, represented Lewis county as having the least amount of crime in proportion to its population, of any county in the state; and on many occasions the criminal courts have adjourned without having had any business before them. Up to 1827 but nine persons were sent from this county to the New York state prison, and from 1819 to 1834 inclusive but 17 were sent to Auburn prison from Lewis.

CHAPTER III.

LAND TITLES.

An unfavorable impression as to the value of northern lands had been acquired from the survey of Totten and Crossfield's purchase before 1776. This tract, embracing the central part of the great northern wilderness, still as wild and inhospitable as when first traversed by surveyors, was found to become worse towards the north, and the inference very naturally followed that the northern border of the state was not susceptible of tillage.

On old maps this great northern region was variously named, as *Irocoisia*, or the land of the Iroquois; *Coughsagraga*, or the dismal wilderness; and the *Deer hunting grounds of the Five Nations.* An old map has inscribed across the northern part of New York this sentence: "Through this tract of land runs a chain of mountains, which, from lake Champlain on one side, and the river St. Lawrence on the other side, show their tops always white with snow; but, although this one unfavorable circumstance has hitherto secured it from the jaws of the harpy land jobbers, yet, no doubt, it is as fertile as the land on the east side of the lake, and will in future furnish a comfortable retreat for many industrious families." A map drawn in 1756, says this country by reason of mountains, swamps and drowned lands, is impassable and uninhabitable.

Sauthier's map, published in England in 1777, and supposed to represent the latest and most accurate information then possessed, remarks that "this marshy tract is full of beavers and otters," and no map of a date earlier than 1795 has any trace of the Black river. The shores of the St. Lawrence and lake Ontario had long been familiar to voyageurs, but Black river bay was evidently regarded as only one of several deep indentations of the coast; and in Morse's geography of 1796, this river is represented as flowing into the St. Lawrence at Oswegatchie.

The fertility of lands in the western part of the state had

become known in the course of military expeditions through them, but no such occasion led to a knowledge of the Black river valley,[1] and it is highly probable that when a proposition for purchase was submitted to the land commissioners, the offer was regarded as favorable upon any terms conditioned to settlement.

The Oneida Indians, sole native owners of our county, by formal treaty at Fort Stanwix, on the 22d of September, 1788,[2] ceded to the state all their lands, excepting certain reservations, among which was a tract one half mile wide on each side of Fish creek, from its source to its mouth, which, according to Cockburn the surveyor, was retained on account of the "salmon fisheries."

On the 22d of June, 1791, Alexander Macomb submitted an application[3] for the purchase of all the lands within certain specified boundaries, including the tract since known as Macomb's purchase, excepting certain islands in the St. Lawrence. One-sixth part of the purchase money was to be paid at the end of one year, and the residue in five equal annual installments, without interest. The first payment was to be secured by bond, to the satisfaction of the commissioners, and if paid within time a patent was to be issued for a sixth part, and new bonds for the next sixth were to be issued. If at any time the purchaser chose to anticipate the payments, a deduction of six per cent. per annum was allowed. The price offered was eight cents per acre, deducting five per cent. for roads, and all lakes of more than one thousand acres in area. The proposition was accepted, and the lands were ordered to be surveyed out at the expense of Macomb,[4] under the direction of the surveyor general.

---

1 Belletres' expedition against the settlement at the German Flatts, in 1755 and that of Lery, which captured fort Bull, near Rome, in 1757, are supposed to have passed through this valley. In 1779, Lieutenants McClellan and Hardenburgh were sent through the interior to Oswegatchie, more with the view of drawing off the friendly Oneidas and preventing them from being disturbed by the expedition against the Indians of the Genesee country, than in the hopes of effecting much against the enemy. Several musket barrels and other military relics have been found in Greig on the line of this route, which may have been lost in these expeditions. Their occurrence has, as usual, occasioned idle rumors of buried treasure.

2 Given in full in the History of Jefferson Co., p. 39.

3 Given in full in the History of St Lawrence and Franklin Counties, p. 253.

4 Alexander Macomb was a son of John Macomb, and emigrated from Ireland in 1742. He resided many years in New York and held a colonial office, and in 1787-8 '91, he was in Assembly. During several years he resided in Detroit as a fur trader, and in passing to and from Montreal had become acquainted with the value of the lands of northern New York. He furnished five sons to the army in 1812, one of whom was the illustrious General Macomb of Plattsburgh memory.

The sale of such enormous tracts of land at a merely nominal price, attracted public notice throughout the state, and the occasion was not lost by the opponents of the state administration to charge the land commissioners with the basest motives of personal gain, and even with treason itself. On the 20th of April, 1792, Dr. Josiah Pomeroy of Kinderhook, made oath to his belief from hearsay, that a company, planned by William Smith, Sir John Johnson and others, chiefly tories living in Canada, had been formed under the auspices of Lord Dorchester as early as 1789, to purchase an extensive tract of land upon the St. Lawrence, with the ultimate design of annexing it to Canada, and that Gov. George Clinton was privy to their scheme, and interested in the result.[1] To this absurd charge the governor's friends opposed a letter of Gen. Schuyler, and the affidavits of Macomb and McCormick, fully denying any direct or indirect interest of the governor in the purchase. In the Assembly a series of violent resolutions was offered by Col. Talbot of Montgomery evidently designed as the basis of an impeachment, but, after a most searching investigation, that body cleared the commissioners of blame and commended their course.[2] Aaron Burr, then attorney general, was absent at the time of the sale, and escaped censure at the time, but in his after career he was directly charged with basely selling his influence to obtain the grant. The clamor against the governor was raised for political effect, and had its influence on the next election.

From letters of these negotiators it appears that the immense purchase was the fruit of years of preliminary management, and allusions to some great operation as early as 1786 have reference, no doubt, to these events, which appear to have originated with Constable. With a keen eye to the *public* interests, the very parties who had secured this tract, influenced the passage of a law in 1794, fixing the minimum price of the remaining 2,000,000 acres of the public lands at six shillings per acre, thereby giving this value to their own. The unsettled state of the frontiers, and the refusal of the British to surrender the posts, had a serious influence upon the first attempt at settlement. The surveyors were turned back at Oswego from proceeding further, and the Indians at St. Regis drove off the first intruders. In a speech to the Indians in 1794, Lord Dorchester said, that there was prospect of war impending, and that the warrior's sword must mark the boundaries of the country. In the

1 Handbills, 1775 to 1802, p. 41, 43. Library of Albany Institute.

2 Assembly Journals. Hammond's Political History of New York, i, 58. Parton's Life of Burr, 176.

war of 1812–15 it was proposed to render the highlands south of the St. Lawrence the national boundary, and some such hope may have led to these embarrassing interruptions in the surveys.

Alexander Macomb, Daniel McCormick and William Constable were equally interested in the original contract, but Macomb became soon involved in an immense speculation styled the "Million Bank," in which Isaac Whippo, Wm. Duer, Walter Livingston and others were concerned, and a great number of men were pecuniary losers; Macomb was lodged in jail April 17, 1792, and even there owed his life to the strength of his prison walls. This failure interrupted a negotiation with the Holland land company, who afterwards bought in western New York.

The Fish creek reservation was not regarded in this sale, probably because it was supposed not to extend up into the tract. In the course of the survey this became a subject of anxiety, and while some considered that the reservation would extend up only so far as the salmon went, others would limit it to the union of the principal branches, and others only by the sources of its main tributaries. The proposition was made in 1794, to meet the Oneidas, and request a person to be sent to fix the uppermost limit of the creek, and see the half mile run out on each side of it. Upon examining the patent it was found that the state had undertaken to sell the reservation, and must settle whatever damages might result to the Indians. In a treaty held September 15, 1795, the latter engaged to sell all north of a certain creek falling into Fish creek, on Scriba's purchase, for an annuity of $3 per hundred acres, to be ascertained by survey. On the 5th of March, 1802, a provisional agreement of sale of this and other parts of reservations was made, and on the 4th of June of that year it was confirmed in the presence of John Tayler, U. S. Com'r, thus forever canceling the native title to the lands of Lewis county.

Macomb's purchase embraced 3,816,960 acres, from which deducting five per cent. there remained 3,670,715 acres. On the 10th of January, 1792, the first payments having been made, a patent for 1,920,000 acres was issued to Macomb, embracing the whole purchase excepting what lies in St. Lawrence and Franklin counties. The conveyance was that of a full and unqualified freehold, with no reservation but those of gold and silver mines, and no condition but the settlement of one family to every square mile within seven years. The purchase was subdivided into six great tracts, of which I, lies in Franklin, II and III in St. Lawrence, and

IV, includes 450,950 acres, or all of Jefferson and Lewis counties north of a line near the 44th degree of north latitude. The division line between V and VI was never run, and they have never been recognized in land sales, being indefinitely regarded as including the remainder of the tract. In an early map, a line drawn from near the S. W. corner of the purchase, about N. 16° E. and crossing the Black river at the northern bend, east of the Watson bridge, is theoretically given as the line between Nos. V and VI. Macomb conveyed to William Constable of New York, June 6, 1792, great tracts IV, V and VI, for £50,000,[1] and this conveyance was renewed by Macomb and wife, Oct. 3d of that year. Constable conveyed, Dec. 17–18, 1792, to Col. Samuel Ward, 1,281,880 acres, embracing tracts V, VI (excepting 25,000 which had been contracted to P. Colquhoun and conveyed to Wm. Inman), for £100,000.[2] On the 27th of February following, Ward and wife re-conveyed these lands to Constable, excepting 685,000 acres which he had sold.[3] This sale to Ward is understood to have been a trust conveyance, and the sales made by Ward, to be hereafter specified, were virtually sales by Constable. We now arrive at a point in the chain of title from whence several lines diverge, and to convey a clear idea of each, they will be traced separately down to the sales of single towns. Such changes as occurred within the limits of towns, will be noticed in connection with their history.

Lewis county comprises two whole and parts of seven other great tracts, which have been known in land sales by distinct names. To the townships west of Black river, separate names were applied by Simeon DeWitt, surveyor general, in his state maps published in 1802 and 1804. These tracts, with the numbers and original names were as follows:

Black River Tract (in part), including,

Township 5, *Mantua,* now Denmark.
do 9, *Handel,* do Pinckney.
do 10, *Platina,* do Harrisburgh.
do 11, *Lowville,* do Lowville.

The remainder in Jefferson county, south of Black river.

---

1 Deeds, Sec. office, xxiv, 300. 2 Deeds, Sec. office, xxxix, 6.

3 Deeds, Sec. office, xxv, 208. In this conveyance it is understood that Wm. Constable, Col. William Stephens Smith, and Samuel Ward were equally interested. A balance sheet of the accounts of these three proprietors, brought down to July 1, 1796, shows an amount of £69,092 2.0, cost and expenses, and £50,475.10.9 profits, leaving to each one a share of $74,778.57. The current of this affair did not always run smooth, and in a letter to Macomb, dated Oct. 29, 1794, Constable complained that Smith had never disbursed a sixpence, and was profiting by the labors of others, while Ward was bound for the bills. Smith died at Lebanon, Madison county, N. Y., June 10, 1816. He was a member of the 13th and 14th Congresses.

BOYLSTON TRACT (in part), including,
Township 3, *Shakespere*, now Montague.
do 4, *Cornelia*, do Martinsburgh.
do 5, *Porcia*, do do
do 8, *Hybla*, do Osceola.
do 9, *Penelope*, do High Market.
do 13, *Rurabella*, do Osceola.
The remainder in Jefferson and Oswego counties.

CONSTABLE'S FOUR TOWNS, including,
Township 1, *Xenophon*, now Lewis.
do 2, *Flora*, do Lewis, High Market and West Turin.
do 3, *Lucretia*, do High Market, Turin and Martinsburgh.
do 4, *Pomona*, do West Turin and Turin.

INMAN'S TRIANGLE, including Leyden and a part of Lewis.

BRANTINGHAM TRACT, in Greig.

BROWN'S TRACT (in part). The western border of four townships extend into the eastern part of the county, viz :
Part of Township 1, *Industry*, now Greig and Herkimer co.
do do 2, *Enterprise*, do do do
do do 3, *Perseverance*, do Watson, do
do do 4, *Unanimity*, do do do
The remainder in Herkimer and Hamilton counties.

WATSON'S TRACT, including part of Watson. The remainder in Herkimer county.

CASTORLAND, including parts of Greig and Watson, the whole of New Bremen and Croghan, and in Jefferson county the parts adjoining Black river on the north side.

GREAT TRACT NUMBER FOUR, or the Antwerp company's purchase, including Diana and a large tract in Jefferson and a corner in Herkimer counties.

The Black River Tract.—Samuel Ward and wife, on the 12th of December, 1792, conveyed to Thomas Boylston of Boston,[1] for £20,000, all of Macomb's purchase south and west of Black river, excepting Inman's triangle. The only knowledge then had of the course of the river was derived from Sauthier's map, a copy of which, corrected at the office of the surveyor general, from the latest data in his possession, was used in these early sales. Black river was entirely omitted on the printed map, and when thus laid out upon vague information, was represented as flowing in a

1 Boylston proved to be a partner of Lane, Son and Fraser of London, who soon failed for a large amount, and the title was subsequently conveyed by their assignees. Boylston was related to the wife of Col. Wm. S. Smith, who is mentioned in connection with Samuel Ward's operations.

nearly direct line from the High falls to the lake. The lands south of the river were sold for 400,000 acres, but upon survey they measured 817,155 acres. To rectify this enormous error is said to have cost Constable £60,000 sterling. On the 21st of May, 1794, Boylston gave a deed of trust of the land since known as the Black river tract, to George Lee, George Irving, and Thomas Latham, assignees of the firm of Lane, Son and Frazer of London, and they in turn conveyed to John Johnson Phyn of that place,[1] June 2, 1794, with whom by sundry assurances in law the title became vested in fee simple, with all the rights and appurtenances pertaining thereto.[2] Phyn appointed Constable his attorney to sell any or all of these lands, April 10, 1795,[3] and the latter sold, on the 15th of July following, to Nicholas Low, William Henderson, Richard Harrison and Josiah Ogden Hoffman, all of New York city, the land between the Black River and a line running in a course S. 81° E. 3100 chains, from the mouth of Sandy creek to the river.

In a letter from Wm. Henderson to Constable, dated Feb. 6, 1795, the writer stated a difficulty in the lodging of American stocks as security instead of personal responsibility. All the advantage he expected was to be derived from the credit allowed, and to buy stock and pledge it would cost more than to advance the money and make full payment at once. Constable was offered an interest in the tract if he preferred to become an associate. Mr. Henderson added: "The room for speedy profit on waste lands in general above a dollar an acre, I do not, for my part, think very great; indeed the sudden rise which they have taken may be considered in a great degree artificial. You will say, perhaps, 'Why then do you purchase?' I reply, because they have been an article in which there is great speculation, and therefore *may answer to sell again.*"

The proposition of Hamilton for bringing the western territory into market at a cheap rate, was looked upon as an alarming indication of ruin by those making this investment.

To give a better idea of these speculations in northern lands, we will quote from a letter written late in 1798, by one of the parties concerned, to his agent in London. After stating that the capital invested might lie unproductive a few years, but would certainly return several hundred per-

---

[1] James Phyn married a sister of Constable, and traded at Schenectady with John Duncan before the revolution. John Johnson Phyn, his son, was an unmarried man.

[2] Deeds, Sec. office, xxiv, 35.

[3] Deeds, Sec. office, xxxix, 64.

cent. in the end, he says that in 1786, he received 3000 acres in Bayard's patent, on the Mohawk, valued at four shillings the acre, which, in 1796, he brought into market and sold at twenty shillings. He then mentions the purchase of the Boylston tract in 1794, estimated at 400,000 acres, at two shillings, and adds:

"On my arrival here in 1795, I had it surveyed and explored, when it appearing that from the course of the river by which it was bounded, it comprehended double the quantity, or upwards of 800,000 acres, the purchase being so much larger than I had contemplated, I was under the necessity of proceeding immediately to sell a part of the tract. This I found no difficulty in doing, as the land was found to be uncommonly good. Messrs. Nicholas Low and his associates purchased 300,000 acres at 8*s.*, or 4*s.* 6*d.* sterling, one-fourth of the money payable down, the balance in five annual installments, with interest, the whole of the land remaining security on mortgage. In 1796, I had the whole of the remaining 500,000 acres laid out in townships of 25 to 30,000 acres, and sold in that and the succeeding year about 100,000 acres from 6*s.* 9*d.* to 9*s.* sterling, receiving ¼ the the money down, and taking mortgage to secure the balance in five annual payments with interest at 7 per cent. as is customary. I interested a Mr. Shaler in one-half of two townships, on condition of his settling on the tract, and selling the lands out in small farms of about 200 acres, he to be charged 9*s.* per acre for his part, and to have half the profit on the sales. He accordingly went out and had the lands surveyed, made a road from fort Stanwix into the midst of it, and built a saw mill and a grist mill. His accounts last rendered show the disposal of about 10,000 acres for nearly $40,000, of which he has paid me all the money received, being $10,000, and has made an account of expenses for roads buildings, &c., of about $4,000. He sells alternate lots at $4 the acre, the settlement of which will immediately give an additional value to the intermediate ones, which we mean to reserve."

A deficiency of 24,624 acres being found on the survey of the Boylston tract, this was supplied from township 2 [Worth], in Jefferson county. On the 15th of April, 1796, Phyn confirmed this sale.[1] One quarter of the purchase was paid down and the balance secured by mortgage, which was paid and canceled June 16, 1804. It had been assigned to the bank of New York with other accounts of Constable.

The Black river tract was divided by ballot between the owners on the 11th of August, 1796. Low drew 2, 7, and 11, or Watertown, Adams and Lowville, and 1,578 acres of the surplus tract; Henderson took 3, 6 and 9, or Rutland,

[1] Deeds, Sec. office, xxxvii, 214.

Henderson and Pinckney, and 649 acres of the surplus; and Harrison and Hoffman together, 1, 4, 5, 8, and 10, or Houndsfield, Champion, Denmark, Rodman, and Harrisburgh, and 1283 acres of the surplus. As their guide, in making this division, Mr. Benjamin Wright who surveyed the outlines of the towns in April, and May, 1796, reported with a minute description of soil, timber, and natural advantages, the following general summary of his views with regard to their relative value:

"Numbers 1, 2, 5, 6, 7, have very little to choose in point of quality. 6 is best situated, but 7 is a most excellent town. 5 would be called best by New England people on account of the luxuriancy of its soil on Deer creek. 2 is an exceeding good town, but is not so good as 7. 8 and 9 are very good towns. 10, the north part, is exceeding good. 11, the west part is excellent. 7 has the preference of the whole for quality and situation together, and 6 for situation only. 1 is well situated, but I fear has not good mill sites on it. 8 has excellent mill sites, and 9 also, but are some broken. 10 is bad on the south line, and 9 also being cold and hemlocky."

The prejudice against hemlock timber is historically connected with the titles, and had an influence upon opinion as to the value of lands, which experience has not sustained. The indifferent quality of these lands when first brought under cultivation, is found due to the large amount of tannin in the leaves, and as this disappears the capacity of the soil increases until it may equal the best, other circumstances being equal.

Boylston's Tract and Constable's Four Towns.—On the 10th of April, 1795, Phyn reconveyed to Constable 105,000 acres for £10,000, which tract was subdivided into four towns adjacent to Inman's triangle, and almost reaching the S. E. corner of the eleven towns of the Black river tract.

On the 1st of April, 1796, Phyn reconveyed to Constable 406,000 acres for $400, this being the residue of the Boylston tract. This land was subdivided into thirteen towns, which in common language have been denominated the "Boylston Tract," although strictly speaking, that tract included every thing between Black river, the lake, and Inman's triangle, amounting to 817,155 acres. The separate numbering of the townships surveyed out from the lands released in 1795 and 1796, has resulted in some confusion as, from 1 to 4, the numbers are duplicated. The outlines of these towns were mostly surveyed by Wm. Cockburn & Son of Poughkeepsie.

The contract with Wright for surveying townships 3, 4, 6, 8, and 9, into lots in 1805, provided that one acre of land in townships 1 and 10 was to be paid for every mile run. It appears that the survey of 4, amounted to 152 miles 42 chains; of No. 6 to 136½ m.; of No. 8 to 154 m. 36 ch.; of No. 9 to 110 m. 39 ch.; and of No. 3 to 161 m. 43 ch.; making 715½ acres due for the survey of 5 towns.

On the 29th of December, 1795, Constable sold to Nathaniel Shaler of Middletown, an undivided half of 52,418 acres being numbers 3 and 4 of Constable's four towns, and made him his agent for selling the other half.[1]

On the 15th of November, 1798, Wm. Constable, on the eve of his departure for Europe, appointed his brother James an agent to sell lands,[2] and under this authority the latter sold most of township 5, or 8000 acres, to Walter Martin on the 18th of June, 1801, receiving $5,400, and a mortgage for $6,600 due in two equal annual payments.

Upon the death of Wm. Constable, May 22, 1803, John McVickar, James Constable, and Hezekiah B. Pierrepont, became the executors of his estate, and in 1819, the latter by purchase acquired the interests of the several heirs. By virtue of marriage with a daughter of Mr. Constable, he had previously become an owner of a share of the estate. The remaining heirs were paid about $25,000 each, principally in lands. By this means Edward McVickar became owner of lands in the west subdivision of No. 5, and in No. 9. The remaining interests in 3 and 4 of Constable's four towns became the property of William Constable, who settled at Constableville, and other members of the family became interested either in lands or contracts.

In the beginning Wm. C. adopted the plan of deeding lands and taking mortgages, but this being found expensive and troublesome, it was superseded by that of contracts, guaranteeing an ample deed upon full payment. This contract, originally prepared by Alexander Hamilton, has not been changed. It secures legal interest annually to the proprietor, requires the purchasers to pay all surveys, taxes, and assessments, binds them not to abandon the premises, or sell or assign the contract, or cut, or suffer to be cut for sale, any timber without the consent of the proprietor, or commit any waste, actual or permissive, upon the premises. In case of default, it is optional with the party of the first part to abide by the contract, or consider it void, and if the latter, to re-enter and dispose of the pre-

1 Transcribed Deeds, Lewis Clerk's office, p. 155.
2 Deeds, Sec. office, xli, 623; Regr's office, N. Y., lvi, 169.

mises as in case of a tenant holding over without permission. The inflexible rule of requiring one quarter payment upon purchase was never relaxed by Constable, but was changed by his executors.

On the 1st of March, 1817, Judge James McVickar, who had acquired an interest by marriage with a daughter of Wm. Constable, conveyed by three several deeds, to George Davis of Belleville, N. J., 5,224¾ acres in townships 3 and 4, then Turin, for $14,225. He also on the same day, conveyed about 3,760 acres to Thomas Alsop, for $11,500, and on the 1st of January following, for $6,000, an undivided half of 46 lots in townships 3 and 4, of Constable's towns. On the 18th of December, Alsop sold for $7,000 to Davis, portions of his improved lands.

Both Davis and Alsop came to reside at Constableville as further noticed in our account of West Turin.

David I. Green of New York, became a purchaser under his brother-in-law Davis, June 16, 1818, and a few days after, conferred upon him powers of attorney to sell lands. Green was for many years cashier of the Phœnix bank, N. Y., and by a long course of exemplary attention to its business, had secured the confidence of the directors to such an extent that they at length made but superficial examinations of his accounts. Soon after the purchase above noticed, he was found a defaulter to the amount of about $140,000, and large packages of bills which had for some time previous been coming through the mails to Capt. Davis, together with mysterious arrangements for expediting the journey of some traveler, should he need to be forwarded in haste towards Canada, leave little room for doubt that a part of the stolen money was used in buying these lands, and that Davis was to some extent, at least, privy to the crime. Green was also deeply concerned in cotton and other speculations, which proved failures, and brought to light his robbery of the bank. He got a few hours' start of the officers of justice, and escaped by way of lake Champlain to Quebec, from whence he sailed to France. In two or three years some arrangement was made, by which he could return, and after going to Michigan, he came back to Davis' house near Constableville, and died, Sept. 5, 1826, aged 45 years.

The Phœnix bank became from this transaction an interested party to the title of a portion of the lands previously held by Davis.

On the 25th of July, 1801, Wm. Constable, in part payment of notes and endorsements of the firm of Wm. & Jas.

Constable, and in consideration of $95,704.50, conveyed townships 1 and 13 on the south border of this county to John Jones, John McVickar and John Rathbone, in trust for the owners of the notes. These towns were conveyed to the trustees above named, July 15, 1802, and proving more than sufficient after making several conveyances amounting to 43,704 acres, they reconveyed the balance to Constable.[1] Of the lands retained to pay the creditors for whose benefit this arrangement was made, 6,118¼ acres in No. 1, and 5,431¼ in No. 13, were deeded to John Jacob Astor, Jan. 28, 1804;[2] and a further quantity of 3232½ acres was conveyed March 10 of that year.[3] On the 1st of June, 1806, Astor sold the whole of his lands in these two townships to Hezekiah B. Pierrepont, for $18,477.50, receiving a mortgage for a part of the amount, due in five, six and seven years.[4]

The trustees above named on the 28th of Jan., 1804, deeded 743 acres of township 1, and 10,074 of township 13, to H. B. Pierrepont.

Inman's Triangle was conveyed Feb. 12, 1793, by Wm. Constable to Wm. Inman, in trust, chiefly for Patrick Colquhoun. The history of this transaction will be given in our account of Leyden.

Brantingham Tract.—S. Ward and wife, conveyed Aug. 18, 1793, to the name of Wm. Inman a tract of land supposed to be 50,000 acres, east of the river, in trust for P. Colquhoun, in pursuance of a contract with Constable of Feb. 13 of that year. The price was £5,000 sterling, and it was the intention of the European owner to offer 10,000 acres to Capt. Charles Williamson at first cost, and he instructed Inman to do so. The latter wrote as directed, but added: "I have no doubt of the propriety of your refusing to accept the share of the 18,000 acres, and I confess I had little hopes of your doing so, although I am certain it would have been highly advantageous to you. I can speak my mind freely to you; and I do not hesitate to say that Mr. C.[5] is capable of expressing sentiments he does not, when they are calculated to serve his own particular purposes; and I am authorized to say, his friendship for you was merely a name, and his boasted attachment and profession

---

1 In township 1, lots 1 to 19 and part of 20=4880 acres; and in 13 lots, 1 to 62, and part of 140=15,484 acres.

2 Deeds, Lewis county, A., 187.

3 In township 1, 2320¼ acres and in 13, 912½ acres. Deeds, Lewis co., A., 190. 4 Deeds, Lewis county, A., 186.

5 Referring to P. Colquhoun, who had loaded him with kindness.

for me was no better, and people would do well to be on their guard in their transactions with that gentleman." Within two months the writer of this letter, offered to buy these lands himself, stating that Williamson declined to purchase. The transaction needs neither note nor comment. Upon survey by Cockburn in 1794, the tract was found to measure 74,400 acres. In August, 1793, Brockholst Livingston became a purchaser in trust for himself and certain alien owners, of whom he alone was allowed to hold lands. There were two associations formed, for holding the Fellowship location, of 50,000 acres, and the Surplus lands, of 24,400, the latter of which belonged exclusively to B. Livingston and Patrick Colquhoun, high sheriff of London. In Dec., 1793, a contract was made between B. L. and Robert Morris,[1] for the 50,000, in behalf of the latter, and Mr. Nicholson and James Greenleaf; but this conveyance was never made, and on the 10th of April, 1794, Wm. Inman, acting for another, sold to Thomas Hopper Brantingham[2] of Phila. for $23,073, the whole tract. The latter soon after executed three mortgages for £7,692,[3] and appointed, Aug. 9, 1794, Arthur Breese his attorney to sell a certain tract of 18,000 acres,[4] but no sales appear to have been made by this agent. Brantingham and wife on the 21st of Jan., 1795, sold 10,000, an undivided part of the tract to Richard W. Underhill of N. Y., for £7000, and other claimants became incidentally interested,[5] but the mortgages being unpaid, two of them were foreclosed and the lands sold[6] according to statute. The lands were re-leased to Inman, and were further confirmed by the assignment of the judgments, upon which a sale was made Nov. 17, 1796, by the sheriff of Herkimer county to Inman,[7] in trust. The latter soon after mortgaged the whole to Thomas Walker, agent of Colquhoun; and by sundry conveyances the title became vested in Brockholst Livingston, Samuel Ogden, James Kerr and Patrick Colquhoun.

The tract was surveyed into lots by Benjamin Wright in 1806, and the tract was divided Nov. 25, 1815, into four parts, of which the N. E. and S. W. marked 2, were drawn

[1] Deeds, Oneida co., iv, 263. Consideration $30,000.

[2] B. was allowed to hold lands in this state by an act of April 9, 1792. He failed in business in the spring of 1794, and in 1795 was imprisoned for debt. [3] Deeds, Lewis co., 149, 151.

[4] Deeds, Oneida co., ii, 224.

[5] Wm. Bird, Joseph Brantingham, Philip Grim and others are named in connection with this title. [6] April 1, and Sept. 1, 1796.

[7] Deeds, Lewis co., 160.

by Kerr and Colquhoun, and the S. E. and N. W., marked 1, by Livingston and Ogden.[1] Lots 253 and 235, including the High falls, were not included, but remained common property of the four proprietors.

By an order of chancery dated June 17, 1822. Elisha Wilcox, Uriel Hooker, and Nathaniel Merriam, were appointed commissioners for making a partition so far as concerned Ogden and Livingston.

In September, 1818, Caleb Lyon was appointed sole agent of John Greig, the agent of Kerr and Colquhoun, and purchased about 10,000 acres on his own account. He subsequently brought Livingston's interest, and continued in the agency until his death, when he was succeeded by his son Lyman R. Lyon, and son-in-law Francis Seger. This agency continued until about 1851, when L. R. Lyon bought out the remaining interest of Kerr and Colquhoun, or rather of Greig who had succeeded them in the title,[2] and a part of the Ogden interest. About 25,000 acres of the Brantingham tract are now in the hands of actual settlers.

Brown's Tract.—This term strictly applicable to a tract of 210,000 acres, or 8 townships of land, extending across Herkimer and including small portions of Lewis and Hamilton counties, has come to be applied as a generic term to the whole northern wilderness.

Samuel Ward and wife conveyed, November 25, 1794, to James Greenleaf, a tract of 210,000 acres from the eastern extremity of great tracts V, VI, and the latter mortgaged the premises July 29, 1795, to Philip Livingston. This was foreclosed, and Thomas Cooper, Master in Chancery, united in a deed to John Brown, a wealthy merchant of Providence, R. I., on the 29th of December, 1798.[3] The tract was surveyed into towns by Nathaniel Smith in 1796, and township 2, was surveyed into lots by Cliff French, in 1799. Townships 3 and 4 were never lotted. There were several conveyances of this tract not essential to its chain of title, of which we have not the exact data. John Julius Angerstein, a wealthy London merchant, Henry Newman, Tho.

---

[1] In the S. W. corner 62 lots or 12,804.77 acres. In the N. E. corner 126 lots, 24,647.71 acres. In all 188 lots of 37,452.48 acres. The lands drawn by Livingston and Ogden were in the S. E. corner 56 lots of 12,179.83 acres; and in the N. W. 125 lots of 24,753.01 acres making in all 181 lots of 36,932.84 acres.

[2] In 1834, 42,298 acres of the Brantingham tract were sold for taxes, the greater part of which was bid off by Seger and deeded to Greig. We are not informed of the transactions between Greig and his principals, or the dates of connection with the titles. Mr. Greig became owner in 1821.

[3] Brown named his towns Industry, Enterprise, Perseverance, Unanimity, Frugality, Sobriety, Economy, and Regularity.

and Daniel Greenleaf, Col. Wm. S. Smith, Aaron Burr, and others, were incidentally concerned before Brown's purchase.[1] An expensive but ineffectual effort was made by Brown to plant a settlement upon this tract, and three roads were opened to it. One of these led from Remsen, another from Boonville, crossing the Black river a little south of the county line, and a third from High falls. Mr. Brown died in 1803, and the land was held by his family until a few years since, when it was purchased by L. R. Lyon and others. It is now contracted to the Lake Ontario and Hudson River R. R. Co.

Watson's Tract.—In April, 1796, Constable conveyed to James Watson, by warranty deed, 61,433 acres, comprising two triangular tracts connected by an isthmus. The first deed being lost, it was reconveyed May 13, 1798. The outlines were surveyed in 1794, by Wm. Cockburn. This tract was originally contracted to the French company, but their tract having a surplus, this was sold to Watson at two shillings the acre. Watson's first agreement Dec. 2, 1793, included 150,000 acres.

Castorland.—The romantic scheme of settlement connected with this tract and the probable results that would have ensued, had the location been more favorably chosen, and the affairs more judiciously managed, give interest to this title, and justify a somewhat extended notice of the company formed under it.

On the 31st of August, 1792, Wm. Constable, then in Paris, sold to Peter Chassanis of that city, 630,000 acres of land south of great tract number IV, and between the Black river and a line near the 44° N. latitude.[2] From the mistaken notion of the course of the river before alluded to, it was estimated that this amount of land lay between these two boundaries. Chassanis in this purchase, acted as agent for an association, and the lands were to be by him held in

---

1 Burr was concerned with Ward, and afterwards with Smith, in this purchase, after the title had been held as security by Angerstein. He became involved in a contract Sept. 22, 1794, for the purchase at £50,000, which he found a hard bargain, and the means he took to get released from Constable showed him the polished scoundrel. He wrote a letter Nov. 6, 1794, referring in an insulting manner to an assumed liability of escheat from alien title, and the personal obligation of Constable to convey notwithstanding, and alluded to his ability in influencing legislative action. He professed a mock sympathy with his correspondent, expressed a nice sense of honor as to obligation, and ended with a proposition to pay £10,000 less than the sum agreed upon, or to forfeit £1,000 and be released from the contract.

2 In a deed in Oneida Clerk's office (c. 405) this is called great lot No. V, of Macomb's purchase. It appears that the French originally contracted 1,255,000 acres on all south of No. IV, both sides of the river, but soon relinquished a part.

trust for Constable until paid for, and disposed of in sections of one hundred acres each, at the rate of eight livres tournois per acre.[1] The state reservations for roads, &c., were stipulated, and a deed for 625,000 acres having been made out, was delivered to Rene Lambot, as an escrow, to take effect on the payment of £52,000. Constable bound himself to procure a perfect title, to be authenticated and deposited with the consul general of France in Philadelphia, and Chassanis agreed that the moneys paid to Lambot should be remitted to certain bankers in London, subject to Constable's order, on his presenting the certificate of Charles Texier, consul, of his having procured a clear title. If the sales should not amount to £62,750, the balance was to be paid in six, nine, and twelve months, in bills upon London. The preëmption of great tract No. IV, for one month, was granted at one shilling sterling per acre.

The purchasers immediately set to work to perfect a scheme of settlement, and in October, 1792, issued a pamphlet,[2] embodying the following programme of colonization under the auspices of a company organized under the laws of France, by the name of LA COMPAGNIE DE NEW YORK.

Like many transcendental schemes of modern times, it appeared very beautiful upon paper, and the untried experiment promised every advantage which associated capital and active industry could claim, or the most ardent hope, promise.

Peculiar circumstances, at that time, favored schemes of emigration from France. The kingdom had been three years distracted by a revolution which, for savage atrocity, has no parallel in history, and the reign of terror had deluged the royal palaces in blood, and thrown a lurid gloom over the future. During the negotiation of Constable and Chassanis, the fearful insurrection for which Danton, Murat, Robespierre, and their kindred spirits had been long preparing the Parisian mob, burst forth; the palace of the Tuilleries was surrounded, the faithful attendants of the royal family butchered, and the king, himself, imprisoned. While the scheme we are noticing was preparing, the mock trial of the sovereign was going on, and a few days after it was published, Louis XVI was brought to the guillotine.

---

[1] Eight livres tournois would equal $1.52 4-10.

[2] The official copy annexed to the original contract and certificates (subsequently cancelled as hereafter to be noticed), was presented to the State library by the Hon. Wm. C. Pierrepont in 1853, at the suggestion of the author. A full translation is given in the History of Jefferson County, page 46.

Amid these scenes what law-and-order-loving citizen could feel safe! More especially would those who possessed wealth, or rank, or titles, tremble before this whirlwind of ruin, and gladly invest their money, and trust their lives in any scheme which promised a retreat from the dangers threatened from their fellow men. A wilderness had no terrors to such, and the perils of sea and foreign climes, sank into nothing when placed beside the fearful desolation around them.

The programme of colonization offered by Chassanis, after a glowing allusion to the fertility of the domain, the fine distribution of its waters, its facilities for commerce, its proximity to older settlements, *and the security of its laws*, offered the 600,000 acres for sale in 6000 portions, to as many associates. To maintain an essential unity of interests, the projectors proposed a division by lot, which should give each associate at once a clear title to fifty acres, and leave a like quantity to be divided at the end of seven years, when the whole domain should have been enhanced in value by their common improvements.

The price of one share was fixed at 800 livres ($152.38), upon paying which, the subscriber received the following receipt:

> "The bearer of this certificate has paid the sum of eight hundred livres, which renders him the owner of a hundred acres in six hundred thousand acres which have been sold to us as representatives of the company of proprietors, according to the present contract, which requires us to pass the necessary titles of this portion of the estate in favor of the holder of this certificate, whenever he may wish to receive it in his own name. The present certificate is for an integral part, and a fraction of the purchase above mentioned, by virtue of which the bearer is entitled to all the rights of this association, of which the articles and rules are fixed by the terms of the agreement annexed to this common title.
>
> This certificate bears the number ——. In evidence of which, it has been signed by myself, countersigned by the commissaries of the company, and inspected by M. Lambot, notary."
>
> *Paris, this —— of ——.* PIERRE CHASSANIS.

One tenth part of the money received was to be paid to the commissaries to defray the expense of the concern, such as the purchase of tools, materials, and provisions, surveys, roads, and other necessary investments.

The 30,000 acres additional were to be divided as follows: 2,000 acres for a city upon the great river in the interior, 2,000 for a second city upon lake Ontario, 6,000 acres to poor artisans, to be charged to them after seven years, at at a rent of twelve sous per acre, and 20,000 acres to be spent for roads, bridges, and such other purposes as the society might direct. The two cities were each to be divided into 14,000 lots, of which 2,000 were reserved for markets and edifices, such as churches, schools, and other public establishments, and for poor artisans; and the remaining 12,000 lots, in two classes, were to be distributed among the 6,000 proprietors; one class immediately, and the other at the end of seven years, when a final report was to be made, and those who elected might receive their remaining shares and withdraw. Those who did not declare this intention two weeks before the advertised day for division, were to be deemed to have chosen the continuation and non-division of the common property.

The affairs of the company were to be managed by three commissaries living in Paris, and two residing upon the tract, who were to be chosen by an absolute majority at a general assembly to be held in Paris, at which each owner might vote in person or by proxy. Each share up to five, was entitled to one vote, but no person could have more than five votes, whatever the number of shares he might possess. The articles might be modified by a general assembly convened for the purpose, by a majority of two-thirds.

The second section of the programme related to government, and was as follows:

Article 1. Within one month, there shall be held a meeting of the subscribers, at the rooms of Sieur Chassanis at Paris, No. 20, *Rue de la Jussienne*, for the election of commissaries.

Art. 2. The commissaries residing in Paris, shall have the care of proving the certificates with the depository, and of personally examining each to guard against errors: the notary shall also compare them as received and paid, after which they shall be signed by the said Chassanis, to be delivered to the shareholders. Consequently no certificate shall be issued until after these inspections and signatures, and the subscribers shall in the mean time, only receive a provisional receipt of deposit.

Art. 3. To guard against errors in distribution, the certificates shall be registered by their numbers, by Chassanis, upon their presentation by the holders, in the record kept in his office, and without this entry, of which notice shall be written upon the certificate by the said Chassanis, or by the one whom the commissaries shall appoint for the purpose, no holders of certificates shall be admitted to the meetings, nor allowed to take his chance in the selection of his location.

Art. 4. The commissaries chosen for removal to America, shall be bearers of the instructions and general powers of the assembly; shall survey the land, fix the location of the two cities, and there prepare for the company within three months after their arrival, a report of their examinations and labors, with a detailed plan of the common property.

Art. 5. The commissaries shall be chosen from among the holders of certificates.

Art. 6. The commissaries shall decide the location of the fifty acres to belong at first to each certificate, after which the holders shall have the right of choice.

Art. 7. The locations shall be marked upon two registers, in the hands of the commissaries in America, who shall retain one, and transmit the other annually to the General Assembly in France.

Art. 8. The titles directed to be delivered to the holders of certificates who make known their wish, shall contain a declaration by Chassanis, that in his general purchase there belongs a certain portion to —— as his own, in accordance with a common title, and a social regulation of which he is a party; this declaration shall bear the number of the certificate, which shall remain attached under pain of forfeiture of the share, even though the certificate had been previously cancelled, and this title shall not be completed, till after the registration of the commissaries to whom it shall be presented.

Art. 9. The commissaries in America, shall be clothed with similar power by Chassanis, for granting like titles to those who require it. This power shall be granted after a model of the declaration, for the purpose of securing uniformity of registration.

Art. 10. All decisions and acts of the company done in France, so far as relates to commissaries, have no need of public formality when they are legalized by the minister or other public functionary of the United States in France.

Art. 11. There shall be delivered, upon demand, a duplicate of title to the holders of certificates, containing a copy of the original, and in it shall be mentioned that it is a duplicate.

It does not appear in what manner public attention in Paris was invited to this project. The *Moniteur* of Nov. 29, 1792 (page 1,413), has an article on the extraordinary profits of the potash manufacture at Cooperstown, and from time to time it notices with commendation, the fine opportunities which the state of New York offered to emigrants, without specially naming the scheme of Chassanis and his associates. Other journals appear to indicate an interested desire to favor the formation in France, of companies of emigrants for settling upon property bought and held in common, in the northern states of the American union, and several French authors published romantic accounts of the soil, climate, and resources of this country, with plans for associated settlement.[1]

On the 28th of June, 1793, the second of the French republic, at five o'clock in the afternoon, the actual holders of provisional receipts convertable into shares of the *Company of New York*,[2] met at the rooms of citizen Chassanis, in the street of Jussienne, section of Mail, in Paris, and proceeded to organize the basis of their society, establish its rules, and deliberate upon all points relative to its division, survey, preparation for market and sale.

Before proceeding to this business, Chassanis recounted the origin of the title, and described its successive changes, from the Indian purchase to its sale by Constable, as certified by John D. Coxe and Jared Ingersol, on the 19th of November, 1792, and deposited in the office of the French consulate in Philadelphia.[3]

The prospectus issued in October, had in December (the period when Constable counted upon a part of the funds which the sale should have procured), failed to obtain purchasers, and Constable directed Col. Ward, his agent, to withdraw the lands from market. Nevertheless, upon the representation of citizen Chassanis, Col. Ward consented to the sale in France of 2,000 shares, and he was assured that 200,000 acres near Black river, and extending to lake Ontario, would be reserved to these 2,000 shares. Upon this basis the provisional receipts had been delivered to the purchasers, and to meet this new engagement, Constable, by a contract passed in London on the 12th and 13th of April, 1793, had, according to all the forms of law, transferred to citizen Chassanis, not only 200,000 acres and 5 p. c. over, for roads and public objects, but also 10,000 acres to facilitate the bringing into market the 200,000 acres. In this instrument, Constable was further bound to transmit to the company the indemnities granted by the state of

---

1 Of these writers J. E. Bonnet, was perhaps the most zealous. In a work of two volumes entitled *Etats Unis de l'Amerique a fin du XVIIIe siecle*, and another several years after; *Tableau des Etats Unis, de l'Amerique au commencement du XIX siecle*, he proposed elaborate plans for colonial association. In the latter, he gives central and northern New York the preference of all other sections of the union, every circumstance being taken into account. He was enthusiastic in his admiration of the sugar maple, which he foretold would yet supply Europe and America with sugar, extinguish African slavery by superseding the cultivation of the sugar cane, and introduce a new era of human happiness.

2 Tillier in his Memorial, p. 3, says that 41 shareholders representing 1,808 shares, attended this meeting.

3 This instrument was acknowledged before Clement Biddle, notary, on the day it was executed.

New York, in cases of lands covered by water. He also recognized the payment in full of £25,000 by Chassanis, for the lands above mentioned.[1] These statements being examined and found to agree with facts, the assembly having listened to the report of the provisional commissaries, and discussed article by article, the project of an association which they offered, unanimously agreed upon the following

CONSTITUTION.

Seal.

TITLE I.—*Declaration of the Rights of the Company.*

Article 1. Citizen Chassanis declares, that all the lands and rights by him definitely acquired of Wm. Constable, by the final contract of the 13th of April last, have been, for the benefit of the purchasers of 2,000 shares of 800 livres each, amounting to the total price of the said purchase, which has been paid to Constable, as appears from the receipt inserted in the said instrument of sale, and repeated by him upon the fold of the said contract. Citizen Chassanis acknowledges, that this payment has been made from funds received from the sale of nearly all of the shares, of which it is well to notice, that one-tenth of the price has been remitted by Constable to the shareholders. Consequently, citizen Chassanis cedes and conveys, so far as need be, to the said shareholders, all the rights of property or otherwise resulting from the said contract, to them collectively, consenting that from this time forth they shall enjoy and dispose of the whole property.

Art. 2. The bearers of receipts controvertable into shares of the said property, who are here present, stipulate, as well for themselves as for those absent, that they accept, as far as need be, and collectively, the property which has been anew declared and ceded by the said citizen Chassanis, with the original conditions annexed to the cession by the state of New York, by letters patent hereinafter mentioned, it being well understood that the said shareholders are not held by these conditions, beyond the proportion of the land which they have purchased under the name of the said citizen Chassanis, by the final contract of April 13th last.

Art. 3. Citizen Chassanis has exhibited and placed upon the table, the documents which establish the original and actual property in the lands and rights which he has bought, to wit:

1*st.* A copy, in legal form, of the letters patent of Jan. 12, 1792.

2*d.* A copy, also in legal form, of the contract of sale made by Alexander Macomb to Wm. Constable, dated June 6, 1792.

3*d.* A copy, in legal form, of the renewal of the said contract of sale by Alexander Macomb and Jane his wife, dated Oct. 3, 1792.

4*th.* Certificate delivered by the Secretary of the Consulate General of France, of the act of deposit of the three above named instruments in the said office.

5*th.* The originals of two certificates of a Master in Chancery of New York, proving that the lands sold are not encumbered by any debt of Alexander Macomb.

6*th.* The original contract of sale of Wm. Constable to Pierre Chassanis, of April 12, 1793, in parchment, with the original pledge of possession.

7*th.* The original bond of the said Wm. Constable in behalf of P. Chassanis, of £50,000 sterling, dated April 12, 1793, to be paid in default of ratification by his wife.

---

1 Constitution de le Compagnie de New York, pp. 1, 3.

Moreover, a printed copy of the prospectus issued by citizen Chassanis, upon the faith of which the shareholders were led to the purchase of their shares.

Lastly, a printed copy of the provisional receipts delivered to the purchasers of shares, to which is annexed a reduction of title of the sale proposed by the prospectus.

Art. 4. The Assembly deposits all of these papers in the hands of citizen Chassanis, and charges him with providing a place of deposit for the archives of the Company of New York.

TITLE II.—*Title of the Shareholders as a Society, and Name of their Property in America.*

Article 1. In adopting as for this, the arrangement implied in the prospectus above mentioned, the Assembly declares that all the said shareholders, as well present as absent, are, by the act of their purchase, co-proprietors in common and of, the lands and rights declared in the first title, and by these presents are constituted dormant partners under the title of *Company of New York*, for the occupation of the said lands and rights, excepting, however, the exceptions and modifications hereinafter specified.

Art. 2. The lands of the Company of New York shall henceforth be known under the name of *Castor Land.*[1]

TITLE III.—*Specification of the Rights which the Company Enjoys and those which it Does Not.*

Art. 1. The ends proposed by the association founded under the preceding title, are: 1*st.* To extend more rapidly life and improvement over all the extent of the lands acquired by the company. 2*d.* To relieve the greater part of the shareholders who can not consent to a passage beyond seas, from the embarrassment and expense attending the first settlement of a large portion of the lands. 3*d.* To aid them with regard to the surplus. *And 4th, and lastly.* To accelerate in that country the population, which will one day become its wealth.

It appears indispensable, that in order to more speedily work these happy results, there should be established over a great part of the purchase that is to remain undivided and in common, a general and capable administration, by the union of the common interests, to give value to that portion, and cause it to realize advantages above what could be derived from the separate exertions of the shareholders through their several agents.

Art. 2. The portion of the said purchase which shall remain with the company, and be held undivided by the associated shareholders, to be enhanced by a general administration, shall be,

1*st.* 100,000 acres of land, to be taken from the 200,000 acres forming the principal object of the said purchase.

2*d.* 20,500 acres, granted as above, to the shareholders by Constable, to wit: 10,000 for roads, canals and public establishments on account of the 5 acres per 100, and 10,000 to be derived from the indemnity. It is observed that in the 220,500 acres mentioned, lands covered by water should not be included, according to the terms of the patent, and the sale of Constable.

3*d.* The tenth part remitted by Constable as an encouragement to the shareholders, upon the whole of the 2,000 shares, in the 1st Article of Title I, amounts to 160,000 livres. This sum is now in the hands of Mr. Lambot, Notary, subject to the order of the shareholders, and is represented by 80,000 livres in credit paper, and a like sum in 100 shares of 800 livres each, which alone remain of the 2,000 shares above mentioned, and were left by Constable to the shareholders, to complete the tenth which he remitted to them, and of which values the Assembly declares its acceptance on account of the said remission.

Art. 3. That portion of the said purchase to be owned separately by the

1 Castor, signifies *Beaver*.

shareholders immediately, shall be divided as soon as may be, in the manner specified in the Title IX, and is composed—*1st*, Of 100,000 acres of land; and *2d*, Of the land which 2,000 divided lots shall occupy in the plan of the first city which shall be projected by the Company of Associates.

TITLE IV.—*Form and Duration of the Society.*

Art. 1. The society which has been formed for the possession and enjoyment in common of the objects specified in Art. 1 of the preceding title, shall consist of 2,000 proprietary shares.

Art. 2. The said shares shall be numbered from 1 to 2,000. These shares instead of being in the form announced in the prespectus, shall be divided into two coupons. The one shall be called *coupon divis*, and shall confer the right to 50 acres in the 100,000 acres divided, and to a divided lot in the plan of the first city which shall be projected upon the lands. The other shall be a stamped *coupon indivis*, and shall give an interest in a two-thousandth part of the objects remaining undivided and in company among the shareholders; and the coupons shall bear the same number as the shares. These coupons shall be drawn in the following form:

Company of New York.

Purchase in the name of Peter Chassanis, of 200,000 acres of land and dependencies known by the name of *Castorland*, and situated in the state of New York, Montgomery co., upon the banks of lake Ontario and of Black river. By deed of April 12, 1793. No.—— Divided coupon. The bearer by full payment of the price of a whole share, of which the present coupon forms a part, is owner by virtue of the said coupon, of divided lot which shall correspond in division with No.—— as well in the plan of the first city which shall be laid out upon the company's land, as in the 2,000 lots of 50 acres each which shall be formed in the division of the divisible property of 100,000 acres making a part of the purchase above named, after the manner determined by the organization of the said company dated June 28, 1793, of which a quadruple remains in the archives of the company and another shall be registered and deposited in the city of New York. Note. This coupon shall be exchanged for a deed upon delivery of the lot.

GUYOT,	CHASSANIS,	GUINOT,
Commissary.	Director.	Commissary.

Inspected according to the act of June 28, 1793.
LAMBOT.

(The second part or undivided coupon is similar, excepting that it gives the holder a final right to one two-thousandth part of the undivided property of the company upon its dissolution.)

Art. 3. Agreeable with the prospectus, the coupons forming each share shall be signed by citizen Chassanis and two commissaries of the company, and inspected by citizen Lambot, notary at Paris.

Art. 4. The provisional receipts delivered by the said Lambot, notary, who has been instructed to receive the payment of the said shares, will need to be exchanged for shares in the above form, which shall bear the same numbers as the receipts to which they correspond.

Art. 5. This exchange shall be made at the company's office, and when done, the exchanged receipts shall be canceled and left with the director of the company, to be sent to the said Lambot as they become worthless by exchange, and by the discharge of the said Lambot to Constable, shall operate by the release inserted in the contract of sale aforesaid.

Art. 6. The society, beginning to-day, shall continue twenty-one years from the 1st of July next, with the privilege of dissolving before the expiration of this term, as will be hereafter explained in Title XII.

Art. 7. None shall be regarded as true members, except the bearers of *coupons indivis* of the two thousand shares aforesaid.

Art. 8. The *coupon divis* of each of the said shares, shall never give the privilege of the society, except as an action against it, to compel the delivery to the bearer of the divided lot mentioned in the coupon, in the manner hereinafter explained in title IX.

TITLE V.—*Government of the Society, a Director and four Commissaries living in Paris, their Functions and Powers.*

Art. 1. The interests of the company shall be managed by a director and four commissaries living in Paris, where the government of the society shall remain fixed.

Art. 2. The director and commissaries, shall always be chosen at a general meeting of the shareholders, by an absolute majority of votes and viva voce.

Art. 3. They can only be chosen from the company, and a person to be director or commissary, must be the owner or holder of at least ten entire shares or of twenty *coupons indivis*, of which deposit shall be made into the hands of citizen Lambot, notary, within eight days after their nomination to the said places, and their powers shall cease if they become the owners of a less amount than above named.

Art. 4. The director once chosen, shall hold his office during the existence of the society, without the power of change, unless in a general assembly called for the purpose, and by a majority of two-thirds.

Art. 5. The commissaries in Paris, shall be renewed seven times in the course of the society, namely, the first time in three years from the 1st of July next, and at intervals of three years after, until the complete revolution of 21 years which the society is to last.

Art. 6. The director shall be charged with the correspondence, and the preservation of the titles, registers, papers, and in general with whatever may enter the archives of the company. He shall convene general assemblies of the shareholders and those of the commissaries, shall provide a convenient place for meeting, and preserve the record of general and special meetings. He shall deliver shares to the bearers of receipts of citizen Lambot. He shall have a consultive voice in the meetings of commissaries, and a casting vote when they are equally divided. He shall hold the funds of the society, and pay and receive money, but he shall make no payment but upon an order signed by two commissaries. He shall keep or cause to be kept for the company, the necessary registers, namely:

1st. A stock-register, for the verification of shares and their coupons.

2d. A record of correspondence.

3d. A record of deliberations.

4th. A register of accounts.

5th. A register which shall show the numbers of *coupons indivis*, and the names of the proprietors who might wish to make this known.

Lastly. He shall, conjointly with the commissaries at Paris, pass to the credit of the shareholders, all titles of property that may fall due, for all of which acts the company confers upon him the necessary powers.

Art. 8. The commissaries at Paris are charged with deliberating and deciding among themselves upon all the affairs and interests of the company, with following and regulating all the operations in which it may be interested; with carrying into effect the decisions of the general assemblies of the company, and with giving, in the name of the company, to the director and the commissaries in America, the instructions and orders that may be necessary; with directing the employment of the funds of the society, and watching the recovery of sums due to it; with ordering payments; with making purchases to send to America; with passing conjointly with the director all declarations of property to the name of the proprietor of shares or coupons when they fall due; with signing the coupons of shares, to deliver to the shareholders, and with watching the operations of the director and commissaries in America. They shall audit annually the accounts of the director, and lastly, submit to the general assemblies all projects they may deem useful, and for these services the company confers upon them all needed powers.

Art. 9. The commissaries in Paris shall receive no salary, but in recognition of the care which they may bestow upon the common concerns, there shall be given them an attendance fee (*droit de presence*) for each special or general assembly where they may meet on the affairs of the company. This fee is fixed at two Jettons of silver, of the weight of 4 to 5 *gros*. They shall be made at the expense of the company, under the direction of the commissaries, who shall decide upon their form and design.[1]

Art. 10. The commissaries in Paris, shall meet at least once a month ; their deliberations shall be held before the director, and shall be determined by a plurality of individual votes.

Art. 11. All decisions thus made, and signed by three commissaries, or by two of them and the director in case he shall have had a deliberative voice, shall have as full and entire force as if they had emanated directly from the majority of the society, and hence the engagements and decisions which result, shall be binding upon the company.

Art. 12. Nevertheless, the commissaries shall neither make nor authorize any loan in the name of the company, without having received a special order at a general assembly of the associates.

Art. 13. The assembly confirms anew the nomination which the shareholders made in their deliberations of the 19th and 20th of the present June, of citizens Guyot, Maillot, Guinot and la Chaume, as commissaries of the company at Paris.

Obverse.

1. These pieces occur in coin cabinets, and have been erroneously called "Castorland half dollars." A *Jetton* is a piece of metal struck with a device, and distributed to be kept in commemoration of some event, or to be used as a counter in games of chance. The one here noticed was termed a *Jetton de presence*, or piece "given in certain societies or companies to each of the members present at a session or meeting." (*Dic de l'Acad. Francaise.*)

This custom has its analogy in the existing practice of certain stock companies in New York, in which a half eagle or a quarter eagle is given to each director present at each meeting held on the business of the company. The piece above figured was doubtless designed to be given to emigrants and others as a keepsake, and was not a *coin*, as it wanted the sanction of law, nor a *token*, as it was not to be redeemed. It was engraved by one of the Duvivier brothers, eminent coin and medal artists of Paris, who became a shareholder in this company, and drew 500 acres of land. This family was celebrated in this particular art. Joannes Duvivier, the father, died in 1761. The design represents on the obverse the head of *Cybele*, as indicated by the turreted mural crown. In Classic Mythology, this goddess personified the earth as *inhabited and cultivated*, while Titæa or Tellus, represented the earth taken in a general sense, Ceres, the fertility of the soil, and Vesta, the earth as warmed by internal heat. The laurel wreath is an emblem of victory, and represents Cybele as conquering the wildness of nature and bringing the earth under the dominion of man. The design is arranged with classic elegance, but shows a palpable ignorance of the country. Ceres has just tapped a maple tree, and inserted a *faucet* for drawing off the sap at will, and the grain, flowers and foliage appear strangely brought into the sugar season. The Latin legend reads on the obverse—"French American Colony," and on the reverse it presents a quotation from Virgil, which, with its context, reads as follows :

Reverse.

"*Salve magna parens frugum, Saturnia tellus,*
Magna virum: * * * " GEOR., ii. 173.

"Hail Saturnian Land, great Parent of Fruits, great Parent of Heroes!" The apostrophe thus addressed to Italy, was intended to apply to Castorland, a country situated in nearly the same latitude, and for aught these Parisians knew to the contrary, equally adapted to the vine and the olive.

A *gros* was 59.02 grains, the actual weight of the piece was 206.25 grains, its fineness about nine-tenths, and its intrinsic value 50 cents. Dealers value it at about $3, and Riddel, in his Monograph of the Silver Dollar, states that he knows of but a single copy. Its history was entirely blank until noticed in Hickcox's American Coinage, where a fine steel engraving is given. The figure here inserted, was engraved from a fresh copy, received from Mr. V. Leray, through the favor of P. S. Stewart, Esq., of Carthage.

TITLE VI.—*The Commissaries in America, their Functions and Powers.*

Art. 1. Two commissaries shall regulate the affairs of the company in America; this number shall be increased if there be occasion.

Art. 2. The said commissaries shall necessarily be chosen from among the shareholders: the nomination shall be made in a general assembly of the company, by an absolute majority and viva voce.

Art. 3. The commissaries in America, shall be required within eight days after their election, in case of acceptance on their part, to execute a bond of 40,000 livres, in which shall be included at least ten entire shares of the company of New York, or at most twenty at their original value. These shares shall be deposited with citizen Lambot, notary, who shall give his private receipt. The company leaves it to the commissaries at Paris to judge of the validity of the securities tendered for these bonds.

Art. 4. The mission of the commissaries in America shall be: to verify and mark the exterior boundaries of the whole tract sold to the shareholders by the said Constable; to direct the surveys, divisions and subdivisions of the said lands; to see to the formation of the divided lots mentioned in title IX, that their value may be nearly equal; to put the divided lots herein mentioned, in possession of their proprietors in the manner to be specified, and to give value to that portion of the lands remaining in the society; and for this end,

1st. To cause the erection of all mills, shops, stores and cottages that may be needed.

2d. To cause all cutting and burning of wood, as well as grubbing out and culture.

3d. To purchase all implements, tools, provisions and animals, necessary and of indispensable utility.

4th. To sell at a moderate profit to new colonists, who may settle upon the lands of the society, portions of the tools and provisions which may belong to the society.

5th. To make all treaties, arrangements, estimates and bargains with surveyors, artizans, workmen and day laborers which should be employed for the labor of the lands and woods.

6th. To arrange all rents and sales, in the advantageous manner for the society, but only upon the lands which overrun the 100,000 acres remaining undivided.

7. To fix the conditions and price of leases of farms upon the whole of the undivided lands. These leases shall nevertheless in no cases exceed the time of the duration of the society, and shall be drawn according to the usages of the country, having regard to the progressive increase of the territorial revenue.

8th. To solicit of the government of New York the opening and maintenance, at its expense, of great routes and canals of communication.

9th. To project and cause to be made, special roads from one district or canton to another. Their mission shall also be to receive the price of sales, rents and hirings, and to give receipts, and to make, on account of the company, all shipments to France of the commodities harvested on the lands of the company. In short, they shall carry and administer, with zeal, economy and intelligence, all the interests of the society in America

Art. 5. These commissaries shall be under the surveillance of those at Paris, and shall be held to conform to the mandates and instructions which shall be given them by the commissaries in Paris, for the exercise of the mission confided to them by the preceding article.

Art. 6. The company authorizes the commissaries in Paris, to confer upon those in America the said powers and all others generally, whatever they may deem necessary for managing, usefully, the property and affairs of the company in America.

Art. 7. The said commissaries shall remove directly to New York, and from thence upon the lands of the company, to reside there and execute the operations which the company or the commissaries of Paris may indicate.

The expense of their passage to America, and of their removal to the said lands, shall be borne by the company to the extent of 1,000 livres tournois.

Art. 8. The company, besides the advantages hereafter mentioned in title IX, will allow to the commissaries in America, an annual allowance of $600, to indemnify for their expense of travelling to the place, and of building a house and an office.

Art. 9. Independently of this allowance, the company reserves the privilege of granting to the commissaries, if satisfied with their labors, a commission upon the benefits which they may confer upon it.

Art. 10. The commissaries in America, shall keep a journal of all their operations, and shall transmit annually to the director of the company a duplicate copy of this journal. They shall send at least once in three months to the director, the state of the labors done during the three months preceding, and they shall maintain a frequent correspondence with him.

Art. 11. The said commissaries shall employ upon the spot, a clerk to keep their writings, and aid in their operations, who shall be allowed a salary half as great as that of a commissary.

Art. 12. The functions of the commissaries in America, shall continue until their recall and the revocation of their powers by the commissaries in Paris, authorized to that effect in a general assembly by a majority of the associates present.

Art. 13. In case the commissaries in America can not agree in opinion, relative to the objects of their administration, they shall then take upon the spot an arbitrator to decide between them. He shall be chosen by preference among the shareholders who may be found in the country.

Art. 14. The assembly confirms anew the nomination which was made in the session of June 19 the present month — of citizens [Simon] Desjardins and [Peter] Pharoux, as commissaries in America, the first as honorary only, and the second with the emolument heretofore fixed.

Title VII.—*Of General and Special Assemblies.*

Art. 1. Annually on the 11th day of January, May and September, or in case of a holiday on the morrow, there shall be held a general assembly of the associated shareholders, at which the commissaries in Paris shall render an account of all that has been done since the last assembly, and the news which shall have been received from the commissaries in America concerning the affairs of the company. General assemblies shall also be convened whenever the commissaries in Paris may deem necessary.

Art. 2. General Assemblies shall be held in Paris at the house of the director of the company, at the day and hour appointed, and shall be presided over by one of the commissaries.

Art. 3. There shall be no business done in a general Assembly, unless the shareholders present are collectively holders of at least 1000 *coupons indivis*, of entire shares, or of 500 only if they are to the number of ten persons, besides the commissaries, and the shares shall be deposited before the assembly in the hands of the director, who is to hold the deposit.

Art. 4. To have admission and a voice in the deliberation of the general assembly, one must be the owner or bearer of five *coupons indivis* of whole shares.

Art. 5. The number of votes in the deliberation shall be in the following proportion to the number of shares: Five shares give one vote, and after that each ten shares shall give one vote up to 45 only, but all shares found in the hands of the same person above 45 shall not be counted, to the end that no shareholder shall ever have more than five votes.

Title VIII.—*Of the Survey and Division of the Lands.*

Art. 1. The survey of the exterior of the domain belonging to the shareholders, shall be made at the expense and under the care of Constable, who has stipulated this. This survey shall be verified if there be occasion by the commissaries in America or their agent.

Art. 2. They shall cause an interior survey of the lands after the plan of instructions which may be given them by the commissaries in Paris.

Art. 3. A duplicate of the results of the survey, shall be sent to Paris, to the director of the company.

Art. 4. The general survey of the land being finished, the subdivisions which may be useful and necessary shall be made.

The first shall be the laying out of the public roads; the second, that of the 100,000 acres to be divided among the bearers of *coupons divis* of whole shares, and their subdivision into 2,000 lots; the third that of a city in the most convenient part of the land remaining in common, and the arrangement of the divided lots in this city; the fourth and last, shall be the marking out of lands to be conceded to American families at a moderate price. The subdivisions shall be made in the above order, unless some great interest of the company requires otherwise. The other subdivisions shall be made afterwards, after the order shall have been given by the company or its commissaries in Paris.

TITLE IX.—*Subdivision of the* 100,000 *acres belonging to the bearers of* coupons divis, *into* 2000 *lots, and the arrangements which are designed in the first city projected by the society.*

MANNER OF CHOOSING THE LOTS.

Art. 1. The 100,000 acres designed to be owned separately by the bearers of *coupons divis* of whole shares, shall only be chosen from [the good and medium lands, without including any land of no value, that is to say, which is not susceptible of any cultivation.

Art. 2. The said 100,000 acres shall be divided into several strips, intermixed as much as possible with the lands which are to remain in common.

Art. 3. As soon as the several portions of land which are to form the said 100,000 divided acres be determined, there shall be laid out 2,000 lots of 50 acres each, and of very equal value, and these lots shall be numbered from 1 up to 2,000.

Art. 4. The lots on Black river, lake Ontario or other navigable waters, shall not have more nor a tenth nor less than a twentieth of water front, and there shall be reserved for the undivided portion one-half of the lands upon Black river and lake Ontario.

Art. 5. The bearers of *coupons divis* shall have a right to one-half of the lands which shall be appropriated by the society to a city, deduction being made for the parts occupied by streets and public establishments.

Art. 6. This right shall only be exercised in the location of the first city which shall be marked out by the society, at whatever period this city may be determined upon.

Art. 7. The divided shareholders shall not have the choice of the portion of land which shall be reserved in the location of the said city, but shall be bound to accept whatever portion may be assigned them by the society.

Art. 8. This portion of land shall be divided into 2,000 separate lots, which shall be scattered through the whole extent of the location of the city, and adjoining the property that is to remain with the society.

Art. 9. To facilitate the division of the lots above mentioned in Articles 3 and 8, among those having rights, these lots shall be designated in a statement by boundaries, according to the nature of the ground, and there shall be prepared two maps at the expense of the company. One of the two originals, duly signed and legalized, shall be sent in the month they are finished, to the director of the company, at Paris, to be deposited in its archives, and the duplicate shall remain in the hands of the commissaries of the society in America.

Art. 10. The division of the lots mentioned in Articles 3 and 8, shall be made as follows, according to the prospectus: The choice shall be made in the order of the numbers of the *coupons divis* of the shares, that is to say, that preference of choice shall pertain to priority of numbers.

Art. 11. The choice of divided lots will need to be made within three months after the deposit of the description and plan of division in the archives of the society, and the shareholders shall be advertised to this effect, as well in the public papers as by letters. Each divided shareholder shall be held, within these three months to notify the director of the company of the choice he has made, and note upon the description his signature, the number of his *coupon divis*, and the precise lot which he has chosen, in default of which the choice shall be void.

Art. 12. To facilitate this operation, at the end of the second month, the commissaries shall cause to be prepared a table of the numbers of the *coupons divis*, of which the bearers have not made choice of lots, and in the course of the third and last month they shall indicate the week in which a determinate series of shareholders must make choice, or in default lose the opportunity of selection and be left eventually to the division by lot hereafter mentioned

Art. 13. Those who have not made choice before the end of three months, or who have not given notice in the manner indicated, shall have no further privilege of choice, and the remaining lots shall then be distributed by lot to the numbers of the coupons which have not selected lots.

Art. 14. The drawing of the remaining lots shall be done in a general assembly of the holders of *coupons divis*, convened for this purpose, and in the manner that shall be arranged by the commissaries in Paris.

Art. 15. The bearers of *coupons divis* who share in this drawing shall be bound to accept the lots drawn, without the power of refusal, and shall note their signatures and the number of their *coupons* into several strips, intermixed as much as possible with the lands which are to remain in common.

Art. 16. In derogation of Article 6, and those following as above given, since it is the interest of the society to hasten the population of the tract, to this end it is deemed proper to offer advantages to the shareholders who may remove upon the lands to reside and begin improvement. It is agreed that every bearer or proprietor of *coupons divis*, upon removal to the tract, may choose from time to time as the survey progresses, without waiting its completion and the turn of his number, provided that he shall not have more than ten coupons. The privilege of choosing before his turn shall be restricted to ten lots, and he shall not have more than 2,000 feet of land along the Black river, lake Ontario or other navigable waters.

Art. 17. The choice by virtue of the privilege implied in article 16 above stated, shall be made in the presence of the commissaries in America or their agent, for this purpose, and on condition that the shareholder, before making choice, shall engage in writing to inhabit or cause to be inhabited a house upon the whole of the lots which he may select, and this in the course of the year following his choice, under pain of an indemnity to the company equal to the value of one tenth part of the lot chosen.

Art. 18. The commissaries sent to America, shall have the privilege of choice expressed in the 12th (16th ?) article above named, to the same limit of ten lots, but shall cause to be inhabited at least two houses upon the lands they may have chosen, under pain of the indemnity named in the preceding article.

Art. 19. The choice mentioned in the three preceding articles shall not be made, except in accordance with the plan of division of the 2,000 divided lots, and a distinction shall be made of the lots chosen upon the map.

Art. 20. The commissaries in America, shall keep statements of the selections made by virtue of articles 16 and 18 above named, and shall pass a duplicate to France to the director of the company.

Art. 21. Each shareholder who may make choice either in France or America, and comply with the formalities heretofore prescribed, shall remit or cause to be remitted to the commissaries in America or in France, the coupons representative of the lots of which he may make choice, and the said commissaries shall pass a declaration of property of the said lots by virtue of which declaration he shall enjoy, hold and dispose of all the property in the said divided lots.

Art. 22. The same shall be observed by those who have submitted to the drawing by lot, and to them shall be passed by the commissaries the same declaration of property to the lots which may fall to them.

Art. 23. The coupons surrendered shall be canceled and deposited in the archives of the company, and notice of this shall be made in the title above mentioned.

Art. 24. The declarations of property shall be passed in the form required in the state of New York.

TITLE X.—*Of the Application of the* 160,000 *Livres, Derived from the Remission made by Constable to the Shareholders.*

Art. 1. The company entrusts to the commissaries in Paris, the care and disposal of the funds composing the 160,000 livres in shares and credit-paper resulting from the remission granted to the society by Constable, and allows them to sell as many as the wants of the society might require, of the 100 shares forming a part of these funds, at the best price they can obtain, provided it be not less than 1,200 livres per share.

Art. 2. The product of the said shares, with the surplus of the said funds existing in credit-paper, shall be employed by the said commissaries to the best advantage they may be able, as well in the purchase of utensils, provisions and other expenses necessary for the success of the first labors to be done upon the estate of the company in the purchase of convertible values in goods and credit in the funds of the bank of New York, and the wants of the commissaries in America shall measure these expenses necessary to the putting in value and the survey of the lands of the company.

Art. 3. The employment and destination above indicated shall be governed by circumstances, under the care and orders of the commissaries in Paris.

TITLE XI.—*Of the End of the Society, and the Division or Disposition of the Property and Rights which shall then belong to it.*

Art. 1. The duration of the society has been fixed as above stated, at 21 years from July 1, 1793, although it may be dissolved before, in the manner now to be indicated.

Art. 2. Nine months before the end of the seven or fourteen first years of the term fixed for the life of the society, the commissaries in America shall send to the administration in Paris, a report of the property and rights then remaining to the society and the nature of the improvements of which it is yet susceptible, and in short, their estimate from the best of their knowledge, calling to their aid, if necessary, the opinion of experts near them.

Art. 3. In the month following the receipt of the report mentioned in the preceding article, there shall be convoked a general assembly of the associated shareholders, and they shall deliberate upon the dissolution of the society, both at the end of the first seven and of the fourteen years. If the dissolution is not decided by a majority of the holders of two shares, the society shall continue seven years longer, yielding to effect this, the mode of voting established by article 2 of title VII.

Art. 4. Six months before the period when the society shall cease, it shall deliberate in a general assembly, in the manner indicated in Title VII, what measures shall be taken to liquidate and divide the property and rights which shall then be found to compose the substance of the society.

TITLE XII.—*On the Form of the Shares and on the Execution of the Clauses of the Present Treaty.*

Art. 1. It is observed that the present act of the society, as well as the shares and all other instruments of the society in France, need no further care for their execution but the public formality of their legalization, which will be done by the minister or other public functionary of the United States in France, in the terms of article 10 of the second part of the prospectus heretofore published, and the assembly repeats, as far as need be, this arrangement, upon the faith of the execution of which the shareholders acquired their shares and established their society.

Art. 2. All the conditions embraced in the present treaty are essential to the constitution of the society, and no part of them shall be derogated during its existence unless by virtue of a deliberation of the general assembly, and by a majority of two-thirds of the *coupons indivis*, yielding in this to the mode of voting mentioned in title VII.

Art. 3. In consequence of the present act, the prospectus under which the shareholders purchased their shares, shall henceforth be regarded as a simple record, and as such a copy shall be placed in the archives of the company.

Art. 4. The record of general and special deliberations of the company, and its commissaries, shall be signed by at least two of the commissaries in Paris, and by the director of the company in his character as common manager; provided, with these three signatures, the said documents shall have as much force as if all the deliberators had signed them.

Art. 5. Collated copies or transcripts of the said records, and of the titles relative to the said property of the shareholders in America, shall be made out by at least two commissaries in Paris, and by the director as a further guaranty. The seal of the society shall also be affixed.

Art. 6. There shall consequently be engraved a special seal for the Company of New York, and the design of the seal shall be determined by the commissaries in Paris.

Art. 7. All the titles of the property of the company which are not already registered in New York, shall be registered there under the direction of the commissaries in America, and if need be, in the name of Peter Chassanis.

Art. 8. The present treaty shall be signed in quadruple; one shall remain in the archives of the society, another shall be placed in charge of Citizen Lambot, Notary, another shall be given to the commissaries who are to go to America, to be registered and deposited in New York with a public officer, and the last shall remain in the hands of the commissaries in America.

Done and executed at Paris, at the dwelling of Peter Chassanis above said, the year 1793, *the said* 28*th day of June.* [1]

Desjardines and Pharoux, appointed by article 14, title VI, of the preceding instrument, lost no time in executing their mission, and leaving France July 7, 1793, arrived in just two months at New York, with the design of proceeding upon the tract to explore its boundaries, and take possession in the name of the company. At Albany, they met one of their countrymen, a political exile, who, although but twenty-four years of age, had already become known by his ingenious mechanical constructions, and who has since justly claimed to rank with Franklin, Brindley, Herschell, and Watt, by the brilliancy of his inventive genius, and his magnificent monuments of constructive art. This person was Marc Isambart Brunel, since celebrated as the founder of the machine shops of the Royal Navy yard at Portsmouth, the builder of magnificent rail road structures in England, and the engineer of the Thames tunnel. His son, the late I. K. Brunel, was one of the principal originators of the "Great Eastern" steamship recently built in England.

---

1 Printed by FROULLÉ, Quai des Augustins No. 39. Cap. quarto, 32 pages.

Brunel was prepared for any adventure, and accepted with eagerness the offer made him by the commissaries, not only of receiving him into their company, but of appointing him their captain on this remote and difficult service. Pharoux was an eminent architect of Paris, and an accomplished engineer, and Desjardines, from what little we learn of his history, was an enterprising but visionary adventurer. We may infer that a cordial fellow-feeling arose between these strangers in a foreign land. They were entirely ignorant of the tract, except that it lay somewhere between the Black river and 44° N. lat., but Brunel, who was a proficient in the use of instruments, was just the man to follow a line of latitude in the woods.

The three Frenchmen hired four natives of the country, making a party of seven men. They supplied themselves with every anticipated want for the journey, including two tents, arms, ammunition, and surveying instruments, with such provisions as might be easily carried, depending upon the forests and the streams for the more delicate and substantial viands. They spent two months in the autumn of 1793 upon this service, and Brunel in after life, often recurred to the incidents of this journey as affording the happiest reminiscenses of his life. Many years after, he was relating the adventure to Louis Phillippe while king of the French, and described minutely the precautions which they had observed in fortifying their camp at night, and employing an Indian escort to attend them. The king pleasantly remarked that *they had traveled in the style of princes.* He had himself been a pilgrim in the American forests with his two brothers, like him, exiles from France, but unlike these French explorers, destitute of those little aids to comfort which had made the journey so agreeable.[1] This began Brunel's life as an engineer. He appears to have been favorably impressed with the country, as he became a shareholder, and drew 500 acres of land in lower Castorland.

Early in 1794, Desjardines and Pharoux petitioned for an act to allow Chassanis to hold lands in New York. They stated that from the political relations then existing, he was unable to change his residence, that he was well affected to

[1] Memoir of Brunel, by Edouard Frere, read July 5, 1850, before the academy of Rouen, and published in the *Precis Analitique des Travaux de l'Academie des Sciences, Belles-Lettres et Arts de Rouen*, 1849-50, p. 67, *Chambers' Edinburgh Journal*, XV, 38.

The route of these explorers probably led from the Mohawk across to Moose river, and down that stream to the High falls. Many years since, a silver spoon marked M. I. B., was found above Lyonsdale, which, doubtless, once belonged to Brunel.

the freedom and government of the country, and with his associates was desirous of promoting its welfare. They also asked for themselves the same benefit, and stated that they had determined upon permanent residence as the agents of Chassanis. The petitioners were by an act of March 27, 1794, allowed the privilege asked, but not their principal.

Pharoux was soon after employed to survey a canal route from the Hudson to lake Champlain, with Brunel, and in the course of the summer of 1794, began the survey of Castorland.

The extraordinary deviation of the river from its supposed course occasioned much complaint, especially since the river cut up their lands into several detached parcels, so that they could only pass from one to another by trespassing upon their neighbors. Desjardines and Pharoux, in a letter of June 7, 1795, to Constable, insisted that the lines should be run with reference to the true, and not the magnetic meridan, and that any deficiency should be made up from the south side of the river. They also urged the speedy execution of release of dower of Mrs. Constable, and the completion of surveys which he was to have made, concluding with the assurance that the equity of their case could not fail to arrest his attention, and that their quality as strangers, would give them farther claims to exact justice from an upright man. Mr. Constable replied that he would do every thing consistent with the rights of others, and cheerfully yield in whatever affected himself only. He could not alter the course of the river, any more than he could prevent the British from stopping his surveyors. Pharoux was drowned soon after with seven of his companions, in attempting to cross the Black river near the Long falls in 1795, and his body was found on an island in Black River bay.[1] Many years after, Le Ray caused a marble tablet to be prepared to be set into the rock, bearing this inscription:

"TO THE MEMORY OF
PETER PHAROUX.
THIS ISLAND IS CONSECRATED."

The first survey as finished by Charles C. Brodhead and assistants in this and subsequent years, was made with reference to two cardinal lines at right angles to each other, from which the lots were reckoned in numbers and ranges.

The line from the High falls, running north to great tract No. IV. was assumed as the principal cardinal, and an east

---

[1] See History of Jefferson Co., p. 50, for details of this accident.

and west line, crossing this nine miles from the falls was fixed as a second cardinal. The ranges extended to 19 east, 51 west, 27 north and about 9 south. Except on the margin, the lots measured 450 acres each, and were subdivided into nine lots of 50 acres each, which were numbered from 1 to 4,828. Lower Castorland, or Beaverland, west of the Great bend, measured 964 lots of 40,522.1 acres and upper Castorland, 3864 lots of 182.895 acres, making a fraction over 223,417 acres. No part of the tract crossed Black river, although the principal cardinal crossed the river several times. The isolated tracts thus left, were numbered from the south northward, and of these No. 4 was much larger than all the rest together, including the large triangular area in the northeast part of this county and the adjacent part of Jefferson.

In this survey the principal streams were named, but most of these have since been changed. The following are the principal ones that can be identified:

Old names.	Present names.
Deer Creek.	Crystal Creek.
Siren Creek.	Blake Creek.
Swan Creek.	Indian River.
Pelican Creek.	Swiss Creek.
French River.	Oswegatchee River.
Linnet Creek.	Blake Creek.

The name of Independence creek, Beaver river and Murmer creek are still retained.

The first settlers found their way upon the tract in June, 1794, cutting their way as they came from fort Stanwix; it is generally believed that they mistook the *High falls*, for the *Long falls*, and they settled at the former, upon a tract scarcely wide enough for a garden, and remote from the great body of their lands. The death of Pharoux checked the growth of the colony, and its history during the first three years is nearly blank. Desjardines acted a short time as agent.

On the 11th of April, 1797, Chassanis appointed Rodolphe Tiller, "member of the Soevereign Council of Bern,"[1] his agent, with power to superintend surveys and improvements, form useful establishments, give titles in tracts of 100 or at most 200 acres to settlers and artisans, receive moneys, and solicit of the state the opening of roads and canals, and of

[1] This council consisted of not less than 200, nor more than 299 members. It had power to make war, peace and alliances, raise moneys and provide for expenditures. It appointed the Lesser Council.

the general government, the same privileges to French citizens as were enjoyed by Americans. This privilege of selling lands was limited to 10,000 acres.

The managers in Paris prescribed minutely from their maps, the divisions that were to be made, and the roads that were to be opened, having no reference to the surface, or the local difficulties that might be encountered. Mr. V. Le Ray, in writing to the author from Paris, Nov. 16, 1859, says:

"I would hardly dare state such a fact, if a sample of this folly was not known in the country, where the traces of a road once opened, but of course never traveled, were visible a few years ago in the south part of the tract, which among other obstacles, was to cross an almost impassable precipice; but orders were imperative, and the road was made on both sides, leaving them to be connected when the thing became feasible." The road here noticed was known as the "Old French Road" from the High falls to Beaver river and thence westward to the St. Lawrence.

Tiller appears to have been in America in the service of the company the year previous, and was allowed $600[1] per annum from July 1, 1796, with the privilege of spending four months in the winter in N. Y. on his own business. He was to have his expenses paid, the use of four or five acres for a garden, two horses, two cows, and commissions on specific objects. The whole tract was reconveyed to Chassanis by Constable, Feb. 15, 1797, from more accurate surveys. This deed recited the former misunderstandings, by which among other things, Chassanis had no use of the waters of Black river to the centre of the channel, and stipulated that if upon subdivision it should be found to overrun, the surplus should be conveyed back.

In Feb., 1797, Tillier, in behalf of Chassanis, petitioned the legislature for a law giving confidence to their title, stating that the company had expended large sums in surveys, roads, and other improvements, and were willing to do much more, but that they experienced embarrassment in the doubts that were entertained of the validity of their title, by reason of the general law of alienism. He expressed his confidence in the privileges of French citizens as assured by the treaty of 1778, and hoped the legislature would remove the doubts which had arisen in such a manner as

1 Increased May 10, to $800 and two rations of food from July 1, 1797. A few days after his appointment, the company resolved that he should devote himself entirely to their business, and be allowed 20 p. c. of net proceeds of stores, potasheries and saw mills.

in their wisdom might be determined. As a motive, he intimated that the legislature "might find in the act, gratification to its benevolence, by doing good to many unfortunate persons, who, in embarking in this enterprise, had expected to find some relief to great misfortunes." He further asked some provision for authenticating instruments executed in Paris, to the end that they might be recorded in this state, as had been done with Great Britain. The committee reported that the question of alienism belonged to the federal government, and that the other request was too important to be settled at that late period of the session.

Jacob Oboussier was appointed with a salary of $40 per month, to take charge of the store which was opened near the High falls in the little village built by the French on the flat east of the river, in front of Judge Seger's present residence. The road opened from fort Stanwix, terminated on the west side below the falls, and the river was crossed in small boats. A large stock of farming implements, tools, and goods, was brought on, and about twenty French families, several of them possessing considerable wealth, liberally educated, and accustomed to Parisian society, began the life of frontier woodsmen among the hemlock forests east of Black river. The imagination must delineate the probable results that would have followed the settlement of great numbers of these people upon the fertile limestone and slate lands west of the river, and the differences that would have now appeared in the social aspect of our country, had the first emigrants been followed by crowds of their countrymen, after the usual custom of New England emigration.

Settled as they were, nine miles away from a part of their tract, wide enough for a single farm, history has only to record the speedy and utter failure of their scheme of colonization. Tillier is remembered as a man somewhat advanced in years, fond of display, vain, visionary, and as the sequel indicated, unworthy of confidence, if not a downright villian. No sooner was he away from immediate direction of the company in Paris, than their director began to meet difficulties, and it is not entirely certain that the latter was blameless. In November, 1798, Chassanis wrote to Gouverneur Morris, who had been minister from the United States, and with whom he was well acquainted, asking him to accept the supervision of the company's affairs in America. There were certain items in Tillier's accounts of which he could not see the aim and object, and the returns were so mixed up and confused, that he could not make out their meaning.

Mr. Morris replied that he would prefer not to undertake it, as it was difficult to find a proper man for taking Tillier's place, and the latter had, perhaps, left an impression unfavorable to Chassanis, in his first conversation with Morris, in which he complained that his drafts had been dishonored, and means of efficient service withheld, adding, that "if this want of success should reach the ears of his enemies they would persecute him." In August, 1799, Morris, however, submitted to the company a plan, in which a person was to be appointed to take charge of the store, upon inventory, keep it supplied with goods needed by the colonists at moderate prices, and each year improve a farm of 40 acres in the environs of Castorville, on the undivided lands. A tract which had been sold to a Swiss company, was to be put in their possession, and efforts were to be made to get actual settlers upon the lands.

In September, 1799, Morris appointed Richard Coxe for four years, at $4,000, who immediately came on to make inquiries, and arrange for more active operations next year. To give Tillier no pretext for further charges, the company on the 26th of Feb., 1800, resolved that no expense should be ordered, or new establishment begun by their agency in America. On the 7th of April, they formally declared their rights and powers fully vested in Chassanis, the shareholders being regarded as dormant partners. They appropriated 9,750 acres to to pay expenses, upon sale at not less than $3 per acre, vesting in G. Morris, powers of attorney for selling these lands, and resolved to continue the company seven years longer.

Although stripped of his agency, Tillier was not deprived of the power of mischief, and in an advertisement dated Jan. 8, 1800, and inserted in the Albany papers, he cautioned the public "not to trust to the invidious reports of Gouverneur Morris or Pierre Joulin, or their substitutes Richard Coxe, Jacob Brown, Patrick Blake, or any other acting under their authority, derogatory to the powers, rights, and title of the subscriber as agent for the Company of New York, in Paris, and James Le Ray, as no sales, acts or deeds of the said persons, or any others claiming authority under them, in regard to the lands of the said company in the state of New York, or for James Le Ray, as it regards the lands known by description [as] No. 4, in Macomb's purchase can be valid, being held as a lien and security for the act and demand of the subscriber as their agent, and will be so held until a decision is made of the suit in chancery, now depending and instituted against the subscribers by Gouverneur Morris, the assuming agent of Pierre Chassanis, and Pierre Joulin, the assuming agent of James Le Ray."[1]

Mr. Cox took forcible possession of the store at the falls, the saw mill at Castorville, on the Beaver river, and the property generally, in June, 1800, and on the 12th of that month Morris wrote, advising the erection of another saw mill, and a grist mill, upon a free lease of 20 or 30 years, to some one who might engage to build them. He noticed the flourishing settlement west of the river, and attributed the difference to the mal-administration of Castorland, upon which immense sums had been squandered or embezzled. He advised a road from the High falls direct to Ford's settlement at the mouth of the Oswegatchie.

In October, 1800, Tillier published French and English editions of a memorial justifying his administration of Castorland. He stated that upon his arrival in the United States, he had undertaken, with the counsels of Alexander Hamilton, to perfect the titles and procure their record, and that errors in the first deed from Constable had rendered that instrument invalid, and required another based upon a new survey. He then proceeds with his narrative as follows:[2]

"R. Tillier afterwards directed all his attention to the buildings, only rough hewed upon the lands of Castorland, not finding any of those which had been announced to him; no ground being cleared; no cultivation established in the ideal town of *Castor;* no practicable road; no established communication; only one or two barracks honored with the name of houses; a yard sowed rather than a garden; in a word, nothing which evinced the former settlement of the pretended establishments, still less the expense which had been made thereon. What afflicted him most at first was, the repugnance strongly impressed on the Americans of the neighboring places, to establish themselves upon the lands of the company, where they perceived nothing enticing.

---

[1] Joulin had been the curé of Chaumont, and refusing to take the constitutional oath, was sent off by Le Ray to save his life. Accustomed to the refinements of Europe, he was little prepared to endure the privations of a pioneer life, and in the lonely solitudes of the Black river pined for the comforts of which through his whole life he had never before known the want. In conversing with Jacob Brown, whom he met when about to commence his improvement at Brownville, he said: "Ah! the French revolution came too soon or too late for me!" Had it come sooner he might have cast his energies into the struggle, and shared the fortunes of the civil war: if later, he would not have witnessed its horrors, and felt its disasters.

[2] Taken from the English edition printed at Rome, N. Y., by Thomas Walker.

"R. Tillier struggled some time against these obstacles, but by conciliatory conduct and fair dealing (his situation not permitting any liberality, in such cases so necessary), he was able to procure some workmen, who all seemed desirous to purchase some lands, which he sold them in small portions, in hopes of very soon selling a greater quantity, and to unite a certain number of cultivators which would give a permanent footing to the new colony. This was the object of his ambition. He felt the consequence of a progressive increase to the holders of shares in the Company of New York. R. Tillier was unanimously elected and named a justice of the peace for the county of Oneida, which mark of confidence and esteem from the inhabitants, fortified his hopes of reaping the fruits of all his cares, and justifying the trust which the company had given him;[1] he rendered an exact statement of all that related to his management; his correspondence, journals and accounts, prove his constant attention to conform himself to the act of the constitution. These different papers show his exertions, and how he was employed, and the manner in which the sums have been expended under his administration; and it can not be doubted that the company were sensible of his zeal and care, as he then received, as well as at different other times, acknowledgements of their satisfaction.

"The affairs were in this condition, when the company sent new French settlers to establish themselves upon the lands of Castorland. Their presence only occasioned considerable expenses without being of any utility, and they occasioned a great expense upon the land, consuming the provisions, introducing the spirit of discord and discontent, and finally they went away, threatening to make their complaints known in France, and to impeach those who had deceived them at Paris, by sending them into a desert. Much mildness and moderation were necessary to disperse them, but on going from Castorland they made bitter complaint against the place and persons, by which means they left traces very disadvantageous to Castorland and those interested in the said company. That these circumstances took place at a time when war appeared inevitable between France and the United States, and the greatest prejudices existing against the French, have also tended to destroy these rising settlements, and to injure the concerns of the company very much.

"At the same time Mr. Blake arrived, calling himself the son-in-law of Mr. Lambot, one of the company, and particularly charged with his interests. Coming into the United States without any resource, R. Tillier received him with kindness, and in such an hospitable manner that any other person would

1 This "extraordinary trust," was conferred upon him by the council of appointment, April 12, 1798. It is impossible to tell what office he might not have been promoted to, had he been appointed or elected!

have thought he merited some acknowledgment. Mr. Blake on the contrary, became his calumniator, as well in the United States as in Europe, but it appears the company were not deceived by his calumnies; they did justice to Tillier, and they wrote to him through their director Chassanis, that they were well satisfied with his services.

"In the mean time one Pierre Joulin, also arrived at New York, appearing to be secretly charged with the interests of the company; it is at least presumable, and what we are authorized to believe from the mystery which has enveloped his conduct. This man did all he could to conceal it without showing his powers. He insinuated to Tillier that he desired to see his accounts, who answered him with a frankness that characterizes him, that he had sent to Paris a faithful copy of all his accounts; that those of his current expenses were at Castorland, kept by a secretary who made his residence there, according to the intention expressed in the act of the constitution; that he was besides ready to render them all, having no reason to delay a settlement.

"R. Tillier saw that Mr. Joulin did not treat him with the same good faith and candor that he used towards the said Joulin. He obtained information indirectly, that he was bound by close and secret ties with Mr. Blake, and he was convinced of it by some letters which were sent him from Castorland. Finally he no longer doubted their employing deceit to divert him of his administration in the capacity of agent to the company, without his, however, receiving any direct or indirect advice either from that company or M. Chassanis, his agent or director at Paris.

"The indignation of an honest man in such a case must be great, and Tillier can not refrain from expressing his feelings. It is without doubt right to dispossess an agent when he is not faithful, but before such a step is taken, some proof should be obtained of his bad conduct, and they ought to take suitable measures that he is reimbursed all the expenses he has been at for the concern, and that he should be discharged from all the engagements which he has made by virtue of his powers towards the different persons employed, for supplies, wages and work. To act as they have done toward an honest citizen, who is invested with a public function, who has held in his country a place at the Council of Berne, is being deficient of all respect and good manners. But finally, if they admit that he is irreproachable in his conduct; that he has managed the affairs of the company ably and with honor, and that there is nothing but calumny against him, they must then admit that he has been treated with great injustice without reason. Their conduct must nevertheless appear very contemptible to a reflecting and discerning nation, whose confidence it was the interest of the company to have cultivated.

"Finally the plot of which these gentlemen were the agents is unveiled. Gouverneur Morris, late ambassador of the United

States in France, has appeared to be the only bearer of the powers of the Company of New York, or rather of P. Chassanis. He has filed in the name of Chassanis, a bill against Tillier, in the court of chancery of this state, and claims as his property the 220,500 acres of land, when by the constitution of the company, he has conveyed them in the most formal manner to the holders of shares. He moreover pretends to annul all the choice made of divided lots, all the sales to divers settlers by R. Tillier who has acted only in conformity to, and in virtue of sufficient powers, and agreeable to the instructions given him; and this suit having been very generally promulgated, it has resulted therefrom, there are doubts as well as the validity of the original bill as the partial sales of the powers and rights of Chassanis and of the old and new agents.

"These scandalous reports have given rise to every kind of mistrust and suspicion on the minds of the Americans,—disgusted the new settlers, and occasioned the land of the company to be absolutely deserted. Thus the imprudence of Director Chassanis, has produced the unfortunate effect of ruining the holders of shares who are the true proprietors,—of depreciating the land and the titles,—has caused the new settlements to be abandoned which will of course go to ruin, and all the expenses to this time will be useless and lost. It is difficult to conceive how the Company of New York has been induced to adopt such a conduct, so contrary to its interests. If from all these measures, there was only one that had any appearance of utility, it might perhaps be some palliation for the others ; but they are all equally contrary and destructive to the prosperity and success of the undertaking.

"The object of R. Tillier in addressing the present observations to the holders of shares, is, 1st to justify himself in their opinions and prove that his administration has been faithful and free from reproach. 2d, to exhibit all the operations of the company, or of the director Chassanis, and to call their attention to the damages which threaten them, if after having done what he thinks his duty concerning it, the holders of shares remain indolent and careless of their interests, they are perfectly their own masters, but at least they will recollect, when their eyes are opened, the advice which R. Tillier gave them, and they can only blame themselves for the losses they may experience.

"The best method, and it may be said the only one to be convinced whether Tillier's administration has been good and able, is to examine what he has done, and the means he had for doing it. When he came to take possession of the lands of Castorland, every thing was to be done; the land itself was not ascertained, and there was a deficiency of title to assure the property. When one considers a man in such a situation, in a strange country, at a great distance from any inhabited place, with very small funds, to put in order an immense tract of land, the difficulty of success must be evident. But it is very hard to give an adequate idea to a person who has not been a witness to a similar undertaking, of the magnitude and full force of the obstacles to be surmounted, and which R. Tillier had to encounter with. If the holders of shares will carefully examine his correspondence, his journal and accounts, they will therein see the use he has made of his time and of his means. If the interest of Chassanis has induced him to conceal that knowledge from the holders of shares, it is the interest of Tillier that these papers should be made public, as they afford unequivocal proof of his zeal, trouble and attention. They will there see the pains he took to ascertain the lands, his steps to secure a valid title, his activity in causing an exact survey to be made, and to obtain a topographical map, they will there see what he has done, what he has attempted, the lands which he has settled, the roads which he has opened, the journeys he has made, the arrangements which he has entered into with different families to establish themselves upon his lands, and by these means to give them a value. They will finally see the prospect of success which he might naturally flatter himself with, and which would undoubtedly in time have succeeded, if he had not been obstructed in his proceedings by the wrong measures of the director.

"Let them once again ascertain the truth of these facts, and have recourse to the testimony of the neighbors, consider the times and means, examine with attention his correspondence and journal which shew what he has done, and they will be convinced that his administration has been able, good and regular. He does not pretend to say, that no other person would have acted as well, perhaps even his administration may not be totally free from faults; for mistakes are almost inevitable in in every undertaking which requires so many details, in which the objects are not specifically traced, nor the plans fixed, but where, on the contrary, he had in fact, to determine on the first principles of this extensive concern, he can with the utmost truth declare, that no person could have exerted himself with more pains and application than he did, and he thinks that it would not have been found that he was deficient in the necessary experience and knowledge to insure the success of the undertaking, if he had been permitted to wait the event of his designs.

"His plans were well formed and conceived, and he wanted nothing to accomplish them but to be aided by the necessary funds which always came to hand too late, and indeed were undersufficient at any time. He was also injured in his plans by the measures of the director of the company at Paris, who far from executing what was necessary for such an establishment, took such steps as were adverse to its success, and who has uniformly by his actions opposed the views and measures of the agent at New York. The main object of the undertaking was, to give a value to the lands of Castorland, for which purpose they should have cultivated the confidence of the natives of the country, in order to entice them to settle upon places; they should have seen on the part of the company a regular and uniform plan of improving the lands, and to secure the benefit the property of those who were inclined to become purchasers; but instead of that how have the Company of New York acted? Mr. Pharoux the first agent sent, was a well informed and honest man, and he gained the esteem of the Americans, but he was ignorant of their language and therefore he could with difficulty treat with them. He lost his life by an excess of zeal and temority. Mr. Desjardines succeeded him, but he was also ignorant of the English language, which being joined with a haughty character, drove the inhabitants from him, although he expended much of the company's money he did nothing useful for it. He was replaced by Rodolphe Tillier, who thinks he understood well the object of the undertaking, and that he made effort to accomplish it. His being chosen a justice of the peace, is a sufficient proof that he had gained the confidence of the inhabitants.

"Some time after, several Frenchmen came to settle upon the lands, in pursuance to an agreement made with the company at Paris. They had scarcely arrived when disgust, misunderstanding and hatred took place, tranquility was destroyed and they left the land abusing it. Soon after Mr. Blake, a new envoy appeared, whose powers are mysteriously concealed except when he can promote discord and utter calumnies. After him Pierre Joulin, an ancient priest came, who imitated the example of his predecessor and loaded Tiller with injustice and defamation. At length Mr. Governeur Morris, the late American Ambassador to France arrived, who charged with the powers of Pierre Chassanis, revokes Tillier the only agent who had displayed activity and the only one whose zeal and experience had extricated the establishment from confusion and disorder. And to aggravate all these changes and imprudencies, a suit is commenced against Tiller, who offered, and still offers, to render his accounts, and submit them to arbitrators. Much noise and clamor is raised and it is rendered more scandalous as it appears to be designed to annul the titles given by Tiller to the purchasers of lands, although he granted them in virtue of acknowledged and approved powers; they would thus destroy those acts which are legal, and dispossess and ruin the proprietors.

"This true statement, which faithfully points out the actual state of things, is sufficient to excite, and accounts for the astonishment with which the Americans view the capricious, irresolute and ridiculous administration of the Company of New York, which is increased when they compare it with the wise, enlightened and uniform administration of the Dutch Company in the vicinity of Castorland, and to the large concern under Captain Williamson's charge, not far from thence, of which last an able writer (Mr. La Rochefoucault-Liancourt) gives so flattering an account, in his travels through America. Let the holders of shares coolly reflect on the consequences resulting from this multitude of imprudent actions, and they will form some conception of the great injury which they have sustained in the minds of the inhabitants of America by such an inconsiderate series of imprudent, false, impolitic and inconsistent measures. Let them change their plans—let them adopt uniform ones and pursue them—let them trust their interests to honest and well informed men, attached by ties of confidence and esteem—let them give to their agent in America very extensive powers. It is in vain to imagine a great design and a large establishment can be governed at a distance without it. The person actually on the spot can only attain just ideas on the subject. In the execution, his experience will enable him immediately to rectify any mistake that may happen. Let them renounce the idea of selling lands in France, because the execution of such contracts is always attended with some difficulties as to the places and portions of land to be given, which inconvenience can not take place when the purchaser sees before he purchases the proposed property. Let them renounce the idea of selling their lands half divided and half undivided, because a confusion results from it which endangers all the operations of the purchasers, and that plan so fine in speculation, is in fact very bad in execution. Let them always provide funds beforehand, that the managing commissary may be able without delay to accomplish his plans, and that he may with confidence undertake them under the certainty of having it in his power to discharge in time, the engagements which he may enter into. Let them abstain from making any agreement in France, and from engaging people either from France or Switzerland, as they have done, for the lands of Castorland can never be cultivated but by the natives of the country. These will not even settle on the land, without they have an easy access to an agreeable abode, and until they are convinced of the authenticity of their titles to secure them in their possessions.

"In adopting such maxims, the holders of shares may reasonably hope to reap a profit, and that time will give value and credit to the lands of Castorland, and that they may see the settlement flourish and increase to that degree to which the position of the land justly entitles them to expect. Without such measures, it may be, that the design of the holders of lands will totally fail, and ruin be inevitable. They also run another danger, which R. Tillier thinks he ought to warn them of; they are exposed to lose their property—perhaps it is already out of their hands. P. Chassanis has given his new powers—not as director and agent of the company, but in his own name. Mr. G. Morris, who is the bearer of it, has instituted the suit against Tillier, for the purpose of proving Pierre Chassanis to be acknowledged as individual proprietor of the 220,500 acres of land, whilst by the constitution of the company, he has transferred them in the most formal manner to the bearers of shares. Does not this manner of acting announce on the part of Pierre Chassanis a desire to dispose of that property as belonging to himself, to the prejudice of the holders of shares? They will be ready to believe it, when they learn that Chassanis has already disposed of 130,000 acres of these same lands in favor of J. Le Ray, either on a deed of sale, bond or mortgage. These acts have, by chance, passed under the eyes of R. Tillier, to whom they had not an intention of showing them. One of these contracts of alienation is for 90,000, the second of 22,000, and the third of 18,000 acres. Let them add 80,000 acres which had been mortgaged to Carrare & Co., of Lausanne, for what they have lent to the company. It appears, then, that at this moment there are 210,000 shares sold or engaged. These are positive facts which perhaps, may give reason to believe that it is at length time to look into, and take their concerns into their own hands, and watch to their own interests, and let them get possession again of their property, if it is not yet too late to do it; for it is clear, that if P. Chassanis appears to be the only proprietor of all the lands of Castorland, he will have the right of selling them, and that if these sales are once completed in a legal manner, it will be in vain for the holders of the shares to reclaim any portion whatsoever. This danger has appeared to R. Tillier to be of too high importance to the holders of shares to leave them ignorant of it. Tillier still owes them the information of a fact which, in the midst of many others, will give them an idea of the character of P. Chassanis and Le Ray de Chaumont, whose interests appear to be joined and confounded together. Some time before the arrival of P. Joulin, Chassanis sent a bill of exchange to Tillier for $3,772, to provide for the expenses of the Company. It was drawn by that Chaumont, on that same Mr. Joulin. Immediately ,after his arrival, Tillier took the first opportunity to present it to him for acceptance, but he did nothing therein, Chaumont having previously ordered him not to pay it. What can be said or thought of such an action? One may judge of Chassanis' administration from his conduct. R. Tillier will not extend his reflections further. His object is not at present to throw blame on any particular person; he therefore confines himself to a statement of facts, and bringing them to the view of the holders of the lands, in order to let them ascertain them, and that they may thereby convince themselves whether their director in Paris is worthy or not of their confidence, and whether his connections in the affairs and interests of Chaumont are not injurious to the interests of the company. Tillier's object is fulfilled if he has been enabled to persuade them that his administration has been pure and free from reproach. If he has convinced them of the causes which the want of success in the undertaking ought to be attributed, and if he has pointed out to them the means of accomplishing their purpose better in the future, he does not seek to maintain himself in their confidence. He is satisfied in knowing that he has always been worthy of it. He wishes to render his account, and to discharge himself from a trust which he has executed with fidelity and honor; but before he does this, it is just that he should be reimbursed for his advances, and guaranteed from all the engagements which he has entered into in the name of the company. He should not have been forced to suffer a law suit, if the new agent had agreed to this fair proposition, which indeed is only an act of justice and of universal usage in similar cases."

To this memorial Chassanis published the following reply:

"Without doubt one who has been charged with the interests of a company, owes it to himself to justify his conduct; for the same reason the Company of New York two years ago, in vain recalled Mr. Tillier. But instead of justifying his conduct, this agent feared to expose himself to the light, he opposed difficulties, and the course he has taken will only postpone the shame of his condemnation. Tillier would wish, in throwing suspicion upon the direction of citizen Chassanis, to gain the interest of the shareholders, and thus cover his own disorders by a hypocritical zeal; but every shareholder knows, that their director has never written or done anything but in accordance with the deliberations of the company. It would be important could Tillier prove the contrary; but citizen Chassanis defies him to produce a single fact to impair this assertion.

"The company finding but very little result coming from so great expenses, and failing to obtain from Tillier any thing but vague information, took a decisive part against this agent himself. It was impossible for the commissaries and director in Paris to learn exactly the state of things in America, to remedy seasonably and effectually the abuses which were introduced, and this led the company to a precautionary measure upon which depended the fate of Castorland. It authorized its director at its session of May 1, 1798, to confer upon Mr. G. Morris, minister plenipotentiary of the United States to the French government, the 'powers necessary to investigate, reform and settle the accounts of Tillier, acting commissary of the company in America; to take cognizance of the details of the administration of Castorland, its actual condition, the ability and conduct of its chief and subordinate agents employed in its service, to suspend or discharge those who might have compromised the interests of the company, or shown themselves incapable of filling the places they occupied; and lastly, power in advance, of removing Tillier in case his functions ought to cease.' This appointment was demanded by circumstances, and although of the highest importance, Tillier terms it *the recklessness of director Chassanis*, and that *by the scandalous scenes which it occasioned, it had ruined the shareholders.* But if it had produced these scandalous scenes, were they not caused by Tillier, who, under the false pretext of serving the shareholders, had rejected the deliberations of the company, and ignored the signature of Pierre Chassanis until now recognized?

"In Tillier's memorial, there is a grave accusation against citizen Chassanis, which appears specious, and must be refuted; for all the rest are only the declamation of a justly suspected servant, who defends himself with words, but has nothing to show in his favor. He distinctly charges Chassanis with having sold or bargained 210,000 acres of land without the consent of the shareholders. The fact, says he, is positive; and he invites them (page 17) *to take their concerns into their own hands and watch to their own interests, and let them get possession again of their property if it is not already too late to do it.* How can Tillier know this fact without knowing the cause? and knowing the cause, how can he dare to utter a calumny so easily refuted? Can he flatter himself that by misconstruing a fact consigned to the record he can prove his end without challenge? However it may be, the abuse of trust with which Tillier reproaches citizen Chassanis, is only an imaginary phantom to tarnish his reputation, and the apprehensions with which he would inspire the shareholders, have not the slightest foundation. They can regain their property, or rather they have never been deprived of it, for in this operation it has been as in all others. It was at a general assembly held May 14, 1798, that the conveyance of 90,000 acres to Le Ray was decreed. The first article of that deliberation read as follows:

" 'Art. 1. The commissaries at Paris and the director, are authorized to transfer to the name of Mr. Le Ray, citizen of the United States of America, all their real and personal estate of the company in the state of New York, in the name of citizen Chassanis its director.'

"This conveyance did not dispossess the company of its property, but it was a measure required by the circumstances, which had no other end than to consolidate the rights of the shareholders and their creditors, as evidently appears in the next article.

" 'Art. 2. The assembly charges the commissaries and the director, to take all proper measures to the end that in this conveyance the rights of the company be preserved, and that they may be maintained in the enjoyment and improvement of their actual possessions, according to the mode established by the act of the society of June 28, 1793.'

"As to the 40,000 acres for which the director has given bonds and mortgages, and which completes the 130,000 acres that Tillier pretends to have been alienated, it was not a sale, but simply a security to a loan ordered by the general assembly of March 16, 1798, and which the director was authorized to execute.

"Nor was this all. Tillier thought he still owed the shareholders information of a fact *which will give them an idea of the character of citizen Chassanis.* It is stated in the memorial, that the director sent a bill of exchange to Tillier to serve the wants of the company, and that Mr. Le Ray the drawer of the letter, caused its payment so be suspended. Upon this Tillier exclaims: *What can be said or thought of such an action? One may judge of Chassanis' administration from his conduct!*

"But whom does this transaction compromise? We can see only its very obvious bearing, and it was exceedingly bad taste in Tillier to allude to it. It is natural when an agent is charged with having abused the confidence of a company, that he should remove the pretext of further censure, and to this the director will limit himself. Tillier had provoked this by his conduct, and it saved the company $3,772. It is certain that citizen Chassanis ought to appear blame-worthy in the eyes of Tillier, for being knowing to Le Ray's opposition to the payment of the draft. It is a very bad turn that both have shown him, and and he can scarcely pardon them. Thus we may regard the refusal of payment as one of the sources of trouble which excited Tillier to the calumnies which defile his memorial. Had it not been for this fatal counter-order which deprived Tillier, for the moment, of his salary, it is to be presumed that the director would have appeared as showing better management, and above all, greater justice.

"If Mr. Tillier wished to prove that his administration, as he says, has been pure, and that it was free from reproach, he has failed to show the result. It is from the fruit that we judge the tree. We will render him justice, if, by the establishments formed and his model accounts, he can show a good employment of his time and of the funds which he has received. His obstinate refusal upon these points, forces upon us the suspicion that he can not report an honest administration. It is not by telling us that his affairs have been well administered that he can persuade us of the fact; it is not by addressing a memorial full of absurd and calumnious accusations, founded rather upon ignorance of facts rather than upon facts themselves, that Mr. Tillier can conciliate our esteem. The only means of justifying his administration is to render his accounts in a proper manner, with vouchers of their correctness."

The necessity for transferring the title to an American citizen, arose from an act of congress, passed July 7, 1798, by which French citizens were deprived of the privileges previously enjoyed. The convention, with the French republic, dated Sept. 30, 1800, gave that nation no privileges beyond others. Tillier's charges upon settlement as presented in 1803, were infamous, including salary six years, personal expenses, commissions of various kinds, as well on lands sold, as lands of which he had been promised the agency, charges for non-enjoyment of his garden, horses and cows, for the non-erection of the pot ashery and distillery which he had been prevented from building, &c., &c., amounting to $23,493.92, besides a heavy charge for the trouble he had taken in surveys and similar accounts which have few parallels in our history. The company declared March 13, 1803, that it had never promised a commission on land sales.

Chassanis died in Paris Nov. 28, 1803. In June, 1804, Tillier offered to settle for the Ure farm at Illingworth's, a tract of 450 acres valued at $3,000, and then offered to throw off $1,000. We are not informed of the final terms of his settlement or his subsequent history. He is believed to have gone off to the French settlements in Louisania, where he is said to have held some office under the U. S. government. Morris never came upon the tract. In the summer of 1808, he passed through the county on his way to St. Lawrence county, but made no stop. The amount of lands sold by Pharoux in Castorland, was 6,266 acres; by the company itself 12,149.8 acres, and by Tillier 3,945¼ acres.

In 1800, after contracting a debt of 300,000 livres, the company could only show one saw mill, eighteen log houses, and 82 acres of clearing, as the fruit of this enormous expense. There were besides, upon the tract, 11 log houses and 130 acres cleared, besides what belonged to the company. Several roads had, indeed, been made, but these were rendered impassable by the first gale of wind, and from want of population speedily relapsed into the state of nature.

The name of James Donatianus Le Ray de Chaumont, has been mentioned in connection with this title. He was the brother-in-law of Chassanis, and one of the original share holders of the company. His father's house had been the home of Dr. Franklin, and of many distinguished Americans during the revolution, and much of their correspondence is dated from Passy, the suburban residence of Chaumont. The elder Le Ray was an ardent friend of the American cause, and in the hour of need had advanced large sums of money, to obtain which, the subject of this notice had visited America, and become well acquainted with many leading persons, and with public affairs generally. He was conjoined with Morris in the agency of Castorland in 1801, and subsequently he became principal agent of the French proprietors, many of whose rights he purchased. He early became one of the four commissaries at Paris, and induced the company to order the sale of 12,000 acres to an American company of which he had the direction. In 1802, the Company of New York having a debt of 360,000 livres to meet, sold 17,000 acres in Beaverland at $2 per acre, and might then have sold the whole at 52 cents per acre, but the shareholders, true to their character *as dormant partners*, continued to slumber in the quiet anticipation of large dividends ultimately resulting in some mysterious way from enhancement of value by neighboring improvements, or by some happy turn of the wheel of fortune.[1]

In July, 1814, the term fixed by the company for its existence expired, and a public sale was resolved upon to pay the debt of 561,766 livres, owed to its Swiss creditors, who, as no one else offered to become purchasers, bid it in. Le Ray became the principal American agent of this company and acquired a large interest in it. In 1824 he was compelled to apply for the benefit of the insolvent act, and to surrender his estates for the relief of his creditors. The management of affairs passed into the hands of his son, and settlement has since been continued under the name of Vincent Le Ray, for the benefit of himself and certain foreign proprietors who have retained from the beginning, or who have since acquired an interest in the lands formerly owned by the Company of New York. Besides Le Ray, the following families now own interests in these land: Lambot, Desormeaux, De la Chaume, Franque, Moreau, La Tramblaye, Weuves, De Loys D'Orsens, and Houst, the latter, it is believed, as trustee of a Swiss company. The Swansmill company, formerly owned 384 lots or 19,200 acres, but their interests have been nearly or quite canceled.

The elder Le Ray spent the best years of his life in promoting the settlement of his lands in Jefferson and Lewis counties, and in 1832 returned to France. In 1836, he made his last visit to the country, spending the summer there. Upon his return home he continued to reside with his daughter and two sisters, spending his time partly in

---

1 In 1856, upon the death of the head of an old French family, the heirs found the title papers of several shares in the *Compagnie de New York*, authenticated by Chassanis and his colleagues, and wrote to the governor of New York for information as to how to come in possession of the estate, which they doubtless imagined had accumulated enormously by lapse of time, allowing even a moderate per cent. of increase.

Paris, and partly in the country, or in traveling. He died Dec. 31, 1840, aged 80 years.[1]

Great Tract Number Four.—On the 12th of April, 1793, Constable sold in London, with the consent of Chassanis who held a preëmptive claim, this tract of 450,950 acres for 300,000 florins ($125,356) to Charles J. Michael De Wolf of Antwerp. The town of Diana lies wholly in this tract which also embraces a large portion of Jefferson co. De Wolf published in Dutch, a plan of settlement under a company of which he was to be the president. Its affairs were to be managed by himself and four directors whose names were to be made known at the proper time. The capital was fixed at 1,200,000 florins current money, to be disposed of a follows:

First. 800,000*F* for the payment of the 400,000 acres for which good titles will be given and of which copies will be kept at the office of the president and all other papers in relation to this negotiation will be kept there also.

Secondly. 400,000*F* will be invested by the said five directors in such stocks as they may deem advisable for the best interests of the negotiators, and in case they deem it necessary to send emigrants there, or to clear some of these lands, or make other expenses for the improvement of the same, or if they can not pay the yearly dividends the said directors may sell or use so much of the said stock as is necessary to cover the expenses.

Thirdly. The interest which may accrue on the said 400,000*F* shall be for the benefit of the negotiators.

As it was evident that the negotiations would be beneficial to its stockholders, the directors were to issue with each share of 1,000 guilders each, three coupons as a dividend, each of 50 guilders payable in 1794, 1795 and 1796. The tract was to be surveyed into 400 acre lots.

It was evident that this scheme was only a trap, and as such it served its end, for De Wolf soon sold for 680,000 florins to a company of large and small capitalists of Antwerp, who organized the "Antwerp Company." The several schemes which were devised by these people for improving their lands belong rather to Jefferson county.

In January, 1800, Gouverneur Morris received a trust deed of half of the tract and on the next day James D. Le Ray received a like deed for the other half.[2] Morris and

---

1 A biographical notice and portrait of Le Ray are contained in the History of Jefferson Co., p. 441, 447.

2 These conveyances were made by James Constable, under powers from his brother, dated Nov. 16, 1798. *Regr's. office, N. Y.*, lvi., 169. See Deeds, Oneida Co., B., 612, E. 307.

Le Ray exchanged releases Aug. 15, 1802,[1] and the former June 15, 1809, conveyed 326 lots of 143,440 acres to Moss Kent who conveyed the same to Le Ray June 24, 1817.[2] The operations of the Antwerp company like those of its neighbor were a failure, and Le Ray ultimately purchased the most if not all of the rights of the individual shareholders in Europe. Not the slightest settlement had been undertaken by the company before Le Ray's connection with the title.

A large part of Diana, with portions of Jefferson county adjoining, were conveyed to Joseph Bonaparte, ex-king of Spain and brother of the illustrious Napoleon, under circumstances which are thus related by Mr. Vincent Le Ray:

"Mr. Le Ray de Chaumont was at his estate in Tourraine in 1815, when he heard of Joseph Bonaparte's arrival at Blois. He had known this prince before his great elevation and was his guest at Mortefontaine when the treaty of Sept. 30, 1800, between the U. S. and France was signed there, but he had ceased meeting him afterwards. Seeing however that misfortune had assailed the prince, he remembered the man and hastened to Blois. The prince having invited Mr. L. to dinner, said suddenly to him: "well, I remember you spoke to me formerly of your great possession in the United States. If you have them still, I should like very much to have some in exchange for a part of that silver I have there in those wagons, and which may be pillaged any moment. Take four or five hundred thousand francs and give the equivalent in land." Mr. Le Ray objected that it was impossible to make a bargain where one party alone knew what he was about. 'Oh!' said the prince, 'I know you well and I rely more on your word than my own judgment.' Still Mr. Le Ray would not be satisfied by this flattering assurance, and a long discussion followed, which was terminated by the following propositions immediately assented to by the prince. Mr. L. would receive 400,000 francs and would give the prince a letter for Mr. L.'s son then on the lands instructing him to convey a certain designated tract, if, after having visited the country (whither he was then going), the prince confirmed the transaction, otherwise the money was to be refunded."

The purchaser, who in the United States assumed the title of the Count de Survilliers, in closing the bargain, is understood to have made payment in certain diamonds brought from Spain, and in real estate. A trust deed with covenant and warranty, was passed Dec. 21, 1818, to Peter S. Duponceau, the confidential agent of the count, for

1 Deeds, Jefferson Co., A. 358. Deeds, Oneida Co., X, 464.
2 Deeds, Jefferson Co., K., 279.

150,260 acres, excepting lands not exceeding 32,260 acres, conveyed or contracted to actual settlers.[1] This was recorded with a defeasance appended, in which it is declared a security for $120,000, and it provided for an auction sale of lands to meet this obligation. The tract conveyed by this instrument included the greater part of Diana, two tiers of lots on the S. E. side of Antwerp, the whole of Wilna and Philadelphia, a small piece south of Black river at the Great bend, a tract four lots wide and seven long, from Le Ray, and nine lots from the easterly range in Theresa.

Diamonds having fallen to half their former price, the fact was made a subject of complaint, and in 1820, the count agreed to accept 26,840 acres for the nominal sum of $40,260. These lands lay in the most distant portions of No. IV, and Mr. Le Ray, in a letter to one of the Antwerp company, dated April 9, 1821, complimented the count upon his taste in selecting a "tract abounding with picturesque landscapes, whose remote and extensive forests affording retreat to game, would enable him to establish a great hunting ground; qualities of soil, and fitness for settlers were only secondary considerations. * * * He regrets, notwithstanding, that thus far, he has been unable to find among the 26,000 acres of land, a plateau of 200 acres to build his house upon, but he intends keeping up his researches this summer." The attempt of Joseph Bonaparte to establish himself in Diana, is elsewhere noticed. By an act of March 31, 1825, he was authorized to hold lands in this state, without his promising or expecting to become a citizen. In his memorial he alludes to the liberality of other states, especially Pennsylvania, in allowing aliens to hold lands, "and not being of the number of those who would wish to abandon this land of hospitality, where the best rights of man prevail, but nevertheless bound to his own country by ties which misfortune renders more sacred," he solicited the privilege of holding titles in his own name.[2]

Duponceau executed to Joseph Bonaparte July 31, 1825, a deed of all the rights he had before held in trust.[3] In 1835, John Lafarge bought for $80,000 the remaining interests of Count Survilliers in Lewis and Jefferson counties,[4] and attempted more active measures for settling these lands.

---

[1] Mortgages, Jefferson Co., A, 626; Deeds N, 1.

[2] This memorial is preserved in Assembly papers xii, 37, 41, Sec. office, and is given in full in the Hist. of Jeff. Co., p. 566.

[3] Deeds, Jefferson co., N, 181; Lewis co., I, 16.

[4] Deeds, Jefferson co., U, 2, 43.

The hard reputation he had acquired in the sale of Penet's square, and the severe measures he had adopted in ejecting squatters and delinquents, however prejudiced the minds of settlers to such an extent that but few in this county ventured to commit themselves to his "tender mercies." La Farge had been a merchant at Havre, and afterwards resided in New Orleans. While in France he purchased the title to much of Penet's square, and in 1824 came to reside upon it. In about 1838, he removed to New York, where he became concerned in extensive pecuniary operations on his own account, and as agent of Louis Phillippe, who, while king of the French, invested large amounts of funds in American stocks. A magnificent hotel on Broadway, N. Y., was named from its owner, the La Farge house. The La Farge fire insurance company was also named from him. He died two or three years since in New York.

On the 3d of June, 1825, William and Gerardus Post, for $17,000, purchased 11,888 acres (out of which 3,503 acres were excepted) in the present towns of Wilna and Diana, portions of which have since been conveyed to T. S. Hammond of Carthage.[1]

The Swiss company that made the first investment at Alpina, received July 28, 1846, a conveyance from La Farge of a tract embracing two ranges of lots in Antwerp, and 122 lots in Diana,[2] and the whole of La Farge's interest has since been sold in this county. The principal owners of the unimproved lands of his tract in Diana, are L. Paddock of Watertown, and David C. Judson of Ogdensburgh. Their agent is Joseph Pahud[3] of Harrisville.

A considerable part of Diana and the adjoining parts of Antwerp are still a wilderness, but the demand for lumber and bark recently created, will before long lead to the clearing up of these lands.

---

1 Deeds, Jefferson co., X, 108; mortgages B. 3, p. 311.
2 Deeds, Jefferson co., 81, p. 532.
3 Pronounced *Pi-u.*

CHAPTER IV.

HISTORY OF TOWNS.

The county of Lewis upon its organization embraced five towns, viz: Leyden, Turin, Martinsburgh, Lowville and Harrisburgh. The present number is seventeen and their names and dates of erection are as follows:

CROGHAN,.....1841.	MARTINSBURGH, 1803.
DENMARK,.....1807.	MONTAGUE,....1850.
DIANA,........1830.	NEW BREMEN,..1848.
GREIG,........1828.	OSCEOLA,.....1844.
HARRISBURGH,..1803.	PINCKNEY,....1808.
HIGHMARKET,..1852.	TURIN,........1800.
LEWIS,........1852.	WATSON,......1821.
LEYDEN,.......1797.	WEST TURIN,..1830.
LOWVILLE,....1800.	

CROGHAN.

This town was formed from Watson and Diana, April 5, 1841, and named in honor of George Croghan, whose military services had then been recently brought to public notice in the presidential campaign resulting in Harrison's election.[1] The name of Tippecanoe had been proposed, and that of New France had been applied to the bill as passed in the senate, but on its third reading in the lower house, the present name was substituted. New Bremen was taken off in part, in 1848. An unsuccessful effort was made in 1859, to procure a division of this town into two. The first town meeting was ordered to be held at the house of John C. Fox, before Willard Barrett, Lodowick Snyder, and Joseph Hamen.

---

1 Croghan was a native of Locust Grove near the falls of the Ohio, where he was born Nov. 15, 1791. His father was Major Wm. Croghan, an Irishman who had rendered efficient service in the revolution, and his mother was sister of William Clark, who with Capt. Lewis explored the Missouri country in 1805-7. In 1810, Croghan graduated at William and Mary's college, and began the study of law; but the war soon opened a more inviting field of enterprise, and in the battle of Tippecanoe, and the sieges of fort Meigs and fort Stephenson, he won the applause of the Union. He rose from the rank of captain to that of inspector general; and in 1825 he received from congress a gold medal for his brilliant military services. He died at New Orleans, January 8, 1849. His name was pronounced *Craw-an*, although that of the town, is uniformly spoken *Cro-gan*.

Supervisors.—1841, Benj. R. Ellis; 1842–4, Bornt Nellis; 1845–50, Darius G. Bent; 1851–60, Patrick Sweetman.

Clerks.—1841–3, Abraham Fox; 1844–6, Joseph Hamen; 1847–8, Joseph Virkler; 1849, Foster L. Cunningham; 1850, Hartwell F. Bent; 1851–4, Joseph Rofinot; 1855, Joseph Catillaz; 1856, J. Rofinot; 1857–9, Augustus Valin.

Bounties for the destruction of wild animals have been voted as follows: For wolves $15 in 1841, $10 in 1845, and $5 in 1842, 6. For panthers, $10 in 1841, 5, 6, and $5 in 1842. For bears, $5 in 1841. In 1856, the town meetings of this town and New Bremen were held in the same house, the town line passing through near the middle.

In this town, the Company of New York had intended to lay out a city by the name of *Castorville*, on the north side of the Beaver river, half a mile above the head of navigation, and at the lowest water power on that stream.[1] The details of this plan have been already stated, but it is believed the city was never surveyed into lots, further than as a part of the Castorland tract. The reservation amounted to 663 acres, and upon it was built about 1798, the first saw mill east of Black river. From this mill the first lumber used by the settlers at Lowville, was obtained. The mill stood on the site of the upper part of Lefever's tannery, but its last vestige had disappeared long before the modern occupation of this site. Tillier made a clearing at the head of navigation, on Beaver river, four miles from its mouth, and a few log huts were erected. The only access to and from this place, was by river navigation. A few French emigrants settled on the banks of the Black river; among whom were, it is believed, J. T. Devouassoux, A. Tassart, Louis François de Saint Michel, and perhaps others. Mr. D. was a retired officer, who owned a good lot on the river, and had built a log house a few feet from the water, on a beautiful flat piece of ground, which he hoped before long to see changed to a smooth verdant lawn. One day as he was sitting by the door in his morning gown and slippers, Mr. Le Ray came along, on his way down the river, to visit his lands. After the usual salutations and a little general conversation, the visitor asked Mr. D. whether he was not afraid the water would reach his house in the spring? This was a new idea to the old soldier, and he was asked to explain. "Well," said Mr. L., "this river does not, by any means, cause such ravages as most rivers

[1] The steamers Lawrence and Norcross each ascended the stream to this point, and canal boats are loaded within half a mile of the tannery, on the lowest fall in Beaver river.

do in snowy countries, but it does overflow its banks in very low grounds. I think I even saw some marks left by it on some trees near your house, and according to them, you would have been about two feet under water in your house next spring!"

At these words our Frenchman felt as perhaps he had never felt before the enemy. "But," resumed Mr. L., after giving him time to compose himself, "have you not on your lot some higher ground?" "Indeed, sir, I can not say." "Why, have you not explored your lands before building?" "Indeed, no: I thought I could not possibly find a better spot than the banks of this beautiful river. I like fishing. Here I am near my field of operations." Mr. L. could not see without apprehension such apathy and levity, for knowing well that Mr. D. was not an exception among his countrymen, he read in his fate that of many others. He persuaded Mr. D. to take a little walk upon his lot, and in a few minutes they found a beautiful building spot on a rising ground.[1] We are not informed precisely upon which side of Beaver river this location was, and it may have been in the town of New Bremen.

Saint Michel arrived in New York in November, 1798, and undertook the improvement of a tract of 1200 acres, owned by three daughters of Mr. Lambot, and from them named *Sistersfield*. The agreement was made with Patrick Blake, husband of one of the sisters, and the owner of 200 acres of the tract. The two other sisters were named Renée Jeane Louise, and Reine Marguerite Lambot. Blake returned to Europe in 1802. Saint Michel had seen better days in France, and is believed to have held an office under Louis XVI., the unfortunate royal victim of the French revolution. His household affairs were managed by a daughter who had been tenderly reared at the schools in Paris, but who applied herself to the duties of her father's home with a cheerfulness that did much to lighten the gloom of solitude and lessen the sadness of both. About 1803, as Gouverneur Morris, Nicholas Low and one or two other landholders, had met at Brownville, Saint Michel came down with Richard Coxe to see them and enjoy the luxury of a conversation with some one who could speak his native language with fluency. The meeting is described by an eye witness as affording a scene worthy of a painter. Their visitor was a tall, thin man, with a keen and intelligent eye, and a vivacity peculiar to the French character.

---

[1] Related by Vincent Le Ray, Esq., in a letter to the author.

The eagerness with which he grasped the hand of the dignified Morris, and the satisfaction he evinced, was as interesting to the spectators as it was gratifying to the parties.[1] Saint Michel in dress and manners, indicated that he had been bred in polished society. He was a man of fervent piety and deep thought. His daughter married Louis Marselle, and adopted with grace the coarse fare and rustic accommodations of a new country, without a murmur. Her father moved to a farm a little south of Deer River village, where he died. Upon the death of her husband she married Louis de Zotelle, who, in the summer of 1838, was supposed to have died; preparations were made for the burial, and a premature notice of the death was printed in the Northern Journal. In a few days he called upon the editor to request that no notice be again printed unless he informed *in person*. He died "in good faith," about 1854, but in the absence of the authentic notice promised, we are unable to give the date. Still further down, and just beyond the border of the county, Jean Baptiste Bossuot, settled at the present village of Carthage, where he held an acre of ground under a verbal agreement with Sauvage, its owner, and kept a ferry and tavern. Other men would have made an independent fortune out of the opportunities which his location offered, but the bridge destroyed his occupation the village of Carthage which sprung up around "the meagre field of his slothful farming," failed to enrich its tenant, and he died a few years ago at an advanced age, leaving a world that was getting along without him!

A few miles from the last, on the north bounds of Castorland, lived a man whose name is familiar to the visitors of Mont Blanc, as that of a family of one of the best guides to that mountain. Mr. Balmat's descendants still reside in the town of Fowler, St. Lawrence county. A neighbor of his, Mr. Carret, a man of good education, would have fared better had he been brought up on a farm. His eldest son, James, a youth of bright natural talents, was obliged to seek service, and while tending ferry at the Long falls, fell under the notice of Le Ray, who received him into his office, and found him so very useful that he took him to Europe. While transacting some business with Joseph Bonaparte, the latter formed so favorable an impression of the young man, that he prevailed upon Le Ray to allow him to become his secretary, and he afterwards appointed him his general land agent. He subsequently returned to France, and settled near Lyons,

---

[1] Related by Mrs. B. Skinner, sister of Maj. Gen. Brown.

where he now resides. The three last named settlers located in what is now Jefferson county.

The little improvents made by the French were soon abandoned, as the would-be pioneers became disheartened and moved away to older colonies or returned to France.

There was scarcely a perceptible progress in settlement during the first twenty-five years after the French removed. Their clearings grew up with brambles, and their rude cabins rotted down, leaving but slight traces of their industry, and few evidences that this region had been traversed by civilized man.

In 1824, Thomas W. Bent, from Watson, took up a farm on the ridge between the Oswegatchie and Indian rivers, about fifteen miles from neighbors, at what is still the frontier clearing in this quarter, and known as Bent's Settlement. The post office of Indian River is a mile and a half south of this place.

In 1830, P. Somerville Stewart, now Le Ray's agent at Carthage, removed to Belfort, on Beaver river; built a saw mill and store, brought in settlers, and two or three years after erected a grist mill. A fire occurred May 30, 1831, from a fallow, which consumed the only two buildings then finished. A post office named Monterey, was established here some years after, but the route has been changed, and the office discontinued. A large tannery has been recently built at this place, by Wm. H. Pier.

About 1830, an immigration began from Europe, and has since continued, mainly through the exertions of agents employed by Le Ray, and the representations sent home by those who had taken up land and settled. The first of these was John Keefer. In the winter of 1848–49, a census taken in this town and New Bremen, showed 247 European families, of 1,275 persons, classified as follows:

From France,....	190	families, of	987	persons.
" Germany,..	46	"	230	"
" Switzerland,	11	"	58	"

Their religious belief was found to be:

Catholic,.......	150	families of	787	persons.
Protestant,.....	57	"	297	"
Muscovite,.....	39	"	189	"

Their residence in America had been, 1 family 21 years: 3, 19: 5, 18: 17, 17: 6, 16: 10, 15: 21, 14: 4, 12, 9, 10: 16, 9: 49, 8: 14, 7: 6, 6: 9, 5: 2, 4: 6, 3: 24, 2: 35, 1: and 10 less than 1 year. They owned or occupied 12,413 acres, of which 4,338 were fenced and improved, and 500 partly cleared. They owned 59 horses, 388 sheep, 513 swine and 1,256 horned cattle, and their produce the year previous had been 2,770 bushels of wheat, 4,430 of corn, 7,513 of rye, 3,127 of buckwheat, 10,640 of oats, and 33,339 of potatoes, 1,447 tons of hay, 17,068 pounds of butter exclusive of that used in families, and 27,925 pounds of maple sugar.

From a pamphlet issued in 1858, it appears that there were then over 500 European families, numbering 3,000 persons, upon Le Ray's lands, the greater part in this town and New Bremen. They were chiefly from the east of Françe, and the adjacent parts of Germany and Switzerland.

In a list of settlers numbering over three hundred names, the departments of Moselle, Meurthe, Lower Rhine, Upper Saône and Doubs in France, had furnished 154, Prussia 56, Mecklenburg-Schwerin and Mecklenburg-Strelitz 4, Hesse Darmstadt 5, Kur Hessen 14, Holstein and Lauenburg 3, Bavaria 8, Saxony and Saxe-Weimar 7, Baden 9, Wurtemberg 10, and Switzerland 36. In 1849 this town had a population of 1,168, of whom 646 were Americans and Irish, and 522 French, German and Swiss.

Mr. Le Ray employs as his sole agent in France, for the procuring of emigrants, M. Vanderest of Dunkirk, and has issued several circulars, maps and other publications in French and German, with the view of calling favorable notice to his lands. The terms advertised in Europe are, one-fifth payment at the end of one year after the selection of lands by the purchasers, and four-fifths in six years in equal annual installments, with interest. The amount offered in the two counties is 80,000 acres. M. Vanderest gives a contract, binding Le Ray to sell a tract of land to be selected within fifteen days or later after their arrival in New York, at a price varying from three to six dollars per acre, according to location, excepting lands near villages and water falls, and such as have timber convenient for sawing or manufacture, and engaging the emigrant to remove within three months to New York, and from thence, by way of Watertown, to Carthage. This instrument, drawn up with due formality, includes the names of all persons, old and young, belonging to the emigrating company, and is evidently intended to keep those removing, out of the hands of emigrant runners interested in other localities, until they may have an opportunity of visiting the lands and selecting for themselves.

The foreigners settling in this town, are mostly industrious, frugal, and disposed to avail themselves of every advantage that their situation affords.[1] Settling together, they retain in common use their native languages, in their families and religious meetings, but most of them readily acquire the English; while their children attending the district schools with Americans, speak English without the slightest foreign accent.

French Settlement (Croghan P. O.), on Beaver river and partly in New Bremen, is a scattered village or rather a vicinage, half a mile long and mostly on the south side of the river. It has a Catholic and a Methodist church, a large tannery owned by Blair, Rice & Bros., a grist mill, two saw mills, two inns, and several mechanic shops.

In 1852, a tannery was built at Beaver falls, the site of ancient Castorville. It is now in the hands of W. C. Lefever, has 80 vats, and produces 16,000 sides of sole leather annually. It is designed to extend it sixty feet and increase its capacity to 25,000. A gang saw mill is built here on the New Bremen side. Besides these, a small Evangelical church, and two or three houses; it has no claims to the rank of a village. This place was formerly called "Rohr's Mills."

Upon a street parallel with the river, leading from Beaver falls to Carthage, is a scattered neighborhood known as the "Prussian Settlement." It has a post office named "Naumburg," and two small chapels.

On the 29th of March, 1843, the house of Jonathan Aldrich was burned, and his son nine years old perished in the flames. The remainder of the family were compelled to walk three-fourths of a mile barefooted in the snow to their nearest neighbors.

Religious Societies.—There are two Roman Catholic churches in this town. St. Stephen's church was erected at the French settlement in 1847, and sermons are preached on alternate Sundays in French and German. Its trustees were incorporated under the general statute, March 14, 1853, the first being Nicholas Gaudel, Christopher Milles, and F. E. Rofinot, Jr. There is also a small Catholic church at Belfort.

The "German Evangelical Lutheran and Reformed Congregation" in Croghan, was formed Sept. 15, 1847, and elected Ernest Schlieder, Christian Rayser, C. Frederick Bachman, Frederick Wilk, and Weiss Katlen, trustees.

A church styled the Evangelical association, was legally

---

[1] To this there are exceptions. A company of 16 Italians who came over a year since, have proved entirely unfit to settle a new country, or encounter the hardships of pioneers.

formed Dec. 1, 1854, with August Stoebe, John Holler, and Jacob Rohr, trustees, and in 1857 erected a plain wood church at Beaver falls. Another, but smaller church, is built in the Prussian settlement. They are sometimes called Methodists, or Albright Methodists.

A society said to have been originally Lutherans, but now mostly Reformed Protestant Dutch, was formed several years since in the Prussian settlement, and has erected a church edifice.

A number of Anabaptist families reside in this and the adjoining town, and of these there are two classes, one being usually termed the new, or reformed Anabaptists. These people have no church edifice, worshiping after the manner of the primitive Christians, in private houses, and in all their dealings and social intercourse, are as much as possible restricted to their own circle.

The First Croghan Methodist Episcopal Church, was incorporated August 14, 1857, with Wm. G. Dealing, Aley Thomson, and Jacob House, trustees. A church edifice was built in 1858 at the French settlement.

DENMARK.

This town was formed from Harrisburgh, April 3, 1807, with its present limits, comprising township 5 of the Black River tract, or *Mantua,* as named by the surveyor general, on his published maps of 1802, 4. The first town meeting was ordered to be held at the house of Simeon Dunham, and the poor and poor moneys were to be divided with Harrisburgh according to the last tax list. The act took effect on the first Monday of February following.

The first town officers were, Lewis Graves,[1] *supervisor;* Wm. Derbyshire, *clerk;* Levi Robbins, Willis Secombe and Eleazer Sylvester,[2] *assessors;* John Clark, Wm. Clark and John Hurd, *commissioners;* Stephen Parson and Sueton Fairchild, *poor masters;* Aaron Nash, *constable,* and Eleazer S. Sylvester, *constable and collector.*

Supervisors.—1808, Lewis Graves; 1809, John Canfield; 1810–2, L. Graves; 1813–4, J. Canfield; 1815–6, Samuel

1 *Mr. Graves* was from Greenfield, Saratoga co., N. Y. He represented this county, Jefferson and St. Lawrence in assembly in 1808, and this county alone in 1810. He was several years judge and supervisor, and died May 10, 1816, aged 61 years. His widow survived until 1852. A brother named David also became an early settler.

2 Mr. Sylvester died February 17, 1835, aged 54 years.

Allen;[1] 1817–8, Israel Kellogg; 1819–23, S. Allen; 1824–37, John Clark, 1st; 1838–9, Apollos Stephens; 1840–1, Abner A. Johnson; 1842–50, Lewis Pierce; 1851, John H. Allen; 1852–3, Albert G. Thompson; 1854, Lewis Pierce; 1855–6, Lucian Clark; 1857–8, L. Pierce; 1859, Philander Blodget; 1860, L. Pierce.

Clerks.—1808, '09, Wm. Derbyshire; 1810, '11, Willis Secombe; 1812, Levi Robbins; 1813, Eleazer S. Sylvester; 1814–19, Asa D. Wright; 1820–4, Absalom Sylvester; 1825, Apollos Stephens; 1826, A. Sylvester; 1827, Daniel A. Higley; 1828, A. Sylvester; 1829–33, A. Stephens; 1834, '35, Amos Buck; 1836, '37, Otis Shaw; 1838, A. Buck; 1839, '40, Lewis Pierce; 1841–3, Charles Loud; 1844, '45, John M. Hulbert; 1846, Sidney Silvester; 1847, Wm. N. Angle; 1848, '49, Elon G. Parsons; 1850, C. Loud; 1851, W. N. Angle; 1852, Edward L. Hulbert; 1853, E. G. Parsons; 1854, '55, John H. Angle; 1856, E. L. Hulbert; 1857, Darwin Nash; 1858, '59, Silas Slater, jr.

In 1810, '11, '12, '13, a fine of $10, was voted for allowing Canada thistles to go to seed. A bounty of 50 cents was voted in 1821, for killing foxes, and $10 for panthers in 1828.

As noticed in our chapter upon titles, this town formed a part of the purchase of Harrison, Hoffman, Low and Henderson, and fell to the lot of the two first, as joint owners, together with townships 8 and 10, or Rodman and Harrisburgh. On the 1st of May, 1805, Josiah Ogden Hoffman sold to Tho. L. Ogden his half of these towns, and the securities upon them in trust, to pay, *first*, to the bank of New York his share of debt due the bank as assignee of Constable; *second*, the personal debts of Hoffman to the

[1] *Dr. Allen* was a native of Massachusetts, studied with Drs. Guiteau of Trenton, and Willoughby of Newport, settled in practice at Lowville in 1808, and in April, 1809, became a partner with Dr. Perry. He removed to Copenhagen in 1811, engaged in trade with David Canfield, and through the war was concerned in heavy contracts with the navy. The peace which followed brought ruin to this firm, although they kept on doing some business from about 1820 to 1828. They succeeded in recovering from government, a portion of the claims which the suspension of contracts occasioned, and while on this business at Washington, Dr. Allen formed acquaintance of many prominent public men. He became the agent of Varick, in the rope manufactory at Copenhagen, and afterwards engaged in farming a little S. E. from the village, and adjacent to the High falls. He died, June 12, 1849, aged 66 years. Dr. Allen was ardently attached to the Whig party and once nominated by them to assembly, but not elected. With literary tastes, polished manners, and uncommon conversational powers, he was eminently fitted to please and instruct, while his prompt reply and keen wit, made him the life of the social gathering.

Saml Allen

Constable estate; *third*, a debt due to Abijah Hammond; *fourth*, to Wm. Harrison the sum due on a bond of $9,093.50, given January 1, 1805; and lastly, what remained to Hoffman. The first and second trusts were executed in the summer of 1809, and on the 1st of June, Harrison and Hoffman made a division of contracts, bonds and mortgages. On the 19th of July, Hoffman and Ogden conveyed the whole to Harrison, to satisfy his demands in full. The amount of securities in the three towns thus transferred, was $86,600.80.[1]

The first definite knowledge of this town was ascertained by Benjamin Wright, who surveyed around it in April, 1796, and recorded in his field book the following:

"This is a most excellent township of land, and is beautifully watered with small streams, with a large creek called Deer creek running through the middle of it. On this creek is a cataract,[2] about four miles from the mouth, of about 20 or 30 feet, and very curious mill seats. There are several large creeks of fine water running through the town, with mill seats on them. There is an exceeding large intervale on Deer creek near the mouth, which is of the richest kind of land, and will be equal in quality and extent to any flat in the state of New York.[3] The south line of this town is of an excellent quality, excepting a swamp near the Black river, which is timbered with pine, ash, cedar, beech and soft maple. This township needs no other remarks, but only to say, that it is the best township in the 300,000 acres, and has every good quality that can be contained in a township of land: mill seats, excellent timber, finest quality of soil, excellent water, and pretty good situation. Area 31,951 acres, strict measure."

The proprietors appointed Abel French of Albany, their agent, and the latter employed Joseph Crary, in 1798–9, to subdivide the township into farms. It will be observed, upon examination of the map, that this survey was made with reference to a line since adopted as the route of the

---

[1] Hoffman while concerned in these titles, was attorney-general. He was seven years in assembly, in 1810–13, '14; was recorder of New York; and at the time of his death, which occurred January 24, 1838, he was associate judge of the superior court of that city. He was a lawyer of great ability and strict integrity.

[2] Probably King's falls. The High falls appear to have been unknown at this time.

[3] The extent of these flats is about 2,000 acres, and their richness is not over estimated. They are not ordinarily flowed over their whole extent, but in the winter of 1856, '57, the flood came up to the foot of the hill, a few rods below Deer River village. On the 12th of May, 1833, the inundation was higher than ever before or since known.

east road, which was called the Base line; and that the lot lines were run nearly parallel, or at right angles to this. The principal lots were intended to measure seventy chains on each side, and were sold as *right angled,* although uniformly, and no doubt purposely, run at an angle varying 6° from this, thus falling a little short of reputed contents in every case. It is said that Crary remonstrated at this irregularity, but was overruled, and directed to proceed as the surveys now indicate.[1]

The lands of this town were offered to settlers upon terms that were considered very favorable, varying from two to three and a half dollars per acre, one-half being required at purchase. About 1806, Morris S. Miller became agent, and soon after Isaac W. Bostwick, under whom its settlement and conveyance by deed was mostly completed.

The first location of land was made by Abel French, the agent, at Deer river, and the next by Jesse Blodget,[2] at Denmark village. The latter became the first settler in town, and arrived with his family in the spring of 1800. Joseph Crary, Peter Bent,[3] Solomon Farrell, William and Daniel Clark, James Bagg, Charles Moseley, Simeon Dunham, and others settled in the lower part of the town. Freedom Wright[4] and his sons Jabez, Douglass and Freedom, Charles Wright[4] and his sons Charles, Tyrannus A., Stephen, Erastus, Chester, Nathan and Matthew, and his son-in-law Wm. Merriam,[4] Joseph Blodget,[4] his son Calvin,[4] and son-in-law Shadrach Case,[4] Andrew Mills,[4] Freeman Williams,[4] Darius Sherwin,[4] Levi and Reuben Robbins, David Goodenough, John Williams, Nathan Munger and his son Nathan, Levi Barnes, John Clark, Joseph and Bezaleel I. Rich, David King, Isaac Munger, Abner Whiting, Robert Horr, Henry Welch, and perhaps others, in the central and western part of the town, are believed to have settled in 1801–2, having in most cases come on the first year to select land and begin improvements, preliminary to the removal of families. The Wrights were from Winstead, Ct., the Mungers from Ludlow, Mass., Blodget and Rich from New

---

1 It is a prevalent belief among the first purchasers, that Mr. French saved a valuable tract of land to himself, by this arrangement. He represented Oneida county in assembly in 1799, 1801, '02, '03, and Albany county in 1810. He died in Albany, where he had resided most of his life, on the 17th of November, 1843, aged 78 years.

2 Mr. B. died January 9, 1848, nearly 84 years of age. His wife, the first woman who came into town, died August 5, 1844, aged 70 years. The first male child born in town was Harrison Blodget, their son, in 1801. Mr. B. erected the large stone hotel in Denmark village in 1824. Harrison Blodget was member of assembly in 1831.

3 Died, Nov. 30, 1833, aged 56 years.

4 Men with families.

Truly Yours

H. Blodget

Hampshire, Crary from Vermont, the Robbinses from Saundersfield, Mass., Clark from Barre, Mass., and with scarcely an exception, all who arrived during the first five years were from some of the New England states.

The town settled with great rapidity, and in less than three years, most of it was in the hands of actual settlers.[1]

In the winter of 1800–1, it is believed no family but that of Jesse Blodget, remained in town. The next winter was remarkably open, and land was plowed in March. This may have created a highly favorable opinion of the climate of the new town, although the occurrence was not peculiar to this section in that year.

That portion of the town south of Deer river, between Copenhagen and Denmark village, early acquired the name of Halifax, and prejudices were raised against it, but fifty years of cultivation have shown that it is equal to any part of the town.

The first physician who settled at Copenhagen was Dr. Dunn, but he removed to the Genesee country in 1804, and in the year following Dr. John Loud settled and remained till his death, March 3, 1831, at the age of 52.

The first framed house in Denmark village was built by Freedom Wright, first inn-keeper, and the first in Copenhagen by Levi Barnes.

In the spring of 1801, the Nathan Mungers (father and son), millwrights, having had their attention called to the Black river country, came down the river and followed up the Deer river to half a mile above the falls where they selected a site for mills, and in that season finished a saw mill and got it in operation. The proprietors to encourage the enterprise gave them the water privilege from the High falls up over two miles. In 1803, they got a small grist mill with one run of burr stones in operation, in time to grind the first wheat raised in the town as soon as it was in condition for use. The mill stood directly below the upper saw mill in Copenhagen village, and its vicinity gradually receiving a number of mechanics acquired the name of *Munger's Mills*.

The first store was opened at this place by Urial Twitchell and the first inn on the hill south, was kept by Andrew Mills. A beaver meadow, now a broad and beautiful intervale just above the village, afforded the first hay used in the settlement.

---

1 Jonathan Barker, Nathaniel Sylvester, William Root, Uriel and Timothy Twitchell, Solomon Wedge, John and David Canfield, Ichabod Parsons and others were early settlers.

It so happened that most of those living at this place were federalists, and as politics then ran, were presumed to sympathize with British measures. Soon after the arrival of the news of the bombardment of Copenhagen in Europe, in 1807, by a British fleet, in time of peace, and under circumstances that were regarded throughout Christendom as highly disgraceful to the assailants, a political meeting was held at Munger's Mills, by the Republicans as then styled. Their business being done, some one proposed to christen the place *Copenhagen*, in derision of the party who were in duty bound to justify the recent outrage in Europe. The name was at once adopted, and a few years after it was applied to their post office. The town had previously been named by the legislature, which rendered the new name to this village the more appropriate, as the largest village in town.

About 1807, P. Card, began a cloth manufactory below Copenhagen, which was continued by himself and sons many years. The cloth principally made was satinett, but more recently the business has chiefly been limited to carding wool.

In 1806, most of a militia company at Copenhagen failed to appear at a training, on account of some grievance at the change of their captain, and were accordingly summoned to a court martial to be held at the inn of Andrew Mills, half a mile south of the village, in January following. Their numbers inspired confidence in the belief that the proceedings of the court might be embarrassed or interrupted, and they agreed upon a course of proceeding, perhaps natural, under the circumstances of time and prevailing customs. Procuring a keg of spirits at a distillery, they marched to the court, and when called up for trial, assigned whimsical reasons for delinquency, alleging the want of decent clothing, short funds, the existence of various infirmities, and other frivolous causes tending to throw ridicule upon the court, and rendering it necessary to order the arrest of the greater number of the party. The prisoners were confined in the room over that in which the court martial was held, and finally by their boisterous conduct, compelled an adjournment without trial.

The offending parties were indicted for riot, and their trial came off at Doty's tavern in Martinsburgh, but resulted in acquittal. The rioters had in the meantime prepared a song, entitled *The Keg and the Law*, which recited minutely the transaction, and when the county court had adjourned, after the trial, this song was sung in the court room with great force and effect. The presiding judge is said to have jocosely remarked, that if this had been sung during the trial, witnesses would have been needless, as it embodied every fact in the case. One year after, the anniversary of their acquittal was duly celebrated, by an address, and the well remembered song was repeated. It was written by Charles Wright, and a friend has furnished us a written copy, as taken down half a century after, from the memory of one of the party. It is destitute of rhyme, poetical measure or literary merit, although it might appear quite different in its appropriate tune, now forgotten, or so changed as not to be applicable to the subject. A company of silver greys or exempts, was formed in this town, under Charles Wright, during the war. It never found occasion for service.

In June, 1815, Henry Waggoner was found dead below the High falls, in Deer river, under circumstances that excited suspicions of murder. A coroner's jury was called, but could not agree, and the body was buried, but the clamors of the public led to the holding of a second inquest before a jury of twenty-three persons, summoned from the central and southern part of the county, of whom twelve united in a verdict of suicide.

It appeared that Simpson Buck of this town, had been on terms of improper intimacy with the wife of a son of Mr. Waggoner, who resided on the Number Three road, south of Copenhagen. The old man publicly denounced this conduct, and in a recent suit against Buck, had appeared and testified against him. It is related that the latter swore that Waggoner should never appear against him again in court. When last seen, Mr. W. was going to his work of hoeing potatoes in a field about a mile south of the falls. When found, some days after, the body was much decayed, and showed marks upon the skull as if made with the head of a hoe. It is said there was also found a trail of blood for some distance from the bank, and on a tree fence over which the body was supposed to have been taken. Forty-two witnesses were sworn by the coroner, and the evidence taken led to the verdict that the deceased, about the 12th of June, 1815, "came to the south bank of Deer river, about one or two rods above the High falls, and then and there, by accident, or intentionally fell, threw himself into the said river, and then and there passed over said falls, a distance of 164 feet, and in so doing bruised and drowned himself."

Buck soon after went off with the young man's wife, resided some years in Penn Yan, and then removed to Michigan, where he is said to have perished by violence. At the time of the event he was very strongly suspected, even before the body was found, and in accordance with a superstition that should rather belong to the days of Salem witchcraft, he was brought and required to touch the dead body, to ascertain whether blood would flow afresh from the wound! Upon conversing with many cotemporaries of Waggoner, we find the belief in his murder to be very generally prevalent, although two or three express doubts whether an old soldier, who had been living in the place some time before, and also went off soon after, was not employed to execute the deed, or to assist in it. There is reason to believe that the coroner and jury were conscientious, as they certainly were disinterested in the discharge of their duties.

On the 9th of July, 1832, a board of health, consisting of the supervisor, overseers of the poor and justices of the peace, was appointed in this town, to guard against cholera, and Dr. Erasmus D. Bartholomew was appointed health officer.

In December, 1850, Wm. Cratzenberg of this town, was indicted for the murder of his wife in the spring preceding, and tried but acquitted. The judge, in charging the jury, stated that the prisoner had been guilty of great cruelty and brutality; but the evidence failed to establish a verdict of guilt.

About 1820, Allen & Canfield,[1] who had several years transacted a heavy mercantile and manufacturing business, failed, and their mill property was subsequently bid in by Abraham Varick of Utica.[2] Dr. Samuel Allen was appointed agent for the erection of an extensive rope factory, and the farmers of this and adjoining towns were induced to engage largely in the culture of flax and hemp, hundreds of acres of which were raised. In 1832 a rope walk, 575 feet long, was erected, and about 1836 machinery was introduced for the preparation of hemp. The rotting of hemp was not found economical by the process employed, and its culture quickly fell into disuse. The rope works were burned in the spring of 1843, doubtless by an incen-

---

1 David Canfield died Dec. 17, 1849, aged 71.

2 Mr. V. was a son of Richard Varick, an eminent citizen of New York. A fire once occurred near his rope works, when he was in the village, but by the most active exertions it was subdued before extensive damage was done. He was not allowed to stand an idle spectator, but was pressed into the line for passing buckets. When advised to get the works insured without further risk, he declined, saying, that among such people insurance was needless.

diary, and again built soon after, 400 feet in length, by Archibald Johnston, and the business has continued more or less regularly till the present time. Varick lost a large sum in this investment.

In 1853, surveys were made with the design of securing the location of the Rome R. R. to this place. The highest point on the surveyed route was 611 feet above Felt's mills, and about 40 above Copenhagen. At that time, a square mile was surveyed, and preliminary measures adopted to obtain a village charter. The census taken for this purpose, gave on the proposed limits, 610 inhabitants.

The water power at this place and below is valuable for manufacturing purposes, and may be improved to a much greater extent than at present. The river is however somewhat liable to extremes of flood and drouth, and the bridge at the village has been several times swept away. The last time this accident occurred was in the winter of 1842–3.

In 1849, a steam saw mill was erected by Kitts & Broadway, on the East road near the Lowville line and in 1858, C. S. Cowles & Co. erected a manufactory of staves, shingle and heading upon the Black river, at Blodget's landing.

About half a mile below Copenhagen occur the celebrated High falls on Deer river. The stream has here worn a broad deep chasm in the Trenton limestone down which the torrent plunges a nearly vertical slope a distance of 166 feet. The bank on the south side is 225 feet high. On the north side of the cascade, the rock presents a very steep inclination, and has been broken away, leaving a succession of small narrow steps, with occasional projections, along which the adventurous visitor may creep a considerable distance up the bank, but not without imminent danger.

About 1806, Miss Lodema Schermerhorn, in attempting rashly to climb this perilous steep, had crept over half way up before she was aware of the danger, when she found that descent was impossible, and her only chance for life depended upon her reaching the top. With cautious and steady nerve, she continued on, now clinging with one hand in a crevice of the rock while she found a firm hold for the other a little higher, she finally gained the summit, exhausted with fatigue, and overcome by the extraordinary nervous excitement which the effort occasioned. A female associate had followed her lead, and also found it necessary to go on or perish in the effort. She also reached the top of the precipice in safety. Some years after, Thomas Parkman attempted to scale the cliff, and got so far up that he could neither advance or recede. His companions ran to the nearest house, procured a bed cord, and drew him to the top.

On the night of Sept. 17, 1853, Wm. Ferguson, a British deserter, working in a foundry, having drank freely the day previous and retired late, sprang up from sleep, saying that a man had fallen into the river above the falls, and ran towards the precipice. A person followed, but before he could be overtaken, the delirious man had climbed a tree that overhung the chasm, when the branch on which he stood broke, and he fell to the bottom, a distance of 130 feet, striking half way down, and bounding into deep water. He was instantly killed by the fall.

King's falls, two miles below, form a cascade about 40 feet in height and are excelled by few localities of the kind in picturesque beauty of scenery. They were named in compliment to Joseph Bonaparte, ex-king of Spain, by whom they were visited and much admired. The banks of Deer river from the High falls to Deer river village, present the finest section of the limestones for the study of geology that the county affords.

Settlement at Deer river was begun by Abel French, a few years after his arrival as agent. In 1824, a large stone mill was built by Richard Myers and A. Wilson. A large saw mill was built in 1848, and the place has gradually grown to one of some business, having besides a large grist mill, two saw mills, a shingle mill and several mechanic shops, two churches, a store and about thirty dwellings. The principally traveled road formerly crossed half a mile above, where there is an oil mill, once a cloth-dressing mill. This village has at various times borne the name of the mill owner, as French's Mills, Myer's Mills, &c., but since the establishment of a post office, it has been known as Deer River. The name was adopted at a meeting called for the purpose.

Denmark (P. O.) is the oldest village in the town, and its post office was one of the first in the county, having been established in January, 1804. As a business place it is now probably the least important. It has a hotel, store, two churches, and a thinly settled street of nearly a mile in length.

Almon M. Norton[1] and Amos Buck[2] were many years prominent merchants in this village. The first merchant

[1] Mr. Norton died at Lockport, Ill., Nov. 23, 1859, aged 73.

[2] Mr. Buck died, July 11, 1855, aged 60. He was in assembly in 1825 and 1843.

was Jabez Wright, in 1805. Freedom Wright was the first inn keeper.

The first school in Copenhagen was taught by Tyrannus A. Wright, and the first school house in town was built near the inn of Freedom Wright in Denmark village. The first school commissioners were Lewis Graves, Charles Wright, jr., and Stephen Parsons, and the first school inspectors were John Canfield, Israel Kellogg and Charles Squire. These were chosen in 1813.

In 1829, Charles Brown erected a wooden building in Denmark village for an academy, and taught with much success for several years. Since his removal, about 1840, several others have taught, but the premises have now fallen into ruin.

The Alexandria library of Denmark was formed, May 6, 1811, by Willis Secombe, Lewis Graves, jr., Charles Squire, Asa Pierce, Gardner Cottrell, Solomon Wood and Isaac Horr, trustees. It was dissolved before the introduction of school libraries.

Religious Societies.—The first meetings in town were held by travelers. On the 9th of July, 1805, the Harrisburgh Ecclesiastical Society was formed, with Levi Robbins, Edward Frisbie, John S. Clark, Charles Wright, jr., and James Buxton, trustees, with the view of erecting a place of worship. The division of the town having made the name inapplicable, the Denmark Ecclesiastical Society was formed in its place, Sept. 21, 1810, with Gershom Sylvester, Chester Wright, Daniel Babcock, Wm. Root, John Canfield, John Loud and Freedom Wright, trustees. This was also unable to erect a church, and in 1815, a third organization. termed the First Ecclesiastical Society in the town of Denmark, was formed, having as its trustees, Josiah White, J. Loud, David Canfield, Lemuel Dickenson, Asa D. Wright and G. Silvester. Unfortunately for the interests of religion, the Presbyterians of this town employed as a minister, a man wholly unworthy of confidence, and as the sequel proved, utterly abandoned in principle. This was Walter H. Gerry, who was installed in 1815, and at a special session of the St. Lawrence presbytery, August 19, 1817, was deposed. The records show that he was "a man of considerable native talent, and in his preaching advocated sound doctrines, but it was found that his credentials were *forged*, and that he had never been admitted to church membership. His moral character was also bad, and at length he abandoned his family and went to South America, where he became a friar." Before leaving he borrowed as much money as his credit would allow.[1] The Rev. Luman Wilcox was ordained and installed, March 16, 1824, and dismissed in 1826. A Presbyterian society was legally formed at Copenhagen, January 20, 1824, with Hezekiah Hulbert, Philo Weed, Wm. Root, John Loud, Gideon Smith and Malachi Van Duzen, trustees. The Denmark first and second churches remained one till 1827, when they were separated by the presbytery. The Rev. Wm. Jones, Abel L. Crandall and others were subsequently employed.

A small wooden church was built at an early day in Denmark village, and used by several denominations many years. The present Union church at that place was built in the fall of 1848. A Universalist church was built in Denmark about 1830.

The first church in Copenhagen was built by Presbyterians and Baptists, on the northwest corner of Main and Mechanic streets, and was burned Feb. 16, 1832. The Presbyterians thus deprived of a place of worship, united with the Methodists and built the church now held by the Unionists, and occupied it alternately until the present Methodist church was erected. In the month of July, 1839, these denominations also united in holding a camp meeting in a grove half a mile south of the village. A Congregational church was legally formed at Copenhagen, May 3, 1841, with Malachi Van Duzen, Silas Chapin, Allen Kilborn, jr., Lorenzo Baker, Warren Murray, Gideon Smith, Nathan Lawton, J. H. Allen and John Newkirk, trustees. Many of the members of this society and others have formed a church upon what is termed the Union principle, professing to be kept together by Christian fellowship rather than creeds. A legal society styled the Church of Christ in the village of Copenhagen, was formed May 11, 1858, with Wm. Canfield, Wm. C. Lawton, Ezekiel Collins, Nelson Munger, Lyman Waters, Stephen Thompson, John D. Loud, Wm. L. Tompkins and Abel G. Sage, trustees.

The first Baptist ministers in town were Stephen Parsons and Peleg Card, the latter of whom settled about 1807 in Copenhagen and engaged in the business of cloth dressing.

---

1 After he absconded, various rumors of his operations came back, among which was the sale of a large quantity of water for whiskey. This was done by placing bladders filled with spirits at the bung, in such a manner that the proof glass could dip into them. When examined as a candidate for the ministry, he affected to be terribly in pain from toothache. Once in preaching he evinced great emotion without apparent cause, turned pale, trembled and could scarcely go on with his discourse. When questioned about the cause, he admitted that the thought had occurred to him, that whilst thus ministering religious truths to others he might himself be damned!

A church was formed from churches in Rutland and Champion in April, 1808, numbering six males and five females. After losing their interest in the first church by fire, they, in 1834, built a church since owned by them. In 1835, Eld. Jacob Knapp, the eccentric revival preacher, held meetings here. Elders Geo. Lyle, Orrin G. Robbins, P. Nichols, W. J. Crane, M. Thrasher, A. S. Curtis, O. Wilbur and others, have preached here.

The first Methodist preacher in town is said to have been Mr. Willis. A society was formed in the west part at an early day, but not organized as a separate circuit until 1840. The preachers since assigned to the Copenhagen circuit have been: 1840, Wm. W. Wood; 1842, Silas Slater, 1843, Harris Kinsley; 1844, David Ferguson; 1845, G. Hall, B. S. Wright; 1846, G. Hall, A. S. Wightman; 1847, Hiram Shepherd, G. W. Plank; 1848, H. Shepherd, Silas C. Kenny; 1849, Alban M. Smith, T. D. Brown; 1850, A. M. Smith; 1851–2, Orman C. Lathrop; 1853–4, W. W. Hunt; 1855, L. Clark; 1856-7, R. E. King; 1858–9, L. L. Palmer.

The 2d Soc. of the M. E. Church of Denmark, was formed Feb. 3, 1841, with Orlando Babcock, Abner Munger, John Clark, 2d, Stephen Nash and John Whiting, as trustees. They have a church edifice in Copenhagen.

The Baptist church in Lowville and Denmark, locally known as the "Line Church," was formed Aug. 25, 1819, a society having been organized under the statute, as the 1st Baptist church of L. and D. Feb. 9, of that year, Moses Waters, Luther Horr, Elijah Clark, Benjamin and Charles Davenport, Nelson Burrows, Samuel Bassett, Ichabod Parsons and Jacob Kitts, 2d, being the first trustees. An edifice was built on the town line on the state road, in 1819, rebuilt in 1850, and rededicated Jan. 10, 1851. Its early ministers were elders Stephen Parsons,[1] Elisha Morgan, John Blodget, Ruel Lathrop and others. In the anti-masonic troubles of 1828–30, the church was

[1] *Eld. Parsons* was born Sept. 5, 1748, and ordained to the ministry, Jan. 31, 1788. He was an early, zealous and successful missionary in the Black river settlements, and active in the organization of nearly every Baptist church in the county. He removed from Middletown to Whitestown towards the close of the last century, and in 1802 came to Leyden, from whence, after several years, he removed to this town. His sons became heads of families and most of those of this name, now living in the county, are his descendants. The circumstances of his death were so peculiar that they made a deep and lasting impression upon the public mind. He had preached on a Sabbath, in the forenoon, from a favorite text, Psalms, xc., 12, and in the afternoon from II. Samuel, xix., 34: "*How long have I to live?*" On going to the barn to feed his horse on the same day, he fell from a scaffold, receiving an injury, from which he died unconscious, Jan. 7, 1820—within the same week that this sermon was preached.

nearly broken up, and some twenty members withdrew at one time. The Presbyterian church at Denmark village had become nearly extinct, when one was formed at Deer river, in 1826, as the second Presbyterian church of Denmark. It was changed in 1833 to the first Congregational church of Denmark, and a legal society was formed July 8, 1841, with Lyman Graves, Wm. Shelden, L. S. Standing and Abner A. Johnson, as trustees. A plain stone church had been previously erected at Deer river by this sect and the Methodists. In 1859, the Congregationalists of Deer river erected a neat church edifice, 36 by 63 feet, at a cost of $3,000.

The Methodist Episcopal society of Deer river was incorporated April 13, 1852, with Rev. Horace Rogers, Tyrannus A. Wright and C. A. Poor, as trustees.

DIANA.

This town was formed from Watson (by request of town meeting), April 26, 1830, and named in compliment to the wishes of Joseph Bonaparte, who then owned most of its wild lands and had begun small improvements. In his favorite pastime of hunting, he had here found an ample field for enterprise, and fancying that Diana herself, might covet this region as her home, by a happy turn of poetic fancy, he conferred upon it the name of the goddess of huntsmen. In classic mythology, Diana was reputed the daughter of Jupiter, from whom she received a bow and arrows, and a train of sixty nymphs. The poppy was sacred to her, and her temple at Ephesus was ranked among the proudest trophies of art. As a huntress she was represented as tall and nimble, with a light flowing robe, her feet covered with buskins, armed with a bow and arrows; and either alone or followed by her nymphs or a hound. Sometimes she rode in a chariot drawn by two white stags, and as goddess of night, or the moon, she was painted with a long starred veil, a torch in her hand and a crescent on her forehead.

The first town meeting was held at the house of Robert Blanchard, at which Chapman Johnson was elected *supervisor;* Geo. W. Bingham, *clerk;* Silas D. Stiles, John Wilbur and Enoch Cleveland, *assessors;* Willis Edwards, Caleb Blanchard and Jesse Palmer, *coms. of highways;* Daniel Robert, C. Blanchard and G. W. Bingham, *coms. of schools;* E. Cleveland and Mills Sly, *poor masters;* James Edward, *collector,* and Thos. Brayton, John Wilbur and Norman Stevens, *inspectors of schools.*

Supervisors.—1830-1, Chapman Johnson; 1832, Thos. Brayton, jr.; 1833, C. Johnson; 1834–5, T. Brayton, jr.; 1836–9, Caleb Blanchard; 1840–1, David D. Reamer; 1842, John Wilbur; 1843–9, D. D. Reamer; 1850, Sherman Blanchard; 1851, Eugine Burnand; 1852–3, Jonathan Aldrich; 1854, Howard Sterling; 1855, Horace Clark; 1856, Wm. Hunt; 1857–60, Joseph Pahud.

Clerks.—1830, G. W. Bingham; 1831–2, John Wilbur; 1833, James G. Lyndes (removed and J. Wilbur appointed July 11); 1834, Silas D. Stiles; 1835–9, J. Wilbur; 1840–5, Horace Clark; 1846, Reuben Tyler; 1847, Henry Allen, jr.; 1848–9, R. Tyler; 1850–3, H. Allen; 1854, Nathan R. Carley; 1855–9, H. Allen.

The south line of the town was fixed between the 19th and 20th north ranges of Castorland, but in the erection of Croghan, in 1841, the north line of that tract was made the south line of the town. The poor and the public money of Watson were to be divided in the ratio of the last tax list. While a part of Watson, the north line of this town was twice changed. On the 10th of April, it was made to run so as to include about 30 lots now in Wilna, and leave off several now in Diana, and on the 2d of April, 1813, the county line was fixed as it now exists.[1] The Checkered house and adjoining neighborhood in Wilna, were under the former arrangement included in Lewis county, and residents in that section could only enjoy the privilege of voting, by a journey to Leyden, distant about forty miles.

A panther bounty of $5 was voted in 1831–2–5, and of $10 in 1836 to '42–50–51. A wolf bounty of $5 was voted in 1835—and of $10 in 1832–4–6–7–8–9–'56. Fox bounties of $1 were voted from 1837 to 1842, inclusive. In 1845, a special law, allowing $5 on panthers, was asked by this town of the legislature.

Settlement began on the old St. Lawrence turnpike by one Doharty, but the first farm improvement was made by Thomas and Jeremiah Brayton, about 1818. Caleb, Robert and Sherman, sons of Isaac Blanchard, came about 1824, and afterwards their brother Daniel. They were originally from R. I., but then from Wilna, from whence also many of the other early settlers removed. Geo. W. Bingham, John Wilbur, Enoch Cleveland and others, settled about 1830, or a little before.

About 1828, the Count de Survilliers (Joseph Bonaparte), having acquired the title, first came to explore his lands,

---

[1] These changes are fully described on p. 29 of Jefferson Co. History.

and spend a few weeks in rural pastimes. He directed a road to be cut, and went in a stage coach through from the old turnpike to the lake, which has since been known as Bonaparte lake. He caused a boat to be taken through the woods and launched upon this water, and a log house to be built on an elevation, commanding a fine view of the lake and its shores.

This sheet of water covers about 1,200 acres, has several wild rocky islands within it, and is environed by bold rocky shores, alternating with wooded swamps and intervales, presenting altogether one of the most picturesque and quiet woodland scenes which the great forest affords. The place chosen for the house, was on lot 928, on the most commanding site that the shores of the lake presented. On the outlet of the lake at the present village of Alpina, the count had a clearing of some thirty acres made, and a framed house erected with ice house, cellars, out houses and other conveniences, with the view of making this a summer residence. He also built in 1829, at the Natural bridge, a large house, still standing.

The count visited his lands four times, upon each occasion spending a few weeks, and always accompanied by a number of chosen companions, some of whom had witnessed and shared the sunny fortunes of the ex-king of Naples and of Spain, the favorite brother of the great Napoleon. Upon one occasion, in returning from the Natural bridge to Evans's mills, the cortege halted upon the pine plains, and partook of a sumptuous feast which had been prepared with great care, and embraced every delicacy that the country afforded, displayed upon golden dishes, and served with regal ceremonies. Liberal in the use of money, and sociable with all who were brought in business relations with him, he was of course popular among our citizens, and his annual return was awaited with interest and remembered with satisfaction.

He soon, however, sold to La Farge; the house on the outlet, still unfinished, rotted down, and the log house on the lake was some years after burned.

This episode in the life of Joseph Bonaparte has been made the subject of the following poem by Caleb Lyon of Lyonsdale. It has been extensively quoted in the newspapers of the day, and presents a favorable specimen of the style of our Lewis county poet:

BONAPARTE LAKE.

From the Louisville Journal.

Waters enwound with greenest woods,
And jewelled isles, the gift of Pan,
Unsought, unseen, where Silence broods,
Unwelcoming the feet of man.

Gray clouds in liquid opal burn
Above the jagged hemlock's height,
A sunset sky outpours its urn
In ripples of the rosiest light.

By sinuous shore the baying hound
Tells the stag seeks on silver sands
Diana's mirror; here is found
One of Endymion's haunted lands.

The lilies on thy glowing breast
Loll languidly in crowns of gold,
Were pure Evangels speaking rest
Unto an Exile's heart of old.

Brother of him whose charmed sword
Clove or created kingdoms fair,
Whose faith in him was as the word
Writ in the Memlook's scimiter.

Here he forgot La Granja's glades,
Escurial's dark and gloomy dome,
And sweet Sorrento's deathless shades,
In his far off secluded home.

The hunter loved his pleasant smile,
The backwoodsman his quiet speech,
And the fisher's cares would he beguile
With ever kindly deeds for each.

He lived for others not in vain,
His well kept memory still is dear—
Once King of Naples and of Spain,
The friend of Bernardin St. Pierre.

In 1832, Fannel and Jomaine,[1] French capitalists of some experience in the iron business, began the erection of a blast furnace on Indian river, at a place which they named Louisburgh. As built by them, the furnace was thirty-three feet square at the base, of the kind technically termed a *quarter furnace* and intended for a cold blast. They

[1] Of the latter name there were two or three brothers. They were directly from Porto Rico. One of them afterwards died of cholera in Canada.

got the furnace in operation in 1833, but their European experience did them more harm than good, and after running two or three short blasts upon bog ore, their capital was expended, and their property, including about five thousand acres of land, was sold.

Isaac K. Lippencott, Joseph M. Morgan and David D. Reamer[1] became purchasers in 1836, and continued the business with better success, about ten years. They rebuilt the furnace, twenty-eight feet square, (seven and a half feet inside measure), introduced the hot blast in 1839, and for some time made stoves and other castings, by dipping directly from the furnace. The establishment had been founded upon the expectation of finding ores in the vicinity, but this failing, a supply was drawn from the Kearney mine in Gouverneur, and elsewhere in St. Lawrence county. The yield was generally three tons per day, and towards the end, much of it found a market in Rochester.

In 1850 the premises were bought by James Sterling who procured a change in the name of the post office, to *Sterlingbush*, and resumed the manufacture. He paid $10,000 for the premises and spent about $13,000 in rebuilding. Several blasts have been run since this change, but the work is now suspended.[2] The village consists of but little else than the furnace and its dependencies. The Sterlingbush and North Wilna plank road, built in 1853, connects this place by plank with the R. R. at Antwerp, and the iron mines, between Antwerp and Somerville.

In 1833, Foskit Harris[3] of Champion, under a promise of two acres of land and a waterfall on the Oswegatchie, with other inducements, from Judge Boyer, agent of Bonaparte, hired several men, and on the 25th of September of that year, pushed three miles beyond settlement, and began the erection of mills at the present village of Harrisville. A saw mill was built the first season, and a grist mill with one run of stones in 1835, several mechanics came in, roads

---

[1] Mr. Reamer died at Watertown, Aug. 12, 1858. He was sole manager at Louisburgh, the other associates being non-residents. In 1848 he was elected from this county to assembly, and soon after removed to Watertown, where he became an unsuccessful merchant. He was afterwards a clerk in the R. R. freight office.

[2] The cost of drawing ore from the Kearney mine, in Gouverneur, averaged $2.25, besides $1.75 for the ore delivered on the bank. It yields readily 50 per cent in the large way, although, theoretically, it should produce more. Most of the ore used by Sterling was drawn from his mine in Antwerp.

[3] Son of Asa Harris, who removed from Newport, N. Y., to Champion, the second year of its settlement. Mr. Harris died at Harrisville, Dec. 17, 1842, aged about 56 years. Mr. La Farge presented fifty acres of land to his widow.

were opened, lands cleared, and the place appeared destined to become a central business point. Several families were from Le Ray and towns adjacent; but no sooner was it known that Mr. La Farge had become the owner of the lands in this section, than they resolved to quit the place. The reputation of La Farge was exceedingly bad among the settlers on Penet square and elsewhere, and cases of marked severity had created so bitter a prejudice, that no inducement, not even that of a free gift at his hand, could induce them to remain. Thus deserted, the place retained little besides a name, until about four years since, when Joseph Pahud, a Swiss gentleman (who had become concerned in the Alpina works, towards the last of the Swiss company's operations), came to reside at this place. Under his auspices, a grist mill of superior finish was erected in 1858, and a saw mill, with double saws, in 1859. Inducements were offered, which led, in 1859, to the building of a chair factory, a sash, door and blind shop, and several buildings in the village. In May of that year, Messrs. Beach and Dodge[1] began an extensive tannery on the east side of the river, half a mile below the village, and in the midst of a forest. It is 288 feet long, has 160 vats, and is intended to turn out about 40,000 sides of sole leather annually. A new saw mill has been got in operation a mile above, and other manufactories are in progress. The village as yet, embraces, besides the above, only an inn, two stores, and about fifteen houses. It is half a mile from the St. Lawrence co. line, and by the nearest practicable route, thirteen miles from Keene's station, on the Potsdam and Watertown R. R., to which place a common or plank road, will, probably, before long, be laid out. The Oswegatchie was declared a public highway, by act of April 13, 1854, as far up as the junction of the middle and west branches.

Eugine Burnand, a Swiss, about 1844, purchased 48,513 acres from La Farge, embracing two ranges of lots in Antwerp, and 122 lots in Diana, and returned to Switzerland to find purchasers to settle upon his tract. While traveling upon the lake Neufchatel he met Louis Suchard, the proprietor of the steamer upon which they then were, and in conversation got him much interested in the chances of speculation, which his tract afforded, especially when he learned that iron ores occurred in this region and that forests of wood were abundant. Selecting, at random, a lot upon the map, (No. 920), he paid for it, and took a deed upon the

[1] Samuel Henry Beach of Catskill, and Robert Wm. Dodge of Gouverneur, son of the Hon. Edwin Dodge.

spot.[1] Suchard came over in 1845, and after two days spent in personal exploration and conversation with settlers, this ardent and credulous adventurer returned and in the winter following, organized a company with a capital of 300,000 francs, for the purchase of the tract, and erection of an iron furnace.[2]

Charles Favarger was sent over to conduct operations, receiving a salary at first, and promised eventually an interest in the enterprise. He selected a site on the lot 886, on the outlet of Bonaparte lake, and began the erection of a furnace, giving the location the name of *Alpina.* Mr. F. was not a practical iron master, but the furnace which he erected was of superior construction, and after an expenditure greatly exceeding the estimates, it was got in operation in the spring of 1848, at a cost of $20,000. The local supply of ore proved insufficient[3] and it was obtained from the Kearney and other mines in St. Lawrence co. After running two blasts with hot air, making from two to five tons per day, the company failed. By F.'s contract with Burnand, he was to have a deed of 1000 acres whenever he had paid $1000, and under this arrangement 17,000 acres had been conveyed at the time of the assignment.

Frederick de Freudenrich, to secure his own interests and those of his nephew, the Count de Portalis, in this Swiss company, bought the property of the assignee, and by careful management secured both without loss. The stock remaining at the furnace was worked up by Sterling, under an agreement with Freudenrich.

The furnace and its dependencies, with a large tract of land, passed into the hands of Z. H. Benton of Ox Bow, Jeff. co., who, on the 6th of June, with his associates, organized the St. Regis Mining Co. with $1,000,000 capital, in shares of $10 each. The parties named in the articles were Thomas Morton, John Stanton, Lyman W. Gilbert, Wm. Hickok and Albert G. Allen, and they stipulated the right to work mines in various towns of St. Lawrence, Jefferson and Lewis counties. It is needless to add that this scheme proved a failure, and that certain parties lost heavily by the speculation. We are not able to follow the

---

[1] This lot afterwards proved to be chiefly swamp and lake. Burnand, when this was found, made a satisfactory change of other lands.

[2] The company consisted of about twenty persons, and its capital was afterwards doubled.

[3] A few hundred tons of ore were obtained on the lands of the company and proved of good quality. About 1000 tons of iron were made under Favarger. Some poor sandy bog ores, obtained from the vicinity, were used as flux only.

intricate management of this affair, or to state further, than that there is a prospect of a continuance of operations at the furnace. One blast has been run by Benton, two by Emmet, and one by Pahud, since the above company was formed. About 1853, Loveland Paddock of Watertown, and D. C. Judson of Ogdensburgh, became the owners of about 30,000 acres in this town, to secure certain interests growing out of the Alpina management, and are now the owners of most of the wild lands in great tract number 4. Their agent is Mr. Pahud of Harrisville.

There are four post offices in this town: Harrisville, Diana, Diana Centre and Sterlingbush.

In 1852, Prince Sulkowski of Belitz, a political exile from Polish Austria, became a resident of Harrisville. His uncle had been a general under Napoleon, and fell in the battle of the Pyramids. The subject of this notice, in the revolutions of 1848, became obnoxious to the government, but managed to reach America with his family, and to secure a small stipend from a once large estate. He removed to this section from the opportunities it offered in the pursuit of his favorite diversion, that of hunting, and perhaps from the number of families who could speak his native language. In 1856 he removed to Dayanville, and he has recently been restored to his hereditary titles and estates. About two years since some attention was called to this person from a report that he was to marry the infamous Lola Montez; but the story, originating from parties in Europe who were interested in preventing his restoration to the royal favor, was easily refuted and had none of its intended effect.

There are at present no church edifices in Diana, excepting an Irish Catholic chapel at Sterlingbush, begun in the fall of 1858 and still unfinished. The Methodists organized a class about 1830, and have since held meetings, more or less regularly, in, school houses. The Seventh Day Baptists organized a church of 11 members in 1846.

GREIG.

This town was formed from Watson under the name of *Brantingham*,[1] March 1, 1828, and changed to its present name, Feb. 20, 1832. It is named from John Greig, who was born in Moffat, Dumfrieshire, Scotland, August 6, 1779.

[1] Named from Thomas Hopper Brantingham of Phila., in whom the title of a large portion was, for a short time, vested. He is understood to have been an unsuccessful merchant. The letters of cotemporaries, allude to him as unworthy of trust and destitute of honor.

His father was a lawyer, the factor of the earl of Hopeton, and a landholder, who ranked among the better class of Scotch farmers. He was educated in his native parish and at the high school in Edinburgh, and at the age of eighteen emigrated to America with John Johnstone, a Scotch gentleman who had previously been concerned in Mr. Williamson's settlements in western New York. After spending a short time in New York and Albany he went to Canandaigua in April, 1800, and became a law student at the office of Nathaniel W. Howell. In 1804 he was admitted to the bar, and becoming a partner with Judge Howell, continued in the practice of his profession until the death of the latter in 1820. In 1806, upon the death of Mr. Johnstone, he succeeded him as the agent of the Hornby and Colquhoun estate, and continued in that relation till his death. He was relieved of a portion of the duties of this trust, at his own request, in August, 1852, by the appointment of William Jeffrey as associate agent. In 1820 he became president of the Ontario bank, and held this office until the expiration of its charter in 1856. In 1841 he was elected to Congress, but resigned at the end of the first session, and during several of his later years he was one of the managers of the Western house of refuge. In 1825 he was chosen a regent of the university, and in 1851 he became vice chancellor of that board. He held many years the office of president of the Ontario county agricultural society, and was one of the founders and corporators of the Ontario female seminary. His death occurred at Canandaigua, April 9, 1858.

Through a long and active life, he discharged the duties entrusted to him with an industry, method and success, which earned him the implicit confidence of his employers, while his indulgent kindness towards those who settled under him, is remembered with gratitude by hundreds of the pioneer families. Of his private life, the village paper, in an obituary notice, remarks:

"Mr. Greig, though sometimes drawn from home by necessary business relations and interests, was eminently domestic in his habits and predilections. His chosen enjoyment was found in the indulgence, amidst the treasures of his select and ample library, of a refined literary taste—in the cultivation and adornment of the grounds about his stately mansion—in the society of a numerous circle of personal friends, and in the dispensation of a generous and tasteful, though unostentatious hospitality. Almost to the close of his life, nearly every stranger of distinction that visited the place, found a welcome and a home at his hospitable dwelling. Indeed, our beautiful village, owes much of its reputation abroad, for social courtesy and refinement, and for a frank and liberal hospitality, to him and his generous hearted and worthy lady."

The first town meeting in this town was held at the house of Dr. Simon Goodell, at which Mr. Goodell was chosen *supervisor;* Joshua Harris, *clerk;* Jedediah Plumb, George Pinney and Henry Harris, *assessors;* Gilbert Ford and Ezbon Pringle, *overseers of poor;* Johannes Saut, Simeon N. Garratt and Otis Munn, *coms. of highways;* Henry Harris, *collector:* Henry Harris and Daniel T. Seares, *constables*; Wm. Parkes, Jedediah S. Plumb and John R. Myers, *commis. of schools;* S. Goodell, E. Pringle and G. Pinney, *school inspectors;* John Fisher, D. T. Sears and Milo Clark, *fence viewers;* John W. Southwick, Chancy Carroll and Judah Barnes, *pound masters.*

Supervisors.—1828, Simon Goodell; 1829–33, Joshua Harris; 1834–6, Wm. Dominick; 1837–9, Aaron Perkins; 1840–3, Francis Seger; 1844, Wm. Dominick; 1845, John I. Dominick; 1846, Dean S. Howard; 1847-8, David Higby; 1849–50, Lyman R. Lyon; 1851, Aaron Perkins; 1852, J. I. Dominick; 1853–4, Adam Deitz; 1855–6, Thomas Rogers; 1857–9, Henry S. Shedd; 1860, Francis Seger.

Clerks.—1828, Joshua Harris; 1829–33, Henry Harris; 1834, Joseph Atkins; 1835, Geo. W. Sharpe; 1836–8, Adam Deitz; 1839–40, H. Harris; 1841–4, J. Harris; 1845–7, A. Deitz; 1848–9, H. Harris; 1850, Aaron Perkins; 1851, Adam Shell; 1852, Asa Beals; 1853–4, Chauncey Munson; 1855–6, Seymour Benedict; 1857–8, James Springsteed, jr.; 1859, Emmet Harris.

This town has since 1832 voted money annually for the support of ferries across Black river, upon the condition that town's people should go free. The towns of Martinsburgh and Turin have, during several years, united in the support of these ferries. The first bridge from this town to the west side was the Davis bridge, first built in 1820 by Caleb Lyon, and since twice rebuilt by the towns. It is two miles above the High falls. Port Leyden bridge was first built in 1823, by the towns. A bridge from the point between Moose and Black river to the west side, was built by C. Lyon in 1824, and lasted three or four years. A bridge was built opposite Turin village in 1824–5 by the towns but did not last long, and the travel has since been supplied by a ferry. A bridge was first built over the High falls in 1836, and rebuilt in 1842.[1] In 1849 a new bridge was built at the junction of Moose and Black river, so as to accommodate both sides of Moose river.[2]

A bridge at Tiffany's landing was built in 1846[3] by this town and Martinsburgh, and maintained until it was cut away by the state authorities in 1854, as obstructing the navigation. A ferry had existed several years before at this place, and has supplied the place of a bridge since the removal of the latter. Two bridges have been authorized to be built at the expense of the state, between the falls and Watson bridge, and the decision of their location will have probably been made before this volume is in the hands of readers. Concerning the upper one of these, there has been an active controversy between those advocating its location at the steamboat dock at Lyon's falls, and those who wish to have it constructed opposite Turin village, at or near the present ferry. A bridge has been recently built across the Black river, one mile below the Oneida county line at Hulbert's saw mill.

The first location by actual settlers was made just below the High falls in 1794, by the French, and their colony received from time to time accessions in number but not in strength. It may be questioned whether any number of tradesmen, jewelers and barbers from Paris could form a flourishing establishment in this wild wooded country, without a long previous course of misspent labor and fruitless expense; for of what avail is industry when applied, as it was here, from dawn till twilight, in clearing land with a *pruning hook?* or of what use was money, but to purchase provisions and other necessaries of life, which could be obtained much cheaper in cities. These tender exotics from sunny France soon found the privations of the northern wilderness beyond their capacity of endurance and quickly began to drop off and return to New York, from whence numbers went back to their native country, wiser and poorer from the bitter lessons which experience had taught.

A romantic account of this settlement, under date of Sept. 9, 1800, appears in the appendix of an anonymous

---

1 Act of April 12, 1842, allowing the question of tax upon West Turin, for this object, to be submitted to a town vote.

2 The town of Greig was authorized by the supervisors Nov. 15, 1849, to borrow $1,000 for this purpose, which was done.

3 Act of May 12, 1846, allowing $400 to be taxed on Greig, and $300 upon Martinsburgh.

work published in Paris in 1801, from which we here offer several extracts :[1]

An event, as unfortunate as unexpected, has much hindered the prosperity of this colony. The death of a young man of much talent, whom the Castorland company had sent from Paris, to render a wild and hitherto unknown country fit to favor the reunion of a new born society, to divide the lands, open roads, begin the first labors, built bridges, and mills, and invent machines, where man is so rare. A victim of his zeal, in taking the level of a bend of the river, he perished in trying to cross above the great falls. His comrades so unfortunate as not to be able to assist him, have collected the details of this disastrous event in a paper, which I have been unable to read without emotion and which I send.

Our rivers abound in fish, and our brooks in trout. I have seen two men take 72 in a day. Of all the colonies of beavers, which inhabited this country and raised so many dams, only a few scattering families remain. We have destroyed these communities, images of happiness, in whose midst reigned the most perfect order, peace and wisdom, foresight and industry. Wolves, more cunning and warlike than the former, live at our expense, and as yet escape our deadly lead. It is the same with the original elk. It is only seen in this part of the state, and our hunters will soon make it disappear, for you know, that wherever man establishes himself, this tyrant must reign alone. Among the birds we have the pheasant, drumming partridge, wild pigeon, different kinds of ducks, geese, and wild turkey, &c. Our chief place, situated on the banks of the pretty Beaver river, and from thence so appropriately named *Castorville*, begins to grow. It is still only, as you may justly think, but a cluster of primitive dwellings, but still it contains several families of mechanics, of which new colonies have so frequent need. Several stores, situated in favorable places, begin to have business. The Canadians, on the right bank of the river, come thither to buy the goods which they need, as well as sugar and rum, which, from the duties being less at our ports than at Quebec, are cheaper with us than with them. The vicinity of these French settlements are very useful to us, in many respects. Cattle are cheaper than with us, as well as manual labor. Such are the causes of communication between the inhabitants of the two sides, that it is impossible for the English government to prevent it. * * * Among our families we have some, who, driven from their country by fear and tyranny, have sought in this an asylum of peace and

[1] The article is translated in full, in the Hist. of Jefferson Co., p. 52—55. The work is in three volumes, and purported to be from a manuscript cast ashore on the coast of Denmark, from the wreck of the ship *Morning Star.* The authority of this letter is unknown, but that of the work is known to be J. Hector Saint John de Crévecœur.

liberty, rather than wealth, and at least of security and sweet repose. One of these, established on the banks of Rose creek, came from St. Domingo, where he owned a considerable plantation, and has evinced a degree of perseverance, worthy of admiration. One of the proprietors[1] has a daughter as interesting by her figure as by her industry, who adds at the same time to the economy of the household, the charms or rather the happiness of their life. Another yet is an officer, of cultivated mind, sprightly and original; who, born in the burning climate of India, finds his health here strengthened. He superintends the clearing of a tract of 1200 acres, which two sisters, French ladies, have entrusted to him, and to which he has given the name of *Sister's Grove.* He has already cleared more than 100 acres, erected a durable house, and enclosed a garden in which he labors with an assiduity, truly edifying. He has two Canadians, whose ancestors were originally from the same province with himself. Far from his country, the most trifling events become at times a cause of fellow feeling, of which those who have never felt it, can have no idea. As for cattle, those raised that only bring $9 a pair, at the end of the year, are worth $70 when they are four years old. Fat cattle, which commonly weigh 700 to 900 lbs., sell at the rate of $5 per hundred. Of swine, living almost always in the woods, the settler can have as many as he can fatten in the fall. It should not be omitted to give them from time to time an ear of corn each, to attach them to the clearing, and prevent them from becoming wild, for then there is no mastering their wills, for they pining for their wandering life will not fatten on whatever is given them. Butter is as dear with us as in old settled countries, and sells for a shilling a pound. * * * I have placed your habitation not far from the great falls, but far enough distant not to be incommoded by the noise, or rather uproar which they make in falling three different stages. The picturesque view of the chain of rocks over which the waters plunge, their tumultuous commotion, the natural meadows in the vicinity, the noble forests which bound the horizon, the establishments on the opposite bank, the passage of travelers who arrive at the ferry I have formed, all contribute to render the location very interesting, and it will become more so when cultivation, industry and time, shall have embellished this district, still so rustic and wild, and so far from resembling the groves of Thessalia. The house is solid and commodious, and the garden and farm yards well enclosed.

I have placed a French family over the store and am well pleased with them. I think, however, they will return to France, where the new government has at length banished injustice, violence and crime, and replaced them by the reign of reason, clemency and law. The fishery of the great lake (On-

[1] St. Michel, noticed in our account of Croghan.

tario) in which I am concerned, furnishes me an abundance of shad,[1] salmon and herring, and more than I want. What more can I say? I want nothing but hands. You who live in a country where there are so many useless hands and whose labors are so little productive there, why don't you send us some hundreds of those men? The void they would occasion would be imperceptible; here they would fill spaces that need to be animated and enlivened by their presence. What conquest would they not achieve in ten years! and what a difference in their lot! Soon they would become freeholders and respectable heads of families. The other day a young Frenchman, my neighbor, seven miles distant, and established some years upon the bank of the river, said to me: "If it is happy to enjoy repose, the fruit of one's labors and ease after having escaped the perils of the revolution, how much more so to have a partner of these enjoyments? I am expecting a friend, a brother; it is one of those blessings which nature alone can bestow. What pleasure shall I not enjoy in pointing out to him the traces of my first labors and in making him count the successive epochs of their progress and the stages of my prosperity, but above all to prove to him that his memory has been ever present to me. The objects which surround me I will tell him are witnesses to the truth of this: this hill upon the right, covered with sombre pines, is designated upon my map under the name of *Hippolites Absence*, the creek which traverses my meadow under that of *Brothers Creek*, the old oak which I have left standing at the forks of the two roads, one of which leads to my house and the other to the river, *Union Oak*, the place of my house *Blooming Slope*. Soon he will arrive from St. Domingo, where Toussant L'Ouverture has allowed him to collect some wreck of our fortune."

The reminiscences of the French colony in this town have been made the subject of the following poem, written by Caleb Lyon of Lyonsdale, entitled

LEWIS COUNTY IN THE OLDEN TIME.

From the Evening Post.

In the lands of vines and olives, over three score years ago,
Where the Bourbon Rulers perished in unutterable woe,
Plans matured for emigration sanctioned were with revel gay,
In saloons of *la belle Paris*, by the friends of Chassanais.

On an hundred thousand acres, never trod by feet of men,
He had mapped out farms and vineyards, roads o'er precipice and glen,
And, like scenes of an enchanter, rose a city wondrous fair,
With its colleges, its churches, and its castles in the air.

---

[1] White Fish.

Then was struck a classic medal by this visionary band :
Cybele was on the silver, and beneath was Castorland ;
The reverse a tree of maple, yielding forth its precious store,
Salve magna parens frugum was the legend that it bore.

O'er the Atlantic, up the Hudson, up the Mohawk's dreary wild,
With his flock came Bishop Joulin, ever gentle as a child ;
Kind words of his dispelled their sorrows and their trials by
the way,
As the darkness of the morning fades before the god of day.

By *la Riviere de la Famine*, ocean-tired and travel-sore,
They up-reared a rustic altar, tapestried with mosses o'er ;
Crucifix they set upon it where the oak tree's shadows fell
Lightly o'er the lighted tapers, 'mid the sweet *Te Deum's* swell.

Never *Dominus Vobiscum*, falling upon human ears,
Made so many heart-strings quiver, filled so many eyes with tears.
The Good Shepherd gave his blessing — even red men gathered there,
Felt the sacrifice of Jesus in his first thanksgiving prayer.

After toils and many troubles, self-exile for many years,
Long delays and sad misfortunes, men's regrets and women's tears,
Unfulfill'd the brilliant outset, broken as a chain of sand,
Were the golden expectations by *Grande Rapides'* promised land.

Few among this generation little care how lived or died
Those who fled from Revolution, spirits true and spirits tried ;
Or of loves and lives all ended, orbs of hope forever set—
These the poet and historian can not let the world forget.

Among the ruins of the French houses at the Falls, there have been found brick of a peculiar form and a light yellow color. If these were made in the locality, the source from whence they obtained the clay is well worth inquiry. If they were brought hither from a distance, the circumstance has scarcely less interest, especially since stone, well adapted for building, could be procured abundantly near the spot, and must have been noticed by the first explorers, had they been in the least degree observant.

The earliest criminal trial relating to this region, occurred in 1795, in the Herkimer court, at which D——— C——— of Litchfield, was tried for stealing $1000 from a Frenchman at the Falls, and sent to state prison. In 1799, a white man came in at the High falls from towards lake Champlain, stating that a negro in his company had died some miles back on the Beaver river road. From his having some property of the other, suspicions were raised that he had murdered him, and upon search the body was found at some distance from where it was reported, but so decayed that nothing could be ascertained. The fellow traveler was arrested, but released from want of evidence against him, and it was thought that the negro had arisen

Caleb Lyon

from where he had been left, and come on some distance before lying down to die.

The first permanent settlement in this town was begun in 1819, under the agency of Caleb Lyon,[1] although improvements had been made by John H. Dickinson, several bro-

---

[1] *Caleb Lyon* was of Scottish ancestry, who removed to Hertfordshire, Eng., during the troubles of the Covenanters, and from thence to New England about 1680. He was a son of a captain in the Revolution. His grandmother was a daughter of Judge Sherburne of the Province of Massachusetts Bay, and his mother was Margaret Hodges of the Island of Jamaica.

The name *Caleb* has been applied to the youngest son in this family through many generations. He was born at East Windsor, Ct., in 1761, and removed when a child to Greenfield, Mass. He entered at Harvard college, but did not graduate, and removed, about 1800, to western New York, where he settled as an agent in what is now Walworth, Wayne county. He was for several years engaged, in the winter months, in the manufacture of salt at Salina. He removed in 1810 to the mouth of Four Mile creek, now North Penfield, Monroe county, where he laid out a village, projected a harbor and formed a settlement, but the enterprise not succeeding, he removed to what is known as Carthage landing, on the Genesee, below Rochester. He there purchased 1000 acres, erected buildings, and in 1816 sold to several associates. Having been for some time an agent of the Pultney estate, and thus brought to the acquaintance of Mr. Greig, he undertook, in 1819, the agency of the Brantingham tract, in which that gentleman was concerned. In 1823 he settled at Lyonsdale, where he built a bridge in 1829, and a grist mill in 1830–1. There were but one or two settlers in town when he came on as agent. He was elected to the assembly of 1824, and took an earnest interest in the construction of the Black River canal, but died before it was assumed as a state work. He was found dead in the woods, about a mile from the Davis Bridge, Sept. 15, 1835, having probably been stricken by apoplexy. Mr. Lyon was a frequent contributor to agricultural journals, especially to Fessenden's New England Farmer. His temperament was ardent and poetic, and his plans of business were pursued with an energy that allowed no common difficulty to prevent their accomplishment. He was the friend and correspondent of De Witt Clinton, and an enthusiastic friend of the great public improvements, brought forward under his administration. Mr. L. married Mary, daughter of Maj. Jean Pierre Du Pont, nephew and aid of Montcalm, last French commandant at Quebec.

Of his two sons, *Lyman R. Lyon* was born in what is now Walworth, Wayne county, in 1806, and was educated under the Rev. John Sherman, at Trenton, and at the Lowville academy. From 1830 to 1835 he was deputy clerk in assembly, and during several years after was employed upon government contracts, in dredging the channels of western rivers and harbors. He was several years cashier and president of the Lewis county bank, and in 1859 was in assembly. He is at present the most extensive resident land proprietor in the county, and is largely concerned in business affairs. He resides in this town, near the river, and a short distance below the falls.

Caleb Lyon of Lyonsdale, widely known as a poet, lecturer, traveler and politician, was born in this town about 1821. He was educated at Norwich, Vt., and in Montreal, and at an early age became known in this county as a lecturer, while his poems and essays rendered his name familiar in literary circles throughout the country. He was commissioned as consul to Shanghai, China, Feb. 15, 1847, but entrusted the office to a deputy, and in 1848 he removed to California, where, after some months spent in the mines, he was chosen one of the secretaries of the constitutional convention. One of the first duties of this body was the adoption of a state seal, and the design offered by Mr. L. was adopted Sept. 2, 1849. He was paid $1000 for the design and seal—(*Journal of Convention*, p. 304, 323). In 1850 he was elected to

thers named Chase and others. At the present day much the largest part of the town is a forest, affording for many years to come, immense resources for the manufacture of lumber[1] and articles of wood[2] and bark for tanning leather.[3] Its water power, especially along the course of Moose river, is of great amount, and as yet mostly unimproved.[4]

---

assembly. He resigned April 26, 1851, to run against Skinner for the senate. While in the legislature he took an active part in favor of free schools, the completion of the canals and other public measures, and upon final adjournment was presented a silver tea service by his friends. In the fall of 1852 he was elected to the 33d congress. Soon after the expiration of his term he visited Europe and extended his travels to Turkey, Egypt and Palestine, from whence he returned with many souvenirs of foreign lands. While at Constantinople he addressed a letter June 28, 1853, to Com. Ingraham of the U. S. corvette St. Louis, highly approving the measures of Mr. Brown, in the case of the exile Martin Koszta, which excited much interest in this country and led to a sharp diplomatic correspondence—(*Executive Docs.*, *vol.* 11, *No.* 91, *p.* 19, 1*st sess.* 33*d Cong.*). In 1858 Mr. Lyon was defeated at the congressional election. In each instance that he has appeared before the public as a candidate he has been self-nominated and has always canvassed the district, holding frequent meetings by appointment and discussing the public issues of the day with his views of the policy which should be pursued with regard to them. The degree of LL. D. was conferred upon Mr. Lyon by Norwich University, the college where he graduated, in 1851. He is also an honorary or corresponding member of several state historical societies. Mr. Lyon is a popular lecturer upon subjects relating to history and the fine arts, as well as upon Egypt, the Holy Land, Italy and southern Russia, and his manner of delivery is animated, earnest and often eloquent. During Mr. Lyon's congressional term, he enjoyed the friendship of Thomas H. Benton and other eminent statesmen. He is a good classical and somewhat of an oriental scholar.

1 Marshal Shedd, jr., and Henry S. Shedd, have a gang saw mill on Moose river, a mile from its mouth. A gang saw mill was put up about 1854, on Otter creek, by Richard Carter, upon the tract purchased by Governor Seymour, and there are numerous other lumber mills of less extent in town.

2 A match box and match factory have been in operation on Otter creek since the fall of 1855. There is an extremely thick growth of pines, soft maple, birch and ash, upon a level tract extending along the creek from half a mile above its mouth, five or six miles up, and from one to three miles from its bank. The pines are small and doubtless of second growth. An old map has a record that this district was burnt over by hunters about the time of the revolution. Running fires have at different times caused great destruction of timber, especially in July, 1849, when the woods, near Port Leyden, were ravaged by the flames.

3 In 1850, Cyrus W. Pratt, son of Ezra Pratt, of Greene county, built a large tannery on Fish creek, three miles below the High Falls. Mr. Wm. Williams of Troy, erected another the same year on Crystaline creek, one mile from the former. This, after several changes of ownership, in the fall of 1856, also passed into the hands of Mr. Pratt, and both have since been run by him. They are capable of tanning 50,000 sides of sole leather annually, and would require 5000 cords of bark. Mr. P. was in our county the pioneer in this business which has come to form an important element of its manufacturing industry.

4 Besides a saw mill and grist mill at Lyonsdale, the only manufactory on this river is a paper mill, built in 1848 by Ager and Lane, and now owned by the Ager brothers. It turns out of wrapping, book and news paper, about 500 pounds daily.

CALEB LYON of LYONSDALE.

The point at the junction of the two rivers has been surveyed into village lots, and mapped, but is still woodland, with no building but the forest church. It is owned by the five daughters of the late Caleb Lyon.

No settlement has been attempted upon Brown's tract within this county. The proprietor endeavored to establish settlers in Herkimer county about 1795, but failed entirely. In 1812, Charles Herreshoff, a son-in-law of Brown, formed a project of establishing a sheep farm on what he called The Manor, made a clearing and got on a flock of sheep, but this also failed. He afterwards built a forge and attempted to open a mine, and after spending all the money he could draw from the family completed this failure also, by suicide, Dec. 19, 1819. The soil of Greig is, in most parts, a light sandy loam. Many years since, Dr. S. Goodell undertook to dig a well in coarse gravel, alternating with hard fine sand. The latter often indicated water, but failed to afford it in quantities, and the shaft was sunk 116 feet before reaching a full supply. A neighbor, the next year, in digging a post hole, found durable water; and a well twelve feet deep, not twelve rods from the deep well, gave an abundant supply.

There is no village in this town. The three offices of Greig, Lyonsdale and Brantingham, are supplied by a side route from Turin village.

Religious Societies.—A Presbyterian church was formed in 1825, and joined the Presbytery, Feb., 1826. No legal society was formed by this sect until Aug. 29, 1854, when the "Trustees of the Forest church, in connection with the Presbytery of Watertown," were incorporated by their own act, the first set being D. G. Binney, E. Schoolcraft, Hezekiah Abbey,[1] Edmund Holcomb, Lyman R. Lyon, Henry S. Shedd and Cyrus W. Pratt. A neat gothic church was built of wood in the forest, on the point near the junction of Black and Moose rivers soon after, at a cost of about $3,000, including a bell worth $200. Of this sum, the Rev. Thomas Brainerd, of Phila., formerly of Leyden, raised $700 abroad.

A Free Will Baptist church was formed in this town Nov. 30, 1844, but never built a place of worship.

The Union Society of Greig, was incorporated Aug. 2, 1856, with Alex'r Hess, Waitstill Cleaveland and Adam Shell, trustees.

The Church and Society of North Greig, was formed Jan. 26, 1859, and Cyrus W. Pratt, Richard Carter, Wm. L.

---

1 Dea. Abbey was born in Windham, Ct., Jan. 31, 1786; settled in Greig in 1825, and died in this town March 5, 1858.

Phillips, Wm. Hillman, Caleb Brown, Wellington Brown, A. F. Cole, Simeon Crandall and Stephen Burdick were chosen first trustees. Neither of these have erected church edifices.

HARRISBURGH.

This town was formed from Lowville, Champion and Mexico, Feb. 22, 1803, embracing townships 5 and 10 of the Black river tract. By an act of March 24, 1804, number 9 or *Handel* was annexed to this town from Mexico. Denmark was taken off in 1807, and Pinckney in 1808, leaving it with its present limits, comprising township No. 10, or *Platina*, of the tract above named. The first town meeting was appointed at the house of Jesse Blodget, and adjourned to Freedom Wright's, in Denmark village, where Lewis Graves was chosen *supervisor;* Jabez Wright, *clerk;* David Graves and Solomon Buck, *assessors;* Andrew Mills, Francis Saunders and Jesse Blodget, *commissioners of highways;* Charles Wright and Freedom Wright, *overseers of the poor;* Nathan Munger, Jr., *constable and collector;* and Charles Mosely and Andrew Mills, *fence viewers.*

Supervisors.—1803–7, Lewis Graves; 1808–13, John Bush; 1814–15, Ashbel Humphrey;[1] 1816, Geo. A. Stoddard;[2] 1817–21, A. Humphrey; 1822–25, Simeon Stoddard; 1826, A. Humphrey; 1827, Amos Buck, Jr.; 1828, S. Stoddard; 1829–30, A. Humphrey; 1831, S. Stoddard; 1832–3, Wm. C. Todd; 1834–7, Elias Gallup; 1838–9, Henry Humphrey; 1840, Julius A. White; 1841–2, H. Humphrey; 1843–7, Horatio N. Bush; 1848, Bester B. Safford;[3] 1849–50, John M. Paris; 1851, H. Humphrey; 1852–4, J. M. Paris; 1855–60, John Chickering.

Clerks.—1803–5, Charles Wright, Jr.; 1806, Andrew Mills; 1807, C. Wright, Jr.; 1808, John G. White; 1809–15, Sanford Safford;[4] 1816, Simeon Stoddard; 1817–19, S. Safford; 1820, Palmer Hodge; 1821, S. Safford; 1822–24, Amos Buck, Jr.; 1825–6, S. Safford (May 6, Wm. Allen); 1827–30, Wm. Allen; 1831–3, Elias Gallup; 1834–50, B. B. Safford; 1851, Rufus Scott; 1852–5, E. Gallup; 1856–9, John Young.

From 1836 to 1846, the bounties authorized by special statute in this county were voted in this town for the killing

---

[1] Born June 20, 1771; died September 9, 1855.

[2] Died Jan. 11, 1844, in his 72d year. He removed from Westfield, Mass., March, 1802. His wife died Dec. 6, 1847, aged 75 years.

[3] Died March 30, 1852, aged 55 years.

[4] Died April 21, 1826, aged 53 years.

of wolves. In 1846, '47 and '48, a $5 bounty was voted for bears.

B. Wright, in surveying the boundaries of this town, in the spring of 1796, made the following memoranda:

"The north line of this town is, in general, an excellent soil, timbered with basswood, maple, elm, beech, birch, butternut. There is one small cedar swamp near the 5 mile stake on this line. The country is level in general, and very finely watered. A large creek crosses this line near the one and ½ mile stake, which makes a N. E. direction, on which there is a fine country. The E line is excellent and very finely watered. There is some near the S. E. corner which is rather indifferent, but very little; the timber is maple, bass, elm, beech, birch, butternut and hemlock. On the South line there is middling country, some considerable swamp and some beaver meadow, on which excellent hay may be cut. Along the W line there is a good country of land. Some small gulfs along it which are made by the streams and a considerable gulf where the Deer creek crosses the line. The timber, in general, is maple, beech, bass, ash, birch, elm and some butternut and hemlock. Towards the South part, the land is swampy and timber sprucy." Measures 24,992 acres.

This town was subdivided into 49 lots by Joseph Crary of Denmark. It was named in honor of Richard Harrison of New York, former proprietor of the town. Mr. Harrison was of Welsh origin and a prominent lawyer. In 1788–9, he was in assembly, and from Feb. 15, 1798 to Aug. 1801, recorder of that city. He died Dec. 6, 1829, aged 81 years. After the death of Hamilton he became counsel for Constable and Pierrepont in their landed transactions.

The transfers of title in this town have been related in our account of Denmark. Settlement was mostly made under the agency of I. W. Bostwick of Lowville. The first improvements were made about 1802, along the line of the West road, which crosses the N. E. corner of the town, and among the first settlers on this road were Wait Stoddard, John Bush, Ashbel Humphrey, Joseph Richards,[1] Jared Knapp,[2] Sylvanus Mead,[3] Palmer Hodge and John Lewis.

In 1806, Silas Greene, Thomas and Ebenezer Kellogg, John Snell, Mark Petrie, John F. Snell and Jacob Walrod, with families named Lamberton and Weston, settled on

[1] From Cummington, Mass; settled in 1803; died Feb., 1813, aged 58 years. David R. settled in 1804, and died in this town in 1845. They were descendants of Joseph Richards, of Abington, Mass.

[2] Col. Knapp died at Copenhagen, March 29, 1854, aged 73 years.

[3] Died Aug. 15, 1848, aged 61 years.

what is since known as the State road, across the south border of this town. Several of these were Germans from the Mohawk valley, and from them the settlement acquired the name of Dutch Hill, by which this region is still known. They have all since removed, and their places are held by others.

In 1821, Jacob Hadcock, and soon after, Michael Parish, Peter Picket, Henry Cramer, Jacob Biddleman, Thomas and Gilbert Merrills, settled on the river road above Copenhagen.

A pompous advertisement was issued in Jan., 1849, announcing the beginning of a village on Watson creek, in the south part of this town, to be named California. The affair ended as it began—in nothing.

Schools were first legally formed under the statute in 1814, when John Bush, John Lewis[1] and Micah Humphrey were chosen first school commissioners, and David Richards, Hart Humphrey, Nathan Look, Jr., Charles Loomis and Seth Hanchet, inspectors.

RELIGIOUS SOCIETIES.—A Free Communion Baptist church was formed in this town July 16, 1822, by a council appointed from Lowville, Martinsburgh and Turin, and subsequently a regular Baptist church was formed and a church edifice erected on the West road. In 1847, this first edifice was removed and a new one, 34 by 44 feet, erected on its site. It was built by Philo Hadcock, at a cost of $945, and is owned in equal shares by the two Baptist organizations.

St. Patrick's church (R. C.), was erected a few years since in the west part of the town, and is attended from Carthage.

HIGH MARKET.

This town was formed from West Turin by the supervisors, November 11, 1852, by the same act that organized the town of Lewis. The first town meeting was directed to be held at the house of Schuyler C. Thompson.

Supervisors.—1853, S. C. Thompson ; 1854–5, Michael H. Coyle ; 1856–8, Michael Walsh ; 1859–60, Charles Plummer.

Clerks.—1853, Lynville M. Beals ; 1854, Wm. Dolphine ; 1855, G. R. Thompson ; 1856, L. M. Beals ; 1857, Charles P. Felshaw ; 1858–9, William Rowlands.

This town embraces township 9, or *Penelope*,[2] of the

1 This settler was from Westfield, Mass. Silas Bush died Jan. 21, 1829.

2 Penelope was the wife of Ulysses, king of Ithaca.

Boylston tract, with 35 lots of township 2 or *Flora*[1] and 64 lots of township 3 or *Lucretia*,[2] of Constable's Four Towns, its present name was borrowed from that of its post office. established in March, 1849, but since discontinued. It was invented by S. C. Thompson to distinguish this place from *every other*, and in this view it was entirely successsful. The Irish settlers wished to have the town named *Sligo*, and usage had long before applied to an undefined region, west of Constableville, the nondescript name of *Kiabia*, by which it is still, to some extent, known.

Township 2, of which nearly half lies in this town, was subdivided by Benjamin Wright in 1797, and measures 26,266¾ acres. The bearings and distances of its outlines are as follows:

N. W. side,	N. 37° 30′ E.	412 ch.	48 lks.
N. E.	N. 52° 30′ W.	632	50
S. E.	S. 37° 30′ W.	412	48
S. W.	S. 52° 30′ E.	63	23

At the second town meeting, the owner of the premises, at which, by adjournment, the voters were to meet, refused to open his house. The majority of the voters, who were Irish, and not accustomed to the usages proper in such a case, were quite at a loss to know how to proceed, and came near losing their organization by failure to elect town officers. Just before sunset, they however organized in the street, as near the place of meeting as practicable, and adjourned to some convenient place the next day. With the advice of a lawyer they went through with their meeting, and have since retained the management of town affairs. In 1858 the town voted, with but one dissenting voice, tc petition for re-annexation to West Turin, but without success. In 1857 they purchased for $200 a store for a town house.

Settlement was begun about 1814, by Alfred Hovey and Liberty Fairchild, and in 1815, John Felshaw,[3] became the third settler. Ebenezer Thompson[4] and others subsequently located in town.

Upon the suspension of the public works in 1842, great numbers of Irish families removed to this town, and took up small tracts of land. The census of 1855 shows that 320 persons (about one-fourth) were natives of Ireland.

---

1 Flora was the Roman goddess of flowers.

2 Lucretia was a noble Roman lady

3 Died June 24, 1857, aged 82 years. He settled in the county in 1813.

4 Mr. T. removed from Rockingham, Vt., in 1821, and died June 6, 1843, aged 69 years. He was the father of S. C. Thompson, Esq., of Constableville.

These, with their children, born in America, would form over half of the present population of the town. There are also a few French or Germans.

A large part of this town is still a wilderness, including almost the whole of township 9, near the west part of which Fish creek flows southward across the town.

The highest point of land in the county is said to occur on lot 50, township 3. Streams flow from this lot in several different directions, and in a clear day distant glimpses of the hills in Madison county, as well as more than half of the distant eastern horizon, are seen. There are at present neither village, church, store nor grist mill in town.

LEWIS.

This town was formed from Leyden and West Turin by the supervisors, Nov. 11, 1852. The first town meeting was ordered to be held at the house of Orlando S. Kenyon. Its name was derived from that of the county.

Supervisors.—1853, Orson Jenks; 1854–5, Charles Pease; 1856, O. Jenks; 1857, Hiram Jenks; 1858, Jonathan A. Pease; 1859, 60, O. Jenks.

Clerks.—1853–4, David Crofoot; 1855, Orson Jenks; 1856–7, Daniel H. Buell; 1858, O. Jenks; 1859, William Gray; 1860, Jay Pease.

This town embraces very nearly that part of Inman's triangle, known as the "New Survey," the whole of township No. 1, or *Xenophon*, and three rows of lots from the S. W. side of No. 2, or *Flora*, of Constable's Four Towns. The principal settlements are in the eastern part, and its drainage is southward, by the head waters of the Mohawk and by Fish creek, and south westward by Salmon river. The soil is well adapted to grazing and the coarser grains, but fruits and corn have not been extensively or successfully cultivated. Its soil is inclined to clay, and in places is a gravelly loam, or covered with flat stone derived from the underlying slate rock.

That part of this town taken from Leyden, was sold to settlers by Storrs and Stow. Township 1 was surveyed into lots by Benjamin Wright in 1797, and its outlines were run in 1795, as follows:

N. W. line:	N. 37°, 30′ E.	520	chains,	3	links.
N. E.	do	S. 52°, 30′ E.	631	do	62	do
S. E.	do	S. 37°, 30′ W.	339	do	07	do
S. W.	do	N. 68°, 50′ W.	559	do	20	do

The latter is the patent line, and was surveyed in 1794.

Practically 3° further W. are allowed to the magnetic meridian to make present surveys coincide with the original field notes. Township 1, measures 27,105 acres, and the whole of Tp. 2, 26,266¾ acres. The connection of John Jacob Astor, with the titles of this town has been noticed on page 31. Lots 1 to 19 and half of 20, in township 1, were conveyed by Pierrepont to Charles Ingersol of Philadelphia, agent of Consequa, a China merchant, in payment of a debt of $12,000 which the captain of a vessel owned by Mr. P., had incurred. John G. Costar, afterwards became agent, and paid the taxes many years from a fund provided for that purpose. They were finally sold for taxes and are now chiefly owned by the Costar heirs. Fifteen lots,[1] owned by Judge Wm. Jay of Bedford, by virtue of a marriage, were sold in 1840, to R. T. Hough, with certain conditions of opening roads and forming settlements. Jas. S. T. Stranahan of Brooklyn, the Lawrence heirs and John E. Hinman of Utica, are owners of considerable tracts of wild lands in this town.

Settlement was began at West Leyden (now included in the town of Lewis), in the summer of 1798, by two families named Newel and Ingraham, who came by way of Whitestown and fort Stanwix, and located, the former on the farm of George Olney, and the latter on that of Amos B. Billing, adjacent to the east line of this town. Fish then abounded in the streams, and game in the forests, affording partial support, with no care but the taking, and incidents were not wanting to diversify the life of the first pioneers of this lonely spot. On one occasion, as the wives of the two first settlers were returning on foot from fort Stanwix (Rome), they saw a bear on a tree near where Jenk's tavern now stands. One of the women took her station at the foot of the tree, club in hand, to keep bruin from escaping, while the other hastened home a distance of two miles, procured a gun, returned and shot the bear.[2] These families remained about two years and went off.

Col. John Barnes came in 1799, and brought potatoes for planting on his back from Whitestown. A saw mill was built in the winter following, near the present mill of Ashael Fox, by Joel Jenks,[3] Medad Dewey, John and Cornelius Putnam[4] who came on with their families, Maj. Alpheus

---

[1] Numbers 26, 27, 32, 41, 50, 52, 53, 55, 56, 58, 61, 64, 65, 68, 69.

[2] Related by Josiah Dewey of Delta, N. Y., who has furnished ample notes upon the early history of this town.

[3] Mr. Jenks was from R. I., and held the first appointment as magistrate He died, February 9, 1838, aged 77.

[4] From Somers, Ct.

Pease,[1] took up four or five lots in 1801, and built the first grist mill, one or two years after, a little above the Mohawk bridge, in the present village of West Leyden. Nathan Pelton[2] and Wm. Jenks, from Stafford, Ct., Stephen Hunt,[3] ——— Graham, ——— McGlashan, Levi Tiffany,[4] Winthrop Felshaw, and perhaps others, settled within four years after. Most of the lands first taken up, were sold at $5 per acre. Samuel Kent and Jeremiah Barnes, were early teachers, and the first school was taught at the house of Joel Jenks. The first death that occurred in town, was that of a child in the family of some travelers, but the first adult person that died in town, was Mrs. Calvin Billings, a sister of Stephen Hunt, in the spring of 1810, about twelve years after the beginning of the settlement.

The first road to Constableville was cut in 1803, by Mr. Shaler, but the first direct road was not opened until 1816, by commissioners appointed for the purpose. This became the line of the Canal turnpike, and still later of a plank road, which in its turn has been abandoned to the public, and is now maintained by the towns through which it passes.

An occurrence happened in November, 1804, which caused much alarm in this settlement, and might have led to a most melancholy result. Joseph Belknap, Cornelius Putman, jr., and Josiah Dewey, jr., set out from the former Dewey tavern stand, westward, on a deer hunt. The snow was about ten inches deep, and they found tracks of deer plenty, but no game. They had no compass, the day was cloudy, and towards night they attempted to return, and as their track was crooked, they concluded to take a direct line for home. After traveling some distance, they came around to the same place, a second and a third time. They were evidently lost, and no longer trusting to their own estimate of direction, they concluded to follow down a stream of water which they took to be the Mohawk, which would of course lead them home. They passed a number of beaver meadows, and were frequently obliged to wade the freezing stream, and at other times were forced to wade down its channel instead of climbing its steep rocky banks. They tried to kindle a fire but failed, and finally kept on traveling till daylight, when they came to a foot-

---

[1] Mr. Pease died April 8, 1816, aged 54 years.

[2] Died June 7, 1856, aged 92 years.

[3] Died June 14, 1853, aged 79 years.

[4] From Somers, Ct.

path, which in two or three miles, led out into a settlement which proved to be in the town of Western, twenty miles by the nearest traveled road from home. They had followed down the Point-of-Rock stream, to near its junction with Fish creek. The half starved wanderers having fed, pushed on over a miry road, and reached home at midnight, when they found the country had been rallied, and a dozen men had gone into the woods in search of the lost.

About 1831 ten German families settled in this town, and these have been followed by others, until the population of foreign birth equals half, and with their children, born in this country, considerably more than half of the whole population of the town. Of these Europeans, 376 were reported by the state census of 1855 as Germans, 171 French and 21 Swiss. They are divided between the Catholic, Lutheran and Reformed Protestant Dutch denominations, in the relative order here named, and although they use their native languages at home, are mostly able to speak English with more or less facility, and the rising generation will learn to use it fluently. These foreigners are mostly an industrious, hardy and frugal people, obedient to the laws, and a large number of them naturalized citizens. The European settlement in this town was preceded by that in West Turin.

In 1841 a bridge was built over Fish creek, and a road opened from Lee, near the line of the old road of 1805, noticed in our account of Osceola. It led only to the line of township 13. The first deeds to actual settlers in this part of the town, were issued in May, 1840, amounting to 1,746¼ acres, for $3,194.60. The bridge was swept off in the winter of 1842–3, and soon rebuilt, and in 1843 a mill was built by Mr. Herron.

Several branches of lumbering have been followed in this town, for which it appears to afford special facilities. About 1840, the manufacture of oars from white ash was begun and continued some seven years. The quantity is estimated at about 500,000 feet per annum, during that period, and the principal market was Boston. Whaling oars were sold in sets of seven, of which two were 14, two 15, two 16, and one 18 feet long. The price ranged about 6 cts. per foot, linear measure.

Of birdseye maple, Lewis county has, during twenty years, produced about 100,000 feet (board measure) annually, mostly from this town, and the greater part sent off by Richardson T. Hough. Of this quantity, nine-tenths seeks an European market by way of New York. This accidental variety of the sugar maple is found somewhat common upon the range of highlands, extending from this town to Adams. It is estimated that two-thirds of all the timber of this variety, used in the world has, during the last twenty years, come from Lewis county; the market price depends upon the fashions of the day, with regard to styles of furniture, and prices range from $60 to $80 per M. ft., board measure. A mill for cutting veneers was formerly established, four miles west of West Leyden, but was burned in 1845. Of hoops, for oyster kegs, this town and Ava, in Oneida co., adjoining, produce about 4,000,000, averaging $2 per M., shaved and delivered, on the rail road. They are mostly used at Fairhaven and Cheshire, Ct. They are made of black ash and bought in a rough state by a few dealers who shave and forward them to market. Considerable quantities of hard-wood lumber, chiefly maple and birch, for flooring, turning, &c., are sent from this town.

West Leyden is the only post office in this town. The village of this name is located upon the Mohawk, here a moderately sized mill stream, and has a few shops, two saw mills, a grist mill, two inns, two churches and 170 inhabitants.

RELIGIOUS SOCIETIES.—Meetings were first held in 1804, by Justus Billings, a Presbyterian,[1] at the house of John Putnam. A Congregational church was formed in the summer of 1806, consisting of Josiah Dewey,[2] Justus Billings, Cornelius Putnam, Solomon Washburn and their wives, Maj. Alpheus Pease, Widow Horton, Cyrus Brooks and a Mr. Wood and their wives, of whom the last four lived a mile east of Ava Corners, and the others in this town. This church erected a house of worship a mile north of West Leyden, many years after, and in February, 1826, it joined the Watertown Presbytery. The church has become nearly or quite extinct.

A Baptist church was formed May, 1829, with 14 members. Elders Marshall, Ashley and Salmon were present at the organization. A legal society was formed Sept. 9, 1837, with Winthrop Felshaw, Jonathan A. S. Pease and Nathaniel Wadsworth, trustees, and a small plain church edifice has been erected. The Revs. —— Burdick, Wm. Rice, R. Z. Williams, R. W. Chafa, D. D. Barnes and others, have preached here.

---

1 Died July 31, 1847, aged 80 years.

2 Died Jan. 14, 1838, aged 80 years. Mr. D. was one of the first deacons of this church.

The United German Lutheran and Reformed Congregation of West Leyden, was formed Aug. 16, 1847, with Frederick Meyer, Frederick Schopper and Geo. Fries, trustees. It was formed of the German Lutheran and Reformed churches, and their new meeting house was to be called the Church of St. Paul. It was to remain a German house of worship, so long as the number of members of the congregation speaking the German language, was more than two. A law suit has occurred between the two sects, in which the Lutherans have gained the case, but the other party have designed to appeal. The Reformed Protestant Dutch church of West Leyden was formed Sept. 12, 1856, under the authority of the Cayuga classis, with John Boehrer, minister, Philip Rübel and Fred'k Meyer. Elders Fred'k Schaffer and Valentine Glesmann, deacons. Another united German Protestant, Lutheran and Reformed Congregation was formed Dec. 7, 1858, with Peter Wolf, Jacob Roser, Peter Kautser, George Trieps and Heinrich Roser, trustees.

LEYDEN.

This town was formed from Steuben,[1] March 10, 1797, embracing besides Inman's Triangle, all of Lewis and Jefferson counties lying east and north of Black river. By the erection of Brownville in 1802, Boonville in 1805, Watson in 1821 and Lewis in 1852, it has been trimmed down to its present limits. It derived its name from the settlement made by Gerret Boon in Boonville, under the auspices of the Holland Land Company, whose members chiefly resided in Leyden, in Holland. In the division of the town, upon the erection of Lewis co., the old name was retained by a section to which it was not strictly applicable in order that Boon's name might be perpetuated in the christening of Boonville.

At the first town meeting held at the house of Andrew Edmonds (Boonville), April 4, 1797, Andrew Edmonds was chosen *supervisor*, John Stormes *clerk*, Asa Brayton, Jacob Rogers and Phineas Southwell *assessors*, Jared Topping and Levi Hillman *constables and collectors*, Bela Hubbard and Luke Fisher *poor masters*, Asa Lord, Reuben King and Elisha Randall *com'rs of highways*, Sheldon Johnson, Eliphalet Edmonds, Amasa King and Archelius Kingsbury, *road masters*,

[1] Whitestown was formed March 7, 1788, embracing the whole of the state west of German Flats. Steuben and Mexico were formed April 10, 1792, embracing all of this county and a vast area north, south and west.

Lilly Fisher, Asahel Hough and Timothy Burges, *fence viewers*, Charles Otis and Joshua Preston, *pound masters*.

Supervisors.—1797–8, Andrew Edmonds; 1799, Phineas Southwell; 1800, Asa Brayton; 1801, P. Southwell; 1802, A. Brayton; 1803, Silas Southwell; 1804, John Dewey;[1] 1805, Peter Schuyler; 1805 (Apr. 18), Lewis Smith;[2] 1806–7, L. Smith; 1808–10, James Hawley; 1811, J. Dewey; 1812–16, Nathaniel Merriam;[3] 1817, John Fish; 1818–23, Stephen Spencer;[4] 1824–30, Michael Brooks;[5] 1831, Amos Miller;[6] 1832–3, Ezra Millor; 1834–6, Isaac Parsons; 1837–8, Allen Auger;[7] 1839–42, Joseph Burnham; 1843–4, Alfred Day;[8] 1845–8, Thomas Baker; 1849, Aaron Parsons; 1850, T. Baker; 1851, J. Burnham; 1852–3, T. Baker; 1854–6, Wm. J. Hall; 1857–8, Wm. J. Olmstead; 1859, Samuel Northum; 1860, David Algur.

Clerks.—1797–1803, John Stormes; 1804, Aaron Willard; 1805–7, Stephen Butler; 1808–9, David Higby; 1810, Benjamin Starr; 1811–2, Augustus Chapman; 1813, D. Higby; 1814–7, Stephen Spencer; 1818–9, Martin Hart; 1820–2, Allen Auger; 1823, Samuel Northum, jr.; 1824–5, Parsons Talcott; 1826–33, A. Auger; 1834–9; Thomas Baker; 1840–2, Lewis S. Auger; 1843–8, E. R. Johnson; 1849, Alfred Day; 1850–4, E. R. Johnson; 1855, David Algur; 1856–8, James M. Malcom; 1859, Chester J. Munn.

The supervisors of Herkimer co. in 1797, allowed £17.-11.2 school money to this town, then a part of that county. A special town meeting was held June 17, 1797, to appoint school commissioners, and Luke Fisher, Eliashab Adams and Jacob Rogers, were chosen. This is the only money received in this region from the state school grants of 1795.

---

[1] Born at Westfield, Jan. 20, 1754, served in the revolution, removed to Leyden in the spring of 1802, and died, Dec. 31, 1821.

[2] Dea. Smith died May 21, 1841, aged 89 years. He was a soldier in the revolution.

[3] *Nathaniel Merriam* was born in Wallingford, Ct., June 3, 1769, and in 1800 removed to Leyden and settled on a place partly new and the remainder first taken up by Asahel Hough. He continued to reside at this place until 1838, during many years as an inn-keeper when he removed to Indiana, but in 1846 he returned to this town. He died Aug. 19, 1847. In 1811, and 1820, he served in Assembly, and in 1815 he was appointed a county judge. He was widely known as an enterprising and public spirited citizen. His son Gen. Ela Merriam is elsewhere noticed. This family name occurs among the founders of Meriden, Ct., and has been till the present time a common and prominent one in that town.

[4] Died, Sept. 24, 1851, aged 72 years.

[5] Died, Feb. 1, 1841, aged 57 years.

[6] Died, Oct. 2, 1840, aged 64 years.

[7] Died, Oct. 6, 1839, aged 64 years.

[8] Died, Nov. 17, 1849, aged 47 years.

Nathaniel Merriam

In 1800, a special town meeting was held, for choosing persons to be appointed justices by the state council, and another, March 19, 1803, to choose two persons to a county convention, to nominate candidates for assembly. The delegates were Nathaniel Merriam and Samuel Snow. They were paid by the town, and present the only instance we have known, in which delegates were thus authorized and paid.

In 1801, John Storms, Lewis Smith and Eber L. Kelsey were appointed to petition for a division of the town. On the 10th of Jan., 1802, and Nov. 14, 1804, other attempts at division were voted. By the latter, it was proposed to divide the town (as was done the next year, on the erection of Lewis co.), the south part to retain the name of *Leyden* and the triangle and part east of the river *Storrsburgh.* On the 3d of Feb., 1804, Stephen Butler, Samuel Snow and Richard Coxe, were chosen delegates to a convention to be held at Champion, Feb. 1st, to take measures for securing the division of Oneida co. On the 18th of Sept., 1802, Asa Lord, Job Fisk and Asa Brayton were delegated to attend a meeting at Lowville, to consult about procuring a road from Albany to Johnstown, and thence to the Black river and down to its mouth. This was the beginning of a movement that secured an appropriation for the state road through the valley.

In 1799, an unique resolution was passed to the effect, that if sleds of less than four feet track were found on the highway more than four miles from home, their owners were liable to a fine of $1, one half to go to the informant, and the remainder to the poor.

Bounties for the destruction of noxious animals have been voted as follows: For wolves, $10 in 1801, 3, 4, 6, 10, 11. For henhawks, 6 cts. in 1815; and for chip-squirrels 2 cts. in 1806–7, if killed within one month after May 20.

This town is comprised within Inman's triangle, and includes the whole of that tract excepting the acute angle taken off in the erection of Lewis in 1852. This was in some early documents erroneously named "Storr's Patent," and its south line running N. 68° E., is supposed to have been the earliest one surveyed in the county. The eastern part comprising its principal area, was surveyed into 126 lots by Wm. and Jas. Cockburn of Poughkeepsie, and the western angle into 28 lots, by Broughton White. The latter is called the "New Survey" and with the exception of the first five lots is now included in the town of Lewis.

On the 5th of June, 1792, Patrick Colquhoun, high sheriff of London, purchased from his friend Wm. Constable this tract of 25,000 acres, at one shilling sterling per acre, and from his friendship to William Inman, interested him in a share of 4000 acres at the original cost; and as the purchaser was an alien, and therefore incapable of holding lands in America, he caused the whole to be conveyed in the name of Inman, in trust, and made him agent for the sale and settlement of the tract.[1] A few of the early settlers in this town received their titles directly from Inman, among whom were Ebenezer Coe, Wm. Bingham, Jared Topping, Thomas Brayton and Asa Lord.[2]

Late in 1793 Mr. Inman returned to England, and through his representations, Mr. Colquhoun was induced to undertake the purchase of what is now known as the Brantingham tract, of which he was entrusted the agency. He sold most of the 25,000 acre tract in February, 1794, and in the sequel his principals found reason to sincerely regret their connection with him. It would be unpleasant to specify details, and it is sufficient to know that Mr. Inman is not

---

1 *Wm. Inman* was allowed to hold lands in this state by an act of March 27, 1794. He was a native of Somersetshire, Eng., and in early life was a clerk of Lord Pultney. He first sailed to America, March 13, 1792, and arrived in June. He soon after was entrusted with the interests of certain Europeans, prominent among whom was Patrick Colquhoun, and took up his residence in Whitestown, not far from the present lunatic asylum, in Utica. He was many years resident in Oneida county, and became extensively concerned in land speculations in and near Utica, where he was engaged in a brewery. He was afterwards a merchant in New York, where he met with heavy reverses. About 1825 he came to Leyden, where he died Feb. 14, 1843, aged 81 years. His wife Sarah died in Leyden, July 24, 1829, aged 56 years. Their sons were William, John, Henry and Charles.

William Inman, the eldest son, resided formerly in Leyden, entered the navy Jan. 1, 1812, and became a commander May 24, 1838. He is at present (1860) in the African fleet.

John Inman was educated to the law, but turned his attention to literature, was connected with the N. Y. Mirror, and soon after, with Col. Stone, engaged as editor of the Commercial Advertiser, of which, in 1847 he became principal editor. He conducted for some time the Columbian Magazine, and died at New York, Aug. 30, 1850, aged 47 years.

Henry Inman early evinced a great talent for painting, and at the age of 15, painted his father's portrait, which is still preserved. He became one of the most eminent of historical and portrait painters, and died at New York, Jan., 1846, aged 45 years. He never resided in this county, but was an occasional visitor.

Charles Inman, a cabinet maker, died in Cincinnati.

2 Topping received a deed of 139 acres, lot 60, Oct. 28, 1795, for £128. Brayton's deed of 100¾ acres, was dated July 2, 1797. Coe's deed for lot 88, 152½ acres, is dated June 12, 1795, and was given by Arthur Breese, attorney for Inman (*Oneida Deeds*, iii., 39). Others were less fortunate, and some were required to make second payment by a transfer of the titles by Inman, before their deeds were made out or their payments completed.

one of those to whom the town owes a grateful recollection.

The purchasers were Lemuel Storrs and Joshua Stow[1] of Middletown, Ct., with whom Thomas and Abel Lyman of Durham, Ct., and Silas Stow, held a small interest; and sales were made by these, as joint proprietors, a few years. Inman reserved a few lots.[2] After the division of the joint estate, Ezra Miller became an agent of Stow. Henry Champion, S. W. Dana, Zenas Parsons of Springfield, Mass.,[3] and others subsequently owned portions of the town before actual settlement.

Great lot No. 7, upon Black river, containing 620 acres, was reserved for a town plot, and the first road traced from from fort Stanwix, led obliquely down to the river at this place, but it was never laid out or traveled. The water power of this point was supposed to offer a chance for important manufactories. Storrs and Stow owed a large sum to the Connnecticut school fund, and an act was passed for receiving lands in this town for security. C. C. Brodhead of Utica, was appointed appraiser, and the price set upon them, being considered too high, they long remained unsold, and finally proved a heavy loss to the fund for which they were pledged. In 1835 an act was passed by that state, providing for the conveyance of lands in this state, and they have since been sold.

Settlement was first made in this town and county by William Topping,[4] who emigrated from Meriden, Ct., early in 1794, with an ox team and his household, consisting of his wife, a son aged seven years, and a girl aged five years. They were two weeks in reaching Whitestown, and turning northward into the wilderness, pursued their course through tangled underbrush and around fallen logs, to the far off tract where they hoped to find a home. The wife assisted in driving the team, while the husband went on before, with axe in hand, to clear the way. After laying by one day to nurse a sick child, they at length reached lot 60 and

---

1 Storrs died in Middletown city, and Stow died in Middlefield, about five miles from Middletown, Oct. 9, 1842, aged 81. He was many years post master at Middletown, and had been chief judge of the Middlesex county county court, state senator, &c.

2 Among these were lots 3, 4, 5 and 6, sold to John I. Glover of New York; 78, 79, sold to Hugh White of Whitestown; 91, 92, sold to David Lyman of Middletown, and perhaps others.

3 Mr. Parsons owned lots 104, 105, 112, 113, 119, which were sold by Jonathan Collins. He is said to have been killed by the Indians upon the Ohio river.

4 Wm. Topping died Sept. 17, 1840, aged 76 years.

selected a spot for shelter. They arrived late in April, and built a bark shanty by the side of a large log, with poles for the sides and a blanket for the door.

This pioneer home was on the east road, a little N. E. of Sugar river, where the road rises from the river flat, on land now owned by Robert Harvey and P. Owens. His neighbors to the south were many miles distant, and none were nearer than Canada to the north. Jared, his brother, came on in June to assist in building a log hut, and the first cabin was hardly finished when Wm. Dustin, Asa Lord,[1] Bela Butterfield and others, came to settle in town. It is believed no families wintered here in 1794–5, besides Topping and Butterfield.[2]

In 1795, Allen Augur, and families named Olmstead, Adams, Bingham, Hinman, Miller and perhaps others came, and in 1796, David Brainerd Miller, Peter W. Aldrich, Eber Kelsey, Brainerd Coe and others. A road warrant dated May 23, 1797, has upon it the following names of tax payers in Dist. No. 5, viz: Asa Lord, Ezra E. C. Rice, Bela Hubbard, Wm. Topping, Rodolphe Tillier, Jonathan Boardman, David B. Miller,[3] David Miller,[4] Calvin Miller, Jared Topping, Ezra Rice, Asahel Hough,[5] Chandler Otis, Amos Miller, Brainerd Coe, Eben Wheeler, Asa Brayton, Elisha Randall, Paul Green, John Worden, Daniel Topping, John Barns, Ephraim Town, Joseph Buttolf, Jonathan Wheeler, Asher Holdridge, Edmund Newell, Jerden Ingham, Moses Warren, Thomas Stone, Eliasheb Adams, Lemuel Storrs, Nathaniel Dustin, Abel Lyman, Peter W. Aldrich, Samuel Douglass,[6] John Allen, and 54 others in what is now Boonville.

The first birth in town was that of Jonathan, son of Wm. Topping, who died, aged 30 years. The birth occurred in June 1796.

The first death of an adult person in town was that of

---

[1] Mr. Lord was born in Franklin, Ct., Oct. 6, 1767. He arrived here immediately after Topping, and built the first log house in the county, on Leyden hill. He was brother of Thomas and Rufus L. Lord of New York, Eleazer Lord of Piermont, and Gurdon Lord of Leyden. He went to St. Lawrence county and was drowned April 9, 1818, with five others, at Madrid, N. Y., while attempting to cross his mill pond.

[2] Mr. B. sold to the Talcotts and removed about six years after.

[3] Died, March 19, 1833, aged 82 years.

[4] Died, Feb. 8, 1859, aged 84 years.

[5] Sold to N. Merriam, and removed to Martinsburgh.

[6] Died Feb. 6, 1856, aged 83 years.

Calvin, son of David B. Miller, March 23, 1797, at the age of 21 years.[1]

A man named Brayton was accidentally killed by a tree early in 1797 or 8. This was the first fatal accident known to have occurred in the county.

The first saw mill in the county was built in 1795, at Talcottville, by Bela Butterfield, a few rods below the present grist mill, but it went off in the next spring flood. In 1798, he sold to the Talcott families[2] from Middletown, Ct., who became prominent settlers in town, but adopted a policy adverse to the building up of a village at the point where natural advantages greatly favored. It is said they refused to sell village lots to mechanics, and retained the water power on Sugar river, although parties offered to invest liberally in manufactures. Bela Hubbard, husband of Stow's sister, removed in 1795, but did not long remain in town. The first framed building after the saw mill, was a barn built by David B. Miller in April, 1798; and the next, a house by Lemuel Storrs, the same year. The latter is still standing and is the oldest in the country. In 1803, the Talcotts built the second grist mill in town. The present stone mill at Talcottville, was built about 1832–3. The river has here a fall of nearly 100 feet within a quarter of a mile.

Many of the early settlers of Leyden were from Haddam, Middlefield and Middletown,[3] Ct. An advertisement in the "Western Centinel" of Whitesboro, dated 1797, and signed by Lemuel Storrs, records the fact that there were at that time 40 actual settlers upon Inman's triangle, and the official records of the earlier years show an unusually large number of *voters*, and of course of men having sufficient property to entitle them to this privilege, many of the pioneers were able to pay down for their lands, and have

---

[1] This historical fact is recorded on his tomb stone in the old Leyden hill cemetery as follows:

"Of all the adults which in this yard do lie
I was the first eternity to try."

[2] Hezekiah Talcott, father of the families of this name who settled in this town, died, March 16, 1813. His children were: *Phebe*, b. 1766, m. David Hall, d. Jan. 1826: *Sally*, b. 1768, m. 1st. Joel Coe, 2d ——— Parsons, d. March 20, 185- : *Elisha*, b. 1770, was killed May, 1807: *Daniel*, b. 1772, d. June 3, 1847: *Joel*, b. 1774, d. April 16, 1813, of the prevailing epidemic: *Jesse*, b. 1775, d. Jan. 15, 1846: *Johnson*, b. Sept. 6, 1778, d. Feb. 17, 1850: *Parsons*, b 1780, d. Jan. 16, 1849; and *Lucy*, b. 1782, m. Ithamer Whetmore, d. March, 1852. Elisha and Daniel were men with families when they settled.

[3] The families of Merwin, Northum, Algur, Thomas, Cone, &c., were from Haddam, those of Coe, Talcott, Brainerd, Smith, Stimson, Starr, &c., from Middlefield.

a surplus to enable them to begin settlement free from debt. In 1799, the number of senatorial voters was 57, and in 1800 it was 79, including of course the territory now known as Boonville. In 1798 the number of persons liable to serve as jurors was 14, in 1802, 61, and in 1805, 64.

In the winter of 1799–1800, a funeral service was held at Talcottville upon receiving news of the death of Washington. We are not informed who delivered the oration, but think it probable that Stephen Butler might have been designated. He was at about this time a teacher in town, and in former years had been one of Washington's life guard. He removed to Ohio many years after.

The first grist mill in this town, and the second one in the county, was built on the Black river, at Port Leyden, in 1799, and got in operation the next year, by Peter W. Aldrich and Eber Kelsey, millwrights,[1] from Killingworth, Ct. They came on to explore in the fall of 1796, selected a site and purchased two lots, extending from the river to near Leyden hill. In the spring of 1797 they removed their families, and during this season put up a frame for a saw mill which was swept off by the next spring flood and lodged on the rocks below. In 1798 the frame was again set up, and the saw mill got in operation, and in 1800 the first rude grist mill was prepared to relieve the early settlers from long tedious journeys to Whitestown in the dry season, and to Constableville at the more favored periods of the year. When first got in operation this mill was but partly enclosed, and its bolt was turned for some time by hand. It stood west of the river, a little below the present bridge. Aldrich sold his share to Jonathan Collins, Oct. 25, 1802. The saw mill was burned in Feb., 1802, but rebuilt by K. & C., and both mills were afterwards burned.

In the fall of 1805 a huge bear was seen on the farm now owned by Jas. S. Jackson, but escaped. Depredations were committed the next night, and Capt. Jonathan Edwards set out in pursuit. He found the enemy on N. Merriam's farm, fired at him without effect, and followed on, till in preparing for a second shot, the bear turned upon the hunter and got within two or three rods of him when the latter hastily fired his half loaded gun and wounded him. Calls for help brought persons to his assistance, and the beast was killed with an axe. It was judged to weigh 500 pounds and had

---

[1] Mr. Aldrich removed to Utica, and afterwards to Ogdensburgh, where he died July 11, 1811. He built the first bridges at Potsdam, Waddington and Ogdensburgh.

Mr. Kelsey died at Cape Vincent, Aug. 18, 1839, aged 76 years.

done much mischief to the settlers. Trout abounded in the streams when first known, and deer were numerous. They used to go east in November and December to winter beyond the Black river, and return as soon as the snow was gone in the spring. Many hundreds used to pass lot 68 before it was cleared. On lot No. 58 was a small strip of land called the Point, just above the junction of Moose creek and Sugar river, where there was a beaten path.

The first store in town was kept by Benj. J. Starr,[1] at Talcottville. Jotham Snow was the first physician in Leyden, and Manly Wellman the next. The latter removed to Lowville and afterwards to the Genesee country.

Silas Southwell taught the first school in town. The first school organization under the act of 1813, was effected at a special town meeting, held Dec. 27, in that year, at which Thomas Wolcott, David B. Miller and Winthrop Felshaw were appointed school commissioners, and Nathan Pelton, Samuel Kent, Israel Douglass, jr.,[2] Amos Miller, Allen Auger and Benj. Starr, inspectors. The first school house in town was built in 1802, at Leyden Hill.

The Leyden Union Library was formed Dec. 24, 1821, with Johnson Talcott, John Fish, Ela Merriam, Parsons Talcott, Allen Auger, Joseph Stimson, Ezra Miller and Thomas Wolcott, trustees. It acquired about 300 volumes and was dissolved two or three years after the introduction of school libraries.

An unsuccessful application was made to the regents of the university March 29, 1826, for the incorporation of an academy at Talcottville, but a sufficient sum had not been raised by the applicants to obtain an incorporation.

On the 22d of March, 1836, Gen. Ela Merriam bought of Eber L. Kelsey an undivided half of 50 acres, lot 17, embracing the water power at Port Leyden and Rock Island, about 60 rods below. On the same day he bought of Daniel Sears his farm on lot 16, adjoining Kelsey's, and immediately sold three-fourths of his interest to Francis Seger, Lyman R. Lyon and Jesse Talcott. The place was surveyed out into village lots by Eleazer Spencer in 1838–9, and the place previously called Kelsey's Mills was named PORT LEYDEN.

---

[1] Mr. S. removed to Rome and kept an inn on the site of the American hotel. He died on a visit to Cleveland.

[2] Mr. D. came to this town Feb., 1805, was two or three years in trade with one Higley, failed, and for several years after was engaged in the manufacture of potash, which, for some time, was the chief article of cash produce in the country. Israel Douglass, sen., died March 28, 1818, aged 75, and I. D., jr., March 22, 1855, aged 85 years.

Mrs. Pamelia J. Munn has since purchased the interest of Talcott. A tannery was run at this place many years by Cornwell Woolworth, who had bought the other half of Kelsey's interest, and in the fall of 1855 the Snyder brothers purchased this tannery, greatly enlarged it and it is now one of the largest establishments of the kind in northern New York. It contains 162 vats, uses 3,800 cords of bark, and produces 40,000 sides of sole leather annually. The village is situated directly upon the Black river canal, and had, until the diversion of the waters of the river into the Erie canal, an abundant supply of water power. Unless the natural volume of the stream can be restored by the construction of reservoirs, the water privilege at this point, as at others above the High falls, will be materially injured.

A short distance below the village, the channel of Black river is contracted to less than twenty feet in width, and the torrent rushes through the gorge with immense force. Several pot-holes have been worn in the gneiss rock to a great depth. Rock Island, at this place, is a rugged bluff, surrounded by water only during floods and easily accessible at other times. Its scenery is highly picturesque and as yet mostly undisturbed by the hand of man. In the map of a survey made before settlement, this narrow gorge is named Hellgate. The rock has been partially excavated west of the island, to afford hydraulic privileges, but the cutting off of the supply by the canals has prevented the completion of this work.

On the Black river, about a mile from Oneida county line, is a mill for the manufacture of lumber, staves, broom handles and other turned work. It stands near the canal, and a few years since was started from its foundations and much injured by a break in the canal directly opposite.

Another highly picturesque locality occurs in this town on Sugar river, about a quarter of a mile above the canal, and below its junction with Moose creek. The river here tumbles down a hundred feet or more through a gorge worn in the limestone, which presents a succession of steps, having a general slope of about 45°. The banks on either side, above and below, are nearly vertical, and from 100 to 200 feet in height. Below the falls, the gorge spreads out into a beautiful vale of some thirty rods in width and forty in length, covered with a dense growth, chiefly of evergreen timber, far above which the massive walls extend on either side. Several very deep pot-holes, worn by pebbles occur above the falls. About a quarter of a mile below, the whole of the river in the summer disappears in the fissures worn by the current, and about fifty rods below, again appears at the surface. The river road passes over this natural bridge thus formed. Near this place and in the same strata are caves which have been explored some 200 or 300 feet in different directions. They are simply natural fissures worn in the formation known to geologists as the Black river limestone. This rock is very soluble, and streams almost uniformly find an underground passage when their course lays across it.

A murder occurred in the northeast corner of this town on the morning of May 4, 1855, under these circumstances: A quarrel arose between two Irish women, near Lyons falls, growing out of the pawning of a pair of flat-irons. One of the parties, who kept a low grog shop, hired Thos. Rutledge and Michael Cavanaugh, two drunken sots, to whip James Cooper, the husband of her opponent. The hirelings assailed Cooper's cabin, pelted it with stones and broke his windows. He resolved to seek the protection of the law, but observing the superstition of his countrymen that "when the cock crows all danger is over," he awaited this signal, and a little after three o'clock, started for Port Leyden, was watched, pursued and killed with clubs, as he fell exhausted with running, at the door of Mr. Philo Post. Rutledge fled, and was doubtless concealed for some time among the Irish in High Market. Rewards were offered by the sheriff and the governor, but he was never arrested. Cavanaugh was indicted May 16, tried June 26, when the jury did not agree, and again before Judge Allen, Aug. 14, 15, when he was convicted of murder and sentenced to be hung Oct. 5. The convict was respited by the governor till Nov. 9, 1855, and subsequently his sentence was commuted to imprisonment for life in Clinton prison. An attempt was made by a low class of politicians to bring discredit upon the governor for this exercise of executive clemency, and on the night of Nov. 9, Governor Clark was hung and burnt in effigy. The governor wrote a lengthy letter in answer to one addressed to him, in which he stated in detail, the grounds upon which the commutation was granted.

There are two post offices in this town. Leyden post office was formerly kept at the village known as Leyden Hill, but in 1836 it was transferred to Talcottville on the Sugar river, two miles south, where it has been since kept. Leyden Hill was formerly a place of some business, but is now only a farming vicinage. Talcottville has but little claims to the title of a village, having only an inn, store, church, a few houses and a partially improved water power. Port Leyden post office is at the village of that name on the Black river and the canal.

RELIGIOUS SOCIETIES.—The Baptist church of Leyden is the oldest church in this town, and the oldest of this sect north of Oneida county, in the state, having been formed at the house of Thomas Brayton, April 22, 1803, by four males and one female. Eld. John Clark, their first minister, was ordained Oct. 4, 1804, by Eld. Jesse Hartwell of New Marlborough, Mass., Eld. Timothy Pool of Champion, Philips Chandler, Maltby, Wm. H. Stevens, Jeduthan, Zaccheus, and John Higby, and Russell Way. In this year the church received an accession of 28 males and 31 females from a revival of religion that occurred. Elds. Thomas Davis, Thos. Morgan, Chandler Hartshorn, Riley B. Ashley, R. Z. Williams, H. Nichols, Henry W. Chafa, Clement Haven, V. R. Waters, J. Lawrence, Reuben Sawyer and others, have preached here.

On the 4th of July, 1820, a subscription was drawn up to procure the means for erecting a church, 35 by 40 feet, which was successful. The edifice was built in 1821 at a cost of $1,660, and on the 17th of Jan., 1825, a society was legally formed, having Dr. Samuel Bass, Daniel Talcott, Samuel Douglass, Jesse Miller, Isaac L. Hitchcock and Nathan Coe, first trustees. The church edifice at Leyden Hill was repaired in 1856. Several years since a plot of ground was purchased adjacent to this church by individuals as a burial place, and the title was conveyed to its trustees.

The Presbyterian church of Leyden was formed Nov. 6, 1803, by the Rev. Ira Hart, and consisted of six males and eight females. The first pastor was the Rev. Jeduthan Higby, who was ordained Sept. 10, 1810, and preached three years. The second pastor was the Rev. Reuel Kimball who was installed May 14, 1817, and dismissed for the want of support in 1826. The Rev. J. Murdock and others were afterwards employed, and Mr Kimball was re-engaged at a later period.[1] The Rev. Evan Evans was employed from June 3, 1838, to Aug. 12, 1843, and one year after the Rev. Augustus L. Chapin began to preach. Others have been engaged for short periods, but for several years no stated services have been held, and the church now numbers (1859) but two males and about a dozen females. The Presbyterian Church of Leyden was built in 1821, and the

[1] The Rev. R. Kimball died Oct. 1, 1847, aged 67 years.

Engraved by J. C. Buttre

Nic W. Low

First Presbyterian Society of Leyden was formed under the statute, Jan. 3, 1826, with Abner Porter, Calvin B. Gay and Wm. Parks, trustees. It was changed to Congregational Jan. 4, 1836. Revivals occurred in 1824 and 1831, and protracted meetings have been held by Burchard, Crandall and Knapp.

In 1825, an effort was made to erect a Union church at Talcottville, but without success. The First Universalist Society in Leyden was formed June 4, 1831, with Otis Munn, James Brooks, Joseph Burnham, Eliphalet Sears, Armstrong Malcom, Alfred Day and Ezra Miller, first trustees. A church was erected[1] and the society has kept up its organization, although for several years it has not, until within the last year, held regular meetings.

The First Methodist Episcopal Church of Leyden was formed March 12, 1832, with Halsey Miller, Levi Hubbard and John Utley as trustees. A church edifice was erected at Talcottville, but this having much decayed, has been removed, and an arrangement recently made by which the Universalist church has been thoroughly repaired and is now owned by the two sects, but chiefly occupied by the Methodists.

An Old School Baptist Church was formed May 22, 1834, in the shed of the Leyden church, consisting of five males. A few days after four females united, and Dec. 17, 1837, the church was dissolved, and united with this sect in Turin.

A church was erected at Port Leyden and dedicated Dec. 6, 1853. It has been used by the Congregationalists and others, and the title of its property has been, or is now, in suit. A Congregational church was legally organized at Port Leyden, May 2, 1859, with Alanson Merwin, Daniel Scrafford and Sylvester Stimson, trustees.

The Calvinistic Methodist church of Port Leyden was formed March 9, 1855, with Rev. Edward Reese, Pierce Owens, David Roberts, Richard Roberts, Evan Evans and John Hughes, trustees. It has not now a place of worship and the members attend at Collinsville.

LOWVILLE.

This town was formed from Mexico, Oswego county, March 14, 1800, embracing, besides its present limits, that part of Denmark, south of Deer river, which was taken off

[1] Joshua Stow, former proprietor of lands in this town, gave $50. He died about 1840.

in the formation of Harrisburgh in 1803. Redfield, Watertown, Turin and other towns were formed by the same act. It embraces No. 11 of the eleven towns, and is the only one of that number that retains the name given by the surveyor general. At an earlier date it was known as Number Eleven, and a few legal writings drawn here are dated in Mexico. The first town meeting was ordered to be held at the house of Silas Stow, at which the following town officers were chosen: Daniel Kelley, *supervisor;* Moses Coffeen, *clerk;* Charles Davenport, Jonathan Rogers and Benjamin Hillman, *assessors;* Ehud Stephens, *constable and collector;* Billa Davenport and Aaron Cole, *overseers of the poor;* Isaac Perry, James Bailey and Benjamin Hillman, *commis. of highways;* Ehud Stephens, David Cobb, Asa Newton, Daniel Porter and and Zadoc Bush, *path masters;* Jonathan Rogers and Elisha Stevens, *pound masters and fence viewers,* and Adam Wilcox, Benj. Hillman, Jonathan Rogers, Daniel Kelley, Asa Newton and John Bush, a committee to select convenient places for burial.

Supervisors.—1800–4, Daniel Kelley; 1805, Silas Stow;[1] 1806–7, Wm. Darrow; 1808, D. Kelley; 1809–10, Benjamin Hillman; 1811–3, Ela Collins; 1814, Solomon King; 1815, B. Hillman; 1816–7, Heman Stickney; 1818–22, Benjamin Davenport; 1823, Chester Buck;[2] 1824–6, Charles D. Morse; 1827, E. Collins; 1828, B. Davenport; 1829–31, E. Collins; 1832–3, C. Buck; 1834, Daniel T. Buck; 1835–41, C. Buck; 1842, John Buck; 1843, Curtis G. Lane; 1844, C. Buck; 1845–6, C. G. Lane; 1847, Phineas Leonard; 1848–52, C. G. Lane; 1853, Jess Brown; 1854–5, C. G. Lane; 1856–7, Joseph A. Willard; 1858–60, C. G. Lane.

Clerks.—1800, Moses Coffeen; 1801–5, Wm. Darrow; 1806, Daniel Gould; 1807, Daniel Kelley; 1808–9, Wm. Darrow; 1810–6, Robert McDowell; 1817–8, Charles D. Morse; 1819–23, Charles Dayan; 1824, Russell Parish; 1825, Andrew W. Doig; 1826, Palmer Townsend; 1827–34, Orrin Wilbur; 1835–8, Wm. L. Easton; 1839, Ambrose W. Clark; 1840–1, Edwin Jarvis; 1842–4, Wm. Thompson; 1845–6, A. W. Clark; 1847, Francis B. Morse; 1848, Wm. A. Chase; 1849–51, F. B. Morse; 1852–4, Geo. S. Case; 1855, Francis N. Willard; 1856–8, Loren M. Brown; 1859–60, Marcellus J. Murray.

---

[1] At a special town meeting, held one month after, Solomon King was chosen supervisor.

[2] *Mr. Buck* came from Lanesboro in 1811. He represented the county in Assembly in 1822 and 1840, and took an active part in public affairs. Superior breeds of sheep were first introduced into the county by him. He died July 3, 1847, at his residence on the west road, aged 58 years.

Notes from the Town Records.—In 1809, 1810, 1812 and 1814, fines were voted for allowing Canada thistles to go to seed.

In 1817 Stephen Leonard and Heman Stickney were appointed a committee to confer with a committee from Martinsburgh about building a poor house. It will be noticed that this was about ten years before one was built.

In 1830 it was proposed to build a town house, and $300 were voted. In 1832 are solution was passed to apply for a law allowing $500 to be raised for a town house. Wm. Shull, Isaac Bailey, John Stevens, Stephen Leonard and Chester Buck were appointed to superintend the building. A petition was presented in Assembly March 15, and referred to Messrs. Doig, Skinner and Moulton, but no further legislative action appears upon the journals.

At a special meeting, July 7, 1832, the town voted $100, besides the $150 previously raised, to build a draw in the Black river bridge, to allow the steamboat then building at Carthage, to pass. The town of Watson also aided in this improvement.

In 1833, voted $150 for the Illingworth bridge, if enough to finish it be raised by other means.

In 1836, resolutions were passed asking for a law to tax the town $500 annually for five years, to aid in rebuilding the academy. This will be further noticed in our account of that institution. A committee, consisting of Chester Buck, Charles Bush, Luke Wilder, George D. Ruggles and Benjamin Davenport, was appointed under these resolutions.

In 1843, the town protested against the tax in this town, for the Carthage and lake Champlain road, and the next year against a county tax for the Tiffany bridge, or a new clerk's office.

In 1851, voted to borrow $1,950 from the state treasurer, under resolution of Nov., 1850, to aid in building Black river bridges.

This town, with Adams and Watertown, fell to the share of Nicholas Low, in the division between the four proprietors of the Black river tract, Aug. 5, 1796.

Nicholas Low, the fifth son of Cornelius Low, and Margarette, his wife, was born near New Brunswick, on the Raritan, N. J., March 30, 1739. Of his boyhood we have no trace, but it may be assumed from the position and easy circumstances of his parents, as well as from his character in after life, that he received careful training. He entered at an early day upon the career of a merchant, in the city of New

York, where his eldest brother Isaac had made himself conspicuous. Both brothers, at the commencement of the dispute between Great Britain and her colonies, embraced the American cause. Isaac Low, in 1774, was chosen by the city a member of the committee of public safety, and also one of the delegates of the continental congress of that year, having for colleagues, John Jay, John Alsop, James Duane and Philip Livingston, but as the quarrel became embittered, *Isaac* Low adhered to his allegiance to the crown, while *Nicholas* cast his lot in with his countrymen,[1] and when the British troops entered New York he abandoned it and only returned after the peace. He then resumed business there as a merchant, enjoying the confidence and friendship of the most eminent men of the nation—Washington, Jay, Hamilton, Gouverneur Morris, Rufus King, the Livingstons and others.

Mr. Low was alive to all the great political questions which agitated his countrymen, and taking such part as he deemed obligatory upon every good citizen, was ever averse to political life, and office he never sought. He was nevertheless sought out by his fellow citizens on occasions of moment. He was a member of the convention that adopted the federal constitution, and in 1788 and 1789 was in assembly. His political sentiments were then of the federal party, as inaugurated under the auspices of Washington, but he was of too independent mind and habits, ever to be a mere partizan.

Late in life, Mr. Low married Alice Fleming, widow of S—— Fleming, and by her he had three children, Cornelius, Nicholas and Henrietta, of whom the last only survives. In 1796, he made the purchase of the Black river tract with others, as we have elsewhere related. He had inherited from his father a considerable amount of landed estate at Ballston, which town in the early part of this century became a place of much summer resort by reason of its medicinal springs, and Mr. Low built there for the accomodation of this travel a large hotel known as Sans-Souci.

When the embargo of 1807 and war of 1812, cut us off from the supply of manufactured goods usually received from England, Mr. Low conceived the project of a great manufactory of cotton at Ballston, and accordingly with his accustomed energy and decision of character, went to work at the enterprise, investing very large sums himself, and

[1] Isaac Low withdrew to England in 1783, having been attainted and banished by an act of the legislature in 1779. He died in that country in 1791

inducing friends to do likewise. For the brief period of the war, the undertaking was remarkably successful, but with peace came ruin to home manufactures, and those at Ballston did not escape the common lot. The capital invested was almost a total loss, and Mr. Low soon after sold all his property at Ballston, of which as a watering place moreover the glories had been eclipsed by the neighboring Saratoga Springs.

With declining years Mr. Low withdrew from business, occupied himself mainly with the care of his estate, and in the society of his family and of attached friends, exempt until within the last year or two of his life, to a remarkable degree, from bodily suffering, though with eyesight and hearing somewhat impaired, yet with mind unclouded, he passed serenely on to death, November 15, 1826, being then in his 83d year.

In personal character, Mr. Low was distinguished for sterling qualities. With a clear head, great self-reliance and independence, much observation and knowledge of men and affairs, he combined a high sense of honor, the most scrupulous integrity, and the most exact justice and truth. His yea was always yea, and his nay nay, whatever might betide. He was a consistent member of the Episcopal church, and for many years a warden of Grace church in the city of New York. In personal appearance he was of compact and robust frame, with a full head, broad forehead, clear steady blue eyes, fine complexion and an expression indicative at once of great kindness and great firmness. His manner was courteous and polished, yet very direct. He was the very type of an independent, upright, honest gentleman.

Mr. Low was accustomed to visit the town annually upon business during many years. His son Cornelius was appointed in 1818, agent with Mr. Bostwick, and remained at Lowville a law partner with him until the death of his father. He died June 30, 1849, aged 54 years. Nicholas Low the second son, died in New York in the fall of 1859, and his only sister, married the Hon. Charles King, now president of Columbia college in the city of New York.

On the 20th of April, 1798, Low deeded to Silas Stow, for $8,000, a tract of 4,168 acres in the central part of the town, excepting 168 acres in a square in the N. W. corner.[1] This tract has from this cause been known as Stow's

[1] Deeds, Oneida Co., vii., 259.

Square, and may be classed among the best farming lands of the county.

Number Eleven was surveyed around its border in May, 1796, by Benjamin Wright, who reported that "this town is very good, especially in the south part, the soil excellent, and timber, bass, maple, beech, birch, ash, elm and butternut and some few hemlock. Along the river there is a fine intervale in many places, which has very fine soil, and is exceedingly handsome." He also notices the swamp along the river and a medicinal spring in the north part, "which may perhaps be of some considerable importance when properly examined." The area reported in this survey was 24,453 acres, and in another made by him in subdividing the town into lots the next year as 24,615 acres. Wright's survey of 1797, divided the town into 40 lots of from 154 to 693 acres. It was further surveyed by John Frees in 1802, J. D. Hammond in 1804, Robert McDowell[1] in 1808, and by others. The swamp near the river extending into Denmark (3,329 acres), was surveyed into 41 lots, of from 72 to 120 acres by McDowell in 1808.

A reminiscence of this town extends back to the revolution, and is supported by very good verbal testimony, to the effect, that a party of tories and Indians having captured a Mrs. Roseburgh and her little boy Henry, in the Mohawk settlements, conducted them through the woods to the High falls. They had here left concealed a birch canoe, in which they came down the river with their prisoners till on arriving at a place above Smith's landing, they left the river and came up to some flat rocks near the present east road and encamped. They had at this place made *caches* of corn, and here they spent the night. They proceeded on the next day to the Long falls, and from thence to Carleton island in the St. Lawrence, where Mrs. R. a few weeks after added one to the number of the captives. Henry was adopted by the Indians, but some time after was stolen away by his relatives. The child born in captivity, afterwards married in this county.[2]

Mr. Low having confirmed the title and caused the survey of this town, appointed Silas Stow, a young man

---

[1] Mr. McDowell was an Irishman of good education and social manners. He removed from Lowville to Waddington, St. Lawrence co., where by the failure of D. A. Ogden, he was deprived of a farm, which had been mostly paid for in surveying. He afterwards taught school many years in Madrid and Ogdensburgh.

[2] She was Mrs. Peter Van Atter. Jacob Van Atter was an ensign in the battle of Oriskany, and an early settler. His wife died, aged 100 years.

twenty-four years of age, who had previously been employed in the settlement of Leyden, as his agent, and 1797 the lands were opened for sale. A strong tide of emigration was then setting from New England, and the central and western parts of this state were being explored by small parties in quest of new homes. One of these companies from Westfield, Mass., consisting of Enoch Lee, Russell Pond, Ehud Stephens[1] and Jonathan Rogers, was returning from a tour to the Genesee country, where it was found sickly. At Whitesboro they met Mr. Charles C. Brodhead, who had but recently been employed in surveying lands on the Black river. He turned their attention to that region, and crossing the Mohawk, set them on a line of marked trees that led to the future homes of three of their number. Mr. Stow,[2] the agent, was then stopping in Leyden, but spent much of his time upon number 11, and from him

---

1 *Ehud Stephens* was a grandson of Thomas Stevens, who was born Dec., 1692, emigrated to America, and died at or near Newgate, Ct., March 20, 1752. His sons were born as follows: Thomas, Nov. 20, 1723, (d. Oct. 17, 1783); Solomon, Feb. 17, 1725; Jonathan, March 15, 1734 (died in childhood), and *Rufus*, Feb. 17, 1740, who accompanied his son to Lowville and died June 26, 1816. The children of Rufus Stephens were,

Ehud, b. Feb. 17, 1771, d. at Copenhagen Aug. 21, 1852. His son Apollos has been many years a merchant at Copenhagen. W. Hudson Stephens, son of Apollos, is a lawyer at Lowville. Harvey Stephens, son of Ehud, was a merchant at Martinsburgh and an agent of the Pierrepont estate. His family reside at that place.

Truman, b. Oct. 20, 1782, resides in Lowville. Settled in June, 1802.

Ira, b. Nov. 29, 1777, d. at Lowville June 21, 1852. Settled in 1801.

Rufus, b. Nov. 20, 1779, resides in Lowville. Settled in June, 1802 and *Apollos*, who died in infancy. His daughters were,

Ruth, married Levi Adams of Martinsburgh.

Electa, married Preserved Finch of Turin.

Paulina, married Heman Stickney of Lowville, and afterwards of Turin.

Each of the above named, except Jonathan (son of Thomas) and Apollos, became heads of families, and their descendants are numerous.

Ehud Stephens married Mercy, a daughter of Jonathan Rogers of Branford, Ct., who became the mother of the first white children born in Lowville and Martinsburgh. She was born in Sept. 28, 1769, and died May 31, 1849. Mr. Stephens was appointed sheriff in 1808 and 1820, holding the office, in all, about three years.

2 *Silas Stow* was born in Middlefield, Ct., Dec. 21, 1773, and was the youngest of a family of eight children. His three older brothers, Elihu, Obed and Joshua, were all in the revolution, and his father, a zealous patriot, rendered all the material aid that could be spared from his farm, and from principle, received continental money at par for everything he had to sell for the army. He was a farmer in very moderate circumstances. His wife was a woman of remarkable energy and devotion to the interests of her family. Mr. Stow was often heard to speak of her with tenderness and respect, and to her were her children largely indebted for whatever distinction they afterwards acquired. He received only a common school education, and his further acquirements were due to his mother's care and his own enthusiasm. He studied law at Middletown, but before settling in practice, became concerned in the agency of Leyden, and 1797 was appointed by Low agent for his towns on the Black

Stephens took the first *contract* in this town, June 2, 1797, for lot 38, at $3 per acre. Rogers, Pond,[1] Daniel Kelley, Moses Waters, and perhaps others, selected land during the summer and fall of 1797, began slight clearings and put up one or two rude shanties, a little south of the lower mill, for the families that were to come on in the following year.

Early in 1798 the first families of this town left their homes in Westfield, Mass., and by slow stages, found their way to the last clearing in Turin. At the High Falls they borrowed a pit saw of the French settlers, and with the aid of such tools as they had, undertook to build a boat of sufficient size to transport their families and goods to their destination. This craft was finished in about two weeks, and ready to launch as soon as the river opened. It was flat-bottomed, about 25 feet long by 7 wide, and might have had a capacity of two tons. It was probably the first vessel larger than a log canoe that had floated on Black river, and may have been regarded by its non-professional boat builders, as a model of its kind.

The ice broke up on the river on the 8th of April, and on the 10th, they launched their boat, loaded it with farming utensils, bedding, grain and provisions until its sides were scarcely two inches above the water, placed upon it their families, and cast off upon the swolen river, on an untried and somewhat perilous voyage. The passengers upon

---

river tract. He came on with the first settlers, and on the 26th of July, 1801, he married Mary Ruggles of Boston, a sister of Gen. Geo. D. Ruggles, formerly of this town. He was appointed a judge of Oneida county, Jan. 28, 1801, and was elected to the twelfth congress (1811–13) from the tenth district, by the Federal party. Following the principles they advocated, he spoke and voted against the declaration of war with Great Britain. In 1814–15 he held the office of sheriff, and from 1815 to 1823, that of first judge of Lewis county. Although educated to the law, he never practiced at the bar, but was regarded as a sound and judicious lawyer, and a man of great native talent. He was succeeded in the agency by Miller, in 1802, and an unfortunate land purchase in Malta (Lorraine) resulted in a pecuniary disaster from which he never recovered. He died January 19, 1827, at the house of Lemuel Wood, aged 54 years. He left three sons, all natives of this town, of whom Alexander W. Stow died at Milwaukie, Sept. 14, 1854, chief justice of Wisconsin. He resided many years in Rochester, from whence, in 1841, he removed to the state which conferred upon him its highest judicial trust. Marcellus K. Stow resides at Fond-du-Lac, Wisconsin, where he is engaged in merchandise. Horatio J. Stow was educated to the law and resided many years at Buffalo, where he held the office of recorder. In 1846 he was elected to the constitutional convention, and in 1857, to the State Senate, in which office he died, at Clifton Springs, Feb. 19, 1859. During several of his later years, he had resided at Lewiston and was extensively engaged in farming. He was a man of brilliant talent and much influence.

[1] Mr. P. never became a settler in town. This location was bought by one Washburn.

this trial trip, were Jonathan Rogers,[1] and his children Bela, Polly and Isaac ; Ehud Stephens, his wife Mercy, and children Clarissa, Apollos and Harvey; Jesse Wilcox, Philemon Hoadley, Zebulon Rogers and Elijah and Justus Woolworth.[2]

The craft was towed into the stream by some Frenchmen but was soon caught in a current that drew it slowly around towards the falls, against the best effort that those assisting could make, when to save themselves, they cast off the line and rowed toward their own side of the river. Four of the men seized their oars, and by hard rowing got within reach of the bottom, when B. Rogers and J. Woolworth, jumped out and swam ashore with a rope, by which the craft was towed down below the eddy, and then rowed across to the French houses opposite. A part of the load was here taken off, and they again started a little after noon. Running down upon the swolen current they arrived just before sunset, at the end of their voyage, as far up the Lowville creek as they could push the boat, and not far from the residence of the late Luke Wilder.

The day was delightfully serene, and they were borne rapidly and pleasantly along, with no effort except to keep their craft in the middle of the stream and no danger but from overhanging trees, by one of which, Clarrissa Stephens was swept off the boat, but soon rescued. They landed upon a tree that had fallen across the creek and prevented further progress, but were yet half a mile distant from the shanty where they were to spend the night. B. Rogers and J. Woolworth started with a gun to look up the spot, and after some time lost in finding a marked line, the rest followed on with such burdens as they could conveniently carry, and which would be most needed for present comfort. Meanwhile it grew dark, and the travelers could no longer see their route, but those who had gone on before, had

---

[1] *Jonathan Rogers*, was a son of Jonathan, who was born Dec. 12, 1715, and died at Westfield March, 1805. His family consisted of,

Eli, b. Nov. 14, 1740, settled in Martinsburgh in 1802, where he died.

Lydia, b. June 1, 1747, maried ——— Frisbie.

Mary, b. Feb. 22, 1753, m. Philemon Hoadley of Turin.

Jonathan, b. March 11, 1756, m. Mercy Rogers.

Abigal, b. Nov. 9, 1758, m. Samuel Danks.

Mercy, m. Ehud Stephens.

Capt. J. Rogers, died in Lowville, April 16, 1841. He was by trade a blacksmith, but in this town chiefly devoted himself to inn keeping and afterwards to farming. He was an exemplary member of the Presbyterian church, and in the various relations of life was highly useful and generally esteemed.

[2] As related by Jesse Wilcox, August, 1859.

kindled a pile of dry brush and logs, and by the sound of a horn, and the gleam of the cheerful fire, they were led to the rude but welcome shelter. A hearty supper was eaten with relish, and such as were entitled to hospitalities of the roof slept *under* it, while the rest made a couch of hemlock boughs, and lay down *upon* it.

Their provisions and furniture were backed up the next day. They had left a number of cattle in Turin to browse in the woods, but finding the spring farther advanced here, and the leeks and wild plants up fresh and green, while the snow still lay in the woods near the falls, some of the number returned in two or three days, and drove their stock down through the woods to Lowville. Two or three trips of the boat, brought the balance of their goods, when the craft was lent and kept running a long time after in transporting the family and goods of other settlers in this and the following seasons. Hoadley and the Woolworths had settled in Turin, whither they returned. Wilcox began clearing in June, upon the place he has ever since owned on Stow's square. Mrs. J. Rogers came on the next week, and during the summer quite a number of families found their way into town, took up land, and began improvements.[1]

The usual landing place of those who came by water, was at Hulbert's afterwards Spafford's landing, at the spot where the road from Lowville to Watson, first strikes the river.[2]

The land books of Mr. Low, show that the following persons took up farms in this town during the first four years of its settlement:

---

1 An early incident is related upon good authority, as having been observed with wonder. Rogers brought on a pair of fowls the first season, old Logan and his mate, and in due course of time, a tender brood of chickens claimed a parent's care. The hen was killed by a hawk, when, with half reasoning instinct, Logan, perhaps thinking these the last of his race, assumed the nurse's care, clucked the half-orphan young around him, fed, guarded and sheltered them with the tenderness of a mother, and reared them to maturity.

2 Col. *John Spafford*, from whom this landing was named, was a native of Ct. and one of the first settlers of Tinmouth, Vt. During the revolution he took an active part at the head of a company of militia. At the taking of Ticonderoga in 1775, under Allen and Arnold, he assisted with his company, and was directed to join Col. Warner, in his attempt upon Crown Point. He reached that important place before the latter, and received himself the sword of the acting commandant, which remained with his family at the time of his death. He died, March 24, 1823, at the age of 71 years. His son Horatio Gates Spafford was author of the first gazetteer of New York.—***Black River Gazette.***

In 1798, James Bailey,[1] Jehoida and Nathan Page, Hulbert and Cooley, Wm. Darrow,[2] and Moses Coffeen.[3]

In 1799, Adam F. and Jacob Snell, Benjamin Hillman, Jacob Eblie,[4] James Craig, John Shull,[5] Jeremy Rogers, John Bush, Daniel Porter, Geo. Bradford, Zadock Bush, Asa Newton, James Parsons, Richard Livingston,[6] Zeboim Carter,[7] Noah Durrin,[8] Ebenezer Hill, Samuel Van Atta, James and Garret Boshart,[9] Wm. and Benjamin Ford, John Kitts, Hooper Boohall, Philes and Kitts, Fisk and Searl, and James Cadwell.

In 1800, Reuben Putney, Luther Washburn, Aaron Coles, David Cobb, Nathaniel Durham, Pardon Lanpher[10] and Francis Murphy.

In 1801, Joseph Newton, Benj. Rice, Jesse Benjamin, Elijah Parks, Z. Plank, E. Newton, David Rice, David Wilbur,[11] Jabez Puffer, Samuel and John Bailey, Joseph Purrinton, Nathan Rowlee, Hezekiah Wheeler, Levi Bickford, Joseph Malby, Eliphaz Searle, Calvin Merrill, A. D. Williams, Benj. Davenport, Daniel Porter, A. and A. Sigourney, Mather Bosworth,[12] Loomis J. Danks, Edward Shepherd, Zuriel Waterman, Amasa Hitchcock, Ozen Bush, Simeon Babcock, Thadeus Smith, Elijah Baldwin, Jonathan Hutchinson, Erastus Hoskins, Robert Barnett,[13] Jesse Hitch-

---

[1] From Lebanon, Ct., and father of Daniel S. Bailey. He settled on Stow's square, and was an early innkeeper. Dr. Ira Adams afterwards owned his place.

[2] Dr. Darrow from Hebron, N. Y., was the first physician in the north part of the county, and settled on Stow's square. He was in assembly in 1812, and died, Jan. 8, 1815, aged 44 years.

[3] Bought on the East road. Sold in 1804, and bought 300 acres on the west road from whence he removed to Jefferson co. His brothers Henry, David and William, were pioneers in that county.

[4] Died, Dec. 15, 1857, aged 82 years.

[5] Died, March 27, 1827, aged 82 years. [6] From Johnstown.

[7] From Westfield, Mass. He served as colonel in the war of 1812–15, and died in this town April 22, 1853, aged 81 years.

[8] The Rev. Noah Durrin, died, Jan. 21, 1853, aged 78 years. He was by trade a millwright.

[9] G. Boshart, died, May 4, 1845, aged 76 years. He removed from the Mohawk settlements with several German families among whom were Shull, Eblie, Snell, Herring, Van Atta, &c., and settled on the hill side, a little north of Lowville village. His smooth, ample and neatly fenced fields, were long the model for whoever might be emulous of success in farming.

[10] Mr. L. removed from Westerly, R. I., in 1797, to Whitestown, and in March, 1800, came to Lowville, where he died Feb. 27, 1827, aged 82 years. The road on which he settled, between the Number Three and West Roads, is still often called from him Lanpher street.

[11] From Worthington, Mass. Died Dec. 27, 1829, aged 60.

[12] From Westmoreland. Died May 17, 1850, aged 84 years. Constant Bosworth died June 21, 1826, aged 80 years.

[13] Died Aug. 13, 1828, aged 67 years.

cock[1], Kent and Bull, John Delap, Nathaniel Prentice and Lewis Gosard.

The first *deed* to actual settlers was issued April 12, 1798, to Daniel Kelley for lot 37, of 250 acres for $650, on the same day that the deed of Stow's square was given. As an interesting subject for comparison the following list of deeds given during the years 1800–1–2, is given:

Name.	Date.	Lot.	Acres.	Price.
John Schull,..............	June 30, 1800.....	18	150	$450.00
Benjamin Hillman,.......	July 1, do	38	300	1,029.00
Wm. Darrow,............	Aug. 20, do		70½	266.37
Jonathan Rogers,........	April 20, 1801.....	29	412½	1,238.25
James Bailey,............	do do	10	101	345.10
John Bush,...............	do do	14	79	237.00
Ebenezer Hill,............	do do	13	101	353.50
Adam F. Snell,...........	do do	23	100	325.00
Jacob Snell,..............	do do	23	100	300.00
Elijah Baldwin,..........	Aug. 20, 1802.....	36	127¼	381.75
Samuel Van Atta,.........	do do	22	129	387.00
Noah Durrin,.............	do do	39	101¼	332.50
Ehud Stephens,..........	do do	38	239	690.00
Hooper Boonall..........	do do	9	259	971.25
Mather Bosworth,.........	do do	9	187½	628.12
Zuriel Waterman.........	do do	4	281¼	984.37

In 1803 the following persons received deeds: Zadock Bush, 103½, David Porter, 104, Simeon Babcock, 154½, Silas Weller, 51, Joseph Newton, 102, and Jesse Hitchcock, 50.

Mr. Stow hired a small piece, cut off and a shanty built in 1797, and a log house, opposite the bridge, at the lower mill, in 1798. In the summer and fall of 1802 he built a mansion, still standing and familiar to many of our readers, on a beautifully chosen spot, a short distance south of Lowville village, and now owned by Charles D. Morse.

Daniel Kelley[2] built a saw mill in 1798 on the south side of

---

From Lanesboro, Mass. Died May 25, 1853, aged 73 years.

[2] *Daniel Kelley* was born in Norwich, Ct., Nov. 27, 1755, married Jemima Stow, a sister of Judge Stow of Middletown, June 28, 1787, and removed from Middletown in 1798 to Lowville. He was appointed first county judge, and in the fall of 1814 removed to Cleveland, O., where he held the offices of post master and county treasurer. He died Aug. 7, 1831, in his 76th year. His wife was born Dec. 23, 1763, and died Sept. 14, 1815. She evinced in a strong degree, the mental vigor and the enterprise which belong to the Stow family, and for many years was an intelligent nurse and skillful midwife in Lowville, freely bestowing her time and services upon the sick.

Datus Kelley is a wealthy proprietor upon Kelley's Island, lake Erie. Alfred Kelley died at Columbus, O., Dec. 2, 1859, aged 70 years. He settled in the profession of the law at Cleveland in 1810, was twenty-two years in the Ohio legislature, was the author of its canal and railroad laws and influential in the public councils to a degree never surpassed in that state. He was acting canal commissioner while the canals were building and afterwards was president of three important railroads at the same time. Irad and Thomas

the creek, in Lowville village, just below the present bridge, and his first log hut built the same year, stood against a huge boulder, adjacent and directly opposite the bridge, as now built. A grist mill was raised the next year, with the aid of settlers summoned from all the country around, and got in operation Sept. 22, 1799. Its stones were dressed from a boulder of gneiss rock by James Parker, the well known mill-stone maker of Watertown, and the gearing was done by Noah Durrin and Ebenezer Hill, millwrights. It is noted by Mr. Stow that this mill, on the 24th of October, about a month after its completion, had ground two bushels of wheat well, in seventeen minutes. Previous to this, milling had been obtained at Whitestown and sometimes in Turin, the boys being generally detailed for this service. A day was usually consumed in going to Turin and returning, and the sun never went down on their way home, if the young pioneers could prevent it by a forced march through the obscure bridle path. The lower mill in Lowville was built by Stow about 1810. In 1803 or 1804, John and Ozem Bush built a saw mill on Sulphur Spring creek, near the Number Three Road, which they sold to Solomon King, who erected the first grist mill at that place. Mr. Kelley's mills, the erection of an inn by Jonathan Rogers, and a store by Fortunatus Eager,[1] determined the location of Lowville village, which sprung up mostly on the farm of Rogers, who cleared the site of its native growth of timber.

The first framed building in the village, was the house of Capt. Rogers, and the second was Eager's store. The second inn was built about 1805 by Preserved Finch in the upper part of the village, and was kept by Daniel Gould, and afterwards by M. W. Welles.[2]

M. Kelley resides at Cleveland, where they are prominent citizens. The latter is president of the Merchants' Bank, and has been for several years in the Ohio Legislature. We find the following incident of his life in the diary of an early settler: *May* 20, 1799.—"At Kelley's, his child Thomas fell into his saw mill pond, and lay there as near as we could judge, at least a quarter of an hour. Every appearance of life and heat was gone. After much pains we restored him to life. He lay floating on the pond."

[1] Mr. Eager was from Lunenburg, Vt., and came the second or third year of the settlement. After trading about three years, he became a partner of Wm. Card, and for several years he carried on the manufacture of potash quite extensively, thus aiding the settlers to means for paying for their lands. He went to Canada, near Brockville, in 1809, where he died. Mr. Card died at Greenbush.

[2] Major *Melancthon Woolsey Welles* was born in Stamford, Ct., Dec. 6, 1770, was some years a merchant at Albany, and removed from Lanesboro, Mass., in 1807. In 1809 he came to Lowville where he resided till his death, Feb.

The first birth in town was that of Harriet, daughter of Ehud Stephens, and afterwards wife of Dr. James M. Sturdevant, which occurred Feb. 24, 1799. The first male born in town was Samuel, son of Jonathan Rogers, June 21, 1800.

The first death is believed to have been that of a child of one Cooley, but the first of an adult, was that of Aaron Hovey, a young unmarried man from Johnstown. He had taken up a lot on the east road, but was then at work clearing land in the upper part of the village, near the present residence of Wm. Root Adams. He was thoughtless and profane, and a little before, upon receiving some slight injury, had intimated that he would soon have a settlement with his maker. He went out on a sabbath morning to cut down a tree, foolishly placing a round stone in the notch, as an experiment, to roll off the trunk from the stump. He was struck and killed by the tree, and was, it is believed, the first person buried in the old grave yard, then a lonely spot in the woods upon the east road below the village.

A few straggling families of St. Regis Indians, occasionally stopped a short time to hunt in the vicinity of the early settlers. One of these savages named "Captain Joe," had brutally whipped his squaw one evening in a drunken fit. She escaped to Capt. Rogers' house for protection, and was sent up a ladder into the garret by Mrs. Rogers, who had then no other company but two of her children. The ladder was scarcely taken down and hid, before Joe came reeling along in quest of his victim, and was the first time deceived and sent away. He soon, however, returned with a torch, following a little dog, who was good on the track, and by snuffing and barking soon convinced his master that the object of his pursuit was in the garret. The Indian sprang up and caught hold of a beam, when the woman and her children seized him by his legs and brought him prostrate to the ground. They held him until the neighbors could be rallied by a conch-shell to their aid, and Joe was deprived of further power to injure until sober and penitent.

On another occasion, a camp of some twenty Indians, on the spot now occupied by Morris Moore, became boisterous from drink, and a party came to Rogers' house, at which

27, 1857, aged 86 years. Mr. Welles was a son of the Rev. Noah Welles, and a descendant of Thomas Welles, whose son was governer of Connecticut in 1655. He was related to the late Commodore Woolsey of Utica, and well known to the citizens of the county. From near the time of his removal to about 1830, he kept an inn at Lowville village. His dwelling was built at the time when it was hoped that the old academic building might become a court house.

no man was present but Eli Kellogg his son-in-law. The Indians were extremely drunk and boisterous, when upon refusing to leave, they were knocked down with a club by the man, and dragged out by the women.

In these primitive times, wheeled vehicles were little known, and had they been owned, could hardly have been used without roads. If a party was to go on a visit to some distant cabin, a rude sled drawn by oxen, and cushioned with a few bundles of straw, afforded a slow, but safe and easy mode of conveyance, nor was the guest less welcome to the coarse fare and rustic hospitality of the bark roofed hovel. Distinctions founded upon the possession of a few more of the conveniences of life than one's neighbors were unknown, and the privations of the present, were relieved by bright anticipations of the future.

In the second summer of the settlement, Capt. Rogers went to the salt springs, now Syracuse, for salt, of which he procured a load, and brought it to near Dexter by water from whence it was drawn to Lowville on a dray made of a crotched limb of a tree. Fish and game were easily procured, and about 1805, two men from Lowville went over to Crystal creek, caught each a hundred pounds of fish and returned the same day. Sixteen years after, an enormous moose was shot in this town, by a lad twelve years of age. His skin was prepared, and exhibited more than thirty years in the Albany museum.

The road as first opened, about 1799, to Turin, was through what was termed the "eleven mile woods." The first road northward was the east road, which was probably run out the same year. In September, Stow hired Joseph Crary to survey out a line to township 3 (Rutland), which has ever since been known as the "Number Three road." John Bush, Peter Swinburne and —— Weller were first settlers on this road. The west road was laid out about 1801 or 1802.

Th street leading from Lowville to New Boston, was settled west of the west road, about 1805–6, by Roswell Waterman, Nathaniel Bement, Malachi Putnam, Sacket and Alvin Dodge, and about a dozen others in Harrisburgh. It is said that at the time of the war, there were about seventy men on this street in the two towns liable to military duty, but not a single family of these first settlers now resides there. The state road from Lowville to Henderson Harbor was afterwards located on this road.

The first settlement upon Stow's square, was begun in the fall of 1797, by Moses Waters,[1] who came on with a back

[1] Died, Feb. 5, 1852, aged 81 years.

load of provisions, and stayed while this lasted, cutting off a small clearing. Jesse and Roswell Wilcox,[1] Charles and Billa Davenport,[2] Dr. Wm. Darrow, Daniel Porter, Joel and Wm. Bates, Isaac Perry,[3] Jacob Apley, Fortunatus and Mayhew Bassett, James Bailey and Absalom Williams, were among the first settlers of Stow's square. A store, church, inn and post office, subsequently gave the settlement upon the state road within this tract some claims to the appellation of a village, but the loss of all those excepting the church (which is falling into ruin), has occasioned the locality to be regarded as only a thickly settled farming neighborhood.

Mr. Stow was succeeded in the agency by Morris S. Miller,[4] about 1802, and the latter by Isaac W. Bostwick in

---

1 These were brothers, sons of Adam and Esther Wilcox. Their brother Elisha, b. Oct. 2, 1768, died in Leyden, and their sister Rebecca, b. Sept. 1770, married Moses Waters. This wedding was the first that occurred in Lowville. Jesse, b. June 8, 1774, resides at Stow Square. Roswell, b. Jan. 22, 1778, died, Oct. 1, 1851. These families were from Killingworth, Ct.

2 The Davenports of this town, are descendants of Thomas D., who settled at Dorchester about 1640, and died, Nov. 9, 1685. His third son, Jonathan (born, March 6, 1658, and died, Dec. 1, 1680), had seven sons, the youngest of whom named Benjamin, was the father of the emigrants named in the text. He was born Oct. 6, 1698, and died about 1785, at Spencertown, N. Y. His family consisted of four sons and three daughters, viz:

Samuel who died in Sheffield, Ct.

Hannah, who married —— House.

Billa, who settled in this town, and had two sons and four daughters. John the eldest son, settled in Delaware co., and gave name to the town of Davenport; he died, wealthy. Billa settled in this town.

Charles, born April 15, 1751, married Elizabeth Taylor in 1778, and died, Dec. 12, 1812. His children were, *Benjamin*, born Nov. 15, 1778, died in Turin, Feb. 19, 1860; *Ira*, b., May 9, 1787, died, May 19, 1819. *Sally*, b. Nov. 7, 1782, died ——. *Betsey*, b. Nov. 17, 1791. *Charles*, b. Oct. 23, 1784, m. May, 1814, to Anna Cole, died July 28, 1855; his portrait is given in this volume. *Alexander*, b. Oct. 25, 1780, d. Jan. 20, 1851. *Roxanna*, b. Aug. 1, 1796, m. Rev. J. Blodget. *Ashley*, b. Feb. 11, 1794, removed to Copenhagen in 1825 and has since resided there; he has held the offices of sheriff and senator. *John B.*, b. Feb. 18, 1798, died in Indiana in 1819.

Jonathan, married a Culver.

Sally, married a Clark.

Zerphiah, married a Bliss.

3 Capt. Perry, originally from R. I., had removed from Hancock, Mass., to Granville, N. Y., and thence to Palmerstown, Westmoreland and Lowville. He settled here in June, 1799, having the year previous located land. One of his daughters married Fortunatus Eager, the first merchant; another a Buell; another Isaac W. Bostwick. He had served in the revolution, and was related to Commodore Perry. His death occurred Nov. 19, 1840, at the age of 81 years.

4 *Morris S. Miller*, had been the private secretary of Gov. Jay, and married a Miss Bleecker of Albany. He removed from Lowville to Utica, where he resided till his death, Nov. 16, 1824, aged 44 years. He was a member of the 13th congress, and held the office of first judge of Oneida Co., from 1810 till his death. He was a gentleman of fine manners and extensive acquirements, but his brief residence in this section scarcely allowed him to become generally known to our citizens.

Chas. Davenport

Engraved by J. C. Buttre N.Y.

J W Bostwick

1806. The latter remained in this station till near the end of his life.[1]

---

[1] *Isaac Welton Bostwick*, a son of Andrew Bostwick, was born in Watertown, Ct., March 6, 1776, and in early childhood removed with his parents to New York city, but in two or three years returned to his native place. After attending several years a school taught by Mr. Punderson, he removed with the family to Roxbury, and in a school taught by the Rev. Mr. Canfield, prepared for the high school at Williamstown. After two or three years attendance at the latter, he undertook his own support by teaching, at first in a public school in South East, and afterwards as a private tutor in the family of Mr. Livingston of Poughkeepsie.

He here became acquainted with a brother of Judge Platt of Whitestown, who induced him to remove in 1797 to Oneida co., where he entered the office of Platt & Breese, and in 1801, he was admitted to the bar of the supreme court, having for a short time previous served as deputy county clerk under Mr. Platt. In 1804, he removed to Turin, and began the practice of the law, residing two years in the family of Judge Collins, and in 1806, he came to Lowville the scene of his future career, with no resource but his profession and a steady reliance upon his own energy. He became Low's agent in Lowville, Harrison's in Harrisburgh and Denmark, and Pierrepont's in Martinsburgh in which he earned the implicit confidence of his employers. A notice of Mr. B. occurs in the diary of James Constable under date of Aug. 7, 1806, which indicates the impression made at that period upon Messrs. Constable and Pierrepont.

"During the last evening and this morning, we had much conversation with Mr. Bostwick, the agent of Messrs. Low and Harrison in this quarter. He appeared to be a very intelligent, well informed and active young man, and very suitable for an agent. He showed us the instruments used for Mr. Low, which we thought well of, and should at once adopt, but our rule hitherto invariable of requiring part of the payment down, is not contemplated, and we therefore reserve our determination."

These landholders on their return, Aug. 23d, from the St. Lawrence country, further remark: "Renewed our conversation with Mr. Bostwick, respecting the agency of town No. 4, which he now showed as well as formerly a great desire to undertake, but the commission which we proposed, of $2\frac{1}{2}$ p. c. on sales, and 2 p. c. for collecting and remitting he thought too low, and during the day it appeared as if he would give it up, stating that it was a lower rate than had yet been given in the country, and would be no object to him. Our answer was, that if the *rate* was lower, the *produce* would be greater, as a considerable part of the town would soon sell at $6 per acre, and $4\frac{1}{2}$ p. c. on that price would be much better than 5 or 7 at $3, at which most of the preceding agents had sold, but he did not agree, tho' he could not reply to such reasoning. He spoke at large of the labors and difficulty in such business, a subject so familiar to us, that we soon convinced him the commission was a full compensation. The subject dropped for the day without coming to an agreement.

24th. Next morning early we prepared a letter to him, in which the commission was the same as verbally, and after a very few words he declared himself perfectly satisfied, and that he would exert himself to the utmost for our interests. We enjoined upon him as one of his first measures, to acquire a personal knowledge of each lot in town, which he promised to do; and recommended him to be mild and conciliatory with the settlers, as they were apt to be apprehensive of an agent of the legal profession. He had before disclaimed all idea of making money as a lawyer, through his situation as an agent, and said he had so expressed himself to Mr. Low and Mr. Harrison when they employed him; and to prove his aversion to harrassing settlers, he told us several anecdotes of his having on his own account, bought in their property at low prices, and delivered it to them. We proposed to him to accompany us to the township which he accordingly did,

The village of Lowville early became a prominent point in the county, from its academy, the spirited efforts of its merchants,[1] and the location of several influential citizens

---

and we introduced him to such of the settlers as were there, being nearly the whole, informing them that he had full powers as agent, that the price of $7, for lots on the road, and those of the first quality in that quarter of the town, and $6 for the remainder; the credit 5 years for the first payment, interest on the whole to be paid in one year, one quarter of the principal with the interest in 2 years, the same in 3 years, the same in 4 years, and the same in 5. They appeared to be well satisfied, and we left them."

We have extended this quotation for the double purpose of embracing the facts, and of showing the business habits of the parties. He continued Pierrepont's agent until 1834, for No. 4, and part of No. 5. Mr. Bostwick's subsequent life, vindicated the sincerity of the intentions, thus early declared, of mildness towards settlers, and his uniformly kind and conciliatory manners, have endeared his memory to multitudes in the towns of Lowville, Harrisburgh, Denmark, Adams, and Watertown, which were mostly sold and settled under his agency.

Although he continued the practice of law many years, his land agencies occupied a large part of his time, and after having been in partnership at different times with Ela Collins, Samuel A. Talcott, Cornelius Low and Russell Parish, he finally withdrew from the profession altogether, and devoted his entire care to his own ample estate, and his land agencies.

He was appointed surrogate upon the organization of the county, and held this office ten years. On the 29th of Sept., 1812, he was married to Miss Hannah Perry, daughter of Capt. Isaac Perry, a pioneer settler. This accomplished partner of his life and solace of his declining years, still resides at his elegant seat in Lowville.

Mr. B., was several years president of the Lewis Co. Bank, and first president of the bank of Lowville. Having held the office of trustee of the Lowville academy many years, he was elected their president in 1840, and continued in that station till his death, ever taking a deep interest in its welfare, and finally leaving to its library, a munificent addition to its literary treasures. The was an active and consistent member of the Presbyterian society and church, liberal in all matters of public improvement, prompt, energetic and efficient in business, and of integrity without stain and above reproach. He died at Lowville, Jan. 3, 1857, at the advanced age of 81 years, universally respected for his great moral worth.

Mr. Bostwick resigned the agency of the Low estate in 1854, and was succeeded by Russell Parish, who lived but a few months after. It then was given to Nathaniel B. Sylvester of Lowville, who still holds it. Mr. Bostwick stated frequently with great satisfaction, that he had remitted to the proprietor more than five times the amount of the original purchase money, and that he left contracts exceeding the said original sum. This is to be remarked alike to the credit of proprietor, agents and settlers, that in the large amount of business transactions between them, ***no occasion arose for an appeal to the courts of law.***

[1] Subsequent to the settlement of Eager and Card, already noticed, James H. and Stephen Leonard came to reside in the village, and during many years conducted an extensive business.

The Leonard families of this town emigrated from West Springfield, Mass., and are descendants of John Leonard, who settled in Springfield in 1639. Abel and Josiah, probably sons of John, settled on the west side of the river in 1660, and died in 1688 and 1690. James and Henry Leonard, sons of Thomas and supposed to be related to these, removed from England before 1642, and built the first forge in America at Taunton, Mass., in 1652. (*Mass. Hist. Coll., I., series* iii., 170).

The descendants of the latter were remarkable for a kind of hereditary attachment to the iron business, which led to the remark that "where you can

Engraved by J. C. Buttre

within the first fifteen years of its settlement. This early prestige has been maintained, and while Lowville village is

---

find iron works there you will find a Leonard." The name is somewhat common in New England, and in 1826, 28 had graduated in the colleges of that section, of whom 12 were of Harvard.

The first emigrants of this name to the Black river country were sons of Elias and Phineas, sons of Moses Leonard. The sons of Elias Leonard were James H., Rodney, Loren and Francis Leonard, and those of Phineas Leonard were Stephen, Chauncey, Phineas and Reuben.

James Harvey Leonard was born at West Springfield, Sept. 22, 1780, and first visited Lowville in 1804 with Stephen Leonard. They came on horseback from Skaneateles where they had been employed as clerks, with the intention of settling and crossed from Rome to Talcott's. The roads were so rough and the settlements so rude that they began to have serious doubts about finding a place that offered inducements, but as they reached the brow of the hill overlooking Lowville, the neat newly painted mansion of Judge Stow, and the thrifty settlement beyond, gave a cheerful aspect to the spot and determined their future course. They were on their way to Chaumont, but did not get nearer that place than Brownville, and returned through Redfield. J. H. Leonard began business in Lowville, Sept., 1804, and in Jan., 1805, was joined by Stephen Leonard. Before this they had leased four acres, at what is now the city of Auburn, for 100 years, at $4 per acre, and J. H. L. had leased 50 acres at $5 for 30 years. The latter lease failed from a refusal of Hardenburgh, the proprietor, to execute the papers, and the former was sold for $150 before a payment was made. J. H. Leonard continued in the firm of J. H. & S. Leonard just a quarter of a century and remained in business here till his removal in 1839, except one or two years at Skaneateles. This firm became widely known throughout northern New York. It supplied rations to the troops passing through the country, and in embargo times were largely engaged with business connections in Canada. They held during the war a contract for supplying 40,000 gallons of whiskey for the navy, and owned one-half of a like contract of Allen & Canfield, making 60,000 gallons at $1 per gallon, to be delivered at Sackett's Harbor. A change in the movements of the fleet, occasioned a transfer to New York where most of it was finally delivered.

Mr. J. H. Leonard was public spirited and benevolent, and was always among the foremost in every measure of public utility. He was an original trustee of the academy and an elder in the Presbyterian church until his removal from the county in 1839. He was also post master at Lowville many years. He became deeply interested in the culture of the mulberry for silk after his removal, and died at Syracuse March 14, 1845. His remains were interred at Lowville. Mr. L., in May, 1805, married Mary, sister of Russell Parish, and his widow still survives. His brother Rodney died in West Martinsburgh, Aug. 13, 1852, and brother Loren in Lowville. Francis Leonard, the youngest brother, resides in Brooklyn. Cornelius P. Leonard, cashier, and James L. Leonard, president of the bank of Lowville, and Francis K. Leonard of Harrisburgh, are sons of James H. Leonard.

Stephen Leonard settled in Lowville early in 1805, and has since, with the exception of a short interval, been engaged in mercantile business. As one of the firm of J. H. & S. Leonard, he was largely concerned in the manufacture of spirits, potash, &c., in milling, and in the trade in live stock, incident to the former. The first distillery in Lowville was begun by this firm in the fall of 1804, and the last one in the county, which had belonged to them, was burned Feb. 16, 1842. He has been many years a trustee of the academy, was an original trustee of the Presbyterian society of the village and from the first, with the exception of one year, has been treasurer of the Lewis county bible society. He marrried a daughter of Gen. W. Martin of Martinsburgh.

Chauncey Leonard, brother of Stephen L., died in Pennsylvania. Phineas, another brother, resides in Denmark, and Reuben died in Brantford, U. C.

the only one in town, it is the largest in the county, affording to the man of business or of leisure, one of the most eligible places of residence in northern New York.[1]

---

[1]Of those who settled within this period in Lowville village, we may, with great justice enumerate, in addition to those already noticed, the following:

Samuel Austin Talcott was born in Hartford, Ct., in 1790, graduated at Williams college in 1809, studied law, in part, with Thomas R. Gold, and came to Lowville in 1812 where he entered into a law partnership with Bostwick, and remained three or four years. He then removed to Utica, and his politics becoming favorable to the then republican party, he was appointed Feb. 12, 1821, to the office of attorney general, which he held eight years. He died in New York March 19, 1836, the admiration and sorrow of his friends. Few men in our country have evinced more brilliant talents, a clearer perception of the great principles of law, or a more powerful and convincing eloquence than Mr. Talcott. His career was an impressive warning to those who apprehend no peril from the wine cup.

Ela Collins was born at Meriden, Ct., Feb. 14th, 1786, and died at Lowville, N. Y., Nov. 23d, 1848. His parents were Gen. Oliver Collins and Lois Cowles. His father served seven years in the revolutionary war as an officer in the Massachusetts troops. Soon after the close of the war he removed to Oneida county, N. Y., and purchased a fine farm, near New Hartford, upon which he resided until his death, Aug. 14, 1838. At the beginning of the last war with Great Britain he held the commission of brigadier general and commanded during the war, the militia of Oneida, Jefferson and Lewis counties. He succeeded Gen. Jacob Brown in the command of Sacketts Harbor, which position he retained till near the close of the war. Ela Collins was educated at the Clinton academy. He read law in the office of Gold & Sill, at Whitesboro, and commenced law practice at Lowville in 1807. He married Maria Clinton, daughter of the Rev. Isaac Clinton, July 11th, 1811. They had eleven children. On the 15th of March, 1815, he was appointed district attorney for the district composed of Lewis, Jefferson and St. Lawrence counties, which office he held several years, until the districts were reduced to single counties. He was then appointed to the same office for Lewis county, successively, until 1840, when he resigned, having held the office for 25 years. He was elected in 1814 a member of the assembly, and was in the legislature when peace was proclaimed. He was a member of the N. Y. Constitutional Convention of 1821. In 1822 he was elected from the double district of Lewis, Jefferson, St. Lawrence and Oswego, as a member of the 18th congress. He was secretary of the last congressional caucus for the nomination of president, when William H. Crawford was nominated. He was for many years a trustee of the Lowville academy.

As a lawyer Mr. Collins attained a high position. He was an excellent and successful advocate and criminal prosecutor. His manner of presenting a case to a jury was clear, forcible and admirably fair. His speeches were always sensible, candid and to the point. And he had rare ability in presenting the questions at issue, in stating the facts, and in argument upon them. His integrity was unsullied, and his manners were simple, cordial and unaffected. In politics he was a republican of the school of Jefferson. For several years he voted the local anti-masonic ticket. He was highly respected and popular throughout the section of the state where he was known. His sons are, *William Collins*, who studied law with his father, was appointed district attorney of Lewis county in 1845, and held two years, when he was elected to the 30th congress. He now resides in Cleveland, O. *Francis Collins*, another son, entered West Point academy, as cadet in 1841, became second lieutenant in the 4th artillery July 1, 1845, and first lieutenant by brevet, " for gallant and meritorious conduct in the battles of Contreras and Cherubusco " on the 27th of August, 1847. In the former of these he

Engraved by J. C. Buttre

Russell Parish

The first trial for a capital crime in the county, was that of Rachel, a servant of I. W. Bostwick, for setting fire to her master's house, and was held before Judge Platt, about 1821. The accused was about eighteen years old, and of bad temper, but as the damage had been slight, the public sympathy in her behalf was strong. The sentiment of that day had not favored commutations or pardons, and execu-

---

was wounded. He became first lieutenant, Sept., 1847, and resigned Dec. 11, 1850. He is now a lawyer at Columbus, O. *Isaac C. Collins*, youngest son of Ela, graduated at Yale college and resides at Cincinnati, O., where he holds the office of judge of the district and circuit court.

Russell Parish was born in Branford, Ct., Oct. 27, 1789, and graduated at Yale college in 1813, in the same class with Professor Fisher, who was lost in the Albion, Profs. Olmstead, Douglass and Mitchell, and Judges Badger, Longstreet and Kane, and other distinguished persons. He was employed in November of the same year as principal of the Lowville academy, and in 1814 he began the study of law with Mr. Bostwick. In due time he was admitted to the bar, and he spent the remainder of his life in Lowville, chiefly in the practice of his profession in which he was regarded as learned, judicious and able. In 1846 he represented the county in the convention for revising the constitution. He died Feb. 21, 1855, and the trustees of the academy and members of the bar testified their respect for his character by calling meetings to express their sympathy with his family and by attending his funeral in a body.

Charles Dayan was born July 16, 1792, at Amsterdam, N. Y., and is a son of Charles D., an Austrian emigrant, who died in 1793, leaving him an infant in charge of his widowed mother, in very indigent circumstances. He remained with Zaccariah Peterson till fourteen years of age, and went to Elliott's mills in Amsterdam, from whence, in August, 1809, he came to Lowville. After working at chopping, and upon Heman Stickney's oil mill (now Gen. Willard's factory), he began going to school at the academy. He was then entirely ignorant of the rudiments of learning and was placed at first in a class of small children, but by great industry and the aid of a Mr. Obits, an old friend of his father, in Germany, he made such rapid progress that in a few months he was able to engage a school in Rutland. He taught four winters in the same district at a monthly price of twenty bushels of wheat, which he sold at $2 per bushel. He entered Bostwick's law office in 1816, and in 1819 was admitted to practice.

From this time, till within a few years, he has been actively engaged in his profession at Lowville, except when withdrawn by the duties of the public offices to which he has been elected, having been at different times in partnership with Edmund Henry, Hiram Carpenter, Russell Parish and Ziba Knox. In 1820 Mr. Dayan was appointed by Le Ray and the Brown family, an agent for settling certain lands east of the river, and he continued agent of the former until 1833. In 1826 he was elected to the state senate to serve out the unexpired term of two years, occasioned by the resignation of Geo. Brayton, and in the extra session, convened in the fall of 1828, to adopt the revised statutes, he was elected Oct. 7, president pro. tem. of the senate. As the office of governor was then filled by Pitcher, elected as lieutenant governor, Mr. Dayan became charged with the duties of the latter office. He presided over the senate until its adjournment Dec. 10th, and was virtually lieutenant governor till Jan. 1, 1829.

On the 26th of Jan., 1829, he became a candidate for comptroller against Silas Wright, Jr., in the legislative republican caucus, in which Wright received 58, Dayan 26, G. B. Baldwin 12, N. Pitcher 4 and G. Sudam, 1 vote. Mr. Dayan was elected to the 22d congress (1831–3) from the 20th district,

tion must have unavoidably followed conviction. The defense was conducted by Micah Sterling and Russell Parish, and as the trial commenced, the latter evinced an elastic buoyancy of spirit which appeared to be unwarranted by the occasion, until it appeared upon the reading of the indictment a second time, that the prosecuting attorney had accidently omitted the word "inhabited" before

---

and in 1835 and 1836 was elected to the assembly upon the canal issue. Mr. Francis Seger was then in the senate, and to these two gentlemen are we largely indebted for the passage of the act for constructing the Black river canal, a work, which, after more than twenty years of delay, we at length enjoy. On the 14th of March, 1840, Dayan was appointed district attorney for Lewis county, and held this office five years, discharging its duties with his accustomed discretion and ability.

Ziba Knox, for several years a law partner of Dayan, is a native of Vermont. He came to Lowville about 1817, acquired his profession, and has since resided at this place, employed in legal practice and as a magistrate.

Vivaldi R. Martin, a native of Saratoga county, settled in Martinsburgh as a lawyer from whence he removed to Lowville. He died Aug. 8, 1850, aged 31 years. His brief career was brilliant and honorable. Possessing talents of a high order, fine oratorical powers and a thorough education, he would have adorned the highest station of public trust had his life been spared to the full term of human life.

Dr. *David Perry* was born in Princeton, Mass., Sept. 13, 1775, studied medicine with Dr. Westel Willoughby of Newport, N. Y., and settled in Denmark in Aug., 1806. In Sept., 1808, he married Miss Nancy Hulburt of Holland Patent, who died Nov., 1812. In April, 1809, he settled in Lowville (the first two years in company with Dr. Samuel Allen) and continued in the practice of medicine until November, 1858, when, in consequence of a paralytic attack, he was deprived of further means of usefulness in the profession in which he had been eminently successful. He now resides in Rutland in feeble health and borne down by the infirmities of age,

He has evinced a great fondness for rural pursuits, and in the intervals of an extensive practice, has found time to devote much attention to his orchard and garden, which were celebrated for the extent and variety of their productions and the precise order in which every thing was kept. His orchard contained about seventy varieties of fruit.

Dr. Perry has been greatly respected by his professional brethren for the soundness of his judgment and the acuteness of his perception with regard to disease, and they have uniformly regarded his diagnosis and treatment as eminently governed by a clear mind and an intelligent understanding.

Andrew W. Doig, a native of Washington county, is a son of Andrew Doig, who was born in Perthshire, Scotland, Feb. 29, 1776, removed to Lowville in 1809, and died March 11, 1854. He was many years a teacher and surveyor. A. W. Doig was elected county clerk in 1825 for one term. He was in assembly in 1832 and held the office of surrogate from 1835 to 1840. He was elected by the democratic party to the 26th and 27th congresses (1839 to 1843) while Lewis was united with Herkimer as the 16th district. In 1849 he joined the general exodus to California, and a few years after returned to Lowville where he has since resided.

James and John Doig are sons of Andrew Doig. The former is ticket agent in the rail road office at Boonville, and the latter a druggist at Lowville.

Joseph A. Northrup from Vermont, settled at an early period as a tanner and conducted this business and that of harness making many years. He was, we believe, the pioneer in these pursuits in this town.

Chas Dayton

"dwelling," and that the trial had reached such a stage that amendment was not admissable. The prisoner upon learning that she would not be hung, from abject terror evinced the most extravagant joy, which met with a sympathizing response in the hearts of many present. She was subsequently tried for arson of lower degree, and died in state prison.

In December, 1828, a vein of galena, calcite, fluor spar and sulphuret of iron, was discovered on the south branch of the creek, about half a mile above Lowville village, which soon became widely celebrated as a *silver mine.* A company was formed, and a small smelting house was erected near the spot, but we are not informed that large dividends were made, or that the stock ever found its way to the Wall street market. This locality is worthy of especial notice by mineralogists, from the beautiful crystalized specimens of green fluor spar which it has produced. The late Luke Wilder,[1] explored the vein for this mineral with great success.

A health committee consisting of Russell Parish with Doctors David Perry, Sylvester Miller,[2] Seth Adams[3] and Josiah Rathbun was appointed June 21, 1832 upon the approach of cholera. They enjoined temperance, cleanliness and care in diet as preventive measures, and advised a course of treatment in case of an attack. The Angel of Death was by the beneficient hand of Providence withheld from our county during this fearful visitation, which nevertheless struck a dread upon the community, which could scarcely have been surpassed had the pestilence been present. On the day the health committee above named was appointed, an act was passed authorizing official action by the town officers, under which Ela Collins, Charles Bush, Orrin Wilbur, Amasa Dodge, Jr., and Roswell Wilcox were appointed, June 29th, a board of health, and Dr. Seth

---

[1] *Mr. Wilder,* died, March 31, 1851, aged 60 years. His zealous researches into the mineralogical resources of northern New York, entitle him to the remembrance of the scientific, while his mild and amiable character have endeared his memory to a wide circle of friends. He was an active member of the Methodist chuch.

[2] *Dr. Miller,* son of Seth Miller one of the first settlers at Constableville, settled in Lowville in 1817, having graduated with the first class in Fairfield, Jan. 30, 1816. He was appointed sheriff in 1821, and from 1823 to 1835, was surrogate. He was called from bed in the night, July 28, 1838, to visit the sick, and mistaking a door in his own house, fell headlong down the cellar stairs. His skull was fractured, and after lingering two days unconscious, he died. He was president of the Lewis co. medical soc. at the time of his death.

[3] *Dr. Adams,* settled in the practice of his profession at Lowville in the spring of 1826, and has since resided there. His son Charles D. Adams is a lawyer at Lowville.

Adams, health officer. On the 30th a committee was empowered to visit the Denmark frontier, to take measures to prevent infected persons from entering the county, the town was divided into four districts and committees appointed in each.

Lowville village.—This is the only incorporated village in the county. Notice of the application was published Feb. 26, 1849, and about one square mile was surveyed by N. B. Sylvester. The legal forms were not complied with until July 10, 1854, when the vote upon the adoption of a village charter, was 109 for, and 33 against the measure. The first trustees were Joseph A. Willard,[1] N. B. Sylvester, A. G. Dayan, S. B. Batchellor, and Geo. W. Fowler. No election was held in 1857, and to remedy this, an act was procured, Feb. 27, 1858, confirming all the privileges of the corporation, directing the annual elections to be held on the first Tuesday of March, and allowing $800 to be raised for a fire engine and fixtures as by vote of Aug. 6, 1857. The trustees elected in 1860, were John Doig, John O'Donnell, Rutson Rea, Geo. W. Stephens and Henry E. Turner.

The first fire company was formed at this place July 24, 1829, at which Stephen Leonard was chosen *captain*, Palmer Townsend, *1st lieut.*, and S. W. Taylor, *2d lieut.* A well was to be sunk in a central part of the village, and in case of an alarm of fire, the captain was to station himself at the head of the company, the 1st lieut. was to form the lines for passing buckets, and the 2d lieut. to act as fire warden in rescuing property. Five buckets were kept in readiness for immediate use. A small fire engine named the ***Eagle*** was purchased, and afforded the only precaution against fires during many years. The burning of Safford's hotel, March 11, 1851, led to the call of a meeting to provide a better one. No efficient action was had until August, 1858, when a new fire engine named ***Rescue No.*** 2, was purchased at a cost of $800. The company to which it is entrusted, numbers (Oct. 1859) thirty eight men.

An independent Union Fire co., was formed June 30, 1858, under E. C. Potter as *captain*, and an engine and hose cart were purchased by him for its use.

---

[1] *Gen. Willard*, was born at Hubbardton, Vt., April 26, 1803, and is a son of Francis Willard. He removed to Lowville upon becoming of age, having previously learned the trade of a clothier. He has since been engaged as a manufacturer at Lowville, and in 1858–9, he represented Jefferson and Lewis counties in the senate.—***Murphy's Biographical Sketches of Legislature***, 1859, *p.* 112.

J A Willard

There is organized in the village a section of light artillery, under Lieut. Moses M. Smith. They have a 6 pounder and a 24 pound howitzer, both of bronze, and are armed with musketoons and sword bayonets.

A Saxhorn band was formed in the fall of 1857, and consists of ten men.

The Union band formed in this village about 1826, was the first that was organized in the county, and maintained existence several years.

The village of Lowville reported in 1855, a population of 908, and must now number nearly 1200. It is much the most prominent business point in the county, and enjoys a large amount of trade with the country around, especially to the east and west. It is situated in a valley environed on all sides but the east with hills, and is about one hundred feet above Black river, and two miles from it.

Seal.

The Bank of Lowville, is among the earliest formed under the general banking law of April 18, 1838. A public meeting was held at Lowville, Oct. 18, 1838, pursuant to a call signed by Wm. L. Easton, Leonard Harding, Merrit M. Norton, Stephen Leonard, John Buck, John Stevens, L. S. Standring, Joseph A. Northrop, H. N. Bush, I. W. Bostwick, Andrew W. Doig, Russell Parish, Charles Dayan, Daniel T. Buck, Chester Buck, W. W. Smith, and Calvin Lewis; the plan was discussed and approved, and Ela Collins, R. Parish, A. W. Doig, W. L. Easton and I. W. Bostwick were appointed to examine the statute and report at a future meeting the probable success of the enterprise.

Articles of association were drawn up, proposing a capital stock of $100,000, in shares of $50 each, with a privilege of increasing to $500,000, and a duration till Nov. 1st, 2301, and on the 27th of October, I. W. Bostwick, C. Dayan, A. W. Doig, W. L. Easton, Chester Buck, Timothy Mills and R. Parish were appointed to receive subscriptions from the 26th of November till Jan. 1, unless the whole amount were sooner taken. On the first two days $37,000 were subscribed, and on the 8th of December the sum had amounted to $78,000. The whole amount was completed Dec. 18, the books were closed, the articles filed that day in the office of the county clerk, and on the 26th in the secretary's office at Albany. The first directors chosen, Dec. 24, were I. W. Bostwick, C. Dayan, A. W. Doig, W. L. Easton, M. M. Norton, L. S. Standring, L. Harding, C. Buck, T. Mills, Harrison Blodget, John H. Allen, Seth Miller and Thomas Baker. Isaac W. Bostwick was chosen president, A. W. Doig, vice president, Kent Jarvis, cashier (pro tem.), and Dayan and Parish, attorneys. Preliminary arrangements were completed, and the bank commenced operations on the first day of July, 1839. The bank has from the beginning occupied rooms in a block of buildings, erected for stores and offices, in the summer of 1837, in the centre of the village.

The officers elected by the directors have been as follows, with the dates of their several appointments:

Presidents:	
Isaac W. Bostwick...........	Dec. 24, 1838, to March 19, 1845.
William L. Easton...........	April 19, 1855.
James L. Leonard...........	Sept. 19, 1857.
Vice Presidents:	
Andrew W. Doig............	Dec. 24, 1838.
Charles Dayan..............	Dec. 20, 1839.
Andrew W. Doig............	Dec. 18, 1843.
Charles Dayan..............	Dec. 30, 1845.
Andrew W. Doig............	Jan. 8, 1847.
Charles Dayan..............	Dec. 18, 1847.
William L. Easton...........	March 18, 1851.
James L. Leonard............	April 19, 1855, to Sept. 19, 1857.
John Stevens...............	Dec. 18, 1857.
Cashiers:	
Kent Jarvis (acting).........	Dec. 24, 1838, to April 1, 1839.
Samuel H. Norton...........	Jan. 21, 1839, to take effect April 1, '39.
William L. Easton...........	March 31, 1840.
James L. Leonard...........	Feb. 16, 1846, to take effect April 1, '46.
Francis N. Willard[1]	Mr'h 28, 1851, to take effect Apr. 1, 1851.
Cornelius P. Leonard........	June 16, 1856.
Tellers:	
James L. Leonard...........	June 19, 1841, to April 1, 1846.
Francis N. Willard..........	Aug. 25, 1847, to April 1, 1851.
Leonard Standring...........	April 16, 1853, to Nov. 1, 1855.

Directors (January 1, 1860).—James L. Leonard, John Stevens, Jared House, Joseph A. Willard, Moses M. Smith, Stephen Brigham, Cornelius P. Leonard, John Doig, Carlos P. Scovil, Hiram S. Lanpher, Charles M. Stephens, Rutson Rea and Charles H. Curtis.

---

[1] Died June 9, 1856. He was a son of Gen. Joseph A. Willard of Lowville.

The statistics of this bank as reported on the 2d of July, 1839, and near the 1st of January, annually since, have been as follows, as shown by the official reports, required by law to be made to the department at Albany.

Years.	Discounts.	Bills rec'd from Comptroller & Sup't of Bank Department.	Circulation.	Deposits.
1839		$15,000	$570	$913
1840	$49,119	45,000	41,520	11,169
1841	54,483	53,000	50,663	20,642
1842	68,254	58,870	46,500	23,148
1843	59,235	54,600	51,436	15,341
1844	77,060	51,000	49,891	22,758
1845	80,384	50,300	49,291	17,780
1846	87,662	60,000	59,213	59,574
1847	93,025	66,000	65,312	33,475
1848	102,940	77,900	75,938	28,049
1849	76,359	84,650	82,781	27,312
1850	83,698	101,900	101,234	33,625
1851	73,968	96,750	95,129	32,797
1852	102,486	100,685	97,112	50,693
1853	102,527	115,000	110,249	50,661
1854	125,403	119,266	115,209	55,748
1855	85,126	125,337	111,802	52,154
1856	81,370	107,050	104,390	57,985
1857	132,386	114,500	108,131	70,984
1858	101,038	68,200	57,643	48,050
1859	106,288	70,850	67,560	68,238
1860	116,197	92,650	84,811	107,737

The capital was reported July 2, 1839, as $27,855. On the 6th of January, 1840, it was $100,411; on the 4th of Jan., 1841, $101,950, and since Jan 1, 1842, $102,450.

During the commercial crisis of 1857 this bank, with assets much above its liabilities, was forced, like most of the other banks in the state, to yield momentarily to the emergencies of the day. On the 10th of Oct., 1857, an injunction was granted upon the request of its president, and on the 27th of that month this was removed upon application of its president and John Stevens. A meeting of citizens was called at Lowville on the 13th of October, and resolutions were passed expressing confidence in the condition of the bank, and an agreement to receive its bills at par as usual. The comparative condition of the bank on the 29th of August (about the time when the panic began), and Oct. 10, was as follows:

	Circulation.	Deposits.	Discounts.
Aug. 22, 1857	$111,034	$54,898	$131,914
Oct. 10, 1857	69,166	41,029	117,447
	$41,868	$13,869	$14,467

From the comparison above given it appears that while the bank had redeemed over 37½ per cent. of its circulation and paid over 25 per cent. of its deposits, it had reduced its discounts less than 11 per cent. The bank did not commence a single suit against its customers during the crisis, as its officers knew their entire inability to pay at that time. With the exception of about $600 (which may yet be collected) it lost no debts from discounts during that period. These statements sufficiently indicate the ability with which the bank was managed during that critical period. Its history through the whole term of its existence has been marked by no event of public interest, and its affairs have been conducted with a steady regard to equity and honor, and the advancement of the interests of its proprietors by promotion of the business of the county.

Two banks, owned by James L. Leonard, an individual banker, have existed for short periods at Lowville, but their bills scarcely became familiar to our citizens before their affairs were wound up. These banks were as follows:

The Valley Bank filed notice and certificate of residence in the department, May 7, 1851. Securities Jan. 1, 1852, $60,290; circulation, $60,287. Removed to Boonville, Feb. 6, 1852, by Ela N. Merriam, who had purchased it, and from thence to Ogdensburgh, where it was closed up.

Bank of the People filed notice and certificate of residence May 11, 1852, the circulation to be secured by public stocks. Securities, January 1, 1853, $51,000; circulation, 50,480. Filed notice of intention to wind up the bank, Sept. 22, 1853, and bond for redemption of bills, Oct. 24, 1856, when its business was closed.

These are the only banks that have been formed under the general statute, although a large business in the sale of drafts and similar banking transactions, has been conducted by Wm. McCulloch, Esq., of Lowville, during several years, and by others to a less extent, in other sections of the county.

The banks of Watertown and of Utica, afforded the only facilities for the transaction of business in this county, from its settlement, until 1834, when the Lewis County Bank was got into operation at Martinsburgh.

Early in the year 1852 sealed proposals were solicited by advertisement for building a court house in Lowville village, with the design of securing, if possible, the removal of the county seat there from Martinsburgh, a

Engraved by J. C. Buttre

Town Hall and Trinity Church.

measure which from the beginning has been the favorite theme of the citizens of this town. The building was begun upon voluntary subscription, and in 1855 the town voted $500 towards this object, upon express condition that the building be free for town purposes, and that the money be not paid until enough were raised to complete it. In 1856 $100 were voted for an iron fence, and in 1858 $325 to pay Hiram S. Lanpher a balance due on the building account. This last appropriation was confirmed by act of April 15, 1858. The edifice was put up in 1852 and finished in 1855 at a cost of less than $6000. The building is of brick with an Ionic portico in front, and is used for town meetings, lectures and other public purposes, with the express provision that it shall be conveyed to the county whenever it may be wanted for the county court house.

The Lowville Franklin society, a library association, was formed in the village, Sept. 20, 1808, having as its first trustees, Isaac Clinton, Manly Wellman, Robert McDowell, Paul Abbot and Ela Collins. Their collection of books some thirty or forty years afterwards was deposited in the Academy library.

The Franklin library of Stow's square, was formed March 28, 1816, with Moses Waters, Constant Bosworth, Beriah Nickelson, Charles Sigourney and Allen Briggs, trustees. The first number of associates was 33, and they began with over $100 subscriptions. After many years this library was, it is believed, divided among its shareholders.

The first school was taught in this town by Miss Hannah Smith, sister of Mrs. Elijah Baldwin of Martinsburgh, in a little log school house near the lower mill. Samuel Slocum taught in 1804, and was one of the earliest male teachers in town. The first public provision for schools was made in March, 1813, under the general school act then newly passed. Amasa Dodge, Robert McDowell, and Moses Waters, were appointed first *commissioners*, and these, with Isaac Clinton, Wm. Sacket, Benj. Hillman, Benj. Davenport, Chester Buck, and Daniel Kelley, *inspectors;* $70 were voted to schools the first year; and in 1815, 456 scholars were reported as attending school, between the ages of 5 and 15. In 1842, the town passed a resolution inviting the resident clergy to visit the schools.

A fine brick school house was finished in the north part of Lowville village in September, 1854, by Morris D. Moore builder and architect.

Seal.

Lowville Academy.—An effort was made in the summer of 1805, by the citizens of Lowville to secure the county seat. A subscription was drawn up for a building that might serve as a meeting house or any other public purpose, as also for an academy and though not expressed, there is not much doubt but that it was designed to offer it for a court house. One term of the court of Oyer and Terminer was held at this place, before the completion of the public buildings at Martinsburgh, at which Judge Ambrose Spencer of the Supreme court presided. The decision of the non-resident commission was, however, sustained, or rather, the attempts made to reverse it were defeated, and the people of Lowville wisely determined to devote the premises to academic uses. The edifice was of wood, 38 by 52 feet, two stories high, and stood on the site of the present stone church in Lowville village, at the head of its principal street. The proposed cost was $2000, in shares of $25, and the five persons highest on the list were to form a building committee. Subscriptions in produce or other articles than cash were to be used or sold to the best advantage, and the committee were to report to the subscribers at the end of one year. The site was given by Silas Stow, Jan. 9, 1807, and the building when finished was used many years for public worship.[1] A charter was applied for March 4, 1808, and granted March 21, 1808, in the words following:

---

[1] The first shareholders were N. Low, 10 shares; S. Stow, 6; Jonathan Rogers and D. Kelley, each 4; J. H. and S. Leonard, Daniel Gould, Asa Newton, Ira Stephens, David Coffeen, Luke Winchell, Rufus Stephens, Wm. Card, Jr., Garret Boshart, each 2; and Ezekiel Thrall, Gad Lane, Fortunatus Bassett, Fortunatus Eager, Daniel Williams, Jonathan Bush, David Cobb, John Spafford, Isaac Perry, Christopher P. Bennett, Thaddeus Smith, Ebenezer Hill, Elijah Woolworth, Morris S. Miller, Joseph Newton, Billa Davenport, Abner Rice, Ziba Cowen, Calvin Merrill, John Shull, Samuel Van Atta, Jacob Boshart, Adam F. Snell, Charles Davenport and Elisha Stephens, each one share. These were soon increased by Isaac W. Bostwick, Wellman & Foot, Asa Brayton, John Smith, Benjamin Hillman, Jonathan Ball, Reuben Chase, Charles Newcomb, Robert Nickels, Ozem Bush, Galen Richmond, Joel Mix, Francis Murphy and David Hillman.

LOWVILLE ACADEMY.

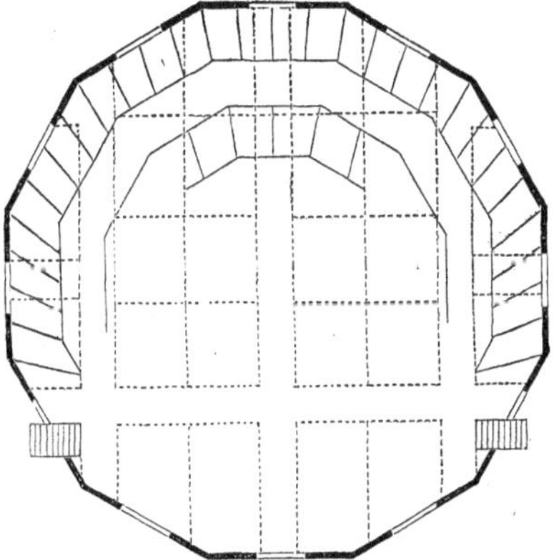

Plan of the Attic Story of the Lowville Academy, as built in 1825.

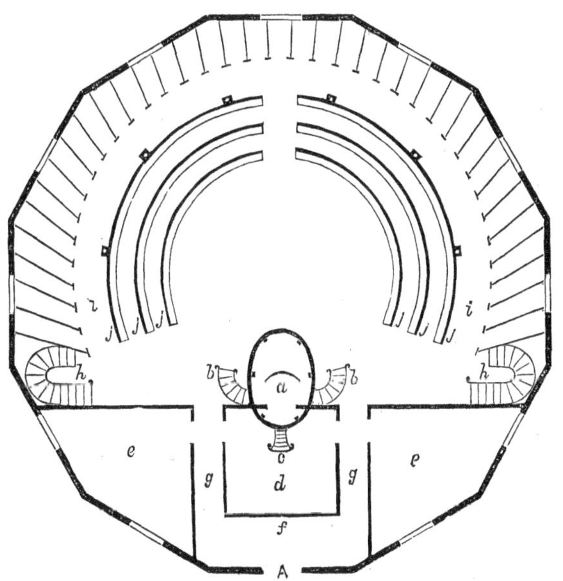

Plan of the Principal Story of the Lowville Academy, as built in 1825.

Charter of Lowville Academy.

The Regents of the University of the state of New York, To all to whom these presents shall or may come, greeting:

Whereas, Nicholas Low, by his attorney Isaac W. Bostwick, Silas Stow, by his attorney Isaac W. Bostwick, Daniel Kelley, James H., and Stephen Leonard, Isaac W. Bostwick, Christopher P. Bennett, David Cobb, Manly Wellman, Jonathan Rogers, Joseph A. Northrup, Elijah Buck, Anson Foot, William Wallis, James Cadwell, Zebina Lane, William Card, Jr., Jonathan Bush, Robert McDowell, Asa Newton, Isaac Clinton, Thaddeus Smith, Paul Abbot, Hosea Lane and Rufus Stephens, by an instrument under their hands in writing and seals bearing date the fourth day of March, in the year one thousand eight hundred and eight, after stating that they had contributed more than one half in value of the real and personal property and estate, collected and appropriated for the use and benefit of the academy erected at the town of Lowville, in the county of Lewis, did make application to us the said Regents, that the said academy might be incorporated and become subject to the visitation of us and our successors, and that Jonathan Rogers, Daniel Kelley, James H. Leonard, Isaac W. Bostwick, William Card, Jr., Benjamin Hillman, John Duffy, Jonathan Collins, James Murdock, Lewis Graves, Moss Kent, Lemuel Dickinson and Manly Wellman, might be trustees of the said academy by the name of Lowville Academy. Know ye, that we the said Regents, having inquired into the allegations contained in the instrument aforesaid, and found the same to be true, and that a proper building for said academy hath been erected, and finished, and paid for, and that funds have been obtained and well secured producing an annual nett income of at least one hundred dollars, and conceiving the said academy calculated for the promotion of literature. Do by these presents, pursuant to the statutes in such cases made and provided, signify our approbation of the incorporation of the said Jonathan Rogers, Daniel Kelley, James H. Leonard, Isaac W. Bostwick, William Card, Jr., Benjamin Hillman, John Duffy, Jonathan Collins, James Murdock, Lewis Graves, Moss Kent, Lemuel Dickinson and Manly Wellman, by the name of The Trustees of Lowville Academy, being the name mentioned in and by said request in writing on condition that tho principal or estate producing the said income shall never be diminished or otherwise appropriated, and that the said income shall be applied only to the maintenance or salaries of the professors or tutors of the academy.

[L. S.] In testimony whereof we caused our common seal, to be hereunto affixed, the twenty-first day of March, in the year of our Lord one thousand eight hundred and eight.

DANIEL D. TOMPKINS, Chancellor.

By command of the Chancellor,

FR. BLOODGOOD, Secretary.[1]

In 1807 the Rev. Isaac Clinton was induced to remove from Southwick, Mass., and began a classical school in the academic building before the charter was procured. He was employed as the first principal, and (with the exception of one year, beginning in November, 1813), continued in this office till 1817, at the same time serving as pastor of the Presbyterian church.[2]

Russell Parish acted as principal one year in 1813–4, and in 1817 Stephen W. Taylor[3] was employed. He entered

---

1 Recorded in Secretary's Office, deeds, vol. 37, page 1.

2 The Rev. *Isaac Clinton* was born at West Milford, near Bridgeport, Ct., Jan. 21, 1759. He was a cousin of DeWitt Clinton. He graduated at Yale college in 1786, and was distinguished in his class for his acquirements in mathematics and the languages. Whilst a student in college, upon an emergency, he volunteered, with other students, as a private in the Connecticut militia, and was engaged in one or more battles.

He studied divinity with Rev. Joseph Bellamy of Bethelehem, Ct. In 1788 he was ordained as pastor of a Presbyterian church, at Southwick, Mass. He married Charity Wells at New Stratford, (now Huntingdon), Ct., in 1787. They had six children, of whom five died at Southwick the same week, from an epidemic, and three were dead in the house at the same time. The only remaining child was Maria, who married Ela Collins at Lowville. Two sons, subsequently born, died at Lowville. He wrote and published, while at Southwick, a work on Infant Baptism, of which a second edition was issued. He preached at Southwick twenty years, and removed in 1807 to Lowville, N. Y. In 1808 he built the house on the beautiful elevation immediately west of the Presbyterian church, where he resided until his death. In 1808 he was installed minister of the Presbyterian church at Lowville, and continued for ten years. In 1807 he was employed as principal of the Lowville academy, and was so engaged nine years (with one year interval), when he was succeeded by S. W. Taylor. He was president of the board of academy trustees for many years, and until his death. When in his eightieth year he completed and published a book entitled Household Baptism. It is a standard work of extraordinary merit, and is in use as a text book in many of the theological seminaries of the country. He owned and cultivated about two hundred acres of land at Lowville, and he was especially devoted to the cultivation of apples and other fruit. Lewis county is much indebted to him for the introduction and distribution of many of its best varieties of apples. He was a handsome man and dressed through his life in the colonial style of his youth, viz: a low-crowned broad brimmed beaver hat, black broadcloth coat, with wide and long skirts, velvet breeches and silver knee buckles, high top boots or shoes, and silk stockings. He died at Lowville, March 18th, 1840, aged 82 years.

3 *Stephen William Taylor*, son of Timothy Taylor, graduated at Hamilton

upon his duties with zeal, and the institution soon gained a patronage which appeared to warrant the erection of new buildings. A contract was made with Mr. Taylor to conduct the school for twenty years, and a plan drawn by Philip Hooker of Albany, under the eye of the principal, was approved late in 1824. The arrangement as applied to academic buildings, was patented by S. W. Taylor and J. W. Martin, April 16, 1825, and consisted in placing the pupils in small separate apartments, open on one side, so that every one, both on the main floor and in the gallery was under the eye of the teacher at his stand, while no one could see any other of the students. The building was erected on a site of four acres purchased from Ela Collins, paid for by Mr. Low and given for academic purposes to the trustees. It was a twelve sided brick edifice two stories high, above a high stone basement, and was surmounted by an attic story of wood and tin covered dome, from the centre of which arose a cupola for the bell. Around the attic was a promenade, whose deck floor formed the roof of the outer portion of the main building. An immense twelve sided column in the centre supported the attic and roof. The building was 70 feet in diameter between its parallel walls, and cost $8,200. It was dedicated Jan. 12, 1826, but it soon proved defective; its walls required support by shoring, and in 1836 it was taken down. Mr. Taylor became sensitive upon the failure of his enterprise, which, aside from defective walls was found objectionable on account of echoes, difficulty in warming uniformly, and especially from the unwillingness of students to submit to the vigilance to which they were constantly subjected. He resigned in 1831 and was succeeded by Eliam E. Barney and Cyrus M. Fay, of whom the former remained two and the latter four years.[1] Henry Maltby was appointed in Aug., 1834, and remained

College in 1817, settled soon after at Lowville, and after his resignation as principal in 1831, continued to teach a family school in the village a short time, and about a year and a half at the Lanpher place, on the West Road, now West Lowville post office. He was then employed as preceptor of the grammar school, and afterwards professor of mathematics and natural philosophy in Hamilton academy. He was one of the founders and first president of the Lewisburgh University, Pa. He returned to Hamilton in 1850, accepted the office of president and Bleecker professor of natural and moral philosophy in Madison university, and continued in this office till his death, Jan. 7, 1856, aged 55 years. His father removed to this town after himself, and died Dec. 8, 1857, aged 90 years.

[1] Both of these graduated at Union College in 1831. Mr. Barney was a native of Jefferson county and now resides at Dayton, O. Mr. Fay was from Montgomery county, went from Lowville to Buffalo, where he taught 16 years, and in 1848 went to California by the overland route. Returning unsuccessful he sickened at Granada and died at San Juan, Nicaragua, Dec. 12, 1850, in his 45th year.

till the close of 1835. The academy was rebuilt nearly on its old site by James H. Leonard and dedicated Dec. 1, 1836. The school was opened by Henry Bannister[1], who was succeeded by Erastus Wentworth[2] in Oct., 1837, Harrison Miller[3] in 1838, David P. Yeomans[4] and David P. Mayhew[5] in 1839, and by Wm. Root Adams,[6] the present incumbent, in June, 1852. The semi-centennal anniversary of this academy was celebrated July 21, 22, 1858, the proceedings of which, published by the home committee, afford many details of its history, for which we have not space in this volume. The number of students that have gone forth from this institution is supposed to exceed 3000. The citizens of Lewis county owe it as a duty to themselves to extend its facilities, so as to meet the increasing demands which the general growth of the county will create. It is the only institution of the kind in the county.

This academy has been designated by the regents for the instruction of common school teachers. It has a valuable library and an excellent collection of apparatus, minerals, &c. In its cabinet is a sword that once belonged to Gen. Pike, and was presented by him to Gen. Brady on the eve of his departure on the fatal expedition against Little York. Gen. Brady afterwards resided in Lowville and presented this memento to Charles D. Morse, who has placed it among other historical relics in the cabinet of the academy.

---

[1] Mr. B. was born in Conway, Mass., in 1812, graduated at the Wesleyan university in 1836, went from Lowville to Auburn seminary, was two years principal of Fairfield academy and went thence to Cazenovia where he remained professor and principal till July, 1856. He is now a professor in the Garrett biblical institute, at Evanston, near Chicago, Ill.

[2] Mr. W. was a native of Norwich, Ct., graduated at the Wesleyan university in 1837, and went from Lowville to Gouverneur. In four years he went to the Troy conference seminary, and about 1845 was appointed president of McKendree college, Ill. In 1849 he became professor of natural science in Dickinson's college, Carlisle, Pa., and in 1854 was sent by the Methodist Episcopal board of missions to Fuh Chau, China.

[3] Mr. M., a native of Champion, was several years at Watertown, after leaving Lowville, and died at Carthage, Sept. 23, 1843, aged 31 years.

[4] Mr. Y. graduated at Williams college in 1837, was afterwards professor of chemistry in Lafayette college, Easton, Pa., and a physician in Canada.

[5] Mr. M., a native of Spencertown, N. Y., graduated at Union college, in 1838. In 1841 he became sole principal of this academy upon the removal of Yeomans. While here he fitted up a chemical laboratory in the academy and procured the addition of important facilities for education. The academy prospered beyond precedent under his management. He removed to Watertown, and in 1853 to Ohio. He is now connected with the Agricultural college at Ypsilanti, Mich.

[6] Mr. A. is a native of Lowville and a son of Dr. Ira Adams. He graduated at Union college in 1851, and was several years an assistant teacher in this academy. He has proved himself an efficient, faithful and successful instructor.

RELIGIOUS SOCIETIES.—On the 29th of November, 1799, a Mr. Cinney, preached in No. 11, and from time to time other traveling preachers visited the settlement, among whom were—Hassenclever, Joseph Willis, and Lorenzo Dow. The latter passed through to Canada in Sept., 1802, and preached at Noah Durrin's house near the landing. Judge Kelley was an occasional exhorter of the Free Will Baptist sect, and held stated meetings in the absence of regular preaching. His meetings were held as early as 1798, and frequently at Stow's square. He was accustomed to take a text, and conduct the service methodically. Judge Stow was an Episcopalian, and is said to have sometimes read the service to his neighbors upon the sabbath.

On the 3d of December, 1803, the Rev. Ira Hart, a missionary from Connecticut, organized a Congregational church at Stow's square, consisting of Mather Bosworth, Benj. Hillman, David Wilbur, Philip Shaw, and their wives, David Scott, Rebecca Waters, Esther Wilcox, Sarah Bates, Abigal Sexton, Lydia Bennet and Sally Richmond. Bosworth and Wilbur served as deacons till their deaths in 1850 and 1829 respectively. It belonged to the B. R. association until 1819, when it united with St. Lawrence Presbytery upon the Plan of Union. The 1st Presb. soc. of Lowville, was formed at Stow's square Dec. 8, 1818, with Levi Brownson, Bela Buell and Thaxter Reed trustees; and in 1819, a church edifice was built by Ezra Brainerd. The society was assisted by the United Domestic and the Western missionary societies.

The ministers who have preached here more or less, were Messrs Lazel, J. Murdock, Royal Phelps, Nathaniel Dutton, Jas. Ells, Wm. Vale, I. Clinton (March, 1808 to Feb., 1816), Daniel Nash (Nov., 1816 till Nov., 1822), Adam W. Platt (June, 1823 till Sept., 1823), Phineas Camp (May, 1824 till July, 1828), Abel L. Crandall (Jan., 1829 till Jan., 1832), Lewis A. Wickes (May, 1832 till May, 1836), Henry Jones (June, 1836, till Dec., 1837), David Dickinson (1838), W. W. Wolcott (Oct., 1840 till Oct., 1842), Charles Bowles (June, 1843 till May, 1846), Calvin Yale (July, 1846 till Feb., 1847). In 1833 the church numbered 160 members. A sabbath school was begun in 1820 and continued every summer since. It is claimed as the oldest in the county. Revivals occurred here in 1816–7, 1822–3, 1828–9 and 1832, at which about 500 are supposed to have been converted, nearly half in the second one. Meetings were discontinued in 1847, and the church is falling into ruin.

The Lowville Cong. soc. was formed Sept. 7, 1805, and

was the earliest legal society in town. Its trustees resided chiefly at Stow's square, and effected nothing. The 1st Cong. soc. of Lowville, was organized Sept. 18, 1807, with six trustees, of whom three were to reside in the village and three upon the Square. The first named were B. Hillman, J. H. Leonard, I. W. Bostwick, Jas. Stephens, Jonathan Patten and Wm. Darrow. The plan of a church between the two places was tried and failed, and although reincorporated Dec. 8, 1808, this organization was given up. A church formed in 1807, invited the Rev. Isaac Clinton to become their pastor, Oct. 13, 1807, and continued to worship in the old academy building until it was burned. On the 22d of Nov., 1820, the Lowville Presb. soc. was formed having Chester Buck, Daniel Williams, Lemuel Wood, Ela Collins, Melancton W. Welles and Stephen Leonard first trustees. The old academy was purchased May 1, 1826 for $390, and arrangements were made for the erection of a church upon its site, when a fire Dec. 26, 1827, consumed the building.

A new wooden edifice, 44 by 64 feet, was dedicated Jan. 15, 1829, and burned Jan. 3, 1830. It had cost $3,500, and was built by Ezra Brainerd. The present stone church at the head of Main street, was built upon the site, and after the plan of the former in 1831, and dedicated Sept. 1, of that year. The church proper, was formed July 11, 1822. Mr. Clinton was succeeded by D. Nash as above from 1816 to 1821. His successors were: David Kimball (Oct., 1821 till Oct., 1830), Jas. D. Pickand[1] (Jan., 1831, till July, 1833), Austin Putnam (Aug., 1833 till Aug., 1834), Dexter Clary (Sept., 1834 till March, 1835), Thomas L. Conklin (Oct., 1835 till May, 1836), Rufus R. Deming (Aug., 1836 till Aug., 1837), —— Bellamy (Dec. 1837 till March, 1838), A. L. Bloodgood (Dec., 1838, till April, 1839), Moses Chase (Dec., 1839 till ——), R. M. Davis (May, 1840 till Nov., 1840), Geo. P. Tyler (Dec., 1840 till Sept., 1853), N. Bosworth (Oct., 1853 till Aug., 1857), Wm. H. Lockwood (Nov., 1857 till the present).

A session room was built in 1853, and a parsonage previously.

About 1801, two ministers attended Mr. Kelly's meeting and requested the privilege of explaining the creed of the Methodist Episcopal church. This led to the organization of a church, and about 1805, the first house was erected in

---

[1] Mr. Pickand was from Phila. He was eccentric and peculiar in his manners, and removed west, where he run a strange career at Akron, O., as a Second advent preacher.

this town expressly for religious worship. It stood west of the village, near the house of Jesse Hitchcock, and continued in use until 1822. At a quarterly conference held June 1, 1822, at Martinsburgh, Daniel Tiffany, Abner Clapp, Henry Curtis, Francis McCarty, Abel S. Rice, Wm. R. Allen, Luke Wilder, Rodney Leonard and Russell Hills were appointed to ascertain when the people in Lowville might safely attempt to build a church at the village. The decision was favorable, and a society was formed under the statute, July 25, 1822, with R. Hills, L. Wilder, D. Tiffany, H. Curtis, Levi Weed, Elias Wood, A. S. Rice, R. Bassett and R. Leonard, trustees. The present brick church was built in 1823, and the parsonage about 1838. The Lowville circuit (first reported separate in 1832), has had the following ministers stationed: 1832, Benj. Phillips, Schuyler Hoes; 1833, Luther Lee; 1834, L. Lee, J. L. Hunt; 1835, Isaac Stone; 1836, E. B. Fuller, F. Hawkins; 1837, Elisha Wheeler; 1838, E. Smith, John Thompson; 1839, E. Smith, John Thomas; 1840, James W. Ninde; 1841, Squire Chase;[1] 1842–3, Jas. Erwin; 1844, Harvey E. Chapin; 1845, Wm. Wyatt, R. Lyle; 1846, W. Wyatt, J. S. Bingham; 1847–8, Geo. Sawyer; 1849–50, Lorenzo D. Stebbins; 1851–2, M. D. Gillet; 1853–4, J. F. Dayan; 1855–6, W. W. Hunt; 1857–8,[2] D. Symonds; 1859, J. L. Hunt.

The Lowville Baptist church was formed from the Line Church, Sept. 8, 1824, to include all south of Moses Waters', inclusive. Eld. M. E. Cook, moderator, Palmer Townsend, clerk; seven united by letter and one by profession. A society was legally formed Oct. 6, 1824, with Moses Waters, Richard Livingston and Calvin Batchiller, first trustees. On the 18th of December they resolved to build a church of wood, 40 by 50 feet, which was done in 1825. It was thoroughly repaired in 1852, and a parsonage was purchased at about that time.

The clergy have been: John Blodget (Dec. 1, 1825, till March 4, 1832), Geo. Lyle (March 11, 1832, till March 11, 1833), Charles Clark[3] (March 14, 1833, till Oct. 20, 1835),

---

[1] Mr. C., went twice to Liberia as a missionary. He died at Syracuse, July 26, 1843, aged 41 years, and was buried at Houseville.

[2] Mr. S. remained only a part of the second year.

[3] The *Rev. Charles Clark* was a son of Elijah Clark of Denmark, where he was born Dec. 29, 1805. He joined the church at 19, studied at the Lowville academy and read theology with Elds. Warner and Blodget, and was ordained at Boonville, Sept., 1830. He preached at that place two years, at Martinsburgh one, and at Lowville three. While here he labored in an extensive revival at Copenhagen. He afterwards preached at Watertown, Adams and Rome with efficiency. For 24 years he was absent from the sanctuary but a

Orrin Wilbur (March 20, 1835, till June 28, 1840), Harvey Silliman (Oct. 1, 1840, till Aug. 28, 1842), Geo. Lyle (Nov. 20, 1842, till March 1, 1845), Charles Graves (March 7, 1845, till Feb. 10, 1849), Lyman Hutchinson (April 7, 1849, till Feb. 1, 1850), Daniel D. Reed (Feb. 9, 1850, till Feb. 7, 1852), Conant Sawyer (Jan. 7, 1853, till May 31, 1856), Wm. Garrett (Sept. 14, 1856, till Sept. 19, 1858), James M. Ferris (March 1, 1859, till the present).

A Free Communion Baptist church was formed Oct. 12, 1816, and Amasa Dodge[1] was ordained April 4, 1818. This sect never owned a house of worship in this town and has long since become extinct.

An Evangelical Luthera nsociety was legally formed Oct. 6, 1827, with Geo. D. Ruggles, Peter Lowks, John Guthermute and Marks Petrie, trustees. It never erected a house of worship or became permanently established.

The Friends held meetings at private houses soon after the war. They were set off from the Le Ray monthly meeting, Jan. 3, 1826, and Lee was set off from Lowville soon after. A house was bought for meetings in 1819, and afterwards exchanged for the present site south of the creek, of which they received a deed Feb. 10, 1825. Their meeting house was built that year. These belong to the Orthodox class of Friends. The Hicksites held meetings for a short time in this town.

An Old School Baptist church was organized about 1834 in the north part of the town, but was given up a few years after.

Bishop Hobart visited Lowville in August, 1818, confirmed several persons and reported the prospects for the speedy formation of an Episcopal church as auspicious. The Rev. J. M. Rogers of Turin occasionally officiated here, but after his removal to Utica, services were only occasionally performed by clergymen who chanced to be passing through.

Trinity church, Lowville, was legally organized Sept. 24, 1838, with Kent Jarvis[2] and Geo. Lyman, wardens, Leonard Harding, L. S. Standring, Albert Strickland, Geo. D. Rug-

---

single Sabbath. He died at Rome, N. Y., Oct. 16, 1852, and was buried at Lowville.

[1] Eld. Dodge came to Lowville in 1806, and died on the West Road, Aug. 13, 1850, aged 82 years. He was remarkable for his loud, boisterous preaching.

[2] Mr. Jarvis came to reside at Lowville in July, 1828, and remained until Feb. 1840, when he removed to Massillon, O., where he now resides. He was a merchant and took a leading interest in public affairs.

gles, Henry Butler, Samuel Wood, Ambrose W. Clark and Merrit M. Norton, vestrymen. The Rev. Edward A. Renouf became the first rector.

An edifice was built in 1846 and consecrated in November of that year. A tower and bell were added in 1853 at a total cost of about $2000. A rectory was built in 1857.

MARTINSBURGH.

This town was formed from Turin, Feb. 22, 1803, in accorddance with a vote of that town, and originally embraced townships four and five of the Boylston tract, or *Cornelia* and *Porcia*,[1] as designated on the surveyor general's maps of 1802–4. The act took effect on the first day of March following, and directed the first town meeting to be held at the house of Ehud Stephens. Harrisburgh and Ellisburgh were created towns by the same act.

By a law passed April 2, 1819, that portion of Turin, north of a line passing nearly east and west, through the point of intersection of the state and west roads, was annexed to this town.[2] It has been stated that this measure was effected against the wishes of Turin, by Levi Adams, then in the senate, and a few settlers east of Martinsburgh village, who found their residence in Turin equivalent to a deprival of their civil rights, on account of their distance from elections. The latter town consented to a change that should fix the line on Whetstone creek, but upon receiving notice of the proposed alteration, called a special meeting, voted against the division with but one dissenting voice, and appointed a committee to petition against it.

The early records of town meetings in this town appear to be lost. In 1806 the town officers were, Walter Martin, *supervisor;* Levi Adams, *clerk;* Ehud Stephens, Asa Brayton Orrin Moore, *assessors;* Truman Stephens, *collector;* Ehud Stephens and Elijah Baldwin, *overseers of poor;* John McCollister, Oliver Allis and Avery P. Stoddard, *commis. highways;* Truman Stephens and Bradford Arthur, *constables.*

Supervisors.—1805, Asa Brayton; 1806–8, Walter Martin; 1809–10, Chillus Doty; 1811–4, Levi Adams; 1815, C.

[1] The latter has been sometimes erroneously written Persia. These names were derived from Roman ladies, conspicuous in classic history. They never received a local application among the settlers, and are perhaps nowhere found as geographical names, except upon the maps quoted, and on the statutes.

[2] The line was directed to be run from the point where the line of lots, 151, 152, township 3,,touched the river, to the place where the line, between the farms of Oliver Bush and Edward Johnson joined on the state road, and on the same course to the east line of township five.

Doty; 1816–7, Bradford Arthur; 1818–22, Baron S. Doty; 1823, B. Arthur; 1824, Barnabas Yale; 1825–9, B. Arthur; 1830–2, Asahel Hough; 1833–5, David Miller; 1836–8, Noah N. Harger; 1839, A. Hough; 1840, David Griffis; 1841, Harvey Stephens; 1842, Henry McCarty; 1843, Morgan Harger; 1844, Edwin S. Cadwell; 1845, H. Stephens;[1] 1846, Eleazer Alger; 1847–51, Diodate Pease; 1852–3, Avery Babcock; 1854, D. Pease; 1855, Horatio Shumway; 1856–60, Edwin Pitcher.

Town Clerks.—1803 and 1806, Levi Adams; (in 1804–5–7–8–9–10, the record not found); 1811–13, Enoch Thompson; 1814, Edward Bancroft; 1815–26, E. Thompson; 1827, John B. Hill; 1828–30, Walter Martin, jr.; 1831–3, Charles L. Martin; 1834–5, W. Martin, jr.; 1836–7, Elijah L. Thompson; 1838–40, Lewis G. Van Slyke; 1841, William King; 1842, John E. Jones; 1843, C. L. Martin; 1844, David Griffis; 1845, Jas. M. Sturtevant; 1846, Wm. King; 1847, Daniel A. Smith; 1849–51, Henry W. King; 1852, Edwin S. Cadwell; 1853, Alonzo J. Buxton; 1854, John M. Michael; 1855, John S. Hill; 1856–60, E. S. Cadwell.

Among the town records of Martinsburgh are noticed in 1809, '12 and '15, a vote imposing a fine of $4 for allowing Canada thistles to go to seed; the money, when recovered, to be applied towards the support of the poor.

In 1823 it was voted that the collection of taxes should be made by the person who would bid to do it *at the least price.* The support of certain town paupers was put up at auction in like manner in 1820, and this practice has precedent in the usages of other towns in the county.

This town was named from the proprietor, under whom settlement was made.

Walter Martin, a son of Capt. Adam Martin, was born in Sturbridge, Mass., Dec. 15, 1764, and in 1787 removed to Salem, N. Y., where he married a step daughter of Gen. John Williams, and became extensively engaged in business. An uncle, named Moses Martin, was one of the first settlers of Salem, and great numbers, from his native town, removed to that place. One of his sisters married Judge Asa Fitch, and another Andrew Freeman of Salem. Silas Conkey and Chillus Doty married two other sisters, and removed with him to the Black river country.

While living in Salem, Mr. Martin narrowly escaped death from an accident which he could never, in after life, relate without emotion. He owned a grist mill, in which it was

[1] Died April 7, 1845, and Harvey Easton elected April 19.

found necessary to cut away the ice on a winter's morning, before it could be started. While engaged at this work, the miller, without knowing the danger, let water upon the wheel which began to revolve with Martin in it, and continued to do so until it was stopped by his body. A leg was broken and he was dreadfully bruised by being thrown repeatedly from axle to circumference, as the wheel revolved.

Early in 1801 Mr. Martin came up into the Black river country, and after spending a short time at Lowville, exploring the lands south, he went to New York in June of that year, and bought of James Constable 8,000 acres of land, including the east subdivision of township five of the Boylston tract. The incidents of his settlement are related in these pages. A few years after his arrival, he again escaped death by the slightest chance. He had gone to a place near the West Road, which was frequented by deer, and climbed a wild cherry tree, for a better opportunity of shooting his game as it passed in the evening. A settler who was also out hunting, came near the place, and seeing a dark, living object in the tree, mistook it for a bear after cherries, and taking deliberate aim was on the point of firing, when Martin discovered his danger, and by giving a timely warning, escaped instant death. It would be difficult to decide which party felt most grateful for this happy escape from a dreadful casualty.

Mr. Martin held successively the offices of assistant justice of the Oneida court, loan commissioner, state road commissioner and state senator. Before the erection of Lewis county he held the rank of lieutenant colonel, and soon after was promoted to that of brigadier general, in which capacity he served a short time on the frontier in 1814. He was appointed post master upon the establishment of a post office, Jan. 19, 1804. His successors have been John W. Martin, May 23, 1831; William King, May 6, 1845; David T. Martin, June 14, 1849; Daniel S. Bailey, Aug. 24, 1853, and James H. Sheldon, Sept. 27, 1854.

In whatever promoted the interests of the town or county Gen. Martin felt a lively interest, and when a measure of public utility wanted *the means* for its accomplishment, he generally contrived to find them, and it appeared to be a governing maxim of his life, that when a thing was to be done it *must be*, if not by one way, by another. He was never backward in aiding to the full extent of his share, however large it might be, in any public enterprise. For some years after his first arrival, he evinced a partiality for a kind of investment which can never be overdone, as regards convenience to the inhabitants of a new settlement, although it may be without profit to the projector. This was the erection of saw mills, of which he owned several in Martinsburgh and Turin, upon which the country around depended for their supply of the essential elements of a comfortable house or a commodious barn. Gen. Martin died at his residence in Martinsburgh village, Dec. 10, 1834. His father was born Aug. 27, 1739, removed with him to Martinsburgh, where he died Aug. 9, 1818, aged seventy-nine. He had been an officer in the French and revolutionary wars and was a member of assembly from Washington county in 1787. His wife died in this town Dec. 2, 1820.[1]

A tract of 8,000 acres, supposed to include the east subdivision of township five of the Boylston tract, was deeded to Walter Martin of Salem, N. Y., June 17, 1801, for $12,000.[2] As early as Jan. 20, 1796, Shaler of Turin, was endeavoring to purchase No. 5, which would then have sold for more than it brought in 1801. At that time Constable refused to sell less than the whole tract of 14,820 acres, and in June, 1798, gave John Stephen a refusal for four months, at twelve shillings per acre. It will be remembered that the political changes in Europe had checked emigration, and that the decline of prices in wild lands was general throughout the country. Just at this time, the land companies in the western states were opening their domains to settlers upon very favorable terms, the hostile Indian tribes in that region had been brought to terms of peace; and the tide of New England emigration, although still strong, was diverted to the broad plains and fertile valleys of the western country.

The purchase of this town was made from James, agent of William Constable, and the tract was familiarly known among the first settlers as The Triangle. Upon its being afterwards found that it fell short of 8,000 acres, 703 acres,

---

1 The three daughters of Gen. M. were married as follows: Jane, to Stephen Leonard of Lowville; Abigail to Philo Rockwell, and Susannah to Dr. John Safford, both of this town. Walter Martin, the oldest son, resides in Marshall, Michigan. Adam Martin, the second son, died May 1826, aged 30 years. John Williams Martin, the third son, was elected to assembly in 1827, became first president of the Lewis county bank, and from 1843 to 1843, was first county judge. He resides in New York. Charles L. Martin, the first of the family born in this town, was for several years cashier of the Lewis county bank, and county treasurer. He is now connected with the bank of North America in New York city. Morgan Lewis Martin has resided many years at Green Bay. David Thomas Martin (named from his uncle, formerly state treasurer,) has always resided in this town, and has been for several years a magistrate.

2 Oneida Deeds, viii, 506.

or parts of lots 2, 4, 15, 17 and 41, in the west subdivision of the same township, were conveyed to supply the deficiency, May 26, 1806. The tract was surveyed the first summer of the purchase, by ——— Montgomery into sixty lots. Township 4, was surveyed into 111 lots by Benjamin Wright in 1805, and belonged to the Pierrepont family, until sold for settlement. Mr. Martin immediately came on with a company of men, to make a clearing and erect a saw mill. He was accompanied by Elijah Baldwin[1] of Salem and wife, who came on to cook for the laborers, and was during the first season the only woman in town. As soon as surveyed, the land was opened for sale in farms at $5 per acre, and with such rapidity was it taken up, that in less than a month, almost the whole of it was under contract to persons intending to settle. The purchasers contracted to clear four acres and erect a house within two years. Numerous small clearings were begun in various parts of the tract, especially along the intended roads, and rude log cabins were put up to be ready for the families that were to arrive the next spring. The first clearing was made by Martin, west of the present mill, and before winter he had built a log house and a sawmill. His millwright was David Waters, from Johnstown, who with his brother John became pioneer settlers.[2]

Mr. Martin arrived with his family March 4, 1802, and during this season, many families came on for permanent settlement. Among those who arrived the first and second years, were Mrs. Richard Arthur and sons,[3] Ehud Stephens, Levi Adams,[4] John and Orrin Moore,[5] Chillus Doty,[6] Silas

---

[1] Mr. Baldwin died at Houseville, Feb. 6, 1857, aged 84 years.

[2] David Waters died in town, March 25, 1843, aged 67. John Waters died, Feb. 20, 1843.

[3] Richard Arthur had died in Westfield in 1790, aged 40, leaving eleven children, most of whom became heads of large families in this town. The sons were named Bradford, Levi, Richard, Russell, Joseph and Elisha. Four of the sisters married early settlers, and the whole family took up large farms on the State road north of Martinsburgh village, the most of which are still owned by their families. Mrs. Arthur died in 1815. Bradford came in 1803, and held for several years the offices of supervisor, coroner, &c. He died, September 9, 1855.

[4] From Westfield, settled in this town March, 1802, elected to the state senate in 1819, and served one term, and in 1820 was chosen one of the council of appointment. He was often elected to town offices, and in 1815-18 was sheriff. He died June 18, 1831, aged 68. He resided on the east road near the line of Lowville.

[5] Orrin Moore died in 1827. The death of John Moore is noticed on page 182.

[6] *Mr. Doty* married a sister of Gen. Martin, was many years an innkeeper, and died in town, October 16, 1824. He was sheriff in 1805-8, and 1811-14; in assembly in 1814-16-17, and a surrogate in 1815-23. He was appointed assessor under the law imposing a direct tax by congress, and was several

Conkey,[1] Wm. Miller,[2] John Atwater,[3] Joseph Sheldon,[4] Jotham Strickland, Elisha and Daniel Tiffany,[5] Nathan Cheney,[6] Justus Sacket,[7] Eli Kellogg, Stephen Root,[8] Roswell Miner, Daniel Ashley,[9] Ephraim Luce, Stephen Searl, Dr. Danforth Shumway, Enoch and Theron Thompson,[10] John McCollister,[11] and others on Martin's triangle. The first settler near West Martinsburgh was Asahel Hough, who removed from Leyden in the spring of 1802. His neighbors along the west road within the next three years, were Lobdell Wood, Arba Jones, James Coates, Samuel Gowdy,[12] David and Chester Shumway,[13] Clark McCarty, Asa Brayton, Wm. Jonas and Watson Henry, Nathaniel Babcock and Truman Stevens. The first settler on township 4 was Nathaniel Alexander, in July, 1805.[14]

In the south part of the town, included in Shaler's tract, and annexed in 1819, the first settlers were Reuben Pitcher[15]

---

years a county judge. Mrs. Sarah Doty was born April 19, 1767, died September 11, 1843, aged 77. James D. Doty their son, removed west at an early period, settled in Wisconsin, and was appointed governor of that territory in March, 1841. Baron S. Doty, another son, settled in Ogdensburgh, and represented St. Lawrence county in Assembly in 1826, '27. He now resides at Portage city, Wisconsin.

1 Married a sister of Gen. Martin, and died in this town April 16, 1813, aged 54. His wife Zuriah, was born May 19, 1763, and died October 16, 1849, aged 86.

2 Father of Dr. David, and Wm. Miller of Martinsburgh.

3 Mr. A. returned to Westfield a few years after. He was the first distiller in the county, and kept an inn half a mile south of the village, which in 1808 he sold to Enoch Lee. The latter died June 17, 1834, aged 77. His sons Winthrop, Charles, Enoch, Shepherd and Williams became heads of families in this town, but several have since removed.

4 Died in Antwerp, May 16, 1844, aged 70. He was the father of the late Ira Sheldon of this town.

5 The Tiffanies were from Montgomery, Mass., and come in 1803. They joined the first Methodist Episcopal Class formed in this circuit.

6 Removed to Ontario county, and died at Richmond, N. Y., about 1826.

7 Died February 28, 1831, aged 52 years. He was from Westfield.

8 From Westfield. Died August 28, 1857.

9 Died June 18, 1816, aged 67 years. He was the father of Stephen, Daniel, Otis, Cyrus, and the Rev. Riley B. Ashley, all formerly of this town.

10 E. T. died March 3, 1845, aged 61. He held many years the office of loan commissioner, and kept an inn at the brick tavern in Martinsburgh.

11 About 1818, McCollister, in fulfillment of a fortune teller's prediction sold, went to Buffalo, kept tavern a while, and then removed to the far west to become the wealthy owner of a township which the hag had promised him. While ascending the Illinois river with two or three other families the party sickened, numbers died, including McCollister, and the survivors were scarcely able to bury the dead on the bank of the river. With great suffering the party at length reached its destination, penniless and wretched.

12 Died April 19, 1840, aged 80 years.

13 From Belchertown, Mass. David died December 5, 1849, aged 74 years.

14 From Chester, Mass. He died February 14, 1829. He had sons, Nathaniel and Gaius.

15 A descendant from Andrew Pitcher, who emigrated from England and settled in Dorchester, Mass., in 1630. Reuben Pitcher died February 15, 1844, aged 81. His sons David, Daniel, Reuben, Moses, Philander and Almond, be-

and Eli Rogers,[1] from Westfield, who settled in 1802. Like many other families who came on in the spring of that year, they were delayed until late in February, by the want of snow. The company in which they came had twelve or fourteen ox teams, and were fourteen days upon the road from Westfield. At Albany the Hudson was broken up, and they were obliged to go up to Half Moon point, now Waterford, to cross, where the ice, although a foot under water was considered safe.

The first blacksmith who settled in town was John Peebles, who removed from Salem in 1804. He was the ancestor of all of the name now living in town. The first birth in town was that of Jane,[2] daughter of Ehud Stephens. Mr. Martin brought on the remainder of a store of goods which he had owned in Salem, to accommodate his settlers until a regular merchant could be established. A grist mill was got in operation in 1802 or 1803, but as Lowville and Turin had been some years settled, the people of this town were relieved from much of the hardship arising from long journeys to mill. The water power wherever considered available, was reserved by Martin in his sale of lands.

In James Constable's diary, under date of September 13, 1803, we find the following notice of this town:

"Travelled on to Mr. Martin's. We had a rain some part of the day, which we were glad of, as it was much wanted in the country. Mr. Martin was not at home, and we went to look at his mills and other improvements. He has a good country grist mill well finished, and a common saw mill, but the creek is dry as is the case throughout the country. There is also a potash work at which they were busy. His house is of logs, the same as first erected, as he has not had time for a frame building. His father lives in a similar one very near. There are several neighbors about him on his land. The cultivation is not very forward, but considering the time he has been here, for he only made the purchase in June, 1801, the improvements do him very great credit. Mrs. Martin being uncertain when he might return home, and it growing late, we took our leave, dined at Capt. Clapp's and returned to Shaler's in the evening."

---

came heads of families, and excepting the last, settled mostly on adjacent farms along the west road, in the southern part of the town. Of his three daughters, Martha married Dr. Horatio G. Hough and is still living; Roxana married Stephen Ashley, and Dema married Paul B. Yale. Moses Pitcher was drowned in Black river bay, December 3, 1846, and Philander in the Black river, near Independence creek, September 15, 1847.

1 Mr. Rogers died April 12, 1849, aged 80. He had a large family, most of whom settled in town, but of whom none now remain, having died or removed.

2 Born February 20, 1802. The second birth was that of Charles Baldwin, and the third that of Charles L. Martin.

The first framed house in town was built by Amos Barnes, in 1805, a mile and a quarter south of the village. It is now owned by Charles S. Lee.

The first regular merchants were Philo Rockwell and Danforth Shumway, about 1806. The former, in 1816, went to Aurora, N. Y., but soon returned and renewed trade with Dr. John Safford.[1] Mr. Rockwell continued a merchant in this town until 1829, when he removed to Utica, and in 1832 became the first victim of the cholera at that place.[2]

The first inn was kept by Chillus Doty, a brother-in-law of Martin, in a log house a few rods west of the brick tavern, where the first county courts were held, and the first town business transacted. Business centered in the north part of the village in early years, and upon its transfer to a more southern locality, this portion long wore an aspect of decay until several of its buildings rotted down or were removed.

The western sub-division of township number 5 was settled under Benjamin Wright of Rome, and much of township 4 by I. W. Bostwick of Lowville, agents of H. B. Pierrepont of Brooklyn, the proprietor. James Constable, one of the executors of his brother's estate, remarks in his journal of Sept. 10, 1804, of the settlement of this portion:

"Passed on from Lowville through the northeast quarter of number four, which is very good, to Capt. McCarty's, on our part of number five, distance three miles. He was from home but we found another of the settlers, Ehud Stephens, who with five or six other men whom we saw, have completed a street of nearly a mile long, of very fine farms in less than two years, and it is quite an animating sight to see them. McCarty, Stephens, and two or three others have paid in full and got their deeds. The rest have paid generally as the money became due, they are all valuable men. The country we are now in, exceeds any part we have seen in the whole journey, and it has the advantage of being well watered. Proceeded on a couple of miles to Squire Martin's, the whole well cleared and cultivated. He is engaged in building a stone house, nearly fifty feet square, after the model of Sir William Johnson's. The walls are up,

---

[1] *Dr. Safford* came from Salem about 1807, married a daughter of Gen. Martin and continued many years in practice. He removed to Watertown about 1826 and died at that place.

[2] *Mr. Rockwell* was from Hadley, N. Y., and married Abigal, daughter of Gen. W. Martin. At Utica he engaged in the hardware trade, in the firm of Rockwell & Sanger, and upon the approach of the cholera he was appointed upon a sanitary committee, and doubtless exposed himself to noxious exhalations in the discharge of this patriotic duty. He had made arrangements to leave for this town upon the first appearance of the cholera, but was stricken and died Aug. 13, 1832.

the roof nearly finished and he expects to complete at least a part of it for the ensuing winter."

The original model of Martin's house, in good preservation and but little changed from the plan designed by its projector, is still standing in the town of Amsterdam, three miles west of the village, and adjacent to the N. Y. Central railroad. It has borne for more than a century, the name of fort Johnson, and in the old French war was fortified against a sudden surprise by the enemy. Mr. Martin had spent a night at this house some years before, and was so well pleased with its arrangement that he sent his builder, David Waters, down to take its plan and dimensions. The structure in Martinsburgh was begun in 1803 and finished in 1805, and is said to have been throughout, in size, style and finish, as far as possible, a faithful copy of Sir William's dwelling. To this day, there is scarcely a residence in the county that has exceeded this in cost, and certainly there is none that excels it in conspicuous site or substantial construction. Early in 1804 Martin was negotiating for the purchase of township four, but failed to conclude a bargain.

The first school-house in town, was built about 1804, on the brow of the hill south of the village, and on the west side of the state road. Erastus Barns was the first teacher. No legal action was taken until the annual town meeting in 1814, when the recent act of the legislature was approved, and double the sum received from the state was raised by tax. The first *commissioners* were Chester Shumway, Horatio G. Hough,[1] and Orrin Moore, and the first *inspectors*, Barna-

---

Horatio G Hough

[1] Dr. *Horatio Gates Hough*, son of Thomas Hough, and the fifth in descent from an English emigrant, was born in Meriden, Ct., January 5, 1778, and at the age of three years, removed with his parents to Southwick, Mass. When sixteen years old he entered the office of Dr. Coit of that place, and in four years was admitted to practice medicine. His classical studies were pursued with the Rev. Isaac Clinton, pastor of the church of which his father was an active member, and a warm personal friendship continued between preceptor and pupil through life.

In 1798, the newly licensed physician received as his only patrimony a horse, saddle, bridle, and a few dollars worth of medicine, made a tour into Maine with the view of settlement, but not finding an attractive location returned and joined the current of emigration then setting towards the Black river country. He came to Constableville and settled as the first physician in the county, taking up a small farm, afterwards owned by Willard Allen, and laboring in the intervals of his professional employment. In the fall of 1803 he married Martha, daughter of Reuben Pitcher, and early in 1805 removed to Martinsburgh and settled on a farm, a mile and a quarter south

bas Yale,[1] John McCollister, Asahel Hough, Levi Adams, Noah N. Harger and Ephraim Luce. The town was soon after divided into five districts, and for many years the sum voted for school purposes was $124.10 annually. The usual amount was afterwards equal to the sum received from the state.

The first settlers of this town, coming chiefly from Salem, N. Y., and Westfield, Mass, or places adjacent, divided off into two parties, between which a certain degree of rivalry, and to some extent of jealousy, existed several years, and its existence was evinced in a wish to control business affairs and town offices. Gen. Martin might have been regarded as the leader of one of these, and Judge Bancroft,[1] an early

---

of the village, where he resided till his death, which occurred from an organic disease of the heart, Sept. 3, 1830.

He was an original member, and at his death, president of the county medical society, and on many occasions he read at its meetings essays upon professional and scientific subjects, which evinced a strong attachment to philosophical studies, and much proficiency in them. In an obituary notice, written by his friend Dr. Sylvester Miller, the hardships of the pioneer physician are thus graphically described:

"How often has he been seen traveling on foot with his saddle bags on his shoulders, making his way through the woods by the aid of marked trees, to some distant log house, the abode of sickness and distress! There has he been seen almost exhausted by fatigue, and suffering from want of sleep and food, reaching forth his hand to restore the sick, and by his cheerful voice pouring consolation into the minds of the afflicted family. He was an obliging neighbor, a kind husband and an affectionate father. In his death literature has lost a friend, and the world a valuable citizen."—*Black River Gazette*, Sept. 15, 1830.

Dr. H. G. Hough left two sons and three daughters. The older son, Horatio Hough, resides upon the homestead in this town. The younger son is the author of this volume.

[1] *Barnabas Yale*, son of Amasa Yale, was born in Rupert, Vt., April 9, 1784, and removed when a child to Salem, N. Y., where his father died, leaving him and two younger children to the care of a poor but industrious mother. He attended the Salem academy two years, and then entered the law office of Mr. Blanchard, where he remained two and a half years. After removing with the family to Schenectady, Amsterdam, Johnstown, Minden and Little Falls, he was, in February, 1807, admitted to practice, and settled in Martinsburgh. He continued a member of the Lewis county bar about twenty-five years, when he settled on a farm, and in 1836 removed to St. Lawrence co. He died October 11, 1854, at the residence of his son Lloyd C., in Norfolk, N. Y. While living in Martinsburgh, he held many years the office of justice of the peace, and in 1820, was appointed surrogate. He was an active member of the Presbyterian church, and took a leading part in the various reform movements of his day. In 1825, he offered his name as an independent candidate for the office of county clerk, and came within 24 votes of election. His brother Paul Baxter Yale, resides near Houseville.

[2] *Edward Bancroft* removed from Westfield 1816, engaged as a merchant, built a grist mill and distillery, was concerned in the manufacture of potash on a somewhat extensive scale, and held the offices of county clerk and first judge. Having proved unsuccessful in business, removed in 1832 to Detroit, and after another crisis in his affairs, he removed to St. Clair county, Mich., where he died April, 1842.

merchant, of the other. It was not observable after the removal of the latter in 1832.

In the month of April, 1807, an unusual fall of snow followed by warm sunny weather, occasioned a flood in all the streams of this region, more destructive than ever before or since, witnessed. The mill of Gen. Martin, which stood a few yards above the present one, was undermined and launched into the stream, when it floated down and finally lodged and partly went to pieces at the state road bridge. Mr. Faxton Dean, father of Samuel Dean[1] the miller, lodged in a small room in the upper part of the mill, and although advised of possible danger from the flood, remained there on the night that the mill was swept away. His cries were heard by the people on the bank, who followed with lanterns the floating building and its inmate, but were entirely unable to render the slightest aid. His body was found among flood-wood some weeks after, and was the first one buried in the old grave yard a mile south of the village. Martin's mill was rebuilt soon after, and in 1822, the present grist mill, a little below the old one was erected. In Jan., 1826, E. Bancroft completed a rival mill, supplied by springs and a small tributary of Martin's creek, a little southwest of the other mill. After being used about ten years, the latter was changed to a manufactory of cotton batting, wicking and wadding. It has since fallen into ruin. In 1833, a building was erected west of village as a woolen factory, but the intention was never fully realized. A starch factory was fitted up in 1847, in a building erected for a tannery, but after the first season it was never used. In the spring of 1844, a company was formed under the style of the Lewis Co. Manufacturing Co., with a proposed capital of $25,000, but the plan was abondoned before it had matured.

A paper mill was built by Gen. Martin in 1807, on the creek, about a mile south east of the village, upon the east road, and got in operation by John Clark & Co., in the fall of that year. Daniel Gould was afterwards in company with Clark. The mill never had any machinery beyond an engine for grinding the pulp, and although kept more or less employed, till about 1832, it never proved a source of much profit to those concerned. In the earlier years writing paper was made, but at a later day only wrapping and wall papers.

A poetical advertisement, a parody of one of Dibdin's

---

[1] Mr. Dean was from Westfield. He removed to Ohio, and died at Brockport, April 8, 1840, aged 85.

songs, which appeared in the Black River Gazette, Nov. 9, 1807, is here inserted, for the double purpose of representing the character of the type used in that newspaper, and the poetical talents of J. Clark & Co.

Sweet Ladies, pray be not offended,
  Nor mind the jeft of fneering wags;
No harm believe us, is intended,
  When humbly we requeft your Rags.

The fcraps, which you reject, unfit
  To clothe the tenant of a hovel,
May fhine in fentiment and wit,
  And help to make a charming novel.

The cap exalted thoughts will raife,
  The ruffle in defcription flourifh;
Whilft on the glowing work we gaze
  The thought will love excite and nourifh.

Each beau in ftudy will engage,
  His fancy doubtlefs will be warmer,
When writing on the milk-white page,
  Which once, perhaps, adorn'd his charmer.

Though foreigners, may fneer and vapor,
  We no longer forc'd their books to buy,
Our gentle Belles will furnifh paper,
  Our fighing Beau will wit fupply.

Forty-five years afterwards, the principal of this firm was a homeless wanderer, seeking to be employed at a fee of a few shillings, to indicate veins of water and points for digging wells, by the pretended traction of a hazel rod.

Capt. John Moore was accidentally shot by Russell Arthur, early on the morning of June 3, 1811. It was on the day of a military muster, and some of his men had come as was the custom, to salute him, by firing guns; when, just as he was crossing the threshold, a ball passed through his neck, which proved speedily fatal. This painful incident cast a gloom over the neighborhood, and was scarcely less afflictive to the unhappy author of the accident and his friends, than to the family of the deceased. Mr. Moore resided on the State road, about midway between the villages of Lowville and Martinsburgh. Otis Ashley, jr., a lad, was killed at a military training, in the village of Martinsburgh, July 4, 1831, by a ball from a rifle, reflected from a stone, at which the weapon was fired, without the owner's knowing that it was charged with any thing but powder.

The scheme of S. Whittlesey and wife of Watertown, to rob the government of $30,000, due the drafted militia of this and adjoining counties, the year after the war, is among the most remarkable incidents of crime upon record. Having concealed the money at home, he traveled carelessly on horseback as far as Trenton, where he announced that he had been robbed, and offered, with well dissembled anxiety, an immense reward for the thief. The sequel, ending in the extortion of the secret, under threats of a terrible death, the suicide of the wife and the disgrace of her husband, are familiar to many of our readers.[1] On his way to Trenton, W. spent a night at the inn of Chillus Doty in this town, where he was cautioned to be more watchful over his treasure. A few days after the discovery of the money, he was seen to leave Watertown on horseback late in the afternoon, and to return the next morning, with his beast jaded and weary, as if he had traveled a long journey without resting. The late Dr. Trowbridge (who related to us the incident, and who, at that time, was almost the only one of W.'s late friends who would harbor him under their roofs,) insisted upon his telling the errand, when he had length reluctantly admitted, that he had on his former journey, concealed about the premises of Mr. Doty a quantity of *marked bills* with the intention of finding them under a search warrant, and thus implicating an innocent man. The plot having been defeated he had gone to recover the money, creeping, at the death of night upon the premises on an errand of guilt, which practiced villainy would have shunned by daylight. Several marked bills were found on the premises of Joseph Sheldon, who kept an inn on the site of the residence of Warren Salmon in Martinsburgh, and were returned to their owners in Watertown. The honorable character of these persons would have ensured them against public suspicion, had the money been found concealed upon their premises.

As Miss Mary Ann Waters, a young lady about twenty years of age, engaged in teaching school in the east part of the town, was returning home on horseback, June 20, 1829, her horse was startled and stopped by a tree falling across the road in front, and directly after another tree fell upon and killed both the horse and its rider.

In the fall of 1828 a thin vein of galena disseminated in calcareous spar, was discovered a short distance north of the village of Martinsburgh, near the brow of the hill, and hopes were excited which further exploration did not justify. In the spring of 1838, as Levi Edwards, in the service of Richard Arthur, was plowing in a field about a mile

[1] This event, derived from those who were intimately concerned, is detailed in the *History of Jefferson county*, p. 262.

northwest of the village, the point of his plow broke off a bright shining ore, which proved to be galena. This led to an examination, and as the rock lay near the surface, the vein was easily uncovered and presented truly an attractive spectacle. The ore from four to ten inches wide stood like a wall several inches above the surface of the rock, and run in a course about N. 80° W. a distance of over twenty rods, and so readily was it obtained that two men in two days threw out over four thousand pounds. Trenches dug across the direction of this vein disclosed others nearly parallel, and the prospect of mineral wealth for a time seemed never fairer. The right of mining was purchased by Thomas L. Conklin[1] for $700, and a company at first of twelve, but afterwards of a hundred shares was formed.

A building, formerly a fulling mill, adjacent to the bridge south of the village was fitted up for smelting the ore, and got in operation in June, 1838, and several tons of the metal were reduced. Meanwhile the cost of mining rapidly increased as the excavations were sunk below the surface, while the yield of ore diminished, and after considerable expenditure during the first year and part of the next the work was abandoned, with heavy loss to all concerned.

In 1853, the mineral right of this locality was purchased on speculation by parties in New York, and a company was legally formed for working the mines. The Lewis County Lead Co., is not "known by its works" in the county, and there is no present prospect of any further enterprise of the kind being attempted.[2]

A serio-comic incident occurred in the western part of this town in the summer of 1836, occasioned by a search after a child lost in the woods. The little wanderer was soon found and restored to its parents, but on counting up after their return it was discovered that a middle aged man named C. N. K., and a lad about 18 years of age in his company were missing. This happened on Thursday, but Friday came and passed without any tidings of the lost. On

---

1 *Mr. Conklin* was from Rensselaerville, N. Y., was admitted to the Lewis county bar about 1824, and for some time was actively engaged in his profession. In 1831, he entered the ministry and removed to Carbondale, Pa., but soon after returned. After the failure of his lead speculation he mostly withdrew from business, and died July 1, 1851, at the age of 55, having mostly secluded himself from society during several years. He was acknowledged by all to be an effective and elegant public speaker, enthusiastic in in whatever he engaged, eccentric in his theories, but withal, the possessor of considerable talent. He studied his profession with Simeon Ford of Herkimer county.

2 This company filed its articles Feb. 4, 1854. Capital $200,000 in shares of $2, each, limit fifty years.

Saturday the report spread generally, and towards the close of that day a public meeting was called, and it was agreed that in case they did not appear by morning, the town bell should be rung at sunrise, as a signal for the inhabitants to rally and engage in a careful search in the woods. The bell was accordingly rung on Sabbath morning, and hundreds of men assembled at the appointed place, agreed upon their signals, formed into a line, and began their search in the forest. About ten o'clock, the signal for "found" was passed along the line, and each hastened to the spot to learn in what condition the lost had been found, and by what casualty they had been detained. The estrays were found in an open beaver meadow, on the head waters of one of the streams, but two or three miles from inhabitants, and almost within hearing of the town bell. The weather had been bright and clear, and the sluggish stream after a few windings in the wood emerged into the clearings. When asked why they did not follow out some one of the hay roads, for winter use, which led into the meadow, Mr. K., with great *naivete* and perfect sincerity, replied, that they had found *a plenty of paths leading into the meadow, but none that led out.*

At the Oneida circuit of Sept., 1844, a suit brought by Abel Fuller, of this town, against Alanson Tyler, of Lowville to recover money alleged to have been paid, disclosed the existence of a combination of swindlers in this and adjoining towns, who had in various ways, for several months previous, been operating to obtain money by fraud. In the case mentioned, perjury was freely offered as evidence, and it subsequently appeared, that numerous schemes of extortion had been planned, and means the most unscrupulous arranged to secure their execution. This club received the name of "the forty thieves." It is said to have met by night in private places, and to have enjoined secresy and fidelity by the most solemn oaths, but the result of the trial in Utica, by removing the leaders to state prison, put an effectual end to their operations.

A distressing accident occurred Sept. 3, 1852, at the Maple Ridge in this town. As a daughter of Timothy Canaan, aged 9 years, was in a field in which the embers of log heaps were still burning, her dress caught fire, and before she could be relieved was literally burned alive

The town of Martinsburgh has three post offices. Martinsburgh (P. O.) village is built upon a bold terrace of Trenton limestone which here rises to a greater elevation than at any other point in the town if not in the county.

In 1855 it reported a population of 210. It has besides the court house and jail, four churches, an inn, four stores, the usual variety of mechanics and on its southern border a limited water power. The scenery, which the surrounding country affords, especially towards the east, is much finer than that of any other village in the county. The most disastrous fire which ever occurred in the county, broke out in this village, on the morning of Feb. 5, 1859, destroying the only hotel,[1] four stores, and all the offices, sheds, barns and buildings attached. The fire occured during court week, and the hotel was filled with guests, who were aroused from sleep, and several of them narrowly escaped with life.

West Martinsburgh (P. O.) three miles north west, on the west road, is rather a thickly settled street, with two churches, an inn, store and a few mechanic shops. As a farming region this vicinity is one of the finest in the county.

Glensdale (P. O.) is a hamlet of about a dozen houses, a mill, store, church and a few shops, in the east part of the town, where Whetstone creek falls over the last terrace of limestone before reaching the river. The post-office at this place was established in March 1855, with S. D. Mason, P. M.

The Lewis County Bank, was incorporated April 20, 1833, and located at Martinsburgh, with a limit of thirty years, and a capital of $100,000. The commissioners for opening subscriptions and distributing stock, were, Geo. D. Ruggles, John W. Martin, Andrew W. Doig, Wm. D. Shaler, Ashley Davenport, John Whittlesey, Ela Merriam, Stephen Leonard and Ozias Wilcox.

In the petition to the legislature which procured this act, the annual surplus products of the county are stated as: cattle $40,000, horses and mules $35,000, flour and wheat $50,000, pot and pearl ashes, $25,000, pork and hogs, $25,000, and whiskey $15,000. It was stated that 75,000 pounds of wool were sent annually, and that hemp, iron, and lumber, formed a large and increasing subject of exportation. It was estimated that the merchants purchased $200,000 worth of goods annually, and that the products of agriculture and opportunities, for manufactures which our hydraulic privileges offered would be largely benefited and encouraged by a bank at the county seat. It will be no-

---

[1] This was originally built in 1807 for Gen. Martin, and afterwards much extended. At the time of the fire it was kept by T. Atwood. The hotel premises are about to be rebuilt by Edwin Pitcher, with the aid of a subscription of $2000 from townsmen.

ticed that no allusion is made to that great feature of productive industry, the dairying interest, which has conferred wealth and reputation upon Lewis county, as this resource was entirely unknown, and did not begin to develop itself until about two years after. A few years before, a merchant in Lowville who had advertised for *three hundred pounds* of butter, payable in goods at ten cents the pound, was considered an adventurer, in a county which now produces over 2,000,000 pounds of butter, and much greater amount of cheese.[1]

The profits upon banking capital had for many years been great, and the prices upon bank stock had been much above par. The franchises implied in a charter were difficult to obtain, and it is not surprising that multitudes should seek this investment, or that an immense subscription should have been offered beyond what could be taken. The charter limited the amount which one person might take at fifty shares, or $2,500, and left the commissioners the invidious task of deciding who should be favored in the assignation of stock. The total amount offered, is said to have been about $1,200,000, which would necessarily leave eleven in twelve on the disappointed list. As an unavoidable result, many were free to charge upon the commissioners the most selfish and ungenerous motives. Each of their number took the amount limited by law.

A bank building was erected in Martinsburgh, adjacent to the court house in 1833, and the bank was opened for business in December of that year, affording the only banking facilities in the county until after the passage of the general banking law of 1838. While the Bank of Lowville was in course of organization, an unsuccessful effort was made to increase the capital of this bank to twice the sum named in the charter. On the 3d of May, 1842, the bills of this bank were rejected by the Commercial bank of Albany, and on the same day an injunction was served upon its officers. Mr. Forbes, one of the bank commissioners, had been for some days investigating its affairs and deemed the measure necessary as large assets were not available for use. The bank was allowed to resume business Jan. 3, 1843, and public confidence had not been entirely restored so as to allow its bills to circulate freely at a distance, when a second injunction was served in 1845, and business was again resumed in September, 1846, with the capital reduced one half. It went on until November, 1854, when it finally failed, beyond prospect of recovery.

---

[1] Black River Gazette, Sept. 18, 1827.

This bank paid 10 per cent dividend upon its stock until 1842, and a single dividend upon its preferred stock after its first suspension. Frederick Hollister of Utica in 1845, bought a large interest, and for time held a controlling amount of stock.

The following is a list of presidents and cashiers of this bank:

Presidents.		*Cashiers.*	
John W. Martin,	1833	Andrew W. Doig,	1833
Isaac W. Bostwick,	1843	Charles L. Martin,	1834
Lyman R. Lyon,	1844	Lyman R. Lyon,	1842
Isaac W. Bostwick,	1845	S. D. Hungerford,	1844
Lyman R. Lyon,	1846	Andrew W. Doig,	1845
		Ela N. Merriam,	1846
		F. W. Grannis,	1852

Statistics as reported annually near the beginning of each year:

Years.	Loans and Discounts.	Circulation.	Total Resources.	Years.	Loans and Discounts.	Circulation.	Total Resources.
1834,..	$116,610	$86,242		1845,..	119,038	97,097	248,407
1835,..	211,484	129,525	$259,116	1846,..	136,787	97,117	223,227
1836,..	245,315	192,656	349,607	1847,..	147,165	101,824	255,649
1837,..	245,882	172,538	355,300	1848,..	166,057	128,807	276,898
1838,..	196,890	147,066	311,123	1849,..	....	117,912	
1839,..	238,108	139,679	308,519	1850,..	....	149,997	
1840,..	236,896	128,555	329,461	1851,..	....	149,988	
1841,..	228,248	137,754	321,180	1852,..	....	48,981	
1842,..	204,763	97,422	274,878	1853,..	....	99,987	
1843,..	162,710	72,864	257,232	1854,..	....	149,995	
1844,..	114,366	72,452	229,239				

The Martinsburgh Library was formed at the house of John Atwater, Feb. 10, 1807, and Nathan Cheney, John Atwater, John McCollister, David Shumway, Truman Stephens, Enoch Bush and Horatio G. Hough, were chosen its first trustees. A good selection of about two hundred volumes was made, and the library was continued till the spring of 1835, when it was broken up and distributed among its remaining shareholders. Asa L. Sheldon, was for many of the later years the librarian.

A wooden building two stories high and furnished with a small cupola, was built in the village in 1828, for an academic school and probably with the ultimate design of obtaining an incorporation. The expense was defrayed by subscription, and the property was to be managed by trustees elected by the contributors. The first Trustees were Rev. David Kimball, John B. Hill, David Waters, Edward Bancroft, Philo Rockwell and Enoch Thompson. It was opened as a young ladies' seminary by Miss M. S. Williams, June 15,

1829, and a few years after was used as an infant school. Calvin B. Gay, the Rev. Calvin Yale and others have taught at different times and scarcely a winter has passed without a select or other school being taught. Since 1854 it has been used as a district school house.

RELIGIOUS SOCIETIES.—The first church edifice in the state north of the Mohawk, was erected in Martinsburgh, in 1806, chiefly through the aid of Gen. Martin, who defrayed the principal share of the cost, and sold out pews to families as opportunities offerred. The first Presbyterian society of Martinsburgh, was formed Dec. 9, 1810, the original trustees being Walter Martin, Levi Adams, John McCollister, Chillus Doty, Chester Shumway, Nathan Cheney, Elizur Stephens, Ephraim Luce and Barnabas Yale. The society began with forty-seven members. The edifice was painted by subscription, and furnished by Gen. Martin with a bell in 1827 in return for the compliment of naming the town after him. It was thoroughly repaired in 1832, furnished with an organ in 1838, again repaired in 1853, and burned by lightning, on the morning of Aug. 1, 1854.

The first bell weighed alone about 800 lbs. and cost $400. It was broken in the fire, and the old metal exchanged in part for the present one, which weighs (with the yoke) 1556 lbs. and cost $450. Both were from Meneeley's foundry in West Troy. The site of the church was not deeded to the society until 1818. A new church edifice was erected in 1858 on the site of the former, at a cost of $3000, and dedicated in November of that year. A parsonage belonging to the society, was burned, Oct. 15, 1849.

The first religious meetings were held by missionaries, in private houses, and afterwards in the school house on the brow of the hill south of the village. The Rev. Mr. Clinton of Lowville, and others preached occasionally in the meeting house, but none were regularly hired until about 1809, when the Rev. Elijah Norton, an old man from Litchfield, N. Y., was hired a few months.[2]

The Rev. Aaron Jordan Booge from Galway, N. Y., having preached a few times, was invited to become the stated supply of the society, Feb. 19, 1810, for a term of four years, from the first of November, preceeding. That he might be "free from worldly cares and avocations," the trustees promised to pay $250 per annum in quarterly in-

---

[2] He had been a prisoner with the Indians in the Revolution, and is remembered as a man zealous in his labors, but somewhat intolerant towards other sects, especially the Methodists. It so happened that an only daughter became an earnest believer in the creed of these people, and chose to leave the paternal roof, rather than relinquish her religious faith.

stallments. He accepted, but stooping to meddle in politics was silenced. While endeavoring to retrieve his position, he yielded in an evil hour, to a besetting sin.[1] The Rev. Mr. Mandeville was next employed a short time, when the Rev. James Murdock was installed first pastor Feb. 11, 1812, and remained about seven years.[2] The Rev. David Kimball accepted a call Dec. 6, 1821, and was ordained pastor of this church and that of Lowville village, June 24, 1822. He continued in this relation until Oct. 19, 1830, when he was dismissed at his own request.[3] After employing one Fisk, a few months, the Rev. Leicester A. Sawyer was engaged, and on the 12th of Oct., 1832, he was installed.[4] He remained about three years and was succeeded by the Revs. Loring, Bushnell, and Joel Osborn in 1835–6, and by the Rev. Calvin Yale, as pastor from 1837 to Feb. 11, 1841.[5] The Rev. Erastus S. Barnes[6] was pastor from Sept. 13, 1841, to to Aug. 24, 1846. His successors have been, the Rev. Herbert W. Morris, from March 8, 1848, to Feb. 1, 1850; Rev. Joseph Rosecrans, stated supply from 1850 to March 8, 1852; Rev. Revilo J. Cone, (do.) from July, 1852 to Feb. 20, 1854; Rev. Samuel L. Merrill from June, 1854 to June, 1857. The Rev. R. A. Wheelock of Deer River has been employed on alternate sabbaths since April, 1859.

This church, originally Congregational, was changed to Presbyterian, Jan. 9, 1812. In the fall of 1830, and winter following, a remarkable revival occurred, and a larger num-

---

1 Having rode to Turin on the 4th of July, he was seen walking home on the 5th with his garments covered with mud and his saddle on his shoulder. He enlisted as a chaplain in the army June 16, 1813, and was disbanded April 14, 1818.

2 Mr. M. was a native of Saybrook, Ct., graduated at Yale College in 1774, in the same class with Mr. Booge; came to Lewis county March, 1805, preached some time in Turin and Constableville. From Martinsburgh he went to Gouverneur, and in 1839 to Crown Point, where he died at his son's residence, Jan. 14, 1841, aged 86 years.

3 Mr. K. was born in Hopkintown, N. H., March 18, 1791, learned the printer's trade at Concord, fitted for college at Phillip's Academy, Andover, graduated at Yale in 1818, and directly after entered the Theological Seminary at Andover. In 1821 he came to this town, and in January, 1831, removed to Plainfield, Mass. He publishes a newspaper at Hanover, N. H., at the present time.

4 Mr. S. was a native of Burrville, Jefferson county; graduated at Hamilton College in 1828, and began his ministry here. He has since become known as an author, and has published a new translation of the New Testament.

5 Mr. Yale was from Kingsboro, N. Y. He graduated at Union College in 1812. Since the dissolution of his pastoral relation with this church, he has preached at Lowville, Watertown, Brownville, and other places, but now resides in this town.

6 Mr. B. was from Gouverneur. He graduated at Amherst College. From this place he went to Chazy, but has since resided in this county and Oneida several years.

bers were added to the church, than at any similar period before or since. A sabbath school has begun in 1821, in connection with this church, and held at first at private houses, in different parts of the town. Over a thousand have been connected with it first and last, as teachers or scholars, Mr. Ezra Botsford has been many years its superintendent.

Methodist meetings were among the earliest held in town, and stated preaching was had by appointment many years before a legal organization was effected. The M. E. church in this town was made a separate circuit from Lowville in 1840, since which the circuit preachers have been: 1840–1, Jas. Erwin; 1842, J. E. Downing; 1843, Lorenzo D. Stebbins; 1844–5, Allen O. Wightman; 1846, Hiram Shepard; 1847–8, H. O. Tilden; 1849–50, Benj. S. Wright; 1851–2, Eleazer Whipple; 1853, W. B. Joyce; 1854–5, R. E. King; 1856–7, L. L. Palmer; 1858, G. W. Elwood, S. B. Shepard; 1859, M. H. Church, A. T. Copeland.

The First Meth. Ep. Ch. of Martinsburgh, was legally formed Sept. 4, 1831, with Abner Clapp, Elijah Baldwin, Sedgwick Coates, Burrage Hough, John C. Hough, Arnold Clapp and Samuel Gordon, Jr., trustees. A stone church was built in 1832, on the brow of the hill east of the state road and on the south border of the village, and dedicated in Jan., 1833. After being used a dozen or fifteen years it fell into decay, and upon the erection of churches in other parts of the town it was discontinued, sold and taken down. A Meth. Ep. church was built adjacent to the clerk's office in Martinsburgh village in the summer of 1857.

The West Martinsburgh soc. of the M. E. Ch., was formed Jan. 30, 1840, with Lobdell Wood, Moses Talmadge, Giles Easton, Henry McCarty, Norman Gowdy, Henry Miner, Henry Curtis, Noah N. Harger, and Moses M. Smith, trustees. In the summer of that year their present church was erected, and about 1846 was furnished with a bell.

The 2d M. E. ch. and soc. of West Martinsburgh was was formed Sept. 8, 1840, with D. Seymour, Joseph Brown and Wm. Peebles, trustees. A small church edifice was erected on Chapel hill, so called, west of the village

A second Advent society in West Martinsburgh village, erected a house of worship in 1851, but meetings have not been regularly continued.

A Baptist church was formed at the school house a mile and a half south of the village, on the 27th of June 1818, under the advice of Eld. Stephen Parsons. It at first consisted of seven members, and worshiped in the school house until the erection of a church in 1825. In 1840, it removed to the village where its meetings have since been held. The first settled minister was Eld. Samuel Marshall, who was ordained Mar. 13, 1822. Elders Martin Salmon, Riley B. Ashley, L. S. Baker, Charles Graves, John B. Ambler, O. Wilbur and others, were afterwards employed.

A Free Communion Baptist Church was formed by a council of delegates from Russia, Lowville and Turin, convened at Martinsburgh Oct. 17, 1818. It continued in existence until about 1840, when by death, removal, and union with other churches it had become so reduced in number, that but four females attended its last covenant meeting. Elder Russell Way, of Turin, was the minister under whom this church was chiefly formed and continued. The sect is considered as extinct in this town.

The Martinsburgh United Baptist Society, was formed Nov. 6, 1824, with Daniel Pitcher, Enoch C. Johnson, Norman Griffis, Jonathan Searle and Daniel Ashley, Jr., as trustees. In 1825 it erected a church edifice one and a half miles south of the village, which continued to be used on alternate Sabbaths by the two Baptist churches about fifteen years, when it gradually fell into decay, until, at length, every vestige has disappeared. The Martinsburgh Baptist society, was formed Sept. 30, 1839, with Levi Bronson, John Waters, Shepard Lee, Samuel Miner, James M. Sturdevant, and David Griffis, trustees. In the year following, a new church was erected in Martinsburgh village, and the congregation worshiping in the former edifice removed thither.

A church was built at Glensdale in 1853, by the joint efforts of the Protestant and Episcopal Methodists, and dedicated Jan. 4, 1854. The society owning this was legally formed April 25, 1854, under the name of the People's Church, Jerrard Stiles, Wm. Glasgow, Alfred Arthur, Walter Hubbard, and Wm. Olivers, first trustees.

A number of persons known as Unionists, professing to be held together by no creed or covenant but such as the scriptural belief and the conscience of every member might dictate and approve, associated in 1857, under the Rev. Stephen P. Taft in Martinsburgh village, and on the 12th of April, 1858, organized themselves into a corporation, styled "The Trustees of the Church of Martinsburgh," of which Charles Peebles, Horatio Hough, Lewis A. Pitcher, Warren A. Peebles, Diodate Pease, Perry S. Hough, Martin Sheldon, Mithra J. Reed and Charles E. Peebles were first trustees. In the summer of that year, they erected a small but neat Gothic chapel for worship on the eastern border of the village.

MONTAGUE.

This town was formed from West Turin by the Board of Supervisors, November 14, 1850, embracing Township 3, or *Shakespere*, of the Boylston Tract. The first town meeting was directed to be held at the school house near Roswell Parmenter's.

Supervisors. — 1851–3, Wheaton Burington ; 1854–60, Joseph M. Gardner.

Clerks.—1851, Stephen A. Green ; 1852–3, Elias Sears ; 1854, Leonard G. Savage ; 1855, Alfred Green ; 1856, Alson C. Rounds ; 1857–8, George D. Moffatt ; 1859, Bildad Woodward, jr.

A bounty of $3 was voted for the destruction of bears, in 1854.

This town was subdivided into 117 lots by Benjamin Wright in 1805. The courses and distances of its boundaries are as follows:

W. side,	north,	533 ch.,	15 lks.	(1795).
N. "	S. 81° E.	551 "	25 "	(1805).
E. "	south,	550 "	36 "	(1795).
S. "	N. 80° W.	554 "		(1795).

The lines of 1795 were run by Medad Mitchell.

This town was named from Miss Mary Montague Pierrepont, a daughter of Hezekiah B. Pierrepont former owner of this town and of large tracts in this and adjoining counties. This lady presented a set of record books to the town in consideration of the compliment. She died in Brooklyn in January, 1853.

The first agent charged with the care of this town, was Dr. Samuel Allen of Denmark, who effected nothing. In 1838, Mr. Henry E. Pierrepont, went with Allen upon the tract, and left arrangements for opening a road from New Boston in Pinckney, southward across this town, but nothing was done, until 1844, when Harvey Stephens of Martinsburgh, then agent, got a road opened. He died the next year, and in August, 1845, Diodate Pease, of Martinsburgh, was appointed agent, and has since continued in efficient service. This town remained the undivided property of the Pierrepont family until 1853; when the east half excepting the parts previously conveyed, fell to the share of Joseph J. Bicknell, and the west half to James M. Miner, both of whom had married daughters of Hezekiah B. Pierrepont.

The first settler was Solomon Holden, who in the fall of 1846, moved into the town with his family, and wintered in a shanty on the land of Foster P. Newton. There was no other family in town during this winter. The first land was taken up by Newton, May 30, 1846, but he never resided in town. Lands were also booked to several others in the year 1846, but they never were known as settlers. Alonzo Garnsey purchased May 10, 1847, and resided a year or two at Gardner's Corners. Joseph M. Gardner became the first merchant, and from him the settlement known as Gardner's Corners was named. A saw mill was raised by S. P. Sears, in the fall of 1847, and finished in July 1848.

Samuel P. Sears, Calvin Rawson, G. Savage, Peter Durham, Oliver Stafford, S. A. Green, Wm. D. Bucklin, Isaiah Burr, Alonzo Garnsey, and Zebulon Marcellus were among the first settlers in this town.

In September, 1848, when Mr. Pierrepont visited the town, 4000 acres were contracted, and 600 deeded. In 1850, 13,000 acres were sold, 40 miles of road were laid out, and a saw mill was in course of erection on Deer river. There were then 100 inhabitants upon the town. Montague P. O. was established about 1856. Most of the settlers were from St. Lawrence and Jefferson counties. The town is about two-thirds taken up by actual settlers. The first death of an adult person was that of Caleb Green, Jan. 23, 1854.

The first framed school house was built in 1850. There are now seven school districts in this town, the first teachers in which were as follows:

Dist. No. 1, Jane Johnson; No. 2, Sarah Kramer; No. 3, Sarah Hart; No. 4, Mary Ann Ten Eyck; No. 5, Anna H. Bent; No. 6, Mrs. Terrill; No. 7, Ellen Terrill.

Religious Societies.—Two Methodist societies were formed in 1851, and one in 1857. A Baptist society was formed in 1854, but none of these have yet erected a house of worship.

NEW BREMEN.

This town was formed from Watson and Croghan, March 31, 1848, with its present boundaries. The first town meeting was held at the house of Charles G. Loomis. Its name was probably applied to render it attractive to European emigrants.

Supervisors.—1848–50, Bornt Nellis; 1851, David Cleveland; 1852–4, B. Nellis; 1855, Roswell Bingham; 1856–7, B. Nellis; 1858, R. Bingham; 1859–60, Jerome Kilts.

Clerks.—1849–50, Squire H. Snell; 1851–8, Jerome Kilts; 1859, Nicholas Gaudel.

Panther and wolf bounties of $5 were voted in 1848. The population of this town when erected, was 1345, of whom 1030 were from Watson and 315 from Croghan. Of the whole number 753 were Europeans.

Settlement began under title derived from the New York Company by Jacob Oboussier, clerk to Tillier, resident agent of the French proprietors. His improvement was made about a third of a mile below the present Illingworth bridge, on the banks of Black river. Oboussier went off about the beginning of this century, leaving some of his property in the hands of Samuel Illingworth,[1] and was never again heard from. He is supposed to have been drowned in the Ohio river, on a journey to the French settlements in Louisiana. The title to his tract was contested by Le Ray, as representative of the French proprietors, upon the ground that Tillier had exceeded his powers in selling more than fifty acres in one tract, and the courts sustained the prosecution by setting aside the claims of Gilchrist, who had acquired the title.

Illingworth remained many years the only inhabitant within the town. His location on the river bank rendered this a convenient crossing place by persons on hunting and fishing expeditions into the forest, and a point familiar to all who passed up or down the river, as was more frequently done when the country was new, and the roads in wet seasons nearly impassable. No effort was made to bring these lands into market until 1821, when Charles Dayan of Lowville was appointed agent by James D. and Vincent Le Ray, for the sale and settlement of some twelve thousand acres, east of the cardinal line, and afterwards of other lands, to the west.

The village of Dayanville was so named by Le Ray, in compliment to this agent. It was surveyed in the fall of 1824 by Jason Clark of Plessis, who, in commencing, found it necessary to trace one of the lines from the river. The party had reached Crystal creek just at sunset, and were preparing to cross the stream and encamp on the opposite bank for the night, when they were startled by the howl of a pack of wolves in their rear. There is something peculiarly dismal in the cry of this animal, especially when heard by night, and the idea of sleeping in this lonely place was especially unpleasant to some of the younger members of the party, who could not be prevailed upon by any argument to remain. They accordingly returned to the settlements on the river, and resumed their labors the next morning.

---

1 Mr. I. was an Englishman. He died May 4, 1847, aged 86 years.

This village is situated on Crystal creek, about one and a half miles from Black river, in the midst of a very level region of light loaming soil, which extends south into Watson and with but moderate undulations, north eastward to the Beaver river. Improvements began about 1826, and one of the first erections was a saw mill. A rake factory was built about 1840 and run several years, and a grist mill in 1847. The first merchant in the village was Samuel Stevens. About 1853 a building, 40 by 100 feet, was erected for a machine shop, in anticipation of the completion of the Sackets Harbor and Saratoga rail road, the route of which passes near, and the work on which had been commenced. The premises remained idle until 1859 when an addition of 40 by 150 feet was made to it for the purpose of a tannery. The firm conducting this business is S. Branaugh & Co., who have fixtures sufficient to tan from 35,000 to 40,000 sides of sole leather annually. Half a mile below are a saw mill, shingle machine, sash shop, cheese box factory and a small manufactory of cotton batting. The village has a methodist church, a large school house of two stories, and about thirty dwellings. The post office was changed in May, 1848, from Dayanville to New Bremen.

At Beaver falls, on the north border of the town, is the gang saw mill and a manufactory of lath and shingles of Prince & Co., formerly known as Rohr's mills.

A small part of the village of French Settlement is in this town. A lager beer brewery has been built two miles above Dayanville on the same stream, and a potato distillery in the north part, near Beaver river. This is, we believe, the only distillery in the county.

The bridge, near Illingworth's place, was built by Thos. Puffer about 1833, and a bridge has since been maintained at this place. The supervisors, Nov. 15, 1850, authorized the town of New Bremen to borrow $1,400, to be repaid by nine equal annual installments, to aid in rebuilding this bridge. The town of Lowville was allowed to borrow $975 for a like purpose, and the state constructed the abutment on the east side, the pier next adjacent and the draw between them. The other two piers, the west abutment and the superstructure, were built at the expense of the two towns.

Religious Societies.—The Methodists had held meetings in this town several years before a church was erected. The large school house in Dayanville had been built with reference to use as a house of worship, but difficulties were interposed by a claim of rent, and on the 19th of Feb.,

1849, a legal society was formed as the First Methodist Episcopal church of New Bremen, David A. Stewart, Griffith Meredith, Peter Van Atter, Wm. Holmes, Egbert Arthur, John Wakefield, Frederick Ford, Simeon Dinslow, and Alexander Y. Stewart were chosen first trustees, and a church edifice was completed and dedicated Sept. 20, 1849, at a cost of $1,206. A camp meeting, held in August, 1848, near the village, by appointment of the B. R. Conference, contributed to strengthen this society. The preachers stationed here have been, 1849–50, O. C. Lathrop; 1851, L. L. Adkins; 1852, Benj. Brundidge; 1853–4, T. D. Sleeper; 1855–6, T. G. Whitney; 1857, B. E. Whipple; 1858–9, O. Holmes.

A Lutheran and a Catholic church were built about 1850, the former on the road to the French Settlement, and the latter on a road leading east from Dayanville.

OSCEOLA.

This town was formed from West Turin, Feb. 28, 1844, in accordance with a vote of that town, embracing townships 8, or *Rurabella*, and 13, or *Hybla*,[1] of the Boylston Tract. The name was applied at the request of a young lady in New York,[2] in memory of the celebrated Seminole chief, whose career forms an important item in the history of Florida. This warrior was a half breed and was first known by his father's name *Powell* but received the title of *As-se-o-la* (as pronounced in the original dialect), because he could drink a greater quantity than others of a drink of this name taken preparatory to the fast and feast of the green-corn dance. He arose to the rank of chief by the force of his native talent, and began and continued the bloody wars which for years wasted the southern frontiers. The superior numbers and discipline of our troops having turned the war against the savages, Osceola with a train of seventy followers, came into the camp of Gen. Jessup in October, 1837. They were detained and sent prisoners to fort Moultrie, near Charleston, where he languished and died in the January following. His detention has been severely censured, but facts seem to indicate that his intention was to capture the place and release some prisoners had he found it practicable, but if not, to return and continue the war.

---

1 Hybly was a town in Sicily. Rurabella is a hog-latin term for "fine country."

2 Miss Jay, now Mrs. Henry E. Pierrepont of Brooklyn. She presented a set of blank record books to the town for the name.

The Indians had been told, that when willing to remove, they should be received and protected, and they were made to understand, that they could not return when they once came in. Osceola's party under these circumstances could claim no alternative but removal.

Some of the settlers proposed to call the town *Greenfield*, in compliment to the resident agent, but upon suggestion of the present name, it was approved at a public meeting called for the occasion.

Supervisors.—1844–8, Seymour Green; 1849, John Marsden; 1850–2, S. Green; 1853, J. Marsden; 1854–6, S. Green; 1857, Henry E. Griffin; 1858, Anthony Rowell; 1859, J. Marsden; 1860, Wm. Rowell.

Clerks.—1844, John Roberts; 1845–6, Roswell A. Hubbard; 1847, Washington Shorey; 1848, R. A. Hubbard; 1849–50, David Dunn; 1851–2, James Roberts; 1853–4, James Mitchell; 1855, Jairus Rowe; 1856, Henry E. Griffin; 1857, Henry J. Baker; 1858, John Gibbs; 1859, John Bain.

The survey of the outlines of township 13, were made as follows:

W. line North, 687 ch., 65 lks. (1795). M. Mitchell.
N. " S. 80° E. 764 " 19 " (1795). " "
E. " S. 30° W. (1795). W. Cockburn.
S. W. (Patent line), N. 68° 50′ W. (1794).

Area 37,041 1-2 acres by Wright's survey. Length of lines, 204 miles, 70 lks. Cost of survey, £204 17s. 6d.

It was subdivided by Benjamin Wright in 1795, into 151 lots, and re-surveyed in 1839. The note book of Moses Wright, an assistant who was running a line in this township in 1797, has the following entry which sets forth some of the hardships of a land surveyor:

"This 9th day of October, it being Monday, had the pleasure of running all day in the coldest rain I ever was sensible of. The rain that fell the day before yesterday, last night and to-day, raised the brooks and creeks over their banks, and what gave me the worst feeling is, that the hard, pinching hand of Poverty, seven days ago took all the rum." In another place the weary and rumless engineer records: "Lots 112, 113: 30 chains up the highest hill that ever was. 5,000,000,000 feet high." Had he stopped seven cyphers short, he might have represented with exaggeration, the rise from the flats of Salmon river to the high lands which border it, but his hand once started on the cyphers, he let it run!

Township 8 was subdivided into 111 lots, by B. Wright in 1805, and contains $28,419\frac{53}{100}$ acres. While surveying in this region in 1795, Mr. Wright remarked, that the beavers were building a dam on the north branch of Salmon river, that would flow 400 acres of land.

In December, 1795, a negotiation was pending for the purchase of township 13 by John Bernard of Rome, who proposed to form a company for this object. The price then proposed was two dollars per acre, payable by installments in four years, with interest from April 20, 1797. The bargain was not closed from the inability of Bernard to find associates.

In 1805 a road was cut out from Fish creek across township No. 1 (now Lewis), and 13 and 8 in this town, to the line of 7, with the design of intersecting the state road in Redfield, but the north end and the portion south of the Macomb purchase were never cut out, and the route soon relapsed into the state of nature. It entered township 13, on lot 137, and in township 8 crossed lots 96, 85, 84, 73, 62, 61 and 50. In the fall of 1805 James Constable and Hez. B. Pierrepont, two of the executors of the estate of Wm. Constable, crossed these towns by this road, and the journal of the former will be read with interest.

"Sept. 7. After breakfast set off from Fairservice's (in Western) towards Fish creek, the first two miles passable for teams, but the rest of the distance to the creek not cut out at all, but it is easy ground and not heavily timbered, and the people promised to do it this fall without fail Forded the creek, and on the other side our road begins. The ascent from the creek very well done, and the cutting appears to be according to agreement, although the clearing out of the timber is occasionally neglected. The soil of the whole of No. 1 is very indifferent, the timber mostly hemlock except sometimes beech or a hard mossy birch, the face of the country uneven and ridgy though not much stony. I fear it will not settle speedily. The southeasterly part of No, 13 not much better, though we have occasionally some better timber, ash, bass, &c. As we advance to the Salmon river we find better land fit for settlers; some good swales and very little hemlock. Forded the river, it being here a small stream, and there being some grass for our horses we stopped to bait them and ourselves. A fire being soon kindled each man cut his slice of pork, toasted or fried it, and we made a hearty meal. The brandy brought with us and the water made a good drink. Passed on, the land improving till we came to the 13 and 14 mile tree, to a good spring and a brook where there was a good hut of the road makers, and although we might have gone two or three miles further before dark, yet Fairservice being doubtful whether we should meet such good accommodations, it was determined to remain here for the night. Another cause was, that we got some hay for the horses. We made our fire, cooked our pork and made our meal with an excellent appetite. Our horses were not neglected.

Sept. 9. After sleeping pretty soundly till daylight, the weather seemed likely to turn to rain, and we resolved to proceed on through the road so far as to insure our getting to Redfield in the course of the day, as the provisions would not hold out longer. Went on to the 18 mile tree, and at another hut prepared and ate our breakfast of pork and bread, with brandy and water for tea. I found these articles less palitable at this meal than the others, however the pork improved (?) very mildly. We went down the road some miles further, leaving No. 13 and going on to No. 8, and found the latter very good land, such as settlers will not refuse. The road is equal to roads as new as it is. The weather looked threatening, and to be sure of reaching Redfield in good time, we took a course southwest to strike the state road, and coming to a good stream which was at first supposed to be Salmon river (it is certainly a branch of it), as it afforded some grass for our horses we thought it a proper place to halt and refresh. Accordingly dinner was provided as usual; we ate heartily, and finished the last of our brandy. We had now to pass through the woods, the south part of No. 7 and north part of Redfield, which was very difficult to ourselves and dangerous to our horses, from the swamps and heavy fallen trees covered with underbrush. We struck one of the main branches of the river, but the brush and fallen logs prevented us from keeping the bank, and the high ground was a hemlock ridge which occasioned us much trouble, but after a good deal of fatigue we came to the state road about two miles from Ingraham's, when it began to rain and we were nearly wet through before we got there. The rain did not continue long, and we set out for Johnson's tavern in Redfield, half a mile beyond Butler's, where we arrived early in the evening a good deal tired with this day's journey. It is a better house than Butler's, and we were well provided for in supper and sleeping.

Sept. 9. Mr. Pierrepont having occasion to see a man who lived off the road respecting his lands in No. 13, set off very early intending to follow us on to Rome, but having found the man near, he came and joined us at breakfast, and we all set off together. They are working upon the road and improving it much. The causeways are mostly new laid and covered three inches with sand or other earth, so that the travelling on them is equal to any part. Stopped at Lyman's, 11 miles, and at Waring's near Fish creek, but we decided to eat the last dinner cooked by ourselves in the woods at the creek and went there, having bought some brandy on the way. The weather was very hot, but after kindling a fire and bathing in the creek, we ate with as good an appetite as ever. After dinner we paid and discharged Fairservice, and set off for Rome, intending to see the new causeway lately finished near that town, but the road not being cut through, we had difficulty to get to it. We succeeded, and it was worth the pains. The length is two miles, of equal sized logs 18 feet long and covered with earth, so that the travelling is excellent. Arrived at Rome late in the evening. Not liking the thought of White's beds we slept in the hay-loft, and made out pretty well."

Portions of townships 1 and 13 were sold by Wm. Constable, July 25, 1801, to John Jones, John McVickar and John Rathbone of New York, in payment of notes and endorsements of Wm. and Jas. Constable, to the amount of $95,704.50. Lynde Catlin received a conveyance, Jan. 28, 1804, of the whole or a greater part.[1] At the time settlement begun about two-thirds of No. 13 were owned by the Pierrepont family, and the remainder by G. Lynch, —— Goddard, —— Bush, J. W. Taylor, J. Lawrence, —— Gentil, —— Stewart, Jefferson Insurance Co., —— Pratt, G. Smith, —— Lyndes, S. Stevens, J. and E. McVickar, L. Catlin, Bishop Moore and Wm. Constable, together amounting to 51 scattered lots.

Township 8 was divided among the Pierrepont heirs Jan. 1, 1853, as follows: To Wm. C. P. lots 17 to 19; 28 to 31; 39 to 44; 50 to 86; 92, 93, W. part of 94, 95, 96, 110 and 111. To Maria T. Bicknell, 87 to 91; 97 to 109; Seymour Green, agent. To E. G. Miner, 1, 2, 6, 7, part of 3 and 8; D. Pease, agent. To M. C. Perry, (in trust) parts of of 4, 5 and 8; 9 to 16; 20 to 27; 32 to 38; 43 to 49; D. Pease, agent. A few settlers have located upon the extreme N. W. corner, but the remainder of that township is still a wilderness. One Saunders was the first settler in this part of the town.

The first persons who came into this town were Jabez Green, Christopher Divine and Harvey Potter, who located on lot 138 about 1822, without title, but did not remain. Samuel W. Nash also located soon after, a little above, but not permanently. In 1826 one Clark burnt off a windfall, a

[1] Deeds Lewis county, A, 53.

mile south of Salmon river, and planted corn, which yielded abundantly, but was claimed and entirely harvested by bears. This wind-fall was the track of a tornado that had passed across the town three years before, and the fire, when applied, ran through it with tremendous energy, sending up columns of flame and smoke, which were observed to an immense distance, the former by its reflections upon the clouds at night, and the latter by its dense sombre masses by day.

The first agent of the Pierrepont estate in this town was James S. T. Stranahan of Brooklyn, but then of Florence. Settlement was delayed by various causes, among which was the failure of the proprietors of scattered lots, to unite in an agency for the opening of roads and other improvements necessary for bringing the town into market. In July, 1839, Seymour Green was appointed Pierrepont's agent in No. 13, with power to sell lands at $1.50 cash, or $2 on a credit of four years. A road was marked out from Florence village northward, nearly across the township, and reports favorable to the tract gaining currency in the surrounding country, the landless rushed forward to secure a homestead with such avidity, that between the first of September and Christmas, nearly 18,000 acres were sold under contract with the intention of settlement. The north part of Redfield (No. 7 or *Greenboro*) was opened under the same agency, and in the above period 1000 acres were contracted upon that township. In May, 1840, the proprietor, in six days, issued 68 contracts and 22 deeds, and received $4,000 in cash. The lands sold amounted to 11,996 acres, and the price to $25,219.35. The following winter was unusually severe, and in 1842 half the lands sold had reverted. As there were no town officers accessible for laying out roads, whatever was done in this line, devolved upon Mr. Pierrepont, the owners of scattered lots being generally indifferent as to these improvements. In 1843, there were 250 inhabitants, two school houses and 60 children. In 1848 1,600 acres were under contract, and 5,491 acres were deeded. In 1850 there were 400 inhabitants in town. The settlers were mostly from the older towns around. Several families came from the factories at Oriskany, and some from the public works upon the suspension of 1842. The northern part of No. 13 is called Vermont Settlement, from the original locality of the settlers. The first family that actually settled with title, on township 13, was that of Robert Russell, on lot 139, in December, 1839. They wintered here alone, and in the spring were joined by Ira and Thomas Hulbert and others. Roswell A. Hubbard, Wm. G. Smith,

Lyman Wellman, David Shorey, Silas A. Fox, Henry J. Baker, Anthony Rowell and others, were also early settlers. Mr. Green,[1] the agent, settled in 1842, and at the first town meeting in 1844 there were 37 voters. The first birth was that of Russell Chase, the first marriage that of Captain Edward Humaston and Jane Smith, and the first death that of Agnes Russell, a child, eight years of age. The first school was taught in 1844 by Jerusha Wetmore, and the first two framed school houses were built in that year. The town has now five framed and one log school houses, and two joint districts, of which the school houses are in Redfield. A road, authorized by law in 1859, has been laid out by S. Green and D. Pease from the Vermont Settlement to Martinsburgh, a distance of about twelve miles from one clearing to the other, and about 23 miles from the court house to Osceola village. At present the distance around is about 70 miles by the nearest public thoroughfare and over 50 by the nearest passable road.

The principal business point in town is at Osceola village and post office, or as it is usually called The River, situated in the deep narrow intervale of Salmon river, five miles from Florence and thirteen from the W. and R. R. R. station at Camden. It has three inns, a store, school house, saw mill, large tannery and about a dozen dwellings. The first saw mill in town was built by Wm. Roberts in 1841. A tannery, 200 feet long, was erected on the south bank of Salmon river in 1859, by Cowles, Sliter & Co., for the manufacture of sole leather, chiefly from Spanish hides.

An Independent (Congregational) religious society was formed in 1850, but there is no church edifice.

PINCKNEY.

This town embracing township No. 9, or *Handel*, was annexed from Mexico to Harrisburgh, Mar. 24, 1804, divided in the erection of the county in 1805, the eastern part being retained by Harrisburgh, and the western attached to Harrison [Rodman]; and finally erected into a separate town Feb. 12, 1808, with its present limits. It was named by the legislature, doubtless in honor of one or all of the three illustrious citizens of South Carolina of this name.

---

[1] Mr. G. is a native of Washington county, and when he received the agency was living in Oneida county. A political opponent many years since, applied to him in derision the title of the "Osceola chief," which has been accepted among his friends, and by which he is widely known. As supervisor, assemblyman and local magistrate, he has taken an active part in public affairs.

Gen. Thomas Pinckney, his brother Charles C. or William, were alike worthy of the honor.

The first town meeting was held at the house of Stephen Hart, but as the early records were burned in 1826, our knowledge of the earlier town officers is derived from other sources.

Supervisors.—1808–9, Ethan Green; 1810–4, Stephen Hart; 1815, Augustus T. Wright; 1816, S. Hart; 1817, G. Waite; 1818–20, S. Hart; 1821, James Hunt; 1822–3, E. Green; 1824–6, S. Hart; 1827–8, J. Hunt; 1829, Benjamin Jeffers; 1830–1, S. Hart; 1832–4, J. Hunt; 1835, Tyrannus A. Wright,[1] J. Hunt; 1836–7, John Spencer; 1838–43, John Lucas; 1844, Joseph Boynton, Jr.; 1845–8, John Newkirk; 1849, Jehiel H. Hall; 1850, J. Lucas; 1851–3, Hamilton Cobleigh; 1854–5, Gilbert E. Woolworth; 1856–7, Phineas Woolworth; 1858–9, Samuel H. Tolles; 1860, John Paris.

Clerks.—1826–8, James Armstrong;[1] 1829–30, John Spencer; 1831, J. Armstrong; 1832–5, J. Spencer; 1836–43, J. Armstrong; 1844–6, Lewis M. Burtch; 1847–8, Jehiel H. Hall; 1849, John Lucas; 1850–5, Samuel H. Tolles; 1856–9, Blodgett Stoddard.

In 1826, 31, 2, 5, a bounty of $10, in 1838, of $15, and in 1834 of $5, was offered for wolves. In 1841, a bounty of $5, and in 1845, of $10, was voted for the killing of bears. In 1834, crow bounties of one shilling if killed in May and June, and 50 cents for foxes within the year, were voted at town meetings.

This town fell to the share of Wm. Henderson, who employed Abel French, and afterward Jesse Hopkins and others as agents. Henderson died about 1824, and Wm. Denning, his brother-in-law, subsequently became principally concerned in the title, and under the Denning family most of the town has been sold. But small remnants now remain in the hands of the former proprietors. From B. Wright's field book of survey around the town in the spring of 1796, we derive the first estimate of its value which was as follows:

"This town is a pretty good one and is extraordinarily well watered with large and small streams. There is a pretty large creek towards the S. E. part of the town known by the name of Deer creek on which probably there are fine mill seats, although I have seen none. A large gulf where the Deer creek crosses the east line of the town. Along the north line of this town there is some very fine land. The soil in general is good and

1 Made ineligible by ordination. Hunt was elected November 6, 1835.

2 Mr. A. died December 7, 1853, aged 74 years.

well watered. There is some gulfs on the branches of Big Sandy which are rather bad. The timber is maple, beech, basswood, ash, birch, elm and hemlock. Along the E. line is very fine soil for about half the distance, from the N. E. to the S. E. corner. The soil is not so good but rather more cold. Some hemlock interspersed in some places with spruce, &c. Along the south line the land is rather cold, some excellent spots but some swampy and bad. The timber is maple, beech, birch, ash, hemlock, bass and some elm, &c.; along the west line there is a very fair country except that it is cut to pieces with small streams which form gulfs."

The outlines of this town lie 9° from the principal cardinals, and its area is 25,045 acres. The first survey gave its N. line 506 chains, its E. 490, its S. 508, and its W. 498. The whole town is elevated from 400 to 800 feet above the level region around Copenhagen, and from many places the blue hills east of Black river, and the waters of lake Ontario with the vessels upon them, may both be seen. The horizon in a serene day, is more clear and bright than in the plains below, as we find in elevated regions, and a perceptible difference is observed in its climate. Haying comes on an average about a week later than in the adjacent town of Denmark, and snows have been observed over six feet deep on a level in the woods. The winter of 1854–5, was remarkable for the depth of snow on this town. Drouth is however, seldom noticed, and the soil is finely adapted to grass and coarse grains, and since the introduction of dairying, the inhabitants have rapidly acquired the means of comfortable support, and a steady increase in wealth.

The streams flow east, west and north from this town, which is entirely underlaid by the Hudson river shales. Weak sulphur springs are common, and were formerly frequented by deer. Game was abundant in early times, especially deer, bears and wolves, the latter of which often proved destructive. Trout were common in the streams when the town was first settled.

Usage has sanctioned the use of the preposition *on*, when speaking of residence or the occurrence of events in this town, as for example a man is said to live *on Pinckney*. This application is by no means peculiar to this town, although perhaps more generally used than in the neighboring towns of Jefferson co. The early land holders adopted the custom of speaking of such and such persons, as living *on* their towns, as we speak of tenants *on* a farm. Hence living *on Pinckney* or being *on the town*, does not imply all that would be understood elsewhere. Although there are over 1000 persons *on the town*, but a very small number are paupers.

Settlement began on this town about 1803, Samuel and Joseph Clear, located in the S. W. part, but soon went off. In 1804, Ethan Russell and J. Greene from R. I., and one or two years after, John Lucas, Levi and Elisha Barnes, Stephen Hart,[1] James Armstrong,[1] James Hart,[1] Phineas Woolworth,[2] Joel Webb, Silas Slater, and several Stoddard families became settlers. The first birth was in the family of James Hunt or John Stoddard, and an early death if not the first, was that of Mrs. Elisha Moody. The first school was taught by Miss Gould, before the war.

There are three post offices on this town. *Pinckney* P. O., at Boynton's corners, *Cronks Corners* P. O., and *Barnes' Corners*. The latter is the only locality in town that has pretensions to the name of a village. It is situated on Gulf creek, a branch of Sandy Creek, and has two churches, a steam saw mill, a saw mill using water power, a small tannery, a few mechanic shops, two stores, an inn, and a dozen houses. The village is quite recent and considerably scattered.

The stream a little below descends into a ravine worn in the slate rock, which presents scenery of some interest. From a swell of land a short distance west, there is presented an extensive view of the lake, and a wide expanse of country north and west.

New Boston is a neighborhood on the Deer river, where it is crossed by the Lowville and Henderson state road. The first improvement was made here by David Canfield, who acting as agent of Henderson, made an extensive clearing and built a bridge and saw mill. About eighty acres of wheat were sowed the first season, which yielded bountifully, but the death of Henderson and other causes prevented the extension of these improvements. Dr. S. Allen was associated in this enterprise and the locality probably receiveded its name from them. The state road although opened through soon after 1816, fell into disuse, until quite recently. It is now well settled and considerably travelled.

A large part of the business of this town tends to Watertown, and the remainder to Copenhagen.

A small social library was formed on this town at an

---

[1] From Stillwater, N. Y.

[2] Mr. W. was brother of Levi, and uncle of Elijah, Justus and Reuben Woolworth, who settled in Turin. He removed from Grayville, Mass. in 1806, and had six sons and three daughters, several of whom became heads of families in this town.

early period, and at one time numbered about two hundred volumes. It was broken up, and the books distributed several years before the introduction of school district libraries.

Religious Societies. — The First Methodist Episcopal Society of the town of Pinckney, was formed Aug. 8, 1831, with Tyrannus A. Wright, Stephen Hart, Rufus Stoddard, Timothy Woolworth and Barney Spalding as trustees. A framed meeting house was erected near Boynton's corners, and is still in use. It was the first, and until recently, the only church edifice in town. The first religious meetings on this town, were held by traveling preachers of this sect. A small Baptist church was built at Barnes' Corners, in 1854, and a Methodist church in the year following. New Boston Mission, of the M. E. Ch. was formed in 1851, supplied at the discretion of the presiding elder, except in 1854, when J. Hall was assigned to this place. A Roman Catholic church was begun on the State road, about one and a half miles west from New Boston, in 1856, but it is not yet completed for use.

TURIN.

This town was formed from Mexico, (now in Oswego Co.), March 14, 1800, including all of the present county of Lewis, west of the river, between Inman's triangle and the south lines of Lowville, Harrisville and Pinckney.[1] It was named from the capital of the kingdom of Sardinia, in Italy, probably upon the suggestion of Nathaniel Shaler, agent and proprietor, under whom the town was settled. Martinsburgh, or townships 4 and 5 of the Boylston Tract was taken off in 1803, another part annexed to that town in 1819, and West Turin was taken off in 1830, reducing it down to its present limits. The statute ordered the first town meeting to be held at the house of Jonathan Collins, at which Jonathan Collins was chosen *supervisor*, Samuel Hall, *clerk*, John Ives, Zaccheus Higby and Philemon Hoadley, *assessors*, Seth Miller and John Salmon, *overseers of the poor*, Nathan Coe, Wm. Rice and Levi Hough, *commissioners of highways*, Elijah Wadsworth, *constable and collector*, Lemuel Scovil, Gershom Birdseye, Edward Johnson, Levi Benedict, Abner Rice and Heman Merwin, *overseers of highways*, Aaron Parsons, *pound master*, Ichabod Parsons, John Salmon,[2] and Elisha Orofoot, *fence viewers*.

---

[1] Redfield, Watertown, Lowville and other towns were formed by the same act.

[2] Died July 26, 1813, aged 56. He lived on the east road.

Supervisors.—1800, Jonathan Collins; 1801, John Ives; 1802–4, Eleazer House; 1805, J. Collins; 1806, E. House; 1807–8, J. Collins; 1809, J. Ives; 1810, J. Collins; 1811, Hamlet Scranton; 1812, Ebenezer Baldwin; 1813, J. Ives; 1814, Levi Hart;[1] 1815, Oliver Bush (Deuel Goff,[2] Sept. 26, 1815); 1816, D. Goff; 1817, E. Baldwin; 1818–9, J. Collins; 1820, Walter Dewey;[3] 1821–2, James McVickar; 1823, Leonard House; 1824–9, J. McVickar; 1830–5, Eli Rogers, Jr.; 1836–9, Royal D. Dewey;[4] 1840–4, Leonard H. Humason; 1845–6, Pardon C. Case; 1847–9, Joseph House; 1850–2, Winfield S. Whitaker; 1853–4, Judah Barnes; 1855, J. House; 1856, Charles G. Riggs; 1857–60, Emory B. Holden.

Clerks.—1800–3, Samuel Hall; 1804–17, Levi Collins; 1818–9, Ebenezer Baldwin; 1820–42, Amos Higby, Jr.; 1843, Henry Paige; 1844, Orrin Woolworth; 1845, Harrison Barnes; 1846–7, O. Woolworth; 1848, Horace R. Lahe; 1849, Charles D. Budd; 1850, Charles G. Riggs; 1851, Walter B. Foster; 1852, Albert H. Litchfield; 1853–5, Harrison J. Thayer; 1856–7, Henry A. House; 1858–9, John O. Davis; 1860, Arthur Pond.

If there has been anything that distinguishes the civil history of this town from all others, it is the unusual number of special town meetings that were held during the earlier years. At the first town meeting Jonathan Collins, Philemon Hoadley, John Salmon, John Ives, Zaccheus Higby, Seth Miller and Judah Barnes were appointed a committee to report a place for future town meetings. They reported the next year, that on the first Monday of May preceding, they had set a stake on the lot of Ebenezer Allen, as the most convenient point for this purpose. This locality was near the old Episcopal church north of Constableville.

---

[1] *Judge Levi Hart* was an early and prominent settler, and in 1818 represented the county in assembly. He was many years a judge of the county court. He died June 30, 1834, aged 61 years.

[2] *Judge Goff* was a pioneer settler. He died at Houseville, September 8, 1852, aged 68 years.

[3] *Dr. Walter Dewey* was the first physician who settled within the present limits of Turin. He was a son of John Dewey of Leyden, and was born in Westfield, Mass., August 20, 1785. He built the first house in Turin village in 1803, and in two or three years removed to Collinsville, where he died February 28, 1821. He was skillful in his profession and generally esteemed.

[4] *Dr. Royal Dwight Dewey*, a cousin of the above, and son of Aaron Dewey, was born at Westfield October 3, 1791, and removed with his father to Franklin, Delaware county, N. Y., where he lived till 1809. He studied medicine with Walter Dewey, at Collinsville, attended lectures at New York and Fairfield, was licensed July 13, 1812, and after practicing in company with his preceptor until 1816, settled at Turin village. He died November 13, 1839. He was appointed a justice of the peace and post master in 1818, and held both offices several years.

In 1802 the town voted to petition for two men for magistrates, and that Judah Barnes and Samuel Hall be the two men.

A call signed by 15 freemen led to a town meeting, Sept. 25, 1802, at which Walter Martin, Eleazer House and Wm. Rice were appointed to consult with delegates from other towns, as to whether there should be two half shires, if a county is set off. On the 25th of Oct. 1802, Jonathan Collins was chosen a delegate to prepare, circulate and forward a petition for a turnpike road from Whitestown down the Black river. In December of that year the town decided not to send a delegate to the legislature with the petition above named, and agreed upon the erection of a new town on the north which was done at the next session.

In December, 1803, Jonathan Collins, John Ives and Ezra Clapp were chosen delegates to a meeting at Denmark, in January, 1804, to discuss plans for a division of Oneida county. In February another meeting was called in Champion, for a like purpose, and J. Collins, E. Clapp and Z. Bush were sent as delegates from this town.

The location of the state road in this town between Halliday's tavern and Dan Taylor's, now A. R. Lee's residence, excited the most active opposition of conflicting interests, and led to several town meetings, at one of which the town clerk was directed not to record the road, and the town voted to indemnify the clerk and road commissioners in any suit that might be brought in consequence of said road not being recorded. They resolved : "that this meeting views with indignation and concern, the shameful and improper conduct of the commissioners in laying and establishing the state road through Turin, in which they have neither consulted the interests of the inhabitants generally nor the town of Turin in particular."

The present village of Turin has since been built upon the proscribed section, and more than a mile of the new road led over a causeway through swamps, which were not brought under cultivation until many years after. A line of well cultivated farms, owned by substantial farmers, had before this been established along the east and west roads, and the location of the commissioners between them was very naturally regarded as hostile to almost every resident interest in town. Their opposition however was unavailing and the new section of road was soon found to offer a more central and convenient point of business than had before been found in the town.

A*

The same year it was voted to remove all foreigners from the town, unless they gave bonds with two sureties to indemnify the town against all charges during their natural lives; to apply to all who had not gained residence.

In 1812 a fine of $10, and in 1816, of $5, was voted for allowing Canada thistles to go to seed.

The division which gave a part of this town to Martinsburgh in 1819 excited active hostility. A special meeting was called, and Geo. Davis, John Ives, Levi Hart, Oliver Bush and Eleazer Baldwin were appointed a committee to to draw up a petition to the legislature to regain the lost territory.

In 1823, a committee, consisting of Levi Hart, Heman Stickney and Leonard House, was appointed to circulate a subscription for a town house at the Four Corners, and another, consisting of Jonathan Collins, James McVickar and James Miller, 2d, for a like purpose, the location to be near the Episcopal church, north of Constableville. In May a special meeting received the reports of these committees, and decided in favor of the former, which united the plan of a town house and church. This resulted in the union meeting house hereafter noticed. In 1824 the wish of the voters upon a division of the town were tested by a vote which gave 40 for, and 200 against, the measure.

In 1836 a bounty of $5 was offered for wolves; the only instance in which this town has offered these premiums.

Turin embraces parts of townships 3 and 4, or *Pomona*[1] and *Lucretia*[2] of Constable's Four Towns. They were surveyed by Benjamin Wright in 1795, and by a deed executed Dec. 29, 1795, Wm. Constable conveyed to Nathaniel Shaler an undivided half of these towns at $2 per acre, and made him his attorney for selling the remainder in farms of 100 or 200 acres, for which he was to have half the profits over the price above named.[3]

Settlement was begun upon No. 4, at the village of Constableville in 1796, as will be more fully mentioned in our history of West Turin. As Mr. Shaler's mills, house and agency was located there, we have only to notice in this connection the settlement of that portion now embraced in this town. The early purchasers paid $4 to $4.75 per acre, and in 1803 new lands were held as high as $17 per acre in favorite localities. The first improvements were made on

---

1 Pomona was the goddess of fruits.

2 Lucretia was the wife of Tarquinius Collatinus, and associated with Roman history.

3 The profits of this speculation are mentioned page 27.

township 4, or the more eastern of the two, about 1797, by emigrants from Meriden and Middletown, Ct., who were joined in one or two years by quite a number from Westfield and towns adjacent in Massachusetts, among whom during the first three years were Edward Johnson,[1] Zaccheus and Amos Higby,[2] Elijah, Justus and Reuben Woolworth,[3] Thomas Kilham,[4] Levi and Stephen Hart,[5] Giles Foster,[6] Zaccheus Bush[7] and sons, Oliver, Walter, Edward, Henry, Enoch and Charles, John Salmon, John Wilkinson,[8] Winthrop and Gideon Shepard,[9] Judah Barnes,[10]

---

[1] *Edward Johnson* removed at an early day to Martinsburgh, near Whetstone creek. He died March 11, 1851, aged 92. He emigrated from Middletown, Conn., to Whitestown, N. Y., when about 30 years of age. He was a soldier of the revolution and a citizen highly esteemed.

[2] *Amos Higby* died at Holland patent, June 14, 1848, aged 95 years. He removed thither in 1843. Zaccheus Higby died February 13, 1816, aged 82 years.

[3] *Levi Woolworth*, uncle to the others, came in 1806 and died October, 1835. He was from Suffield, Conn. Elijah came in 1797, removed to Allegany county, in 1819, and died in 1828. Justus came in 1797. Opened the first inn at Turin village, September 1809, and died October 31, 1845, aged 71 years. Reuben came in 1800, and is still living. Orrin, George, Paris, Cornwell, Edward and Edwin, are sons of Justus Woolworth.

[4] *Thomas Kilham* was born March 23, 1752, and died April 25, 1825, from an opiate given in over dose by a drunken physician. His wife Mary died March 18, 1845, aged 93. Their sons, were *John*, who resides near Copenhagen, *James* and *Thomas*, who are dead, *Heman*, who died October 14, 1847, at his residence two miles north of Turin village, *Solomon*, who resides in Turin, and *Samuel*, who has been many years inspector in the government armory, at Harper's Ferry, Va.

[5] *Stephen Hart* died August 12, 1857, aged 90 years. He was from Wallingford, Conn.

[6] *Giles Foster*, died January 1, 1844, aged 87 years. His sons Sylvester, Isaac, Lyman, Chauncey and Johnson, and several daughters, became heads of families and mostly settled in town.

[7] *Major Z. Bush* died at Houseville, of cancer, November 21, 1811. Major Oliver Bush settled on the state road near the north line of the town. Served as major in the war of 1812–15, and died April 10, 1844, of the prevailing epidemic, aged 75 years. He was highly respected, and in every sense a useful citizen. *Walter Bush* died March 2, 1841, aged 66 years. *Henry Bush* died at Houseville, July 23, 1837. *Enoch Bush*, died August 28, 1849, aged 82 years. *Charles Bush* resided in Lowville, where he died February 21, 1852.

[8] *Mr. Wilkinson* came to Turin in 1798, and died in this town January 23, 1857, aged 89 years. When he settled his was the last house northward until we reached Lowville.

[9] *Captain W. Shepard* died September 24, 1854, aged 82, and his brother, *Major Gideon Shepard* died December 12, 1850, aged 81. Both served in the war of 1812–15. They were sons of the Rev. Charles Shepard of Westfield, and nephews of Gen. William Shepard, an officer of the revolution, and afterwards prominent in the suppression of Shay's rebellion in 1787. He died at Westfield, November 11, 1817. *George Shepard*, son of Winthrop, was sheriff of Lewis county, from 1846 to 1849. He died at Champion, May 1, 1853, on his way home from Kingston, and was buried in Turin with Masonic ceremonies.

[10] *Judah Barnes* was a son of Amos Barnes, who came on afterwards. These men built the first saw mill in the present town of Turin, in 1798. Judah

Dan. Taylor,[1] Consider Williston,[2] Jonathan Bush,[3] Thomas Ragan,[4] Levi Benedict,[5] Beekman Sabin, Geo. and Thomas Hoskins,[6] Elias Sage, Benjamin Dowd[7] and others. The Johnson and Higby families were from Middletown, Ct., the Bush, Woolworth, Shepard and Kilham families from Meriden, Ct., and Salmon, Wilkinson, Ragan, Benedict and Sabin, from Pawling, Dutchess county, N. Y.

Settlement upon township No. 3 was delayed until Oct. 1798 when Eleazer House,[8] Ezra Clapp,[9] Winthrop Shepard, David Kendall,[10] Alexander Cooley, and others, purchased on the east road opposite Houseville, in March, 1799; they returned and worked through the season. Mr. House built a saw mill, put up the frame of a house and barn, and in March 1800, moved on his family. He resided on the east road till 1808, when he moved to the place since known as Houseville. He kept an inn from his first removal till near the time of his death. He was active in opposing Clapp and others in the location of the state road, on the route finally chosen, and labored hard to secure a business point at his mill. A grist mill was built in 1816, and another many years after by his son, Leonard House. The latter stood on the present site of V. R. Waters' mill, and was built Feb. 10, 1851. An incident occurred near Houseville in the summer of 1808, which is worth preserving, as belonging to the primitive days of settlement. The country abounded in wild animals, especially wolves, bears and deer, and the former became so bold as to carry off on one occasion a sheep from the field of Mr. Clapp, by daylight, although

---

Barnes was a judge in the county court several years, and in 1808 '9, was in assembly. He died February 23, 1821, aged 67.

1 Settled on the Williston place, near Turin village. He died in this town October 1, 1813, aged 57.

2 Settled on the place now owned by Winfield S. Whitaker, and afterwards on that of Warren H. Kentner. He died September 20, 1851.

3 Died July 3, 1825, aged 80 years.

4 Died May 13, 1820, aged 63 years. 5 Died June 11, 1833.

6 *George Hoskins* died August 22, 1848, aged 66 years. He settled about 1801. Thomas died west.

7 Died January 6, 1852.

8 *Eleazer House* was born at Glastonbury, Conn., September 20, 1759; married December 25, 1782, to Miss Moseley, and held the first appointment of coroner north of Utica. He died January 30, 1833, and his wife survived only till March. His sons *Jared*, *Joseph* and *Leonard* are well known and prominent citizens of the county. Jared settled at Lowville, where he was many years an inn-keeper. He still resides at that place. *Anson House*, a lawyer, resides in Rochester.

9 *Ezra Clapp* was born May 28, 1760, at Westfield. Married February 22, 1781, to Grace Mather. Settled on the farm now owned by Wm. Thompson, where he kept an inn 30 years. He died in Westfield, Mass, June 17, 1838. Horace Clapp, Esq., of this town, is a son of Ezra Clapp.

10 From Suffield, Conn. He died April 22, 1847, aged 69 years.

Mrs. C. endeavored to frighten away the beast. Upon the date mentioned, Mr. Clapp found a large black wolf in a trap, half a mile west of the house, and with his neighbor's help, beat him with clubs until he was thought to be dead. He then took the wolf before him on horseback, and brought him to his barn, but as he evinced signs of life on the way, it was thought safe to secure him by a chain around the neck, the trap remaining upon his leg. Half an hour after the wolf was as active as ever, and the settlers upon learning the circumstance, assembled from far and near to indulge in savage sport with the chained enemy of their flocks. Many large dogs were provoked to attack him separately, but one snap from his powerful jaws sent them howling from the barn, nor could they be induced to approach a second time. Having wearied themselves with this brutal amusement, his captors at length ended his life by a rifle shot.

About 1812, several teamsters stopping at House's tavern, noticed wolf tracks about, and the party followed until they found the animal concealed under a log. He was killed by one of them with a hemlock knot, within a quarter of a mile of Houseville.

Deer were accustomed to cross over from the hills on the west to the forests east of the river, at the point known as Proven's Hill, at the gate-house of the Turin plank road, and also at a point half a mile south of Turin village. They would begin to appear late in the evening, and in the course of the night, hundreds would cross. On one occasion Mr. Clapp built a yard enclosed with a high tree fence on three sides, the fourth being a steep descent, and in one night forty deer were caught in this enclosure. As late as 1830, numbers of deer were shot at Proven's Hill. The last wolf hunt in this town, occurred in the swamp adjacent this place in the summer of 1836, when three or four of these animals were traced thither, but although many persons surrounded the woods, they mostly escaped.

An anecdote is told of a citizen of this town, who took a number of cattle to sell at Ogdensburgh soon after the war. Upon learning that the Canadians would pay a higher price, he crossed over to make a bargain. He asked a shilling per pound for beef, but could only get an offer for ten pence, and after wrangling a long time, he at length accepted. Upon being paid he was pleasantly surprised at receiving a much greater sum than was expected, for while he had been talking in New York currency, his purchaser was dealing in sterling money.

The first mill in Turin, was a stump mortar, made by Christopher Clobridge[1] in 1797, in the eastern border of the town, on the farm now owned by Nathan W. Douglass. To this the first settlers were accustomed to resort, when Shaler's mill at Constableville was not running. The first grist mill in the present town of Turin was built by Giles Foster, at the present site of Cadwell Dewey's mill, on the east road. It was once burnt. A somewhat extensive woolen cloth manufactory was established by Cadwell Dewey, a short distance below, which has been in active operation nearly a quarter of a century.

There are two villages and post offices in Turin. *Turin Village*, formerly known as *Turin Four Corners*, is a place of about 500 inhabitants, three churches, and limited facilities for manufactures.[2] It has six stores of various kinds, and is a place of considerable business for the country around.

The Turin Brass Band at this place was formed June 1, 1859, and numbers thirteen men.

Houseville has a church, an inn, a store, and about 100 inhabitants.

Schools were first established about 1801. The first measure taken for the visitation of schools was in 1807, when in the entire absence of law upon the subject, the town appointed the Rev. James Murdock, Elder Stephen Parsons, Deacon Timothy Hill, David Kendall, Ebenezer Baldwin and Richard Cone a committee to inspect schools.

Late in 1813 a special town meeting was called to organize schools under the law. The town was divided into eight districts. Oliver Bush, Levi Collins and Seth Miller, sen., were chosen school commissioners, and on the 1st of December the justices appointed Judah Barnes, Wm. Constable, Deuel Goff, Willard Allen, John Hooker and Dr. Walter Dewey first school inspectors.

The Turin Social Library was formed under the act of June 14, 1814, although a subscription had been started April 20 previous. In 1839 its prosperity ceased with the formation of school libraries, and in the fall of 1849 it was dissolved, and its books, about 600 in number, were divided among the proprietors. The first trustees were Levi Hart,

---

[1] Mr. C. was a Hessian, and had been in the British service in the revolution. He died May 8, 1844, aged 98. His son Adam, also a pioneer, died Nov. 2, 1849.

[2] The first steam engine set up in the county was at the tannery of Ethan Perry in this village.

Ebenezer Baldwin, Dr. Walter Dewey, Henry Graves,[1] Deuel Goff, John P. Kentner[2] and Martin Hart. During most of its existence it was kept with scrupulous care by Amos Higby, jr.[3]

Probably the earliest literary association in the county was formed in this town July 28, 1809, as a debating club. Their preamble read as follows: "For the promotion of literature, benefit of society, and advancement of useful knowledge in Turin, we the undersigned do form ourselves into a society with the title of *The Columbian Society*, and knowing that no society can flourish without well regulated laws and strict rules, we do all and each of us bind ourselves in penalty, declared in the following laws, to obey them in every particular, and further to promote the institution as lies in our power." The constitution was signed by Martin Hart, John Hooker, Levi Collins, Homer Collins, Urial Hooker, Chester Hoadley, Walter Dewey and Cordial Storrs.

We are not informed of the subsequent history of this "Institution," nor were the debates reported in any journal that we have seen. The first question discussed probably settled for all time the doubt as to "Which has been the most beneficial to society? the discovery and use of metals, or the labor and use of animals."

On the 30th of April, 1839, the Turin academy was incorporated but it was never organized. The trustees named in the act were Emory B. Holden, Geo. J. Fowler, Nathaniel Hart, Selden Ives, Leonard H. Humason, Orrin Woolworth, Charles G. Riggs, Cadwell Dewey, Albert A. White, Ozias Wilcox and Enoch Lee.

RELIGIOUS SOCIETIES. The first meetings were held by missionaries about 1800. A Congregational church was formed by the Rev. John Taylor of Deerfield, Mass., Sept. 19, 1802, while on a missionary tour. The first male members were Amos and Judah Barnes, Joshua Rockwell, John and Levi Ives, Timothy Underwood, Eliphalet Hubbard, Timothy Johnson, Heman Merwin, Seth Miller, David Pitcher, Timothy Hill, Reuben Pain, Samuel Smith, Jeduthan Higby, jr., Philemon Hoadley, George Palmer and Robert Lewis. About 40 females also united. The church

---

1 *Mr. Graves* was the first merchant in Turin village.

2 *Mr. Kentner* was one of the pioneers. He died November 11, 1836, aged 86 years.

3 *Mr. Higby* was many years town clerk, and resigned when he could no longer hold by unanimous election, as he had previously done. He was a man of exemplary life, eccentric in some respects, but still deserving and enjoying the fullest confidence of the public. He was of the Unitarian faith, and published two editions of a small book explaining his peculiar views of scripture. He died February 17, 1857, aged 63 years.

approved, March 8, 1808, of the articles adopted by the Black river association, and June 25, 1824, it joined the St. Lawrence Presbytery. It again became Congregational March 7, 1831. It joined the Watertown Presbytery, Oct. 5, 1852, and has since remained Presbyterian. The Revs. James Murdock, Reuel Kimball and John Iveson were employed between 1806 and 1830. In July 1841, the Rev. Nathaniel Hurd was installed as first pastor. The Rev. James Morton was employed in 1849, and the Rev. Wm. H. Adams in 1854, for one year. The Rev. Charles B. Pond the present minister, was employed in 1857. This church owned an interest in the union church, but in 1842, built a church on the north border of the village which cost $1500, and was dedicated Nov. 24 of that year. In 1859 it was extended 20 feet in the rear at a cost of $600.

Major John Ives, by will, dated Nov. 16, 1827, gave $300 to this church, of which two-thirds were to lie until it amounted to $1000. It has now reached that sum, and $70 are received annually from this fund towards defraying the pastor's salary.

The Methodists held meetings at an early day, and Turin circuit was formed in 1812, but given up three years after having been attended by Reuben Farley and Chandley Lambert. The 1st M. E. church of Turin was organized Oct. 5, 1818, with Jonathan Bush, Winthrop Weller, Orange Hill, Francis Crane, Stephen Hart and Charles Weller first trustees. They built a church in 1819 on the east road 3 miles N. of Turin village, which continued many years in use. In 1841 the plan of a new church at Houseville was discussed, and in 1842 it was erected by Elisha Wood, builder. The 2nd society of the M. E. church, of Turin, was formed May 20, 1833, from the former, having Ozias Wilcox, Sylvester Hart, Heman Stickney, Deuel Goff, Leonard H. Humason, and Sylvester Foster trustees. A stone church, 45 by 65 feet, was built in Turin village in 1834, at a cost of $3,500. It was extended 20 feet in the rear and rearranged in 1859, and rededicated Oct. 20 of that year.

The Black river circuit, originally embracing the whole country north of the Mohawk, was gradually reduced down to the Turin church, by the formation of other circuits. It was changed July 13, 1844, to the Turin circuit. The preachers assigned have been: 1833, C. Northrup, F. H. Stanton; 1834–5, Elijah Smith; 1836, R. Houghton, J. Downing; 1837, R. Houghton, C. H. Austin, W. Cummings; 1838, Isaac Puffer, E. Whipple; 1839, Darius Mason; 1840–1, John Roper, John Thomas; 1842, M. H. Gaylord, S. F.

Fenton; 1843, S. F. Fenton, Reuben Reynolds; 1844–5, Jesse Penfield; 1846–7, Geo. C. Woodruff; 1848, R. M. Barber; 1849, A. S. Wightman; 1850–1, Royal Houghton; 1852, D. M. Rogers; 1853–4, E. Smith; 1855, T. D. Sleeper; 1856–7, Isaac Hall; 1858–9, Cyrus Philips.

The Baptists formed a church at an early period, the major part of whose members became Free Communion, June 3, 1812, and kept up an organization about 30 years. Jeduthan and Zaccheus Higby, Abner Mitchel, Elijah Wadsworth, Tho. Hoskins, Ebenezer Baldwin, Lydia and Sarah Scovil, and Elizabeth Lane, formed its first members. A Baptist ch. was formed April 12, 1812, by the minor part of the former church, under Stephen Parsons. It agreed to unite with a Leyden ch., Dec. 20, 1816. The associated Baptist church was dissolved Jan. 17, 1818, having got reduced to 8 members. The Revs. Calvin Phileo, Simeon Hersey, Riley B. Ashley, Calvin Horr and others have been employed.

The Turin and West Turin Bap. soc. (old school) was formed March 22, 1842, with Newton Clark, Benham Webb; Jason and Edwin Payne and Horace C. Ragan, trustees; and the next year built a church in Turin village. This sect was formed here in the fall of 1843, under the Rev. Martin Salmon.[1]

The Welsh Cong. ch. at Turin was formed Nov. 5, 1843, by Rev. S. A. Williams of Deerfield, N. Y. It has increased from 9 to 37 members. D. E. Prichard, pastor, Robert Williams and John O. Jones, deacons. They built a church in 1847, on the hill west of the village, and they have a branch that worships in the Baptist church in the village. The legal society has formed May 1, 1848, with John L. Roberts, David W. Roberts, Robert Williams, Wm. Roberts, jr., and D. E. Prichard trustees. A Calvinistic M. E. ch. was formed July 23, 1848, and have a small church. In both of these Welsh churches, worship is held in the Welsh language.

As early as 1807, a religious soc. was formed to build a union church in Turin, but it failed. Its trustees were: Eleazer House, Oliver Bush, Richard Coxe, Timothy Hill, Judah Barnes and Seth Miller. A subscription was opened Nov. 23, 1823, for a union church and town house. It was

---

[1] The *Rev. Martin Salmon* was born in Pauling, Dutchess county. Came when a child to this town, and was many years a preacher in the Baptist churches of this region. He died September 13, 1847, aged 53 years. The O. S. Baptists in this town have sometimes been called from him "Salmonites."

incorporated under the general statute, Sept. 27, 1826, as the Turin Union society, with Levi Hart, Heman Stickney, Amos Higby, jr., Royal D. Dewey and Leonard House, trustees, and a house was built at a cost of $2,350. It was used alternately many years by the two Baptist and the Presbyterian churches, and as a town house. In 1846, it was changed to a school house. A bell was purchased in 1847, at a cost of $300, and first placed upon the union church, but it has been removed to a tower erected on a small lot opposite, belonging to the town. The latter premises afford a convenient place for keeping the town hearse.

WATSON.

This town was formed from Leyden, March 30, 1821, embracing all of Lewis county east of Black river. The first town meeting was held at the house of John Beach,[1] at which Caleb Lyon was chosen *supervisor;* John Beach, *clerk;* Ozem Bush, Phineas Cole, and Joseph O. Mott, *assessors;* C. Lyon, Thomas Puffer, and O. Bush, *commissioners of highways;* Samuel Smith and P. Cole, *overseers of the poor;* J. O. Mott and Daniel B. Baker, *constables;* S. Smith, *collector;* C. Lyon, J. Beach, and P. Cole, *commissioners of common schools;* C. Lyon, John Bush, and P. Cole, *inspectors of schools;* and O. Bush, T. Puffer and David Chase, *fence viewers.*

In this list we find the names of persons who lived in parts of the town remote from each other, and the same name several times repeated. The latter was occasioned by the small number of persons who possessed freeholds sufficient to allow them to hold office. This inconvenience led

---

[1] *John Beach* from Litchfield, Ct., settled in this town in 1814, and was the father of Nelson J. Beach, Esq. He died May 15, 1845, aged 75 years.

Nelson J. Beach came to this town when a lad with his father's family, and was many years a land surveyor in this region. In 1846 he represented the county in assembly, and in 1847 in the senate, but the constitution of 1846 coming into operation, his term in the senate was cut short to one year. In 1847 he was elected a canal commissioner, being one of the first three elected to that office, and in the classification of terms he drew that of two years. On the 11th of January, 1850, he was appointed a canal appraiser, and held about three years. He was subsequently employed in the engineering department of the Hudson River rail road, and at a later period was appointed to the trust of closing up the business of the Rome rail road, projected through this county. After several years residence at Rome, he has now returned to his seat on the banks of the Black river in this town. Mr. Beach is a man of acknowledged ability, zealous and energetic in whatever he undertakes, and well informed upon all subjects relating to public affairs. In regard to the question of the Black river improvement, in which his influence and official position have given his views importance, he has been the steady advocate of the construction of piers for narrowing and deepening the channel, and opposed to the plan of dams and locks.

to an act passed Feb. 6, 1824, authorizing white males, of legal age in this town to hold office, if they had *contracts* for land worth $150. There were, when the town was organized, 44 families, and 481 acres of improved land: 115 head of cattle, 18 horses and 107 sheep within its borders.[1]

Supervisors.—1821–22, Caleb Lyon; 1823, Joseph O. Mott; 1824–27, Ozem Bush;[2] 1828, Simon Goodell (May, 1828, O. Bush); 1829, O. Bush; 1830, Stephen P. Hamilton; 1831–34, Nelson J. Beach; 1835–36, Nathan Lewis; 1837–38, N. J. Beach; 1839–44, Ralph Beach; 1845, N. J. Beach; 1846, Jonathan Perry; 1848–51, R. Beach; 1852, Peter Kirley; 1853, Jehiel R. Wetmore; 1854, Daniel S. Andrews; 1855, Charles Chase; 1856–58, Chester Ray; 1859–60, P. Kirley.

Clerks.—1821–22, John Beach; 1823–4, Otis Munn; 1825–26, J. Beach; 1827, Archibald Benjamin; 1828, Joshua Harris (May, 1828, A. Benjamin); 1829–32, A. Benjamin, 1833, Charles Loomis; 1834–38, Anson Ormsby; 1839–43, Peter Munn; 1844, Thomas Kirley; 1845, John W. Merrile; 1846, P. Munn; 1847, T. Kirley; 1848, Squire H. Snell; (May, 1848, Peter Kirley); 1849–51, P. Kirley; 1852–55, Isaac C. Brown; 1856, Albert M. Gillet; 1857–58, James Garmon; 1859, Isaac H. Brown.

In no town in the county have so large bounties been paid for the destruction of wild animals as this. The records show a vote of $5 in 1827, 28, 32; $10 in 1825, 6, 8, 9, 30, 1, 6, 7, 8, 41, 2, 52 to 59, and $15 in 1835 for wolves; of $5 in 1828 to 36, 1842–6, and $10 in 1839, 40, 1, 57, 8, for panthers; of $2 in 1833 to 8, and 5 in 1841, 2, for bears; of 50 cents in 1833, 5, 6, for foxes, and of 50 cents in 1833, 5, for crows killed between May 15 and June 15. Whether the relief thus obtained from the ravages of these animals, or the knowledge that a large portion of the bounty was raised by *tax upon wild lands*, was a governing motive in these votes of town meeting we may not perhaps be allowed to decide.

Watson was named from James T. Watson, the proprietor of a tract of 61,433 acres lying in this town and in Herkimer co. James Watson, the first owner under Constable, was a native of Litchfield, Ct., and a wealthy merchant in N. Y. during and subsequent to the Revolution. He held a

[1] The census of 1825 gave 121 families, 357 males, 338 females; 89 liable to military duty, 128 electors, 4 aliens and 4 colored. There were 1437 acres improved, 529 neat cattle, 55 horses, 460 sheep, and 307 swine.

[2] Contested by S. Goodell in 1826–7, as hereinafter stated. Mr. Bush was a pioneer settler of the county, and died in this town March 20, 1845, aged 70 years.

captain's commission in the war, served the State in several important offices, and died in 1808 or 9. His only son *James Talcott Watson,* made the first attempt to settle these lands, and for many years was accustomed to spend his summers in the county. He was a man of fine education and affable manners, and in early life was a partner in the house of Thomas L. Smith & Co., East India merchants, in which capacity he made a voyage to China. The death of a Miss Livingston, with whom he was engaged to be married, induced a mental aberration which continued through life, being more aggravated in certain seasons of the year, while at others it was scarcely perceptible. In after life the image of the loved and the lost often came back to his memory, like the sunbeam from a broken mirror, and in his waking reveries he was heard to speak of her as present in the spirit, and a confidant of his inmost thoughts.

In his business transactions, Mr. Watson often evinced a caprice which was sometimes amusing, and always innocent. This was, by most persons, humored, as tending to prevent any unpleasant result, which opposition might at such times have upon him. In the summer of 1838 he undertook to cultivate an immense garden, chiefly of culinary vegetables, upon his farm in Watson, beginning at a season, when, under the most favorable conditions, nothing could come to maturity, and insisting that he would be satisfied if the seeds only sprouted, as this would prove the capacity of his land.

In his social intercourse Mr. Watson often evinced, in a high degree, many noble and manly qualities. With a lively fancy and ready command of language, he had the power of rendering himself eminently agreeable, while many of those who settled upon his tract, will bear witness that he possessed a kind and generous heart. But there were moments when the darkest melancholy settled upon him, utterly beyond relief from human sympathy, and in one of these he ended his own life. He committed suicide with a razor, in New York, Jan. 29, 1839, at the age of 50 years. His estate was divided among 39 first cousins on his father's side and 5 on his mother's, and some of these shares were still farther subdivided among numerous families. The sixty thousand acres, when divided, gave to a cousin's share over 1,600 acres, but some parcels amounted to but 33 acres. Much of these lands have since been sold for taxes.

The Watson tract formed two triangular areas, connected by a narrow strip, of which the outline was surveyed by Wm. Cockburn in 1794. The west triangle was surveyed out by Broughton White of Remsen, in 1808, and the east one by N. J. Beach in 1842.

A large part of the west, and all of the east tract, is still a forest, and much of it towards and beyond the county line, is chiefly valuable for its timber. There is a tradition that Low offered Watson $16,000 to exchange lands, before either knew any thing of the soil, or the relative value of their purchases, which time has shown to belong to the two extremes of agricultural capacity.

At the date of organization there were no roads in Watson, connecting the upper settlements near Lyonsdale, with those opposite Lowville, and for many years the only way of passing from one part to the other was by the roads on the west side of the river, from fifteen to twenty miles around, or upon the river itself. It was therefore a desirable object to secure the location of town meetings, which could not possibly be located so as to accommodate more than a part of the voters. In 1824 the town meeting, held at the house of Daniel Wheaton, at Lyonsdale, was adjourned over to the same place.

The northern section was numerically the strongest, and the next year privately rallying their full force, some from the extreme parts of what is now Diana, attended at the appointed house, which was, at the time, uninhabited, and the barn empty. They opened at 9½, an hour earlier than usually opening town meetings, three justices and the town clerk presiding, and on the pretense of the want of accommodation and inclemency of the weather, adjourned over to the next day at the house of Thomas Puffer, in what is now Watson, and 20 miles from Lyonsdale.

The southerners, upon assembling, found the town meeting stolen, but upon weighing all the circumstances, concluded to go on as if no accident had happened, and called upon a justice present to organize the meeting The latter refused to do so, and the electors proceeded in their own way, elected a full set of town officers and adjourned for one year to the same part of the town. The northern party met the next day, pursuant to adjournment, also elected a full set of town officers, and *probably* adjourned over to the same neighborhood.

During *four years* two town meetings were thus annually held, and a double set of town officers elected. Both supervisors appeared at the county board, and the one from the northern part alone was admitted, and the collector from this part alone received his warrant from the board. The town officers in the southern part received no pay for their services, and their authority in local affairs was limited to their own section, and by sufferance rather than law.

In March, 1828, the upper party quietly mustered their whole force on the night before town meeting day, agreed upon their ticket, and leaving at home a few old men, barely enough to conduct their own meeting, they set out before dawn with a dozen sleigh-loads of voters to assist their rivals in electing town officers. The expedition was conducted with the most profound secresy, and the enemy were taken by surprise. To have contested the passage at the ferry might have been easy, had not the ice furnished a bridge for crossing, or to have privately dispatched a small party to capture the town meeting left behind in charge of the veterans would have been feasible had not the distance prevented.

The result showed a striking unanimity at the two town meetings, the same persons being elected throughout and the adjournment of both being to the same place in the extreme south part of the town. Resolutions for a division had been voted in 1822–4–5–6 and 7, the latter by the northern party recommending Beaver river as the boundary line. In 1828, both town meetings voted against any division until the southern town officers had been paid for their services, but before another town meeting the question of division was settled by the legislature.

A suit brought by Goodell against Baker in the Lewis Circuit, Dec. 14, 1826, before Judge Williams, in a suit of trespass *de bonis asportatis*, for having distrained the plaintiff's horses for a tax, assuming to act as collecter under authority of the northern town meeting, was decided in Goodell's favor. The defendant appealed to the Supreme Court for a new trial, which was granted in February, 1828, and the case as reported,[1] gives the circumstances of the adjournment, and the opinions of the Court briefly as follows:

The people at town meetings may determine the place of holding town meetings from time to time, and may adjourn to a second day and another place if they judge necessary. There could be no injury to the rights of any as all might attend. They were exclusive judges of the occasion; and although they might have been indiscreet, their act was still legal and the officers they elected at the adjourned meeting were legally chosen and the proper town officers.

Both parties voted in their town meetings to raise money to protect the rights of the town, and in Watson the *poor*

---

[1] *Cowen's Reports*, viii., 287.

fund belonging to the town was voted to be applied to this law suit.

Settlement was begun within this town by Eliphalet Edmonds and Jonathan Bishop, who received deeds of Tiller, agent of Castorland, on the 10th of October, 1798, for 100 and 162 acres respectively, at $2 per acre. The lots were surveyed by J. C. Chambers, and the settlers began small improvements on the banks of the river but did not long remain. The former in the fall of 1799, took up land in Adams, and the next spring became a pioneer settler in that town. Isaac Puffer[1] and family soon after settled in this town, and were for several years the only inhabitants. He was the first purchaser under Watson, and built a saw mill for the proprietor on his tract near Chase's lake. In 1807, Melancthon W. Welles became the first agent of Watson, and under his direction surveys were made in Watson's west triangle by Robert McDowell soon after. Unexpected difficulties prevented Mr. Welles from forming a successful settlement at that period, and a few years after he relinquished the agency.

The first agricultural operation of any magnitude was by Puffer, who in 1811 burnt over the great windfall on the plains east of the present bridge; and planted corn. The season was favorable, and the yield among the logs was over forty bushels to the acre. Settlement advanced many years but slowly, and many of those who undertook improvement were of the poorer class, who possessed neither resources nor tact in encountering the difficulties which the wilderness presented. In 1823, over twenty Wurtemburghers were sent on by Watson, who paid their passage and winter's subsistence upon condition of three years' services, but most of them left in the spring. This is believed to have been the only attempt made by this proprietor to settle Europeans upon his lands.

Many hundred tons of bog iron ore were taken from this town to the Carthage furnace. The boat used had a burthen of from fifty to fifty-five tons, and made two trips a week.—It floated down with the current, and was pushed up stream by poles.

In former times the settlers in Watson were much an-

[1] *Isaac Puffer* was from Princetown, Massachusetts, but had resided about ten years in Otsego county. His family were *Isaac, jr.*, (afterwards celebrated as a Methodist preacher,) Sally (Mrs. D. Tiffany), Asa, Ebenezer, Thomas, Polly (Mrs. Russel Stone), and Josiah. Some of these brothers have been successful hunters, and Ebenezer Puffer has killed 47 wolves (five of the black variety), and bears, deer, and other wild game "in proportion." Isaac Puffer, sen., died about 1836.

noyed by wolves, and it was found difficult to keep sheep on this account. It is said upon good authority, that 52 sheep have been destroyed by a single wolf in one night.—A most remarkable event was reported as happening in this town, July 27, 1839, nine miles east of Lowville. The house of James Ranney was left in charge of a girl twelve years old, and a child a little over a year old was sleeping on a bed in an adjoining room; hearing the child scream, the girl sprang to the door and saw a wild animal leap from an open window with the infant in its mouth. She followed about forty rods, thinking it was a large dog, till it reached a pair of bars, where, after several times trying to leap over with its burden, it made off into the woods without it.—The child was not seriously injured. The animal proved to be a huge male panther.

An affray occurred in this town Aug. 21, 1829, between Samuel Shaw and Wm. Myers, in which the former received several large wounds from a knife. Myers was sent to state prison. He had evidently intended to provoke a quarrel, and to kill Shaw as if in self defense.

On the 13th of March, 1837, Isaac G. Puffer, a young man, was accidentally shot by an intimate companion and playmate of childhood, who thoughtlessly presented a gun supposed to be not loaded, and telling him to prepare for death, discharged its contents, killing him instantly.

The only capital execution that has hitherto occurred in Lewis county, was that of Lawrence McCarthy, for the murder of his father-in-law, Asahel Alford of this town, Nov. 15, 1838. Mr. A. had been living with McCarthy sometime, and a difficulty had been known to exist between them. One day when the two were alone, the murderer approached his victim while writing, and killed him with an axe, drew him with a horse by a chain fastened around his legs to an unfrequented spot in the woods, buried him slightly with stones and brush and returned. A snow soon covered the trail, but suspicions led to a successful search, and "Larry" (as he was commonly called) was indicted for murder on the 13th of December, tried on the 13th of June, before Judge Gridley, and hung in the court room at Martinsburgh on the 1st of August, 1839.

In the interval between the sentence and the execution, fears were entertained that the Irish laborers upon the canal at Boonville would attempt the rescue of their countryman, and threats to this effect were freely made. To provide against this, a volunteer company was formed at Martinsburgh, under Elijah L. Thompson, and armed from the state arsenal at Watertown. Sentinels were stationed around the jail, and arrangements were made for resisting any attempt that might be made. The "Larry Guards" and a rifle company escorted the prisoner to the gallows and guarded the Court House while the execution was progressing, and an immense crowd were drawn together by a morbid curiosity to witness the preparation, although but a few were enabled to observe the final crisis.

A few weeks before this execution, the Rev. Michael Gilbride, a Catholic priest of Carthage, applied for a private interview with the condemned, and was refused access, unless in the presence of the jailor. In this refusal the sheriff had followed the letter of the statute, and the advice of the district attorney. The priest at once made personal application to the governor for his interposition or authority, and the latter addressed a lengthy letter to the sheriff, which scarcely amounted to more than his advice to place a charitable construction upon the law. Whether this letter was designed for the public eye may be surmised from the fact, that it was published in the papers before it was received by the sheriff.

In July 1849, extensive damage occurred in this town from running fires in the woods, and an extremely dry season seldom occurs without a liability to this accident. In 1822, a settlement was begun in the eastern border of the town, on No. 4, Brown's Tract, by David Barber and —— Bunce. In 1826, Orrin Fenton settled, and is still with one exception, the only settler living in that part of the town. The station is highly convenient to parties hunting in winter, and fishing in summer, and is chiefly supported by them.

A Union Library was formed in this town July 14, 1829, with Nathan Snow, John Fox, Daniel C. Wickham, Joseph Webb, jr., Francis B. Taylor, Hiram Crego and Lansing Benjamin, trustees. It never became successfully organized.

A ferry, regulated by the law of public convenience, formed the first, and until 1828, the only means of crossing the river with teams in summer to this town. It was owned and kept by the Puffer family. In 1821, those interested in lands east of the river, attempted to raise the means to erect a bridge, but nothing was effected. The question continued to be under consideration until Feb., 1828, when Ozem Bush, Thomas Puffer, J. C. Herrington, Lemuel Tooley and Daniel B. Baker, were designated as trustees to receive subscriptions for a free bridge, and an appeal was published, urging the importance of the proposed measure.

As a further stimulus, an act was procured, March 29, 1828, allowing Nelson J. Beach to erect a toll bridge, and to hold the same twenty years, unless a free bridge was built before Jan., 1829. These efforts were successful, and a frame bridge was built by Tho. Puffer and finished Aug. 6, 1828. In 1832, a draw was placed in the bridge at the expense of the towns of Watson and Lowville, and a few years after, the bridge was rebuilt at the expense of the two towns.

An act passed Jan. 20, 1851, authorized a loan of $1,000 by the town of Watson, to be repaid by a tax, in from two to five years, and a loan by Lowville of $975, to rebuild the Watson bridge. The piers, abutments and draw, were built by the state in a most thorough and permanent manner, and the money raised by the two towns was applied upon the wooden superstructure of the bridge.

The balloon "Excelsior" landed in the top of a hemlock tree on the land of Mr. Nye near Passenger's mill, late in the afternoon of August 3, 1859. It contained Prof. C. C. Coe and C. H. Hull, and had made the passage from Oswego in a little over two hours. It passed over Adams, Harrisburgh, Lowville and Martinsburgh at a great elevation, and it was the intention of the æronants to gain the sea board. Perceiving the immense stretch of forest which lay beyond them to the eastward, they hastened to descend, and finally landed with much peril.[1] This was the first balloon ever seen in the county except those made of paper, and inflated with air rarified by heat. Of the latter the first were sent off about 1837, at our principal villages, by an itinerant juggler as the afterpiece of his performances.

Religious Societies.—The earliest meetings here were held by the Methodists, and in 1834, this town first appeared on the conference minutes as "to be supplied." The numbers then claimed were 77. The Plains M. E. church was incorporated May 12, 1854, with Reuben Chase, Ira A. Stone, Eben Blakeman, Ebenezer Puffer and Adam Comstock, trustees, and the present church edifice was erected the same year. The first minister whose name appears on the minutes as assigned to this charge was the Rev. Isaac Puffer, who had spent a part of his early life in this town.[2]

---

[1] Mr. Coe at the agricultural fair in Rome, Sept. 29, 1859, made an ascension in the presence of 10,000 spectators, and at the height of two miles his balloon burst. By a happy coincidence of circumstances, the descent was made in safety, but soon after Mr. C. received a serious injury in getting his balloon down from a tree which has disabled him perhaps for life.

[2] The *Rev. Isaac Puffer* was born in Westminster, Mass., June 20, 1784, and in 1789, removed to Otsego Co,, and in 1800 to Lewis Co. In 1809 he was received on trial in the N. Y. Conference and appointed to Otsego Circuit with-

Richard Lyle was stationed in 1844; H. O. Tilden in 1845–6; A. S. Wightman in 1847–8.

The Seventh Day Baptists formed a society in this town, May 2, 1841, but have never erected a house of worship. Their first trustees were Burdick Wells, K. Green, Daniel P. Williams and Joseph B. Davis. In 1846, they claimed 73 communicants. They now consist of about 20 families, and the school in their district is held but five days in the week.

WEST TURIN.

This town was formed from Turin, March 25, 1830, including besides its present boundaries Montague, Osceola, High Market and all of Lewis except the portion taken from Inman's triangle. While the plan of a division of Turin was in prospect, the old town was offered townships 3, 8 and 9 by the parties desiring to be set off, and a committee was sent to Albany with a map upon which was marked the course of the hills and the extent of settlement. The county was then represented by a citizen of Turin village who regarded the wild lands then attached to the town as poor; and reasoning upon the principle that poor lands make poor settlers, and that the poor tax of the town would be proportioned accordingly, refused to listen to any plan which left these lands with the old town. The parties asking for a division yielded without a struggle the point which secured to them over $350 in non-resident taxes annually, and the old town's people displayed a black flag at half mast and evinced other signs of displeasure upon receiving news of the division.

The lands rated as poor had not then seen the peep of day, for the dairying interest had not begun to be developed, and tracts which as yet, from their elevated location, had failed to succeed in grain, might have been well regarded as destined to afford a meagre profit to the farmer. These very lands are now found admirably adapted to grazing, and less liable to drouth than the lower and otherwise more favored tracts that were the earliest taken up by settlers.

---

in the newly formed Genesee Conference. He continued to labor in central and northern New York, until 1843, when by his own request, he was placed on the supernumerary list, and in 1848, he removed to Illinois. He preached occasionally until Dec. 1853, when a severe illness prevented further usefulness. He died at Lighthouse Point, Ogle Co. Ill., May 25, 1854. A striking peculiarity in his preaching, was the facility and correctness with which he quoted scripture, always naming the place where found. This custom gave him the appellation of "Chapter and Verse" by which he was often known among his friends. His citations sometimes exceeded a hundred in a sermon, and had generally a close relation to the argument in hand.

Supervisors.—1830, Martin Hart; 1831, James McVickar; 1832, Aaron Foster; 1833–4, Peter Rea; 1835–6, Anthony W. Collins; 1837, David A. Stiles; 1838, Seth Miller; 1839–40, Horace Johnson; 1841–2, Edmund Baldwin; 1843, Owen J. Owens; 1844, S. Miller; 1845–6, Wm. R. Wadsworth; 1847–8, S. Miller; 1849–50, Jonathan C. Collins; 1851, S. Miller; 1852–4, V. R. Waters; 1855, W. R. Wadsworth; 1856, Homer Collins; 1857, Hiram T. Felshaw; 1858, Riley Parsons; 1859–60, Schuyler C. Thompson.

Clerks.—1830, Seth Miller, jr. (resigned), Wm. R. Wadsworth appointed and continued till 1844; 1845, Ela G. Stoddard; 1846, Robert W. Bennett; 1847, V. R. Waters; 1848, Charles M. Goff; 1849, W. R. Wadsworth; 1850, C. M. Goff; 1851, V. R. Waters; 1852, Luman L. Fairchild; 1853–4, W. R. Wadsworth; 1855, C. M. Goff; 1856, John C. Stiles; 1857–9, W. R. Wadsworth.

West Turin now includes parts of townships **2** and **4**, or *Flora* and *Pomona* of Constable's Four Towns. Of these the former belongs to the Pierrepont estate, and its settlement is modern as compared with the latter, upon which Nathaniel Shaler commenced settlement in 1796.[1] In the summer of 1795 Shaler sent a man to explore these lands, and late in that year he concluded the purchase noticed in the history of Turin. The Stows were his competitors for the tract, but Shaler at length secured it and at once took active measures for establishing a settlement.

A road was run from fort Stanwix, and early in 1796, John Ives,[2] the pioneer settler, came on with his family and

---

[1] *Mr. Shaler* was a prominent merchant of Middletown, Ct., and towards the close of the last century, was residing in New York, and concerned in the West India trade. He there became acquainted with Mr. Constable and purchased one half of townships 3 and 4 of Constable's four towns, and became his agent for the undivided remainder. He was accustomed to spend his summers here during several years, but never removed his family. He soon after undertook the settlement of lands on the Connecticut Reserve in Ohio, where he owned the towns of Shalersville, Middletown, Bazetta and a part of Medina. He died at Middletown, Ct., May 1816.

A daughter of Mr. Shaler married Commodore McDonough, the hero of Plattsburgh.

His son, William Denning Shaler, resided many years in this town, and died in New York, May 18, 1842.

[2] *Major Ives* removed a few years after to a farm 2½ miles north of Turin village, where he died of a cancer, March 13, 1828, in his 66th year. His wife survived until Feb. 12, 1841. He was a native of Meriden, Ct., and resided at New Hartford about a year previous to his removal to this town. He was appointed sheriff in 1810, and was a highly esteemed and valuable citizen, systematic and successful in business, and a man of much influence in the county. His homestead is now owned by his son Selden Ives. Another son George, formerly of this town now resides in Chicago. John Ives, the oldest son, died in California.

built his first rude bark shelter by the side of a large elm tree, which was felled late in the evening of their arrival. This formed their dwelling for a few days, until a regular log cabin could be built. In reaching this spot the family was compelled to cross swolen streams upon the trunks of fallen timber, and carry their goods across these treacherous bridges at great peril. The family had tarried in Leyden a few days, while Mr. Ives went forward and explored the town for a location of 400 acres which he was allowed to select from the whole tract. The final removal of the household did not take place till April.

During the summer, about twenty young men were hired by Shaler to put up a saw mill, which was got in operation in the fall, and during the summer great numbers from Middletown, Meriden, and towns adjacent came in and selected farms. Among these were Joshua Rockwell,[1] Levi Ives,[2] Nathan Coe,[3] Elisha Scovill,[4] Daniel Higby, Levi Hough,[5] William Hubbard,[6] James Miller,[7] Ebenezer Allen,[8] and perhaps others, the most of whom began clearings and made preparations for their families but returned back to Connecticut in the fall. But two families spent the long dreary winter in the town, a winter which has had few equals in intensity of cold and depth of snow. Mr. Ives had occasion to go to Connecticut and left his family with a large supply of wood and a stock of provisions, sufficient to last till his return. He was absent six weeks, and in the mean time the snow fell five feet deep, cutting off all communication with the world. At length a young man named Caleb Rockwell reached the cabin on snow shoes to see whether the family were alive and well, and a few days after he returned with his sister, and the tedious solitude was soon after relieved by the return of the husband, and with him several new settlers. Soon after this, the roof of the cabin was crushed in by the snow, and had not the beams of the gar-

---

[1] Mr. Rockwell died March 2, 1825, aged 83 years.

[2] Brother of John Ives and father of Levi Silliman Ives, late bishop of the Protestant Episcopal church in North Carolina, and now an ecclesiastic in the Roman Catholic church. Levi Ives became melancholy from want of prosperity, and drowned himself in Bear creek, near Black river, June 19, 1815.

[3] From Middlefield. He died Feb. 27, 1845, aged 76 years.

[4] From Meriden, Ct. Mr. Scovill had several children who settled in this town and became heads of families. Hezekiah and Elisha Scovill were his sons.

[5] Born at Meriden, Ct., May 2, 1773. Removed to this town in 1798, and to Martinsburgh in 1814, where he died Aug. 21, 1853.

[6] Mr. Hubbard is said to have built the first framed house in town.

[7] Second son of Richard Miller. He came April 29, 1796, when 18 years of age. He is still living in this town.

[8] Died March 1, 1829, aged 60 years.

ret floor been strong, the whole family would have been buried in the ruin.

During the second summer, Jonathan Collins,[1] Seth Miller,[2] Reuben Scovil,[3] Aaron Parsons,[4] Willard Allen,[5] Eli-

[1] *Jonathan Collins* was born at Wallingford, Ct., May 3, 1755, served in the Revolution, for which he drew a pension, and emigrated from Meriden to this town in 1797. He arrived in March, and had great difficulty in crossing Sugar river then swollen by the spring flood. The goods were got across on a tree, the horses were made to swim the stream, and the sleigh was drawn over by a rope attached to the heap. He selected a valuable tract for a farm, and having considerable means, he was enabled to begin settlement to advantage, and to maintain through life an independence in property, which was surpassed by but few in the county. He was early selected as a magistrate and judge, and from 1809 to 1815, he served as the first judge of the county court. In 1820 he was chosen a presidential elector. Few citizens have enjoyed to a greater degree the confidence of the public, and in the various trusts reposed in him by the town and county, he uniformly evinced strict integrity, sound judgment, and a scrupulous regard for the public welfare. His brother, Gen. Oliver Collins of Oneida co., was in service on the frontier in the war of 1812–15. His sons were:

Levi, born Feb. 24, 1778, long a merchant at Collinsville, and a member of assembly in 1813. He died March 31, 1819.

Selden, born May 22, 1780. Died at Ogdensburgh June 13, 1857.

Homer, born May 15, 1788. Member of Assembly in 1858. Resides at Collinsville.

Anthony Wayne, born February 10, 1797. Resides at Turin village.

Jonathan C., born January 30, 1804. Presidential elector in 1852, and member of assembly in 1854. Resides on the homestead. Judge Collins died April 6, 1845, aged 90 years.

[2] This family was from Canaan, Ct. Seth Miller was a son of Benjamin Miller, and settled a short distance west of Constableville, where he died Feb. 20, 1855, aged 75 years. His sons were, *Sylvester*, a physician of Lowville, whose death we have noticed on page 155, *James*, a physician, who settled in Johnstown, *Timothy*, first merchant of Constableville, now deceased, *Benjamin*, who removed west and died, *Seth*, merchant of Constableville, elsewhere noticed, and *Edwin*, who resides on the homestead. He had four daughters.

[3] Died July 9, 1846, aged 77 years.

[4] Died Aug. 26, 1854, aged 84 years. He was a son of Elder Stephen Parsons, and father of Aaron Parsons, jr., sheriff in 1853, and member of assembly in 1855.

Eld. Stephen Parsons was thrice married and had eleven children, six of whom removed to the Black river country before he moved from Whitestown himself.

Aaron was the oldest. His sister *Eleanor* married Elisha Cone and died in this town August, 1853, aged 82.

Stephen died in Denmark in 1832, aged 56 years.

Ichabod still resides in Denmark at an advanced age. He was several years a judge in the county court.

Elihu, half brother of the above, died in Pompey, N. Y., in 1842. His sister *Betsey* married Elijah Clark of Denmark, and died in 1833, aged 53.

Comfort, eldest son by third marriage, resides at Wales Centre, N. Y.

Johnson was a physician, served in the war and was taken prisoner. He died in Florida July 30, 1820. His sister *Sally* married Johnson Foster of Turin. *Grace*, another sister, married Isaac Foster, and died in California in 1859. *Ann*, the youngest, married Mr. Crane of Denmark. The death of Eld. Parsons has been noticed on page 93.

[5] Mr. Allen was a surveyor and farmer. He died Sept. 18, 1850, aged 77 years.

Jonathan Collins

sha Crofoot,[1] James T. Ward, Philemon Hoadley,[2] William and Abner Rice, Elder Stephen Parsons, Jesse Miller, William Daniels,[3] Ebenezer and Elijah Wadsworth,[4] and others. During the second season Mr. Shaler completed the first grist mill erected in the county. It stood upon Sugar river not far from the place where it issues from the hills.

Within the next three years the whole town below the hill, and an extensive tract west of Constableville was taken up by settlers. Among these pioneers were Aaron Foster, [5] Ebenezer Baldwin,[6] Cephas Clark,[7] James and Levi Miller,[8] Elisha Cone,[9] Dr. Horatio G. Hough, Roswell Woodruff,[10] Richard Coxe,[11] Wm. Coleman,[12] and Josiah P. Raymond,[13]

---

6 *Mr. Crofoot* was a native of Berlin, Ct. He removed from Middletown April 25, 1797, having spent the summer previous in this town. He died March 29, 1813, in his 60th year. His wife died March 16, 1813. His children were *Mary* and *John*, who never came to this county; *Isaac*, formerly a judge of the county court, and now of Fond-du-Lac, Wis.; *Rachael*, who died March 11, 1813; *James*, still living in town; Anson, who died July 23, 1825; and *David*, who died Sept. 2, 1814.

2 Mr. H. settled on the old French road where it crossed the east road, south of Collinsville. He was from Westfield, kept an inn several years, and died Jan. 8, 1811, aged 57 years. Jacob Hoadley, his father, died aged 84.

3 Died Jan. 12, 1849, aged 88 years.

4 Elijah W. died Oct. 17, 1836, aged 72 years. Ebenezer W. died in Vienna, N. Y. Seth Miller, sen., and Willard Allen married sisters of these brothers.

5 Died in Martinsburgh, April 3, 1858, aged 87 years. He settled in 1799, near the state road, in this town.

6 Died Nov. 3, 1834, aged 66 years. He settled between the villages of Turin and Collinsville, on the place now owned by his son, Edmund Baldwin.

7 Settled in 1801, from Granby, Ct. Died Dec. 1, 1854, aged 91. He left numerous descendants, many of whom still reside in town, on the road between Turin and Constableville.

8 *Rev. James Miller* died March 31, 1843, aged 67 years. He was a Methodist preacher. His brother Levi, also a Methodist minister, removed some years after to Louisville, N. Y., where he died, Jan. 26, 1853, aged 73 years.

9 Setttled in 1798. Died June 28, 1828, aged 61. He was the first tanner in Turin.

10 W. was from Berlin, Ct. In 1804 he exchanged his place near Collinsville with Coxe for 400 acres in Jefferson county. Many years after he removed to New Hartford, where he died. He was the father of the late Norris M. Woodruff of Watertown, who also resided here several years.

11 *Richard Coxe* belonged to an old and respectable family, on the Delaware, in New Jersey, and his sister Grace married James D. Le Ray. He came in 1800 to supersede Tillier in the agency of Castorland, and continued for some time to carry on the store which the French had established under Oboussier. He was appointed first county clerk, and traded several years on the hill, a little west of Collinsville, where he built a stylish curb-roofed house and store, still standing. He went off about 1816, and was afterwards many years a clerk in the post office department at Washington. Charles C. Coxe, his brother, was several years consul at Tunis.

12 Coleman settled on the Rees Place, east of Collinsville, and went to the Western Reserve six years after.

13 Came in 1800 with Coxe, as clerk to the French store, and still living in town.

Shaler built a house near St. Paul's chapel in the village of Constableville, and was accustomed to spend several weeks of each summer in town but never came to reside. He employed James T. Ward,[1] a man of plausible address and considerable means, to induce people to emigrate to this town; whether the result be due to Ward or Shaler, it will be conceded that a better class of citizens seldom emigrated to a new country than those who began improvements in this town. They were mostly in easy circumstances, and early acquired clear titles to their farms. Excepting the first year or two, the settlers did not suffer those hardships which are often incident to a new country, as the earth yielded its fruits kindly, and the principal difficulties arose from the poorness of the roads, and the difficulty of reaching markets. As an instance of the expense attending the transportation of provisions we may notice that Jonathan Collins upon coming into town in March, 1797, offered to furnish a cart and one yoke of oxen, to any one who would furnish another yoke and bring in a lot of

---

[1] The following anecdote is related by Mr. Alson Clark in his historical articles upon this county :

As Mr. Ward was coming in from fort Stanwix, he met at the foot of the long hill now Lee Corners, two suspicious looking men, who went on before while he stopped at the inn. Two or three miles beyond he overtook them, when one of the men challenged him to wrestle, as Ward thought to try his strength, and if able, to rob him. He accepted the proposal, and having slightly fastened his horse a short distance beyond, took from his portmanteau a bottle of spirits to treat them with, before beginning the contest. He found some other occasion to return to his horse, when springing upon its back he soon disappeared, leaving the bottle in their possession.

Capt. Ward returned to Middlefield, where his habits reduced him to poverty. A pleasing incident occurred near the close of his life. One of his settlers, who in paying for land had given several twenty dollar notes, found the relation of debtor unpleasant and resolved to take them up. They were all written upon one piece of paper. Ward opened the paper, computed the sum due, and stated the amount at less than what was expected. Upon being told of this, he carefully revised his figures, assured the purchaser that it was all right, and gave them up with a receipt in full. The latter on going home discovered that one of the notes had not been unfolded. He had previously lost more money than this through Ward, and finally concluded to let the error offset the previous transaction and he kept the secret. About thirty years after, as he felt death approaching from a slow but incurable disease, this act came up before him, troubling his sleep, and haunting his waking hours with the chidings of a burdened conscience. He at length sought the advice of his family and for the first time related the circumstances of the case. They at once agreed upon the only course that should be taken. Compound interest was reckoned upon the note, and nearly sixty-five dollars were placed in the hands of a messenger to deliver to the owner, with an explanatory letter. The agent found Mr. Ward, enfeebled by age, but forced to earn a scanty support by day labor among the farmers. He had never detected the error, and read the statement with surprise and gratitude, for an act which of itself possessed no merit, but which has too few parallels in the business dealings of mankind.

flour and pork from Whitestown *for half*, and much of his first year's provisions were brought upon these terms. Game and fish formed an important element in the line of provisions, and of the latter, salmon from Fish creek were taken in great numbers. A long stretch of deep still water in that stream still bears the name of Shaler's Hole, from its its being an important fishing ground for his people. Deer, wolves and bears were numerous, and two men coming through from Redfield to Shaler's, once killed an enormous panther over seven feet long, and dragged him out to the settlement.

During the winter of 1799—1800, three deserters from the British fort at Kingston, escaped to this state, and were making their way up the Black river valley, when they were pursued and arrested by a citizen of the district now included in Jefferson co., shut up in an smoke house over night, and the next day taken back to the garrison, for the bounty offered by the British government. The facts spread quickly through the settlements, losing nothing in passing from mouth to mouth, until in reaching this town, they had gained many details of cruelty, that were well calculated to excite indignation. With an impulse prompted by virtue, a prominent citizen of Constableville, seized his gun, declaring that the statutes against kidnapping should not be trampled upon, and that the laws of his country should be enforced against the sordid villain who had sold the freedom of men for a few pieces of silver. He called upon his neighbors to arm and follow, and the expedition gaining a recruit at every cabin, amounted to about forty armed men by the time it reached Champion. A warrant was taken out from Justice Mix, and delivered to a constable, with whom they proceeded to their destination, notwithstanding word was sent, that the offending party had employed Indians to aid in defending him, and that resistance would be made. The warrant was served and the party was escorted up to Champion, where he was bound over to the next term of the Oneida court, and the avengers quietly returned home. The trial resulted in the heaviest fine which could be imposed, amounting with expenses, it is said, to about $800, and a stigma was attached to the culprit, which half a century of virtuous life could not outlive. He died in 1813. The first local agent after Ward was Samuel Hall,[1] who resided here but a few years.

[1] Mr. Hall returned to Middletown, where he died about five years since. He owned extensive brown freestone quarries, which have supplied building material to an immense extent, in New York and elsewhere.

The state of the colony in 1803 is thus described by James Constable in his diary:

"Remained at Rome till Monday, Sept. 12, when I left at 9 A. M. for Shaler's settlement, in company wtth B. Wright. Travelled through a middling good country but well settled, though the lands are principally held under lease from Gov. Clinton and Chancellor Lansing. This tenure is, I am told, very objectionable in the country, and it must be given up when the lease expire. Came to Clark's tavern 6 miles from Rome, in the town of Western. This town the Governor is considerably interested in, but except near Clark's the settlers are few and the soil not inviting. Some places appear to have been occupied, but are now deserted. We saw people going near a mile for water. This is however the driest season ever remembered through the country, and such a circumstance may not happen again. If it does the people will abandon this part.

Passed through Leyden[1] which appears very indifferent, and the settlers were of course few, most of them indeed had not been long there. Arrived at Jones' 15 miles from Rome and expected to find it a tavern to dine at, but they had left off that business as they told us was the case with their neighbors 4 miles further, and that there was no public house nearer than Shaler's settlement, so we baited our horses and proceeded through Adgate's purchase and Inman's Triangle, both of which are and appear very rough and bad, though of the latter Wright tells me the part to the eastward is very good. We do not find a settler in several miles, and the road, bad as it is, is the only sign of improvement. Pass the two main branches of the Mohawk, now nearly dry, though very formidable streams generally. The Triangle improves in quality somewhat, and after some distance we entered Shaler's No. 4, where we immediately saw settlers, good buildings, and crops of corn. His house and other buildings being not far from the south line, we soon arrived there, being 5 o'clock, so that we were 8 hours going 26 miles, which in a new road is pretty good speed. While dinner was getting ready we looked at the buildings. The house is a good large frame house, well finished and grand for that part of the country. The barn, stable and other places for cattle also good. The mill is a common country mill with one run of stone and well finished. The saw mill like others of the country, but not covered in, though the boards cannot be wanting. Neither of these mills had run for some time for want of water. The dam seems firm and good though it has been twice heretofore carried away.[1] There is also a house for potash work which is

---

[1] Leyden then included Boonville and Ava.

[2] The summer of 1803 was the driest upon record in the Black river country. On one occasion a party of 17 men, working for Shaler, rather than to go without flour, mounted the wheel by turns, tread-mill fashion, and ground out sufficient grain for present use. Several of the early settlers went

equal to what I have seen in this country; but knowing that upwards of $10,000 were expended in these buildings, I was astonished to see that so much could have been laid out on them; but of this more hereafter.

After our view it was near dark; we got our dinner, sat an hour or two and went to bed. Everything was well provided for us, and plenty of good liquor from Mr. Shaler's stock. Looking from the house, about 150 acres appear to be well cleared which is called the homestead, and there are also some very fine farms covered with good buildings, but there is a street (as they call it) about a mile west from the house and of that length, of good farms in high cultivation, which the lateness of the hour and my other route did not permit me to see. I had to go to Martin's, 12 miles north of us, next morning, *Tuesday*, *Sept.* 13, and accordingly set off after breakfast, travelling over a road which the settlers by laying out judiciously and using have made infinitely superior to that between this place and Rome.

Our course from Shaler's to Martin's is N. W. through No. 4, and part of No. 3. This No. 4 Wright considers superior to any land belonging to the estate. It is indeed very fine, and being more settled and cultivated than Ellisburgh appears to greater advantage, but the soil so far as I am a judge is not superior. There is however an advantage it possesses over the other in being so remarkably well watered throughout, while Ellisburgh depends upon the two branches of Sandy Creek in the dry season. The buildings are all framed and well finished including barns, &c. We seldom see log houses. On our route we met two men who were desirous of buying lands on the other No. 4,[1] which they had been to view, and which they said contained land good enough for any man. I told them the executors[2] had not yet determined about opening that town for sale but soon would, and make it known. This account of No. 4 was pleasing, as I had formed a very indifferent opinion of it, and Wright says they must have been on the N. E. corner, as the remainder is bad. Crossed from Shaler's No. 4 to No. 3, which seems somewhat inferior though very little. It has few settlers, his whole force having been hitherto applied to the other, but his object now is to settle No. 3, and he is raising the price of the other to $6 and $7 which the people will not at present give, but go to the other at half the price. Passed to Capt. Clapp's tavern 8 miles from Shaler's. The landlord is a very active, industrious and intelligent man, the buildings and farm about him in excellent order, the work of two years. He told me when he set down there, there was not a neighbor north-

---

to Whitestown to mill, and one Wm. Barnes backed home two bushels of corn meal from that place. The first dam at Constableville was built like a log house, and stood less than a year. The house above mentioned was afterwards burned.

[1] In Martinsburgh, No. 4 of the Boylston tract.

[2] Executors of the estate of Wm. Constable, then recently deceased.

ward of him as far as Lowville, and now there are about 40 families in a distance of a few miles. I found from the conversation of him and Wright, that he knows every spot of the country; he informed us that he had been running a line for a road through the whole length of No. 3, and found the soil and ground good. This he did by order of Mr. Shaler, and when the road is cut the town will settle immediately."

Returning the same day from Martin's, he adds:

"*Wednesday, Sept.* 14. Arose and breakfasted by 5 o'clock, that we might go by Shaler's new road through No. 3 and 2. The former appeared in this part rough and hilly, the soil not very good and no settlers, but the road being only just cut, there has not been time for them to sit down. The travelling rather bad, there being no bridges or causeways to cover the mud holes. Passed on 7 miles without seeing a house till we come to Inman's Triangle. I was sorry to find No. 2 so indifferent. The timber was mostly beech and hemlock, which denotes a very poor soil, and the country is rough and uneven without being relieved by intervale."

In the year following, Constable notes under date of Sept. 11, that after leaving Collins for Rome the wind blew very hard, and they heard and saw the trees falling in every direction. One dropped in the wood just before them and obliged them to go around it; and in several places they leaped their horses over trees newly fallen. In 1805 he remarks, Sept. 4:

"Passed on to Coxe's at the High Falls, or rather 1½ mile west of them, where he lives and is finishing a house he bought. He is clerk of the new county of Lewis but has not yet got the books for the papers, and the records are in a very insecure place."

Township No. 2, or *Flora*, was first opened for settlement under Shaler as agent, who was authorized June 13, 1803, to lay out a road, and sell at not less than $2.50 per acre. Abraham Scranton was appointed agent Dec. 15, 1804, through the aid of Shaler. On the 25th of August, 1804, Hamlet Scranton,[1] his son, was associated in the agency, and the rule, hitherto invariable, of requiring a quarter payment down was relaxed by the executors of the Constable estate. The terms allowed were 2, 3, 4, and 5 years, in equal installments. The diary, under date of August 6, 1806, says of this agency:

[1] Mr. Scranton was from Durham, Ct. The family removed to Rochester in April, 1812, where they became early settlers. Hamlet Scranton died of apoplexy, April, 1851, aged 78 years.—*Memorial of the Scranton Family*, p. 61; *Lives of Pioneers of Rochester*, p. 9. Hamlet D. Scranton is the present mayor of Rochester.

"Left Rome and arrived at Scranton's in Turin towards evening, having travelled through the old road from Deacon Clark's in Western, through town No. 2, which appeared a good soil, though not a little hilly. Saw no settlers, and the road requires a good deal of working, which Mr. Scranton informed me was to be done in about two weeks, the people from Leyden having undertaken to meet them and do their part. We find Mr. Scranton (the son) not so sanguine of settling this town as the father was last year, at $5, tho' he thinks settlers will come forward at a less price. We therefore authorized him to proceed in the business on the best terms he could, without adhering to $5. He had a frame prepared for a saw-mill, which was to be raised to-day. The other business remained as last year. The grist-mill was at a stand both for a want of water and itself appearing to be worn out."

The attempt to settle No. 2, except along the direct road to Rome, which crosses the N. E. corner, failed, as from its great elevation, grains did not thrive, and its value for grazing was unknown. In 1826 some Germans came to the office of H. B. Pierrepont in Brooklyn, to buy lands, and selected portions of this town. Among these were Joseph Kochly, Capt. Wider and others, chiefly from Alsace on the Rhine. They were joined by others from the borders of France and Germany, and from Switzerland; and in 1834 Kochly counted 75 German families, on 3,400 acres in No. 2. In 1836, 2,000 acres were under contract, and as much more deeded, and in 1839, 5,000 acres were contracted. These foreigners are chiefly Catholics and Lutherans. They prove a hardy, laborious, patient and well disposed class of people, and mostly become citizens as soon as the legal forms can be complied with. Settlement was begun on Fish creek by one Wright, who was supported for some time by Pierrepont's agent, on condition of his remaining. Others were induced to venture in, and a permanent settlement was formed. Many Irish from the canals settled in 1841, and at present the greater part of the township is settled.

The first birth, was that of Richard, a son of Joshua Rockwell, and the second that of Julia, daughter of John Ives. The second male child born in town was Seth Miller, jr. On the second summer of settlement, a young man named Coe was brought to Shaler's house to be nursed, and died. In 1799 a sickly season occurred, and two men named Platt died of a putrid fever. About thirty persons who came to attend them sickened with the fever. In the early settlement a child of Samuel Hall was drowned at Constableville. The first school was kept by Miss Dorothy Wadsworth, daughter of Timothy Wadsworth and afterwards wife of Willard Allen. A school-house was built in 1798, near the house of Horace Johnson, Esq., in Constableville.

In 1805 an act was procured, allowing Shaler to make conveyances in the same manner as if Wm. Constable, sen., were still alive. It was vetoed by the Council of Revision for the following reasons:

"1st. The bill not only enables Nathaniel Shaler, therein named, to complete the contracts of sale which he had made prior to the death of Wm. Constable, by virtue of attorney from him, but to proceed under the said power and sell the residue of the said lands therein specified, and which are stated in the bill to William Constable, a son of the said Wm. Constable, deceased, and who is now an infant under the age of twenty-one years, thereby absolutely disposing of the estate of the said minor, contrary to the just rights of property and the general principles of law.

"2d. Because if it is deemed necessary that the real estate of the said minor should be sold, it ought to be done under the direction, and at the discretion of the court of chancery, so that the respective interests of all parties concerned might be duly examined, adjusted and secured."

The bill in a modified form passed on the last day of the session.[1]

---

[1] We may in this connection record a notice of the family so intimately associated with the land titles of northern New York.

William Constable was born in Dublin, Jan. 1, 1752. His father, Dr. John Constable, was a surgeon in the British army, and came to Montreal during the French war, and brought his son William, then an infant, with him. In 1762 Governor Cadwallader Colden granted him a commission as surgeon in the first regiment, in the pay of the province of New York. He then removed to Schenectady, where his daughter married Mr. James Phyn, who was there engaged in the Indian trade, in correspondence with Col. Sir William Johnson.

Dr. Constable sent his son to Dublin for his education, to the care of his paternal aunt, Mrs. White, with whom he resided, while a student at Trinity college. By inheritance he became possessed of a valuable estate near Dublin. On his return to America his kinsman, Mr. Phyn, associated him in his business at Schenectady. On the breaking out of the war of the revolution Mr. Phyn and his friend Mr. Alexander Ellice, removed to England under a pass from the committee of safety, in consequence of which their property was not confiscated. These gentlemen established in England the firm of Phyn, Ellice and Inglis—a firm which gave two members to the privy council in the persons of their sons, Sir Robert Inglis and the right honorable Edward Ellice. Mr. Constable joined the cause of his adopted country, and served in the army as aid-de-camp to General Lafayette. He ever afterwards continued in intimate correspondence with him. When the General visited this country in 1824, hearing that the widow of his deceased friend was at Brooklyn, at her daughter's, Mrs. Pierrepont, he paid his respects to her there.

As Philadelphia and Charleston, were at that time, the chief commercial

William Constable, Jr., born April 4, 1786, was carefully educated in Europe, married Eliza, daughter of John McVickar, and in June, 1810, came to reside at Constableville, first occupying the house built by Shaler. He received

---

ports of the country, Mr. Constable associated himself with Mr. James Seagrove and established a commercial house at Philadelphia, while his partner settled in Charleston. Their trade was mainly with the West Indies, and Mr. Constable, in the course of his business, visited Havana, and there took the yellow fever, of which he nearly died. He married in 1782 Ann White, daughter of Townsend White of Philadelphia; a lady of beauty of person, and of character, who had been a school friend of Miss Dandridge, and who afterwards became Mrs. General Washington, whose friendship she retained. After the peace, Mr. Constable, in 1784, removed to New York, and established the firm of Constable, Rucker & Co. On the death of Mr. Rucker, shortly afterwards, the firm of Constable & Co., in which Robert Morris and Gouverneur Morris were partners, contributing £50,000 as their share of the capital. The national debt, and that of the several states, not being yet funded, offered great field for speculation, which the firm was largely concerned in, as they were also in furnishing supplies to Europe. Mr. Robert Morris, who was the chief financial agent of our government, remained in Philadelphia, while Governeur Morris, who was sent minister plenipotentiary to France, aided by procuring contracts, and by his advices from thence. The war between France and England threw the carrying trade into the hands of neutrals. The firm of Constable & Co. took early advantage of this, and in 1786 sent the ship Empress to India and China, and made a very profitable voyage. In 1788 the ship America, of 600 tons, which was the finest ship that had been built at New York, was built by Mr. Constable for that trade. In 1790 he proposed to build a ship of one thousand tons, but the demand for China goods in this country did not warrant it, and he abandoned the enterprise. He fulfilled a large contract with the British government for the supply of their troops in the West Indies. Through the agency of Col. Jeremiah Wadsworth of Hartford, and Joseph Howland of New London, he shipped seventy-eight cargoes of cattle from Connecticut.

Europe continuing to draw supplies of provisions from this country, raised the price of wheat here to two dollars per bushel, and even higher, which induced Mr. Constable to establish a flouring mill. For this purpose he purchased the confiscated estate of Philips manor, at Yonkers, nineteen miles from New York, consisting of 320 acres. Here he resided and built a large mill, which he continued in operation for many years. He sold this estate for $65,000 and bought a country seat at Bloomingdale, six miles from New York. His residence in the city was first in Great Dock street, afterwards in Wall street, till 1797, when he sold to the bank of New York for $27,000 for their banking house. He then leased the dwelling of the Hon. Rufus King in Broadway, where the Astor House has been built.

Mr. Constable at an early day had had his attention turned to land speculation. His first purchases were in Ohio, associated with companies, who with military protection, commenced settlements, mainly of French settlers, on the Muskingum and the Scioto. As the British still retained their outposts, which they did not finally surrender till ten years after the peace, they instigated the Indians to harass these settlers. Besides these lands he made extensive purchases in Kentucky, Virginia and Georgia. Mr. Constable was interested in the grant of two millions of acres made by the state of Massachusetts in the Genesee country, which was sold to Mr. Bingham. He, in 1787, associated with Alexander Macomb, with whom he had been intimate since boyhood, in the purchase of the 640,000 acres on the St. Lawrence river called the Ten Townships. His share of this purchase was Madrid, Potsdam, and the half of Louisville, and the half of Stockholm, in all 192,000 acres. In the year 1791 he associated with Alexander Macomb and Daniel McCormick

from his father, townships 3 and 4, of the four towns, subject to the contract with Shaler, and a bond to Daniel McCormick. He died May 28, 1821.

The elegant mansion erected by Mr. Constable in 1819, a

---

in the purchase from the state of New York of the great tract known as Macomb's purchase, estimated to contain four millions of acres, being one tenth of the state of New York, and comprising the whole of the present counties of Lewis, Jefferson, St. Lawrence and Franklin, with parts of Oswego and Herkimer. In this purchase, each of these gentlemen was jointly interested one-third, but the contract with the Commissioners of the Land Office was made in the name of Macomb, and the first patent taken out in his name, while the remainder of the tract was patented in the name of Daniel McCormick. The price paid was eight pence per acre, which at that time was deemed very advantageous to the state, as Massachusetts had sold at that price two millions of acres of land in the Genesee country, which was deemed far superior in quality to this land. The state was also really the gainer, in consequence of the stimulus given thereby to land speculation, which enabled the commissioners of the land office to sell the remaining unappropriated lands at advanced prices. The clause inserted in the patents, requiring settlements to be made within a specified time, had been usual in all grants previously made by the Provincial government and by the land office. It had, however, never been fulfilled and never enforced. When in 1791 the law granting power to the commissioners of the land office "to sell the waste and unappropriated lands of the state" was under discussion, Mr. Macomb (a member of the Legislature) had this clause, by an unanimous vote, stricken out. It was inserted in the patents by inadvertence, and when attention was drawn to it by foreign purchasers, Mr. Macomb procured a certificate of the nullity of the clause.

Immediately after the contract was made with the land office, Mr. Constable embarked for Europe to sell, where he was joined by his family. He remained till the fall of 1795 and had two children born in Europe. He left his commercial house in charge of his brother James, whom he took into partnership, having dissolved his connection with the Messrs. Morris. In 1792 the patent for Great Tracts 4, 5 and 6, containing 1,920,000 acres, was taken out, and the title immediately transferred to Mr. Constable, who, with the aid of his agents, Col. Samuel Ward and Col. William S. Smith, succeeding in selling the whole, in large tracts, to Messrs. Inman, Chassanis, Angersteen, the Antwerp Company and Thomas Boylston, at prices varying from two to four shillings per acre.

The surveys which were not completed till after these sales were made, located the Black river further north than it was supposed to be. A tract was sold to Thomas Boylston, bounded by the Black river on the north and by the line of the patent on the south as four hundred thousand acres more or less. The subsequent surveys showed this tract to be valuable, and to contain 817,155 acres; whereupon Mr. Constable repurchased it at an advance of £60,000 sterling, and then sold the northern part of it, containing 305,000 acres, for one dollar per acre to Messrs. Low, Henderson, Harrison and Hoffman. This tract is now called the eleven Black river towns.

The remainder of the Boylston tract, containing 512,155 acres, Mr. Constable retained for himself, having bought out the interests of his associates in it. It was subdivided into townships, called the Thirteen Towns, which, with the town of Ellisburgh, and Nos. 1, 2, 3, and 4 of Turin, called Constable's Four Towns, constituted the whole of it.

If the surveys of the 640,000 acres of ten townships, and the great tracts of No. 1, 2, and 3, containing 1,800,000 acres, could have then been obtained, Mr. Constable would have succeeded in selling the whole in Europe. The St. Regis Indians, instigated by the Governor of Canada, Lord Dorchester, drove off the surveyors, and finally did not cease their opposition, till the

little east of Constableville, has since remained the homestead of the family. This seat for quiet seclusion, elegant surroundings and classic beauty, is not surpassed by any in northern New York. The management of the landed

---

Jay treaty, after which the British posts at Oswego and Oswegatchie were given up.

On his return to America, Mr. Constable exerted himself to make improvements in roads, so as to open his lands for settlement. He also took an active interest in forming a water communication between the Hudson and lake Ontario, by improving the navigation of the Mohawk river and Wood creek. The company formed for the purpose was called the *Northern Inland Lock Navigation Company*. This company, after succeeding in conveying boats of ten tons from Schenectady to lake Ontario, with one portage, was bought out by the state, when it was determined to construct the Erie canal. The first township sold was Ellisburgh, which subsequently reverted. Afterwards Nos. 3 and 4, now Turin, were placed in the hands of Mr. Shaler of Middletown, as we have already noticed.

The next township sold was No. 5, to Walter Martin. For this township there were many competitors; but Mr. Constable made it an invariable rule, not to sell but on receiving one-quarter of the payment in money. If he had departed from this determination, he might then have sold all his townships at two dollars per acre, so great was then the rage for land speculation and so scarce was money. The only other township sold was No. 12, called Redfield, which was sold for two dollars per acre. The consequence of the European war was then severely felt in our commercial community, from the the course taken by belligerents in seizing our vessels. France, dissatisfied with an act of neutrality, and under a disorganized government, made seizures of our vessels under various pretexts. The spoliations thus made would have been paid to our merchants by France, but unfortunately for the claimants, they were assumed by our own government, which, to the disgrace of the country, has withheld payment to this day. Among the refugees from France, driven to this country in 1797, were the Duke of Orleans and his brothers Monpensier, and Beaujoli. The duke brought a letter of credit from Gouverneur Morris on Mr. Constable, for one thousand dollars. This money, with interest, was repaid by Louis Phillippe to the son of Mr. Morris.

The patents of Great Tracts Nos. 1, 2, and 3, were not obtained till 1798. Mr. Macomb had failed in 1793, for one million of dollars, in consequence of a wild speculation in stocks, with Col. William Duer and Isaac Whippo. He thereupon assigned his third interest in these tracts to certain creditors, and conveyed his contract with the Land office to Daniel McCormick, who took out the patents in his name, and made a partition with Mr. Constable for his one third interest. On his second visit to Europe, Mr. Constable narrowly escaped being taken by a privateer. He succeeded in France in making some large sales of land to Mr. Le Ray, Mr. Parish and to Neckar. The commercial distress that prevailed in England prevented any success in that country. It was in Paris that he first became acquainted with Mr. Pierrepont, who in 1802 became his son in law.

Hearing that his brother James had involved his commercial house by endorsements, Mr. Constable returned to New York in 1801. Though under no legal obligation to do so, he paid these large obligations, which consumed most of his personal property. The scattering lots in townships Nos. 1 and 13 in Lewis co., were given to some of the holders of these obligations. His health, which had always been delicate, was much impaired by this misfortune. He endeavored to visit his lands, but after going to Rome, he found the road could not be traveled except on horse-back, which he was unable to do. He thus never saw an acre of his extensive possesions in this county. He appointed Mr. Benjamin Wright his general land agent. Mr. Wright, who resided at Rome, had been previously employed by Mr. Constable in

interests remaining with this family, chiefly devolved upon his son John Constable, whose indulgence towards settlers, and whose urbane manners, have rendered him deservedly popular in the community where he resides.

---

surveys for the improvement of Wood creek, when he was interested in the Inland Lock Navigation company. He had also been his principal surveyor in subdividing Macomb's purchase into townships and lots. He continued his valuable agency for the family, till his services were required by the state in the construction of the Erie canal. Under the agency of Benjamin Wright, Nathaniel Shaler, and Isaac W. Bostwick, the sale and settlement of this land progressed satisfactorily.

Mr. Constable died 22d of May, 1803, leaving a widow and seven children. As in questions of title in this county, the names of his heirs are often required, we will add a list of them.

Anna Maria, born 1783, died 1859. She married Hezekiah B. Pierrepont, who died 1838.

Eweretta, born 1784, died 1830. Married James McVickar who died 1835.

William, born 1786, died 1821. Married Eliza McVickar.

John, born 1788, resides in Philadelphia. He married Susan Livingston, and afterwards his present wife, Alida Kane.

Harriet, born 1794, married James Duane, who died 1859. She continues to reside in Duane, Franklin county.

Emily, born 1795, died 1844. Married Dr. Samuel W. Moore, who died 1854.

Matilda, born 1797, married Edward McVickar, and resides at Constableville, and New York city.

The executors under the will, were James Constable, H. B. Pierrepont and John McVickar. The first two gentlemen made persevering efforts to open roads and induce settlement We give elsewhere some interesting extracts from the diaries of Mr. Constable, from 1803 to 1806. He died in 1807, and Mr. McVickar died 1812. Mr. Pierrepont continued his labors till the settlement of the estate in 1819, when he purchased the remaining interest of the heirs of Mr. Constable. The lands in Lewis county, he became possessed of, were townships Nos. 1 and 2, West Turin, 3 Montague, 4 Martinsburgh, with part of No. 5, and No. 8 and 13 Osceola, and parts of Denmark and Harrisburgh; comprising one hundred and fifty thousand acres. On the death of Mr. Pierrepont, in 1838, these lands were subdivided among his heirs.

In concluding our notice of Mr. Constable, which we have somewhat extended, from the connection which his history necessarily has with the history of Lewis county, we will add a delineation of his appearance and character as portrayed by that venerable and distinguished jurist, the Hon. Ogden Edwards:

William Constable was truly one of nature's noblemen. He was a man of sound comprehension and fruitful mind, of high-toned feelings and vivid imagination. He saw clearly, felt keenly and expressed himself pungently. He was endowed with all the qualities necessary to constitute an orator; and was, in truth, the most eloquent man in conversation I ever heard. So impressed was I by his eloquence, even at the early age of sixteen, that I asked my father if he did not think that Mr. Constable was very eloquent in conversation. To which he cooly replied "That he was the most eloquent man in conversation that he had ever heard." Such were his powers, and such the charms of his conversation, that wherever he went he was the king of the company. I first saw him in 1796, at a dinner party. Among the distinguished persons present were General Hamilton, Colonel Burr and Volney. Yet, even in such company, all eyes and ears were turned to him, and he appeared to be the master spirit. He was a man of a princely disposition. Every thing with him was upon a lofty scale. Whatever was laud-

George Davis of Bellville, N. J., formerly a sea captain, in 1817, purchased a large tract of wild land from James McVickar, and several improved farms, and came to reside at Constableville. His maritime associations had deprived

---

able insured his commendation; what was reprehensible, his fiery indignation.

It is a Spanish proverb, "Tell me who your company is, and I will tell you who you are." Testing him by this rule, he must have been truly great, for his most intimate associates were Jay and Hamilton, and Robert Morris, and the other master spirits of the time. Even in early life he was thrown into the society of the distinguished men of the revolution, being an aid to the great and good Lafayette.

His appearance strikingly indicated his character, his countenance beamed with intelligence and expressed every emotion. So striking was his appearance that I heard a very sensible man say, "That although he was not acquainted with Mr. Constable, yet, such was his appearance, that he felt as though he should be pleased to pass his days in his company." He lived in splendid style and his house was the resort of the master spirits of the day. The last time I saw him was in 1802, at Lebanon Springs, the summer before he died. Though in broken health, his spirits were superior to his infirmities. Although more than half a century has since elapsed, yet so striking and so interesting were his characteristics, and so deep the impression they made on me that I retain a vivid recollection of them to this day. I may say in the words of the poet:

> And that the elements were so happily blended in him
> That nature might have stood up and said to all the world
> "This was a man."

Hezekiah Beers Pierrepont of Brooklyn, was known in Lewis county, through his extensive landed possessions in the county, and the intercourse, in consequence, he had with the inhabitants. He was born at New Haven, Connecticut, 3d Nov., 1768, and was descended from the Rev. James Pierrepont, the first minister settled in that colony after its establishment. It is worthy of note that the town plat apportioned to him in 1684, has ever since belonged to the family, and been occupied by them. It has thus never been sold since it was ceeded by the aborigines. The immediate ancestor of the Rev. James Pierrepont, was John Pierrepont, who belonged to the family of Holme Pierrepont, in Nottinghamshire, which family was descended from Robert de Pierrepont of Normandy. John came to America about the year 1640, with his younger brother Robert, as tradition says, merely to visit the country, but married and settled near Boston, where he purchased in 1656, three hundred acres, now the site of the town of Roxbury. The family name being French, became Anglicized in this country, and was spelt Pierpont. The correct spelling has been resumed by this branch of the family.

The subject of this memoir displayed at an early age an enterprising active spirit. While at college he became dissatisfied with the study of Latin and Greek, and the prospect of a professional life. He proposed to his father if he would permit him to leave his studies, he would provide for himself, and not receive a share of his estate. His father consented, and he fulfilled his promise to him, and thereafter provided for himself. He first entered the office of his uncle, Mr. Isaac Beers, at New Haven, to obtain a knowledge of business. In 1790 he went to New York and engaged in the custom house, with the view of obtaining a better knowledge of commercial business. The next year he associated himself with Messrs. Watson and Greenleaf, and acted with them in Philadelphia in the purchase of national debt, in which he realized a small fortune. In 1793 he formed a partnership with his cousin

him of the ability or the inclination to assume that social position, or to enjoy the rural independence and happiness which one differently reared might have attained. He became involved in losses, his health failed, he went to sea,

---

William Leffingwell and established in New York, the house of Leffingwell and Pierrepont.

France being then in revolution, neglected agriculture, and derived large supplies of provisions from America. Mr. Pierrepont went to France to attend the shipments of his firm. The seizures of his vessels by England, then at war with France, so embarrassed the trade that he abandoned it, and in 1795, purchased a fine ship named the Confederacy, on which he made a trading voyage to India and China, acting as his own supercargo. On his return voyage, his ship with a valuable cargo was seized by a French privateer, and condemned and sold, contrary to the laws of nations and our treaty stipulations. He remained in France making reclamations against that government, with a good prospect of recovering the value of his property, when a treaty was made between the two countries, by the terms of which our government agreed to assume the claims of its citizens against France, and France agreed to assume the claims of its own citizens against the United States. To the disgrace of the government of the United States, these claims, among other similar claims known as "*claims for French spoliations prior to* 1800," though brought constantly before congress, have never been paid. Twenty-one reports have been made in their favor, and the bill has twice been passed and been vetoed. The best men of this country have admitted their justice and advocated them.

Mr. Pierrepont was in Paris during the most bloody days of the revolution, and saw Robespierre beheaded. He was detained in England also by the legal steps necessary to obtain his insurance, part of which he recovered. Though war prevailed, his character as a neutral enabled him to travel between England and France. Our country being represented in those countries by able men, as well in as out of the diplomatic circle, he enjoyed their society and cemented friendships which lasted during life. That with Mr. Constable was one, and also that with Robert Fulton, in compliment to whom Mr. Pierrepont named a son Robert Fulton, who died in infancy. After an absence of seven years Mr. Pierrepont returned to New York. He married in 1802, Anna Maria, eldest daughter of William Constable. After his marriage, wishing to engage in some business of less hazard than foreign trade, he traveled through New England to examine its manufacturing establishments, and finding distilling profitable he in 1802 purchased at Brooklyn a brewery belonging to Philip Livingston, and turned it into a manufactory of gin which attained a high reputation, and was very profitable as it was at that time the only manufactory of the kind in the state. He purchased also a country seat on Brooklyn heights, which afterwards became his permanent residence. He was at that time one of only twenty-six freeholders, who owned the village of Brooklyn, now a city the third in population in the United States. When the profits of his manufactory were diminished by competition Mr. Pierrepont abandoned it, and thereafter gave his attention exclusively to the management of his extensive landed estate in northern New York and his real estate at Brooklyn. He purchased in 1806 the town of Pierrepont and subsequently half of Stockholm in St. Lawrence county. He made large additions to his landed estate in the five northern counties by purchases from the heirs of Wm. Constable and others, and became the owner of nearly half a million of acres of land, one hundred and fifty thousand acres of which were in this county. He made annual visits to this county to direct the making of roads and other improvements to facilitate settlements, and spent large sums on turnpike roads, aiding in constructing, among others, the St. Lawrence turnpike, of which he was president, and

HEZ. B. PIERREPONT.

OF BROOKLYN, L.I.

Engraved for the History of Jefferson County by Franklin B. Hough.

and died off the coast of South America. His son is said to have paid the penalty decreed by the law of nations against pirates.

The Welsh settlers on the hills west of Turin, mostly settled under Capt. Davis.

The post office of Constableville, was established Jan., 1826, with Seth Miller, jr.,[1] as postmaster. The receipts of the first quarter were $4.12, and in the first three years averaged $4.01. They began to increase rapidly Jan., 1829, when they had more than quadrupled. The quarter ending March, 1853, gave $65.12, and the whole period of Col. Miller's term, ending Sept., 1853 (excepting from Jan., '45, to May '49), gave a total of $3,744.45 received from postage.

---

which extended from the Black river to Franklin county a distance of seventy miles. He was also one of the principal proprietors of the turnpike from Rome to Constableville, and was interested in the Albany and Schenectady rail road, which was the first constructed in the state of New York.

His first visit to this county was in 1803, with Mr. James Constable. It was then an almost unbroken forest, and he was obliged to travel on horseback. He had the gratification to witness its gradual settlement and improvement, much of which was the result of his own exertions, seconded by his agents, Mr. Bostwick, Mr. Harvey Stephens, Mr. Diodate Pease, and Mr. David Stiles and others. In the treatment of settlers Mr. Pierrepont was uniformly kind and lenient, extending his indulgence in the collection of their indebtedness, much to his own inconvenience. He surrendered the care and management of his lands in Lewis county for five years previous to his death, and by the provisions of his will, to his son Henry E. Pierrepont, who continued during twenty years in their active management, till the year 1853, when they were partitioned among the members of the family.

Mr. Pierrepont died 11th August, 1838, leaving a widow, two sons and eight daughters. His widow died in 1859. We add a list of the children of Mr. Pierrepont, to whom his possessions in this county have descended.

William Constable Pierrepont, residing at Pierrepont Manor, Jeff. Co.

Henry Evelyn Pierrepont, residing at Brooklyn.

Anna Constable Pierrepont who died in 1839, leaving a son, G. Hubert Van Wagenen.

Emily Constable Pierrepont, who married Joseph A. Perry.

Frances Matilda Pierrepont, who married Rev. Frederick S. Wiley.

Mary Montague Pierrepont, who died in 1853.

Harriet Constable Pierrepont, who married Edgar J. Barton. She died 18

Maria Theresa Pierrepont, who married Joseph S. Bicknell.

Julia Josephine Pierrepont, who married John Constable of Constableville.

Ellen A. Pierrepont, who married Dr. James M. Minor.

[1] *Col. Miller* began trade in 1819, and has since been steadily and successfully engaged in business, presenting the longest course of continuous mercantile employment in the county. In the various commercial crises which have happened, he has not been compelled for a day to suspend business or stop payment; an exemption which can be said of but few merchants of equal business in this section of the state. This success has been due to a discriminating judgment, and strict attention to business, qualities which in every pursuit, ensure their appropriate reward. Col. Miller was many years a partner of James C. Duff. He has been influential in public affairs, and a prominent political leader in the Whig and Republican school.

The village of Constableville is the most important business point in the southern part of the county, and enjoys an extensive trade with the country south and west.

Collinsville, on the East road 1½ m. west of the falls, was formerly known as High Falls village, and received its present name from Levi and Homer Collins. It was an important business point in former times, and Jabez Foster, Levi Collins, John Hooker, Richard Coxe and others carried on extensive mercantile operations at or near this place. The Collinsville Institute was incorporated by act of May 2, 1837, which appointed Dr. David Budd,[1] John Whittlesey, Hezekiah Scovil,[2] Ela Merriam, Alburn Foster, Jabez Rockwell, Jehiel H. Hall, Morgan Cummings, Rev. Russel Way, and Sylvester Hart, trustees. A school was taught in the basement of the Union church, a few terms, by A. W. Cummings, when the enterprise died out. It was never recognized by the Regents, and issued but one catalogue. The business of this village has been almost entirely transferred to other places.

Lyons Falls, is the name of a small village and P. O., at the High falls, where the Black River canal enters the river which is navigable from this place to Carthage. The falls themselves, and a narrow strip about three acres in extent on the west side belonged to the Brantingham tract. A lot of 50 acres adjacent, was bought about 1835, upon speculation by an association, and some part is still held in undivided possession. The water power belonged to Caleb Lyon at the time of his death. In 1829, an act was procured for a manufacturing co. at this place, rather to call attention to its facilities than with a view of actual construction. The water power, now amounting to 70 feet fall including the state dam above, has hitherto been improved only by a saw mill, and the importance of the village as a business point is mostly prospective. The high falls during freshets, present a scene of wildness and grandeur well worthy of a visit, but in low water the torrent is confined to narrow channels worn in the gneiss rock, down which it rushes with immense force. Tradition relates that in the revolution, a white man pursued by Indians, leaped safely

---

1 *Dr. D. Budd* was born in Schoharie, Sept. 30, 1798, attended one course of lectures at Phila., received a diploma from the Schoharie Co. Med. Society June 10, 1821, and removed in that year to this town. He died in Turin village Nov. 4, 1848, having held for several years the offices of judge and justice of the peace. He was a man of scientific attainments and devoted some portion of his time to mineralogy. His son Dr. Charles D. Budd is engaged in medical practice in Turin.

2 Died Oct. 12, 1856, aged 75 years.

across these channels and escaped from his pursuers, who paused at the verge of the fearful chasm, and dared not fire their pieces at the heaven protected fugitive. Several fatal accidents have happened here. In May, 1837, two men named Graves and Brown were drawn under the falls in a boat one Sunday and drowned. The body of the former was found a year after at an island below, having apparently been buried in the sand most of the time.

On the 5th of May, 1842, a son of Noble Phelps, aged 5 years, playing in a skiff above the falls, was drawn into the current, Mr. J. Lewis Church seeing the peril, seized a log-hook from the mill yard, sprung upon the bridge, dropped down on the slope of the pier, caught the boat as it was passing down the falls, and saved the child's life at a great risk of his own. On the 9th of Jan., 1857, John Post, jr., aged 22, while cutting ice in a flume above the falls, stepped upon a cake which broke and dropped him into the stream. He probably passed over the falls immediately.

The house of D. H. Green, adjacent to St. Paul's Church cemetery on the West road, was burned on the evening of Dec. 7, 1859, and two boys aged 12 and 13 years, who were sleeping in the chamber, perished in the flames. The family had retired to rest, and were awakened by the fire, which barely allowed Mrs. Green and two younger children to escape. The stairway was already in flames, and the lads stifled and bewildered by the smoke, sank down within hearing of their mother. The husband was away from home, and as the night was intensely cold, no help was rallied until the work of death was accomplished.

Religious Societies.—Missionaries named Hart and Robinson, from Conn., came through the country and held meetings at an early day. During the summer of 1796, regular prayer meetings were held. About 1803, a revival occurred, in which most of the converts joined the Baptists. A church was formed at that time, under Rev. Stephen Parsons from Middletown, and for several years was much the most thriving in town. A Baptist society was legally formed in this town June 15, 1835, with Aaron Parsons, Jesse Miller, and Nathaniel Wadsworth, trustees. After existing at Constableville several years, it has become nearly or quite extinct.

About 1803, a Presbyterian church was formed, which became Congregational, and its meetings were removed to Turin village. On the 14th of Feb., 1843, the Constableville Presbyterian church was organized by the Watertown Presbytery, consisting at first of 4 males and 11 females.

A Presb. soc. had been legally formed June 13, 1835, with Edwin Miller, Nathaniel Wood and James Miller, 2d, first trustees, and changed to Congregational Oct. 22, 1838. This society has no church edifice, but owns an interest in the Union church at Constableville.

The first church edifice built in town, and the first of its denomination north of the Mohawk valley, was St. Paul's church, which stood about a mile north east of Constableville, near where the Canal turnpike ended. This society was organized April 7, 1817, at the house of Levi Collins, in Collinsville. The first vestrymen were Nathaniel Merriam, and Thomas Alsop, and the first wardens John Kentner, James McVickar, Giles Foster, William Constable, Walter Dewey,[1] Willard Allen, Calvin Roberts, George Davis, and Timothy Miller.

Arrangements were first made to build of stone near Collinsville, but the influence of Geo. Davis, T. Alsop and others determined its final location. The first rector was Joshua M. Rogers, who was sent hither as a missionary, and labored with great zeal and success to promote the objects of his mission.[2] He was succeeded by the Revs. Amos G. Baldwin, Edmund Embury, Lawrence Sterne Stevens, and for a short period by others. St. Paul's Church was consecrated by Bishop Hobart, Aug. 16, 1818,[3] and the grounds were deeded to the society in October of that year. The edifice having fallen into decay was taken down, and its location being inconvenient, the society was reorganized Jan. 30. 1835, under the Rev. Mr. Embury for the purpose of rebuilding in a more convenient site. Edward McVickar and Wm. Van Coughnet were chosen wardens, Seth Miller jr., Wm. Constable, Edwin Miller, Brock McVickar, Wm. D. Shaler, James C. Duff, Bryant Collins and Bard McVickar ar, vestrymen. During that year St. Paul's chapel was built on the south border of Constableville village, upon a site deeded to Trinity church, N. Y., from which it received $600 in aid of the building.

After some attempt to build separately, the Presbyterian, Open Communion Baptists, Baptists and Meth. Episcopal churches united in 1835, and built a union meeting house in Constableville. There is at present no stated preaching in

[1] *Dr. Dewey* died at Collinsville, Feb. 26, 1821, aged 35 years.

[2] *Mr. Rogers* was born at Hudson, N. Y., May 15, 1782, of Baptist parents. He was ordained deacon in 1816, and as priest in 1817. In 1833 he accepted a call to Trinity church, Utica, and in 1851 resigned and retired to Easton, Pa., where he died March 1, 1858. He was buried near New York.

[3] Two years before this date, there were but two Episcopal families in this vicinity. In 1817, there were 16 communicants.

this house, except by the Methodists. In the winter of 1842–3, a revival occurred in which nearly all these sects united.

An Open Communion Baptist church was organized in this town about 1812, from the Baptist church previously existing, in which Jeduthan Higby[1] and Russell Way[2] became prominent ministers. They mostly resided near Collinsville. They are now much reduced in numbers, but continue to hold their covenant meetings.

The union meeting house at Collinsville was built of stone, in 1836, by the Presbyterian Congregational, both Baptist, and Prot. Episcopal sects, each to use it in proportion to subscription. The society was formed Sept. 29, 1836, with Ansel Stocking, Lyman Lane and Lyman Hoadley, trustees. The church has been thoroughly repaired within a few years.

An independent Baptist society was formed March 22, 1842, with Newton Clark, Benham Webb, Edwin Payne, Jason Paine and Horace C. Ragan, trustees, but no edifice has been built.

On the 13th of March, 1848, a Calvinistic Methodist church (Welsh) was formed at Collinsville, with John Hughes, Evan Roberts, Edward Reese, Robert Evans and Robert Morris trustees, but no edifice was built by them until 1855, when the society was reörganized Jan. 22, and a neat church edifice built in that year. The first trustees under this organization were Rev. Thomas Williams, Thomas Lewis, Evans Evans, John Lloyd, John Hughes and Griffith T. Williams. A church of this sect was formed in Constableville, March 13, 1848, and has a small edifice. In both of these the Welsh language is used.

The church of St. Michael in this town, four miles south of Constableville, was first built by a society legally formed, Nov. 2, 1843, having as trustees, Casper Houck, Joseph Bali, Jacob Detenbeck, Joseph Ryan and Nicholas Kresbeck. It was rebuilt in 1851, on the plank road near the summit of the land dividing the waters of the Black and Mohawk rivers. It is of ample size and has a bell. Preaching is done in the German language, and a German school was opened adjacent in 1857.

The next Catholic church formed in the town was St.

---

[1] From Middletown, Ct. His son of the same name became a Presbyterian minister, and an associate of Gerry of Denmark.

[2] *Eld. Way* was from Middletown. He died at his home in Collinsville, Feb. 23, 1848, aged 68 years. His father, Moses Way, died in this town April 7, 1813, aged 67 years.

Mary's, mostly supported by the Irish, and situated half a mile west of Constableville. It was built in 1846. A third church of this denomination, named St. Peter's and St. Paul's, was built in 1854, near Fish creek in the extreme south west corner of the town. It is attended from St. Michael's church, and is also almost entirely supported by Germans.

A Methodist Episcopal society was formed in 1849, with John R. Scovill, David C. Higby and James Crofoot first trustees, and a chapel named the Ebenezer was built in that year, about two miles west of Constableville, on Crofoot hill, at a cost of $1,050. About half this cost was defrayed by James Crofoot and his sons William, John, Levi and Benjamin. Other sects assisted, and may use it to some extent.

A German Union Evangelical church was formed Dec. 5, 1854, with Geo. Long, Samuel Miller and Andrew Hays trustees. They have a small church on the plank road, three miles south of Constableville, near Olmstead creek.

CHAPTER V.

STATE TURNPIKE AND PLANK ROADS.

The first road projected through this section of the state was designed to extend from the Little falls on the Mohawk to the High falls on Black river. The measure was urged upon the legislature by Arthur Noble and Baron Steuben in 1791 and received a favorable report but no further action.[1] The first road actually opened in the county, was made at the expense of the Castorland Company and led from Rome to the High Falls. It was cut out about 1798 by one Jordan, and was used several years, but as its course lay across the current of travel as it was soon after directed, it soon fell into disuse and not a mile of it is now in existence. It is said that a branch from this road led to Whitesboro. The French also caused a road to be laid out and cut from their settlement at the falls to Beaver river, but this can now only be traced by a line of second growth trees through the forest, or the rude vestiges of its bridges. It was nearly direct in its course, and appears to

[1] The petition of Steuben and Noble is given in the *Hist. of Jeff. co., p.* 307. The diversion of the Canadian fur trade to Albany was urged as a prominent motive.

nave been laid out rather with a view to shorten distance than to accommodate settlement along its course. It was cut by Judah Barnes in 1797–8.

A bridle path run with a pocket compass, with very little reference to the most favorable location, was opened about the time of first settlement. It led from Collinsville to Tug Hill west of Turin village and across the hill, down to the place first settled by Ezra Clapp; from thence northward along near the line of the state road, passing west of Martinsburgh village and below Lowville to Deer river and Champion. The idea of climbing a hill over five hundred feet high, and again descending on the same side, when a level and nearer route might have been taken, is sufficiently absurd to one acquainted with the topography of this region, and affords a striking proof of the ignorance of the surveyor. Along this path known as "Dustin's track," the first settlers toiled their weary way on foot or on horseback (for it was not passable for teams), until a more favorable route was discovered and opened.

The first routes through the county were surveyed and chiefly cut out at the expense of the land proprietors, but the principal cost of construction was borne by the settlers along their route. One of the earliest of these in the north part of the county, was that leading from the village of Lowville through Copenhagen to Rutland, or township 3, and on this account still named the "Number Three Road." It was surveyed by Joseph Crary, before 1800, and cut through about 1802 or 1803. The east road in Lowville and Denmark is a little older, and has scarcely been changed from its location in advance of settlement. Through Denmark it is often known as the Base Line road from its running along the line from which offsets were made in surveying the lands adjacent to the river.

Nathaniel Shaler, in 1797, caused a road to be cut from Constableville southward to Rome. It meandered along the valleys not far from the present route, but in no place for any considerable distance on the same line. He established a family named Jones at the half way point in the present town of Ava. He also opened a road in the western part of Turin, which did not settle through and is now partly grown up. Both of these routes were known in their day as the Shaler roads.

The first state patronage for roads in this county, was obtained in an act of March 26, 1803, by which the sum of $41,500, was to be raised by a lottery, for public roads, chiefly in the Black River country. The governor and council of appointment were directed to appoint three commissioners to lay out and improve a road from within two miles of Preston's tavern, in Steuben, to within three miles of the High falls on Black river, and thence through Turin, Lowville, Champion, &c., to Brownville, to intersect another road ordered in the same act to be built from Rome through Redfield. Walter Martin, Silas Stow and Jacob Brown were appointed commissioners for constructing this road, but subsequently Stow was succeeded by Peter Schuyler, and Brown was succeeded by Nathaniel Merriam, Feb. 5, 1820. The location through Lewis county was made by Stow and Martin, and an active rivalry was excited, especially in Turin, between settlers who had located on different routes. The east road through that town was already opened and traveled as far north as a mile beyond Eleazer House's location, and the farms on its route were all taken up by actual settlers. The road nearer the hill through Houseville had been laid out, but led through swamps difficult to pass, but the interests of Ezra Clapp, a sub-agent, and incidentally those of one or two of the commissioners, lay in that direction. Professing no concern but for the greatest good to the greatest number, the offer was made that the route should be given to the parties who would subscribe the greatest amount of free labor. Upon comparing it is said that notwithstanding five hundred days signed by Clapp for Shaler, the east road out numbered the west. Whether so or not, the location, perhaps predetermined, was that of the present plank road.

Thus deprived of their object, the disappointed party resolved to connect their road with the east road in Lowville, and by the utmost effort finished in the summer of 1803, a branch five or six miles long, and from a quarter to half a mile east of the state road, connecting the two east roads. It was never much traveled and soon fell into ruin. This route was known as the Oswegatchie road, as it formed a continuation of the road from the Long falls (Carthage) to the Oswegatchie at Ogdensburgh.

The cost of the State road is said to have been about $30,000 to the state, and its commissioners were continued about twenty years. In 1814 they were authorized to change the southern location.

An act passed Feb. 25, 1805, appointed commissioners living in Oneida co. to lay out a road from Whitesboro, through to intersect the State road in Turin. The road was surveyed by John Hammond, but its proposed location gave much dissatisfaction in Turin. In 1807 memorials were sent in for a lottery to construct a road from Whitestown to Turin, but these failed in consequence of the great number of similar grants that had been made.

A road from Turin to Emilyville, or township 15, great tract 1 of Macomb's purchase, St. Lawrence co., was authorized April 15, 1814, and James T. Watson, Robert McDowell and Levi Collins, were appointed to locate and construct it at the expense of adjacent lands. This act was kept alive about 30 years, and a road was cut through from Independence creek to the old Albany road. By a constrained but perhaps justifiable interpretation of the law, a portion of the money was finally applied upon collateral and tributary roads upon which settlement was progressing. the labor spent on the northern end of this route was lost, as it still lies in the great forest and has never been traveled.

A State road from Lowville to Henderson Harbor was authorized April 17, 1816, and Robert McDowell, of Lowville, Eber Lucas, of Pinckney, and Abel Cole, of Rodman, were appointed to lay it out. The route was surveyed, and the map filed in the clerk's office May 2, 1818. It was located chiefly upon roads previously laid out, and the expense of its improvement was assessed upon adjacent wild lands. In 1820, David Canfield of Denmark, Tyrannus A. Wright of Pinckney, and Sanford Safford of Harrisburgh, were appointed commissioners for completing the road. It runs from the stone church in Lowville nearly parallel with the south lines of Lowville, Harrisburgh and Pinckney, into Jefferson county.

About 1824, a road was cut out from the Black river in Watson, north eastward to the St. Lawrence turnpike. It was wholly built by Watson and Le Ray, and still bears the name of the Erie canal road. It passes through Belfort and the Bent Settlement.

A road from Cedar Point on Lake Champlain to the Black river was authorized April 21, 1828, and the commissioners emerged from the forest on a preliminary survey on the last day of August of that year. They reported that 68 of the 73 miles were saleable lands and estimated the cost at $23,-259 besides bridges. The latter would cost but $350. The eastern end only was opened. A bill appropriating money for this road was rejected in the senate April 8, 1829.

A road from the West road on the north line of Lowville towards Denmark village, was ordered to be laid out by an act of Feb. 19, 1829, naming Pardon Lanpher, Harvey Stephens and Homer Collins as commissioners for this purpose. This road was laid out and has been since traveled.

By an act of April 9, 1831, Peter Mann and Silas Salisbury were appointed to lay out a road from one mile east of Watson bridge north to the Lower falls on Beaver river, and the north line of Watson. This road was also opened.

By act of April 14, 1841, David Judd of Essex, Nelson J. Beach of Lewis and Nathan Ingersol of Jefferson counties, were appointed to construct a road from Carthage through township 4, of Brown's tract, to lake Champlain in Moriah or Crown point, the expenses to be defrayed by a tax on the non-resident lands to be benefited. The road was surveyed in the summer of 1841, and opened during the next half dozen years so as to be passable by teams. The eastern portion now forms the usual route from the lake to the Long Lake settlements, but a portion westward has fallen into decay, and is growing up with trees. It is settled upon and traveled from Carthage to about a mile east of Belfort. Several acts have been passed concerning this road, among which was one in 1843, releasing from the tax certain lands in Denmark and Lowville which came within the limits first defined by law.

A road from Port Leyden to the old forge on township 7 of Brown's tract, Herkimer county, and another from the residence of Hezekiah Abbey to intersect this, were authorized June 8, 1853, to be constructed under the direction of Lyman R. Lyon and Francis Seger, by the aid of highway taxes upon unsettled lands adjacent. The act was extended to 1867 in 1859, but as yet the roads are not fully completed. They follow mainly the routes opened by John Brown about sixty years since.

An act passed April 2, 1859, appointed Seymour Green and Diodate Pease to lay out and open a road from the northern settlements of Osceola through to some road already opened in Martinsburgh, and granted most of the non-resident highway taxes upon the lands of the towns through which it passed, for a period of five years for its construction. Surveys have been made and the route has been partially opened.

The foregoing list embraces, with an exception to be noticed, all the roads located within this county by virtue of special acts of the Legislature, excepting turnpikes, of which more have been projected than built and of which the last rod has long since been merged in common or plank roads.

The Mohawk and Black River Turnpike Co. incorporated April 5, 1810, had power to build a turnpike from

Rome to the residence of Ezra Clapp in Turin. It failed to organize.

The St. Lawrence Turnpike Co., incorporated April 5, 1810, constructed a road across the northeastern border of the county, but no settlements were formed upon it and in 1829 its charter was repealed and the road was divided into common districts. In 1830 an act was passed to tax the adjacent lands for improving this road, from the tenth mile post beyond Carthage to the line of St. Lawrence county. The road was surveyed by B. Wright and Chas. C. Brodhead in 1812.

The Black River and Sackets Harbor Turnpike Co. was incorporated March 30, 1811, to build a road from Lowville through Copenhagen to Watertown, capital $37,500. Nothing done. The Sackets Harbor Turnpike Co. formed by the same act had power to build a turnpike from Copenhagen to Sackets Harbor, but did nothing.

The Lewis Turnpike Co. was incorporated April 8, 1811, to construct a turnpike from Steuben through Boonville and Martinsburgh villages to Lowville, but effected nothing. The parties named in the act were Isaac W. Bostwick, Silas Stow, Walter Martin, Chillus Doty and Peter Schuyler, who might associate others with them. Capital $37,500.

The Boonville Turnpike Co. completed their survey in May, 1816, and about one mile and a half of their road extended into Leyden. This road was constructed and maintained many years, but no gate was erected in Lewis county. It was kept up until a plank road was constructed.

The Turin and Leyden Turnpike Co. capital $10,000, was formed under an act of March 26, 1819, and laid out by Pelatiah Ballou, Broughton White and Peter Post. It was surveyed by Mr. White in June 1819, and was constructed from the State road in Leyden, south of Talcotville, directly through to a point on the State road, a mile north of Turin village. It was completed and put in excellent condition, but no gates were ever erected upon it. One of the principal objects of the projectors of this enterprise was, to procure a direct route where every other means had failed, through the opposition of parties interested in other roads. Application to the town commissioners and the legislature had been tried in vain when this measure was resorted to with success, and the route was left free of toll in the hope of diverting travel upon it. It was given up soon after as a common road. The corporators of this road were Jonathan Collins, Wm. Constable, James McVickar, Geo. Davis,

Oliver Bush, Anthony W. Collins, and their associates. The act gave them the existing highway so far as they needed, and power to buy new lands not over $3,000 in value.

The Canal Turnpike Co. was incorporated Feb. 28, 1823, with $15,000 capital to build a road from Stokesville in Lee to Olmstead creek in Turin. Subscription books were to be opened by Seth B. Roberts and Geo. Brown of Oneida, and Ela Collins of Lewis county. In May 1826, Stephen Ward, Ephraim Owens and John Post were appointed (under an act passed a few days previous), to locate the southern end at the court house in Rome, and to extend it northward to the store of Seth Miller jr., and thence to St. Paul's church in Turin. The stock was by this act increased to $20,000, and the rates of toll were raised. The location north of Constableville was actively opposed by interested parties. The route of this road had been surveyed under the direction of Peter Colt, James Lynch and Moses Wright in August, 1808, under an act of April 8, of that year. To open the road an act of April 15, 1815, appointed Moses Wright assessor, and Geo. Huntington, Wm. Constable and Thomas E. Lawrence commissioners to assign a tax to be levied upon adjacent lands, but the supervisors neglecting to raise the tax, the act was modified April 15, 1816, and the road was opened in that year. It was not however passable in wet seasons until improved as a turnpike. It was proposed in 1823, to extend the canal turnpike to Martinsburgh, but the measure was opposed by a vote of town meeting, and means were found to suppress the project.

Early in 1842 the plan of a McAdamized road through the county was discussed, but nothing resulted from it. In the spring of 1847, efforts were made to organize a plank road on an extensive scale, to extend through Oneida and Lewis counties. A meeting was held at Boonville, Feb. 23d, and town committees were appointed, but nothing was effected towards a general union of effort, and each sectional interest began its race of rivalry, which has produced the natural result. Upon neighboring and nearly parallel routes plank roads were laid, all of which have perished much sooner than was anticipated, and most of which have never earned beyond the cost of collection and maintenance, anything worth naming towards paying first cost or rebuilding. With the exception of the roads laid along the line of the State road south of Lowville, they have all been abandoned and again laid out into road districts. In every instance these roads were constructed along old and well settled roads, except at points where to improve the grade it was found necessary to deviate slightly from the former line. The excavations and embankments upon these roads will form a durable monument to their memory, and if the gain in value of farms and their market products, justly due to plank roads, were placed to their credit, it would far exceed the amount expended upon them. Unfortunately the public spirited citizen has in this case, as in others, often paid too liberally to enrich his parsimonious but more wealthy neighbor, and fortune, with partial hand, has dealt out her favors to the undeserving.

Of the eight plank roads, with an aggregate length of seventy-six miles, that have been built in this county, all but three have been discontinued. The history of these roads is briefly as follows:

Rome and Turin P. R., laid on the route of the old Canal turnpike, filed its articles in the Secretary's office Dec. 24, 1847. Capital $45,000; cost $50,000; was 30 miles long; was inspected July 21, Sept. 28, and Oct. 28, 1848, and abandoned to the public Jan. 18, 1855.

Turin P. R., through the town of Turin, on the State road, filed articles Dec. 27, 1847; cap. $8,000; was 5½ m. long, and was inspected July 15, 1848, except 117 rods south of the village, which was inspected July 9, 1849. After paying large dividends a few years, it was bought at a small price by parties interested in its maintenance, and it is still kept up. Large quantities of timber cut for rail road ties, have been used in relaying it.

West Martinsburgh and Copenhagen P. R., filed articles Feb. 17, 1848. Cap. $25,000; length 17 miles; cost 22,000, the whole of which was lost. Inspected July 17, 1849, and abandoned March 19, 1856, and April 5, 1858. It was laid on the West road from the south line of Martinsburgh to Copenhagen.

West Turin and Leyden P. R., on the line of the former Turin and Leyden Turnpike (so called) from its southern end to the Rome and Turin P. R., one mile north of Constableville. It filed its articles Oct. 23, 1848; cap. $6,000; length 5½ m. Inspected August 30, 1849, and abandoned March 3, 1856. It was a total loss to the owners, and made but one or two small dividends.

Lowville and Carthage P. R., along the State road from the line of Martinsburgh to Denmark village, and thence by the direct road to Carthage. It filed its articles Nov. 8, 1848. Cap. $22,000, cost $26,000, the most of which was lost. Length 16 m. Inspected July 30, Aug. 6, and Sept. 11, 1849, and abandoned May 5, 1859.

Boonville P. R., on the State road from the south line of Turin to Boonville, and southward. It filed its articles Nov. 8, 1848. Cap. $30,000; length 20 m. Inspected Aug. 31, 1849, and still maintained.

Martinsburgh P. R , on the State road through the town of Martinsburgh. Filed its articles Dec. 13, 1848. Cap. $7,000; length 5 m. Inspected July 13, 1849, and still maintained.

The Great Bend and Copenhagen P. R., about three miles of which lay in this county, filed its articles Dec. 4, 1848, cap. $13,000; length 10 m.; inspected July 17, 1849, and abandoned about 1856.

Several other plank roads were proposed, among which was one from Lowville to New Bremen; one from near Constableville to the High falls, and another from Turin to the High falls and Lyonsdale. The Lowville and Denmark P. R. Co., formed a regular organization but did nothing. During the summer of 1859, an effort was being made to raise the means to rebuild the road from West Leyden to Stokesville on the line of the old Rome and Turin P. R., but without success.

These several plank roads were chiefly laid with hemlock plank eight feet wide and three inches thick, the track being usually on the west side of the grade, so that teams going southward retained the plank in meeting other teams.

Mail Routes.—The first route through the valley was established Jan. 19, 1804. Daniel Gould is said to have been the first carrier. He was succeeded by Reuben Chase soon after, who began in 1804, and performed one trip each week from Utica to Brownville. Mr. Barnabas Dickinson of Denmark, was the next mail carrier, and by him a two horse carriage was first placed upon the route for the accommodation of travellers. About 1812, or 1814, Parker & Co., run a line of stages. Other parties were afterwards engaged in this service, and in Jan., 1824, E. Backus and Ela Merriam, with N. W. Kiniston and John McElwaine, commenced carrying the mail, and with the exception of four years Mr. Merriam has continued in the business till the present time.[1] It has been carried daily except on Sunday during 36 years, and until 1848 to 50 over as muddy a road

[1] The shortest trip from Utica to Sackets Harbor ever made over this route by stages, was on Thursday, Feb. 19, 1829. The trip was made in 9 hours 45 minutes, and the mail was changed at every office. The stops amounted to 39 minutes, distance 93 miles, snow $2\frac{1}{2}$ feet deep. Mr. Merriam has been concerned in stage routes from Denmark to Ogdensburgh, from Rome to

Ela Merriam,

as could be found in the state. The spirited and sacrificing efforts of Mr. Merriam, in calling public attention to plank roads and other improvements, and in their construction and maintenance, entitle him to the lasting gratitude of the citizens of Lewis county. Without his exertions the only existing plank road southward from Lowville would ere this have been abandoned, and the traveling public left to plod their weary way over the original mud road.

There has been since its first establishment, a daily mail line (except Sunday) through the county with a short interval in 1859. In 1821, a route was established from Martinsburgh to Adams; and about 1826, a route from Rome to Turin. At a later day a side route was established from Turin to the post offices east, and from Lowville through the woods to Edwards, St. Lawrence co. There are at present several short routes supplying offices not on the central line, at intervals of two, three and six days.

CHAPTER VI.

CANAL AND RAIL ROAD PROJECTS.

Black River Canal and Improvement.—Excepting the vague allusion to canals and other public works, in the instructions of Tillier in 1796, no measure was proposed for constructing a canal into this county until 1825, when DeWitt Clinton in his annual message suggested a connection between Black river and the Erie canal, as one of several highly desirable canal routes. Under a general act passed April 20, 1825, a survey was ordered from the Erie canal in Herkimer co., to the head waters of Black river and thence to Ogdensburgh, and another from Rome to the same.

A survey was begun by James Geddes, one of the chief engineers on the Erie canal, July 25, 1825, and the leveling was continued down to Carthage. By this survey the Remsen summit on the eastern route was found 841 feet, and the descent from thence to the lake 985 feet. From Rome to Boonville, the rise was 700 feet, and from thence to the

---

Sackets Harbor, through Redfield, from Oneida to Turin, from Rome to Turin and Denmark, from Rome by Copenhagen to Watertown, from Rome by Western, to Boonville, and now from Boonville to Lowville, in company with Moses M. Smith of the latter place.

river below the falls 422 feet. The Camden route to Ogdensburgh, 129 miles, was estimated at $655,630, and the Boonville route, 114 miles, $931,014. Mr. Geddes advised two dams with locks on the river, and a towing path on the bank. A canal meeting was held at the Court house Sept. 21, 1825, at which James T. Watson reported Geddes's survey, the maps were left with Mr Dayan for reference, and a committee was appointed to gather statistics of transportation from each town in the county, specifying every article of which more than five tons were carried, with the probable increase. Other meetings were held in Jefferson and St. Lawrence counties, and committees of correspondence were chosen to secure unity of action.

A meeting at the court house Dec. 24, 1825, prepared a petition to the legislature, and reported the following estimates of business:

Denmark 1272 tons ; mean distance 60 miles.

Lowville 1310 tons, viz: grain and flour 550 ; ashes 130 ; butter and cheese 10 ; sundries 620. Distance 60 miles at 1½ cents per mile.

Martinsburgh 1280 tons. *Turin* 600 tons. *Leyden, Watson, Pinckney* and *Harrisburgh,* 1200 tons. Total 5,662 tons, amounting to $5,435.80. From Jefferson county the estimate claimed 10,680 tons at $10,146 ; from St. Lawrence 13,000 tons at $23,400, and from Herkimer and Oneida 4,620 tons at $1,386, making with the extra transportation added to the Erie canal a revenue of $69,145.88.[1]

The county papers of northern New York at this period teemed with articles favoring the measure, and a series of statistical essays in the Black River Gazette, signed *Jonathan,* had a beneficial influence upon public opinion.

The canal commissioners reported March 6, 1826, upon the Herkimer, Rome and Camden routes. The first had a rise and fall of 1831 feet, and was deemed inexpedient. The second had 1587 feet lockage, and would cost to Ogdensburgh $931,014, and the third with 635 feet lockages would cost $855,630. No result followed, and on the 2d of Jan., 1827, a canal meeting held at the court house, renewed their memorial, and petitioned Congress to procure the right of navigating the St. Lawrence to the ocean. A meeting at Carthage Oct. 23, 1827, prepared the way for a general convention at the court house in Martinsburgh on the 4th of Dec., at which delegates attended from all the towns in-

[1] A general committee of correspondence was chosen at this meeting, consisting of Russell Parish, Isaac W. Bostwick, Ela Collins, Charles Dayan and James McVickar.

terested in the work. Spirited addresses were delivered, and a resolution was passed for the incorporation of a company to construct a canal.

The address of the Rev. Isaac Clinton upon this occasion, affords data in the highest degree valuable as showing existing resources. It was therein stated that five towns in Lewis co. made annually 100 tons of potash each, and three others about fifty tons each. About 2500 barrels of pork, and 60,000 bushels of wheat were supposed to pass through and from the county to the canal. About 1500 head of cattle were driven from the county and five times as many from Jefferson and St. Lawrence. The county exported 50 tons of *butter* and *cheese*, 20 tons of grass seed, 14 tons of wool, 12 tons of oil of mint, and 325 tons or 650 hogsheads of whiskey. It received annually 400 tons of merchandise, 50 tons of bar iron and steel, 40 tons of gypsum, 15 tons of dyestuffs and 20 tons of *hides.* The increase from the county and beyond had been during twelve years at the rate of 300 tons annually. This address closed with a direct appeal to the enterprise of our citizens. It was as follows:

"Perhaps, sir, it may be said that the remarks are plausible, but the undertaking is great and we can do without it. So we might do without many other things. A farmer on a very small scale might do without a scythe and cut his grass with a jack-knife. What are canals and what are rail roads but great labor saving machines? What a grass scythe is to a jack-knife, so is a canal to a common team. Will it be said, sir, that the undertaking is really too great—we can not accomplish it? Let no such thought lodge in any man's bosom. Say we *can* accomplish it, we *must* and we *will* have a canal. What if the patriots of the Revolution had said—'slavery is truly detestable and liberty is equally desirable, but what are we? We have no army, no treasury, no revenue, no magazines of arms, and such is the mighty power and prowess of Great Britain that we can not withstand them?' What, I say! Then we and our children would have been slaves forever. But they said, we *can* withstand them; and they *did* withstand them, and with their blood and treasure and indescribable hardships and privations procured the benefits and blessings we now enjoy. Let us not say "we can't." This expression has been the ruin of thousands, has prevented many a glorious enterprise,—has kept many a family poor and in the back ground. This was the imbecile language of our committee, last winter! Let us then say we *can* and we *will* have a canal. Many farmers may turn out if need require, with their teams and work out shares. It would be better to do this than be forever wearing out their teams in carrying their produce to market and paying toll at turnpike gates. The enterprise is only worthy of the industrious and spirited citizens inhabiting this section of the state. And from the previous estimates I am confident the stock must be good, and after the canal is made and proved, will sell at any time for ready cash."

A writer in the Black River Gazette, under the signature of *Asdrubal,* at this period also urged the measure proposed at this convention.

The application in the hands of Mr. Dayan then in the the senate, and Gen. Ruggles in assembly, procured an act passed March 20, 1828, incorporating the *Black River canal company.* A subscription of $100,000 by the state was proposed by Mr. Dayan, who was supported by Senators Hart, Waterman and Wilkins, and opposed by Jordan and Carroll. It was finally stricken out in the senate.

The act incorporated Geo. Brayton, Isaac Clinton, Levi Adams, Peter Schuyler, James McVickar, James T. Watson, Seth B. Roberts and Vincent Le Ray de Chaumont and their associates, with $400,000 capital and the usual powers of similar stock companies. The canal was to be finished within three years, and the franchise included the navigation of the river to Carthage. The commissioners above named employed Alfred Cruger[1] to survey and estimate a route, and his report rendered in September of that year, mostly advised inclined planes instead of locks, and placed the total cost of 44.86 miles at $433,571.25. The structures were to include 9 culverts, 8 dams, 7 waste weirs, 52 bridges, 1015 feet rise by planes, and 75 feet by locks. He proposed to improve the river by wing dams, where obstructed by sand bars, eight of which might be built for $4,168. Subscription books were opened at the office of W. Gracie, N. Y., Dec. 15, 1828, but the stock was not taken, and a meeting at Lowville represented from many towns, Jan. 24, 1829, discussed a plan of local taxation, but finally abandoned it, and agreed upon a memorial urging its adoption as a state work.

A concurrent resolution introduced by Mr. Ruggles, was passed April 7, 1829, ordering a new survey in case that made by Cruger was not found reliable, and the canal commissioners were directed to report the result to the next legislature. Canal meetings were held at Lowville June 4, and at Turin Oct. 17, 1829, and an effort was made to procure a nomination of a person pledged to the canal

[1] Mr. Cruger died at Mantanzas, Cuba, in 1845, while engaged in a rail road survey.

alone, irrespective of party, but did not meet with favor. On the 12th of January, 1830, a convention of delegates from Lewis, Jefferson and Oneida, met at Lowville to memorialize the legislature ; town committees were appointed, and again Nov. 22, of that year, for a similar purpose.

On the 6th of April, 1830, the canal commissioners were by law directed to cause a survey of the proposed canal, and Holmes Hutchinson employed under this act, reported his labors the 6th of March following.[1] His estimate based upon a canal 20 feet wide at the bottom, 4 feet deep, and and locks 10 by 70 feet, capable of passing boats of 25 tons, placed the total cost of canal and feeder at $602,544. The first company having expired by its own limitation, a new one of the same name was chartered April 17, 1832, with $900,000 capital, and power to construct a canal from Rome or Herkimer to the Black river, and thence to Ogdensburgh, Cape Vincent, or Sackets Harbor. The work was divided into six sections, of which one must be finished in three and the whole in ten years. Nothing was done under this act.

In 1834, Francis Seger in the senate, and Geo. D. Ruggles in the assembly procured an act (April 22,) providing for an accurate survey of a canal from the Erie canal to the Black river below the falls, and thence to Carthage. The surveys of Cruger and Hutchinson were to be adopted in whole or in part, at the discretion of the commissioners, and the result was to be reported at the next session. Mr. Timothy B. Jervis was employed upon this duty, and his survey based upon a canal 26 feet wide at the bottom, banks 7 feet high, water 4 feet deep, locks and two inclined planes, computed the cost at $907,802.72, with composite locks, and $1,019,226.72 with stone locks.[2]

A report from the canal board in 1835, stated that the actual cost of freight by rail road was 3½ cents a mile per ton, as shown by the Mohawk and Hudson rail road. This is believed to have influenced favorable action upon the Black River canal, although manifestly unfair as regarded rail roads, because based upon the experience of a road only sixteen miles long, then with two heavy inclined planes, and using locomotive and stationary steam power as well as horses.

The construction of the Black River canal was authorized by an act of April 19, 1836, which provided for a navigable feeder from Black river to Boonville, and a canal from thence

1 Assembly Documents, No. 229, 1831.
2 Assembly Documents, Nos. 55, 150, 1835.

to Rome and to the High Falls, and the improvement of the river to Carthage for steam boats drawing 4 feet water. The details of construction and expense were left discretionary with the canal commissioners, who were to receive from the canal fund such sums as the canal board might estimate and certify would be the probable expense, with such additional sums over and above the foregoing, borrowed on the credit of the state, and not to exceed $800,000. The surplus waters of Black river, not needed for the canal, were to be passed around the locks by sluices or turned into Lansing's kill or the Mohawk river.

This act was largely due to the exertions of Francis Seger of the senate, and Charles Dayan of the assembly, whose active labors for the promotion of this measure deserve honorable recognition in this connection.[1] Eleven years had passed since this work was first urged upon public notice by the governor, and the youth who listened with enthusiasm to the glowing prospect of coming benefits from the completed canal, had ripened into manhood before the first positive step was taken towards its realization. Still they were destined to grow old in the anticipation, and while those who had fondly cherished and aided the successive stages of effort, became silvered with age; full many closed their eyes in death, before it became a practical reality! Stow, Clinton, Watson, the elder Le Ray, Lyon, W. Martin, Adams, J. McVickar, Collins, Parish, Rockwell, Bancroft, J. H. Leonard, N. Merriam, H. G. Hough, B. Yale, S. Allen, and many others who had served on committees, and contributed time and money to the promotion of this improvement, died before it was so far completed as to admit boats into the river.

Surveys were placed in charge of Porteus R. Root, and in Sept., 1836, Daniel C. Jenne, resident engineer, began further examinations which were continued through the fall and in the spring following.

The first contract for construction was made November

---

[1] *Francis Seger* removed from Albany county to this county in 1826. He studied law with Marcus T. Reynolds, and was admitted to the bar in 1823, having taught school at various times to aid in acquiring an education. He was several years deputy clerk, and from 1828 to 1833, inclusive, clerk of assembly, but yielded this position at the urgent solicitation of friends of the Black River canal, for a place in the Senate, where he remained four years. He was appointed a master in chancery, and in April, 1843, under Bouck's administration, became first judge of Lewis county. He continued to officiate until 1856, having been elected judge and surrogate, at the first judicial election in June, 1847, and again in 1851. In 1846, he was elected one of the secretaries of the constitutional convention. His highest ambition ever seems to have been the faithful discharge of official trusts, with an ability and simplicity worthy of imitation.

N. ORR—CO.

11, 1837, including 14 miles from Rome and work was at once begun. On the 26th of May following, the work was let to Boonville, including the feeder, and Sept. 7, 1838, eight miles north of that place. Work was begun and vigorously prosecuted until, under an act of March 29, 1842, entitled "An act to provide for paying the debt and preserving the credit of the state," more familiarly known as the *tax and stop law,* work was suspended. The original estimate upon which work had been begun was $1,068,437.20. The third division, extending from Boonville to the river a distance of ten miles, contained 38 locks of which 24 were nearly finished, the gates and docking timbers excepted. The other 14 locks had not been contracted. It was estimated that $276,000 would finish this division, and $809,000 the whole work.[1] There had been expended according to the report of 1842, $1,550,097.67. The sum of $55,222.78 was paid for extra allowances and for suspension of contracts on the part of the state, and much loss was occasioned by the decay of wooden structures, washing away of banks, filling in of excavations, and other damages to which half finished works of this class are liable.

In the constitutional convention of 1846, Lewis county was represented by Russell Parish, an ardent friend and able advocate of the Black river canal. In a speech of Sept. 15th he urged the completion of this work with great zeal, and the clause in the constitution (art. vii. sec. 3), providing for the completion of this canal among other public works, is without doubt to be attributed in quite a degree to him.[2]

An act passed May 12, 1847, appropriated $100,000 to this canal. Work was soon after resumed on the feeder, and the next year on the canal south of Boonville, many old contracts were resumed, new portions were let, and in the fall of 1848, the feeder was finished so far as to admit water on the 18th of October. The first boat passed up the feeder to the river Dec. 13, 1848. The canal from Boonville to Port Leyden was put under contract in 1849, and the feeder was brought fully and successfully into operation in May or June of that year. The first boat from Rome

---

1 Other estimates placed this amount less. A special report by acting commissioner Enos, dated Feb. 23, 1843 (Senate Doc., 49), estimated the cost of completion, with stone locks, at $639,000.01, and with composite locks, at $436,740.96.

2 The vote in Feb. 1854, on amending the state constitution in relation to the canals, was in this county, cast in favor of the change in every town except Montague, West Turin, Turin, Osceola, Lewis, Leyden, and Pinckney, amounting to 1572 *for* and 907 *against* the measure.

came up May 10, 1850, and water was let in down to Port Leyden, Oct. 27, 1850, and it was brought into use in the spring of 1851.[1] The part north of Port Leyden was put under contract in 1850, to be done July 1, 1854, and one mile brought into use in 1852. A dam four feet high was built in 1854 just above the High falls at a cost of $5,000, affording two and a half miles of navigation on Black and Moose rivers. The canal passes 45 chains in the river above this dam.

The canal was finally brought into the river Nov. 13, 1855, by the completion of 2.7 miles of canal comprising 13 locks north of Port Leyden. The canal is 35.62 miles in length. The feeder is 10.29 miles, and the slack water above the dam 2 miles further. A feeder at Delta 1.38 miles, and the river below the falls 42.5 miles making in all about 95 miles of navigation, including 5 miles on Beaver river which enters 10 miles above the falls and is navigable for boats of three feet draft. The canal rises 693 feet by 70 locks, from the Erie canal at Rome to the summit at Boonville. It descends northward, 387 feet, by 39 locks to the river below the High falls a distance of 10.3 miles.

The canal has 6 aqueducts, 12 waste-weirs, 18 culverts, 36 road bridges, 40 farm bridges, 3 tow bridges and 2 dams. Its net cost of construction and working, up to Sept. 30, 1857, was $4,050,406.70. It had not then paid its expenses for repairs in any one year.[2]

The experience of 1849 (a very dry season) demonstrated the necessity of reservoirs on the head waters of Black river to supply the Rome level on the Erie canal. Of these three, known as the Woodhull, North Branch and South Branch reservoirs, having together an area of 2,177 acres, and a capacity of 1,822,002,480 cubic feet have been built. The lakes on Moose river, appear capable of improvement as reservoirs, to an extent sufficient to meet all probable demands for river navigation or hydraulic power below.

The improvement of the river channel has been made a subject of vacillating project, and barren expenditure, which reflects little credit upon the state authorities charged with this duty, and although large sums have been applied to this object, we have comparatively little benefit to show beyond the dam at Carthage,[3] three substantial bridges, and

[1] The estimated cost of completion in 1851 was $397,761.96 including the river improvement. In 1853 the estimated cost of finishing was $155,400, or according to the plan of 1851 $248,784.

[2] Senate Doc. 129, 1858. The deficiency alluded to, is not limited to this canal, and might be said with reference to others.

[3] The dam at Carthage was built in 1854, at a cost of $7,500. One of the bridges above alluded to is at that village.

a few landing places partly built at town or individual cost. In the summer of 1849 two boats were built for clearing the river, one at the Falls and the other at Illingworth's in New Bremen. In 1851 a plan was adopted for constructing jetty dams and piers, for confining the current and thus deepening the channel. The estimated cost of this work, including the dam at Carthage, two bridges and the reservoirs was $153,200. On the 18th of October, 1853, after large expenditures, this plan was abandoned, and that of two dams with locks was substituted, under the advice of John C. Mather, then canal commissioner.[1] This scheme was superseded in 1854, by the canal commissioners, on the ground of fraudulent contracts,[2] and that of 1851 reädopted Dec. 19 of that year, at an estimated cost of $161,000 for completion. Other heavy expenditures were incurred, when on the 3d of Sept., 1857, this plan was again abandoned, and the engineer was directed to furnish plans for a dam and lock just above the mouth of Otter creek. There had then been spent on the piers, $88,320. The dam and lock are now under contract, and unless the plan be again changed, and the half finished work abandoned, they will perhaps be in use in one or two years. The estimated cost of the work at contract prices is $27,309.20, of which $10,840.10 were spent in 1859. The chamber of the lock is 160 by 34 feet, and the lift 4 feet.

It will be noticed that the idea of improvement of the river has been a subject of progressive growth. In 1828 Cruger estimated its cost at $4,168. In 1830 Hutchinson found it would be $12,000. In 1834 Jervis estimated it at $20,840. Its ultimate cost is to be revealed by time and our canal engineers.

The Black river was declared a public highway by act of March 16, 1821, from the High falls to Carthage, and on the 24th of June, 1853, from the falls up to the Moose river tract. The latter act applied $5000 to the improvement of the channel for floating logs, required booms and dams to be constructed with reference to passing timbers, and attached penalties for obstructing the channel. The commissioners for applying this sum were Alfred N. Hough, Gardner Hinkley, and Anson Blake, jr.

The steamer *Cornelia*[3] was built in 1832 at Carthage, by Paul Boynton, now of Canton, for a company in which V.

---

[1] A dam near Lowville was to cost $29,700, and one at Otter creek $35,000, two bridges $6,000, dredging $0,000, and reservoirs $39,600.

[2] For details see Assem. Doc. No. 8, 1855.

[3] Named from Madame Cornelia Juhel a relative of the Le Rays. Among other names proposed was *Dido*, by some one who is presumed to have read the Enead of Virgil.

Le Ray was president and principal owner, at a cost of about $6,000. Its dimensions were, length of keel 90 feet, across the guards 22 feet, and when light it drew 22 inches of water. She measured 70 tons, and was furnished with two upright high pressure engines of ten horse power each, when first built, but before starting one of these was taken out, reducing the draft to 17 inches. The machinery was built by N. Starbuck of Troy. Her cabin was aft, the floor a little below the deck, and the forward part was covered by an awning. Her first trip was made Sept. 22, 1832, having on board a large number of citizens, and everything went on pleasantly until opposite Lowville where she ran on a sand bar, and although the hands jumped into the water and tried to lift her off it was of no avail.

This was but a prelude to numerous like casualties which marked her short and unprofitable career, which ended with 1833. A thrilling incident attended her first visit to the High falls. The man at the tiller, wishing to show the party on board and the spectators on shore the qualities of the boat in rapid water, steered up so near the falls, that as she turned the spray from the torrent covered the deck, and the boat itself came as near as possible being drawn under. Fortunately there was a heavy pressure of steam up, and the next moment the craft was out of harm's way, with only a thorough drenching.[1] This boat was dismantled, and a few years after was privately cut loose from the dock at Carthage in a freshet, and went to pieces in the rapids. Her engine was put on a boat upon Black lake, and her boiler, many years after, was used in pumping water at one of the iron mines near Somerville, St. Lawrence co.

In the spring of 1853, G. H. Gould fitted up a scow with a small portable engine connected with a stern wheel by a band. This craft named the *Enterprise* made a few trips. The little steam tug *William P. Lawrence*, of Lansingburgh, was brought into the river in Sept. 1856, and on the 11th made the first steamboat visit to Beaver falls. She soon after burst her boiler near Independence creek and was completely demolished. The captain was badly injured in the face, a boy was thrown through the window into the river, and the engineer into the hold. The fireman was thrown into the river somewhat scalded, and the boiler itself blown ashore, the steam chest going far beyond over the tops of the trees. The accident was attributed to fastening down of the safety valve.

---

[1] Related by Mr. Boynton, builder and engineer at the time.

In Jan. 1848, notice of an application for the formation of a steamboat company with $50,000 was published but failed. The *Black River steamboat company* was formed at Lowville, April 24, 1856, and in the summer following, the the steamer *L. R. Lyon* was built at Lyons falls; it was launched June 26, 1856,[1] and got in operation that year, at a cost of $8000. When light this boat draws 15 inches of water; she is built with a stern wheel, after the model of the Ohio river boats, with open sides and elevated cabin. She is chiefly employed in towing canal boats. The little steamer *J. W. Norcross*, built at Phœnix, Oswego county, came in from the canal in the spring of 1858, and was employed one season as a packet, making a trip from Carthage to the falls and back daily. She has since run on the Erie canal.

Rail Road Project.—*The Black River company*, incorporated in 1832, was empowered to construct a route by canal or rail road from the Erie canal at Rome or Herkimer to Ogdensburgh, but accomplished nothing beyond a partial survey.[2] In December, 1852, the plan of a rail road through the Black River valley was discussed, and a call for a meeting signed by thirty-four citizens, and published in the Northern Journal in January 1853, led to a favorable response, and the appointment of a committee consisting of five persons in each county interested, for collecting statistics. A meeting was appointed at Theresa on the 20th, and another at Boonville on the 26th of the same month. On the 27th articles of association were drawn up forming the *Black River rail road company,* with $1,200,000 capital, for building a rail road from Herkimer on Mohawk village, to Clayton on the St. Lawrence. Of the proposed directors Ela Merriam, Seth Miller, Moses M. Smith, Wm. L. Easton and John Benedict, resided in Lewis county.

This movement excited immediately an active rivalry between Utica and Rome, and on the 29th of Jan. 1853, the *Black River and Utica rail road company* was formed, and the articles filed two days after in the secretary's office. The capital was $1,000,000 (increased one half Sept. 26, 1853), and the directors were T. S. Faxton, Spencer Kellogg, John Butterfield, Martin Hart, Alfred Churchill, Jas. V. P. Gardiner, Benj. F. Ray, James S. Lynch, Wm. H. Ferry, Hugh Crocker, Harvey Barnard, Jonathan R. Warner, and John D. Leland, all of Utica excepting Leland, who resided

[1] By the fall of a platform on this occasion, about a hundred persons were pcecipitated several feet to the ground, and one, Mrs. Edwin Woolworth, died a few days after, from the nervous shock thus occasioned.

[2] For details see *Hist. of Jefferson Co.*, p. 338.

in Deerfield. They proposed to build a road by way of Boonville and Carthage to Clayton. Daniel C. Jenne was at once employed to begin surveys in the midst of winter, and energetic efforts were made to secure subscriptions to the stock.

The citizens of Rome lost no time in raising means for a preliminary survey, under Octave Blanc, and on the 8th of March at a meeting held at Lowville, the claims of the three rival routes south of Boonville were presented and urged, and a committee of three to each town on the line from Boonville to the St. Lawrence, was appointed to examine the subject and to decide as to which of the three routes had the strongest claims to patronage. This committee was unable to agree and appointed a sub-committee of eight, to visit the several places proposed for junction with the N. Y. Central rail road, and report at an adjourned meeting at Carthage on the 22d inst. The Lowville meeting continued two days, and an intense activity was shown by the rival parties in securing a favorable decision. At the Carthage meeting a rule was adopted, that *two-thirds* majority should decide upon the southern terminus. After two days' discussion it was found impossible to obtain the requisite vote and the committee was discharged. The *Ogdensburgh, Clayton and Rome rail road company* was formed Feb. 19, 1853, with $2,000,000 capital. Its directors were Henry A. Foster, John Stryker, Edward Huntington and Alex. Mudge of Rome, Elijah B. Allen and Henry Van Rennselaer of Ogdensburgh, Augustus Chapman of Morristown, Wm. L. Easton of Lowville, Seth Miller of West Turin, A. H. Barnes of Martinsburgh, Sidney Sylvester of Denmark, Samuel J. Davis of Wilma, and Jason Clark of Plessis.[1] The Herkimer location having been abandoned, the Utica and Rome rail road projects were pressed with enthusiasm by their respective friends. Acts were procured allowing the corporations of Utica, Rome and Ogdensburgh to subscribe to the stock. Subscriptions were urged, surveys completed, and right of way purchased or solicited as a donation.

Work was begun on the B. R. and U. rail road at Utica, with commemorative ceremonies, August 27, and at Lowville, Oct. 27, 1853. Speeches were made, in which many pleasant things were said of Lewis county, and cheerful hopes expressed that the road thus begun would before many months be finished. The road was put under contract Aug. 10, with Farewell Case, Lund and Co., who in

[1] Extended details of the origin of these companies will be found in the *History of Jefferson Co.*, p. 339

Oct. 1853, sub-let a part extending from the north end of Lowville village to south of Martin's creek in Martinsburgh, to Solomon Phelps, Chester Ray and Albert Buel.

Large quantities of ties were got out, the masonry of bridges was built in a substantial manner, the road was extensively graded, and costly excavations in rock and earth were begun, and in some places completed. The road was opened to Boonville, Dec. 15, 1855, and has since been in regular operation to that place, changing entirely the business connection between Lewis county and Rome, and diverting nearly all the travel and business of the Black River valley from Denmark southward to Utica. A large amount of work has been done on this route north of Boonville, chiefly in grading and the masonry of bridges.

Work was begun on the O., C. & R. R. R. at Rome, Nov. 10, and at Carthage, Nov. 23, 1853. Sections 6, 7 and 9 were awarded Nov. 7, 1853, to Clapp and Allen of Lewis co., and Archibald McVickar & Co. of N. J. Sections 10, 11, and 12 in Lewis, to Bebee Williams & Co. of Onondaga. Much of the right of way was secured and fenced, a large amount of grading was done, but no part of the road was ever completed, and five years after the date of organization the project was hopelessly and completely abandoned. A considerable amount of the land granted for the use of the road has been reconveyed, and the shareholders, exasperated by repeated calls for installments to pay large salaries of officers and unavailing expenses, are it is believed mostly free from this reckless adventure. The proposition for two rail roads, side by side, and seldom a mile apart, running through the whole length of the county, both leading to the same markets and supplying the same wants, was sufficiently absurd. There can not be room for the slightest doubt, but that the present business of the county would render the construction of one rail road through it a safe and prudent investment, while the now dormant resources which it must awaken, would ensure it permanent and remunerative support. The wealth of its forests, the extent of its water power, and the still half developed capacity of its soil, are subjects of too much importance to lie long neglected. It is understood that the Black River and Utica R. R. will change owners during the present year, and that it will pass into the hands of the bond holders. If the citizens of Lewis co. prove true to their own interests, they will unite in a strong effort to extend this road through at least to Lowville, and there can be little doubt, but that this would at least double the present business upon the portion already constructed.

The Sackets Harbor and Saratoga rail road co. was incorporated by an act of April 10, 1848, which granted 250,000 acres of the state lands, upon conditions which have since been so far complied with that the lands have been conveyed to the company. The preliminary arrangements were completed and the company duly organized Jan. 10, 1852. On the 8th of April 1852, the ceremony of breaking ground near Dayanville was performed with parade of martial music and oratorical display, but work was not actively commenced until 1854. During the summer of that year, a large amount of grading was done on the southern portion, and in places in this county, but in the fall of 1854, work was suspended and has not been resumed. The intention of the company was to first construct a plank road, to facilitate the travel which the rail road would require until opened, and large quantities of road plank were sold for less than their worth in standing timber upon the suspension of work. The report at the close of 1858, states that the capital stock is $6,000,000; amount subscribed $5,461,100; paid in $2,714,150; expenditures $3,675,858.67; length 182 miles. The legislature by act of April 6, 1857, changed the name of the company to the *Lake Ontario and Hudson River rail road company.*

CHAPTER VII.

NOTICES OF SOCIETIES AND ASSOCIATIONS.

Agriculture, &c.—From 1808 to 1814, premiums for domestic cloths were awarded by the state, to the extent of $15,210, mostly by the judges of the county courts, and specimens of each are still preserved in the *Albany Institute.* The following awards were made to citizens of Lewis county:

1809, Lewis Graves, $80.

1810, Peleg Card, $80.

1811, Peleg Card, $40; Chester Wood, $35; Nathan Munger, $30.

1814, Moses Waters, $40; Ethan Card, $35; Lewis Card, $30.

Under an act of 1819, creating a board of agriculture,

Lewis county was entitled to $100 annually for two years, if a like amount should be raised by subscription. A society was formed under this act in 1820, held four annual fairs, and distributed premiums in money and plate upon farms, tillage, animals and domestic manufactures. The secretary was Charles Dayan, and the president for one year at least, was the Rev. Isaac Clinton. The first fair was held Oct. 23, 1821, at which the address was delivered by Judge Stow, and premiums to the amount of over $300 were awarded. Members were furnished with a badge formed of ears of wheat, worn like a cockade upon the hat. The festival ended with a ball at Welle's tavern, where nearly a hundred couple attended. The last fair was held in 1824.

The Lewis county association for improving the breed of horses, was formed in 1831, and held one or two annual fairs. It may be here noticed, that this county early acquired distinction for its superior breed of horses.

On the 5th of May, 1841, a law gave $53 annually to Lewis co., in aid of a county agricultural society, which has since been continued annually. A meeting called by the county clerk, June 21, 1841, was addressed by Charles E. Clarke, and a constitution adopted, which remained unchanged until Dec. 27, 1859, when the present constitution was adopted, under the law of 1855. Under the former, a president, six vice-presidents, an executive committee of five, a corresponding and recording secretary, and a treasurer were elected every year. Members paid $1 annually, and none other could receive premiums.

The first officers elected were, Clement Whitaker, *president;* Johnson Talcott, Carlos Hart, Charles D. Morse, Harrison Blodget, Elias Gallup, Alburn Foster, *vice-presidents;* Jared Stiles, Enoch Thompson, Timothy Mills, Levi Hart, Oliver Bush, *executive committee;* Stephen Leonard, *corresponding secretary;* Charles Dayan, *recording secretary;* and Harvey Stephens, *treasurer.* The officers of the society have been as follows:

Presidents.—1841–2, Clement Whitaker; 1843–4, Ela Merriam; 1845, Lyman R. Lyon; 1846–8, Norman Gowdy; 1849–50, Hiram Mills; 1851, S. D. Mason; 1852, Ashley Davenport; 1853, Seth Miller; 1855, Sanford Coe; 1856, Lewis Stephens; 1857–8, Edmund Baldwin; 1859, Moses M. Smith.

Corresponding Secretaries.—1841–2, Stephen Leonard; 1844, Charles L. Martin; 1845, Francis Seger; 1846, V. R. Martin; 1847, Wm. King; 1848–9, Cornelius H. Wood; 1850–4, Harrison Barnes; 1855, Chas. D. Adams; 1856, Leonard C. Davenport; 1857, Cornelius E. Stephens; 1858, H. D. Nolton; 1859, Jehiel R. Wetmore.

Recording Secretaries.—1841, Charles Dayan; 1843, Charles L. Martin; 1844, C. Dayan; 1845, S. D. Hungerford; 1846–8, John Benedict; 1849, F. W. Northrup; 1850–1, S. P. Mills; 1852–3, N. Duane Baker; 1855–6, Charles G. Riggs; 1857–8, Mortimer Smith; 1859, Charles M. Goff.

Treasurers. 1841, Harvey Stephens; 1848–9, Ela N. Merriam, 1850–8, Moses M. Smith; 1859, Alfred H. Lee.

Fairs, have been held at Denmark in 1852; Lowville in 1843, 6, 8, 1856, 9, at West Martinsburgh in 1844; at Martinsburgh in 1842, 5, 1850, 4; at Turin in 1847, 9, 1851, 5, 7, 8; and at Constableville in 1853. From 1852 to 1859, inclusive, $1,640 and 270 volumes of books were given as premiums. With two exceptions the receipts have steadily increased, and in 1859, were much greater than ever before. In 1856, the fairs were located alternately at Turin and Lowville for six years; and in 1857, an association at the former place purchased about eleven acres of ground, a little west of the village, the most of which has been enclosed and fitted up for fairs.[1] In 1859, a lot was purchased in Lowville by Norman Gowdy and enclosed at the expense of the society for a like use. The latter has a course about half a mile in length. The society was reorganized Dec. 27, 1859, under chapter 425 of the laws of 1855, and its officers now consist of a president, vice-president, secretary, treasurer and six directors. The officers are, James S. Jackson, *president;* Wm. W. Smith, *vice-president;* F. B. Morse, *secretary;* and Alfred H. Lee, *treasurer;* Norman Gowdy, Charles H. Curtis, Azro H. Buck, Ela Merriam, Sanford Coe and C. G. Riggs are *directors.*

In this connection we may notice the total results of agriculture in Lewis county, as reported by the state and national census for the year preceding the dates of these official inquiries. They may vary from the truth, but are the nearest and most reliable data existing with regard to our productive resources.

---

[1] The owners of the Turin fair ground, are Albert Foster, Jefferson M. Wilcox, Edwin Woolworth, Charles G. Riggs, Alfred H. Lee, and Edmund Baldwin.

Agricultural Statistics.

	1840.	1845.	1850.	1855.
Barley, bushels,	20,271	23,119	23,813	37,513
Beans, bushels,	....	678	....	1,030
Buckwheat, bushels,	8,498	25,803	10,117	10,443
Corn, bushels,	48,984	53,180	83,027	92,398
Flax, pounds,	....	45,281	31,905	65,782
Hay, tons,	43,284	....	67,280	51,802
Hops, pounds,	5,460	....	11,322	8,870
Oats, bushels,	144,880	....	202,515	295,445
Peas, bushels,	....	21,925	....	12,978
Potatoes, bushels,	634,316	498,849	287,715	243,841
Rye, bushels,	2,473	9,278	....	11,383
Sugar, pounds,	257,476	....	....	236,918
Turnips, bushels,	....	22,340	....	5,830
Wax and Honey, pounds,	148	....	17,968	12,743
Wheat, bushels,	85,191	87,406	73,584	63,785
Wool, pounds,	68,173	89,229	44,137	27,047

	1821.	1825.	1835.	1840.	1845.	1850.	1855.
Cattle,	10,417	13,780	25,063	31,130	32,790	32,308	29,748
Horses,	1,887	3,066	4,684	3,931	4,570	4,309	5,106
Sheep,	18,267	34,467	40,234	36,665	40,657	15,368	10,086
Swine,	......	11,739	16,197	18,076	15,813	9,091	8,353

Value of dairy products, 1840,..................................$137,177

In 1855, there were reported 2,423 working oxen and 19,151 cows. The amount of butter produced, was 1,575,515 pounds, and of cheese, 1,896,741 pounds. The amount of cloths of domestic manufacture formerly large had decreased to 15,802 yards.

Of the grains now cultivated, the surplus from the county is now small, and much less wheat is raised than consumed. In most sections, the production of butter and cheese has been found the most profitable and certain, and the true interest of the farmer will generally be found to cultivate grains only so far as by the proper rotation of crops to keep his land in the best condition possible for the growth of grass. Of the less common products of agriculture, several require historical notice.

Dye Stuffs.—The cultivation of saffron (*Carthamus tinctoris*), for dyeing, was about 1846, a prominent business with several farmers in Lowville and Martinsburgh. At a somewhat earlier period, the cultivation of madder was attempted, but without success sufficient to induce a continuance of the enterprise.

Flax has been a subject of culture from the first, but never extensively as a leading business, except during the active operation of the Copenhagen works. In 1845–6, large quantities were raised, chiefly from the high price of the seed. Linseed oil has been extensively manufactured at Lowville and Copenhagen.

Hemp was cultivated to a considerable extent in Denmark and vicinity, soon after the establishment of Varick's cordage manufactory at Copenhagen, about 1832–5. The result was not satisfactory, chiefly from the difficulty of properly preparing it for use when grown.

Essential oils.—The manufacture of the oil of peppermint, has been an important item of business in Lowville and Harrisburgh, and is still followed to a limited extent. The first field of mint in the county was planted in 1811, by Martin Guiteau and Truman Terrill, who continued the business several years. The Buck, Morse, Humphrey, and other families have since been extensively engaged in it. In 1814, three farmers had 40 acres planted, and the profits of some of the earlier adventurers were great. The plant is usually mown three years, and the yield per acre in oil generally averages ten pounds the first year, fifteen the second, and five or six the third. It is distilled soon after being cut, or when partially cured like hay. The price of this article is very fluctuating, and on several occasions, the transition from one extreme to the other has resulted in heavy losses. Other essential oils, as of hemlock, cedar, spearmint, &c., have been made to a limited extent.

Silk.—In 1843, Ira Adams received a premium of $3.79, at the rate of 15 cents per pound, for cocoons, and $1.12 at the rate of 50 cents per pound for reeled silk. This was probably the largest amount ever raised in one year by one person, and but few have ever attempted silk culture in the county. The Morus multicaulis speculation prevailed in this county to only a moderate degree, as compared with other sections.

The Lewis County Mutual Insurance Company, was incorporated Feb. 27, 1837, and Ela Collins, Isaac W. Bostwick, Stephen Leonard, Andrew W. Doig, Jared House, Merrit M. Norton, John W. Martin, Carlos P. Scovil, Enoch Thompson, Isaac W. Bush, Asa L. Sheldon, Ashley Davenport, Abraham Miller, John Whittlesey and Ela Merriam were appointed directors. The directors elected John Whittlesey president of the company, but the organization was never completed and no policies were issued.

The Lewis County Bible Society was formed May 28, 1812, when the Rev. James Murdock was chosen *president;* Rev. Isaac Clinton, *vice president;* Stephen Leonard, *treasurer;* Barnabas Yale, *secretary;* and Jedediah Darrow, jr., Dea. Mather Bosworth, Dea. Samuel Dean, Wm. S. Radcliff and

John McCollister, a *committee.* Members were required to pay $1 the first year and 50 cents annually until it amounted to $3. During the seven first years there was no change of officers except in the committee, which included at different times the Rev. Jeduthan Higby, Dea. Seth Miller, Jonathan Barker, Paul Abbott, Lemuel Dickinson, Chillus Doty, John Ives and Chester Shumway. In Aug. 1827, a Bible soc., auxiliary to the Am. B. S., was formed in this county. Its donations to the parent society have been $599.08, and its remittances for bibles and testaments $3,056.39. Stephen Leonard has acted as treasurer from the beginning, excepting one year. In 1828 it established auxiliaries in each town, but this was found unadvisable. A Bible census has been several times taken, by the first of which in 1829, it was found that 400 families in 2000 were without the Bible. In 1848 it was found that 708 out of 3743 families were destitute, and of that number 278 were supplied, the remaining 430 being all Catholic.

In 1818, John W. Towne of Marlborough, Vt., agent of Holbrook & Fessenden, got an immense subscription list for a $12 quarto family bible in this county.

THE LEWIS COUNTY SABBATH SCHOOL UNION was formed in 1825, and held annual meetings about 5 years. It became auxiliary to the Am. S. S. U. The first anniversary gathering of S. S. pupils was at Lowville July 2, 1829, at which 550 scholars were present. The services were unusually impressive from the funeral of Anna Shepherd, a child of twelve years of age, which was held upon the occasion. In 1830, 400 met at Martinsburgh, and similar gatherings have been held annually or oftener since this period.

THE LEWIS COUNTY ANTI-SLAVERY SOCIETY was formed Aug., 1835, auxiliary to the Am. A. S. Society, and reorganized Jan. 10, 1837, embracing at first members of both of the great political parties, and of all religious creeds. It was soon after merged in a political party which in 1846, numbered 5 per cent of all the votes cast for governor. At no other election has their vote been so high.

THE EDUCATIONAL SOCIETY OF LEWIS COUNTY was formed Nov. 14, 1845, with D. P. Mayhew, *president;* Sidney Sylvester, 1st *vice president;* A. D. Pease, 2d *vice president;* Harrison Barnes, *corresponding secretary;* A. S. Easton, *recording secretary*, and J. P. Clark,[1] *treasurer*. After a few years this organization was given up, and a *Teachers' association* was formed which has since been continued with great

[1] Mr. Clark of Denmark, now a professor in Irving college, Tennessee.

advantage. Teacher's institutes have been held annually since 1846, in different parts of the county, beginning at Turin.

Lewis county was composed of 12 towns in 1844, when acts were passed requiring the supervisors of each county to appoint one or more superintendents of schools. It so happened that the board was equally divided, and from political grounds could not unite upon a candidate for this office. No effort was made until 1843, when after three days' ineffectual balloting the board adjourned. Notice was duly given by the secretary of state that unless the county complied with the statute, the public school moneys would be withheld. This led to a special meeting of the supervisors, and the forenoon of the first day was again spent to no purpose. Upon assembling after dinner, it was found that but eleven persons were present, the twelfth being on his way from the hotel. The vote was at once pressed to an issue and the dilemma ceased. The incumbents of this office until its discontinuance were Sidney Sylvester of Copenhagen, Jan. 16, 1844, and Alfred H. Bush of Turin, Nov. 16, 1846.

Under the act of 1856 creating the office of school commissioner, the county has been divided into two districts, the southern, or No. 1, embracing we believe the towns of Greig, Martinsburgh and towns south, and the other, the remainder of the county.

Society for the Acquisition of Useful Knowledge.—Under this name an association was formed in this county April 26, 1843, and continued till Sept. 2, 1848. It consisted at one time of about forty young men, mostly students, and was designed for mutual improvement by the reading of original papers, debates, &c.

Temperance Societies.—The first society of this kind in the county,[1] was formed at Copenhagen, in February, 1825, and consisted of twelve members. It grew out of prosecutions for the sale of ardent spirits without a license, under an act passed February 18, 1820, requiring poor masters to recover certain fines for the benefit of the poor. These suits were instituted by Levi Robbins, poor master, and although judgment was got, the town would release the parties convicted, by a vote of town meeting. The discussions which these measures raised, led to the formation of a

[1] Turin may incidentally claim an earlier attempt at reform with regard to intemperance. At a town meeting held in 1821, it voted *that no licenses should be granted* (unless the applicant should first produce a certificate of the town sealer, that his measures had been compared and found correct).

society, consisting of Norman Guiteau, Levi Robbins, Wm. C. Lawton, David Goodenough, Dr. John Loud, Austin H. Robbins, Harris Bronson, Edward S. Robbins, Wm. Keen, J. Stoddard, and two others not remembered by our informant.

A town society was formed in Turin, July, 1827, in Lowville in February, 1828, in West Leyden in January, 1829, and in Martinsburgh in October, 1830. Societies were also formed in Stow Square, Leyden and Greig. The first temperance tavern in the state, so far as we are informed, was opened by Douglas Wright of Denmark, in 1817, and continued two years. The first merchants who discontinued the sale of liquors, were Fowler & Woolworth of Turin, in April, 1829, and their trade fell off one-third in consequence.

A County temperance society was formed at Martinsburgh, September 15, 1828, and became auxiliary to the State temperance society, upon the formation of the latter. This county society in a few years fell into neglect.[1] The Washingtonian Temperance movement began in 1843. A society styled the Washington Association of Lewis was formed July 15, 1843, and at the close of that year 5,000 members belonged to it in Lewis county. Anniversary meetings were held June 25, 1844, and July 8, 1845, and the interest continued until the vote upon the license question in 1846 and 1847, divided public sentiment. A Carson League was formed at the county seat, July 13, 1854. Capital $100,000, in shares of $5, of which 25 cents were required to be paid. It is believed a few prosecutions were begun, but a decision of the Court of Appeals terminated its existence.

The B. R. Am. Conf., of the M. E. Church, at Lowville, December, 1826, voted to use its influence to prevent the use of ardent spirits in their society, and in 1832 passed strong resolutions, in which the use, manufacture or sale of liquors was declared strongly derogatory to Christian character and a fit subject of discipline.

Temperance lecturers through the country have been frequent; among which were Rev. D. C. Axtel, in Oct., 1829; Samuel Chipman in 1833, and November, 1845; L. A. Crandall in 1839; Caleb Lyon of Lyonsdale, in the spring of 1842; J. P. Coffin, in December, 1842, and Thomas N. Johnson, in September, 1844.

[1] In 1830, there were 10 town societies, and 677 members; in 1831, there were 9 town societies, and 1,237 members; in 1832, there were 13 town societies, and 2,118 members.

The vote on the license question in May, 1846 and 1847, was as follows, in the several towns:

	1846. License.	1846. No License.	1847. License.	1847. No License.
Croghan,	12	10		
Denmark,	118	285	234	256
Diana,	47	33		
Greig,	30	4		
Harrisburgh,	53	73		
Leyden,	129	112		
Lowville,	168	218	205	176
Martinsburgh,	173	196	214	161
Osceola,	...	14		
Pinckney,	45	84		
Turin,	139	130	184	124
Watson,	90	72		
West Turin,	169	117	189	74
Total,	1,173	1,348	1,026	791

MASONIC LODGES.—A Mark lodge was formed at Martinsburgh, about 1810, at the house of Adoniram Foot, and afterwards removed to Denmark. It was merged in chapters about 1824.

A Master's lodge was formed at a very early day at the house of Jonathan Collins, in Turin. It was the first in the county.

Jefferson Lodge, No. 64, was formed in the winter of 1806–7, in Martinsburgh, with Chillus Doty, Master; Wm. Derbyshire, S. W.; Solomon Rathbone, J. W. It was removed to Lowville, and held for some time in the house of Ira Stephens, from whence it has returned to Martinsburgh. Before its removal it was held at the house of Chillus Doty and A. Foot, and after its return at the house of David Waters. Its charter was surrendered June 3, 1831.

Orient Lodge was formed in Denmark about 1810, with Jonathan Barker, M., Sueton Fairchild, S. W., and —— Van Vleck, J. W. A new charter was granted September 6, 1851, No. 238; and it has been removed from Denmark village to Copenhagen.

Lowville Lodge, No. 134, was chartered June 13, 1848, and has since been sustained.

Turin Lodge, No. 184, was chartered December 3, 1850.

ODD FELLOWS' LODGES.—Six lodges of the I. O. O. F.,

have been formed, of which four continue in this county, as follows:

Lewis Lodge, No. 92. Constableville. Meetings Saturdays.

Copenhagen Lodge, No. 190. Copenhagen. Meetings Saturdays.

Cynosure Lodge, No. 215. Turin. (Charter surrendered).

Adelphia Lodge, No. 308. Lowville. Meetings Mondays.

Central Lodge, No. 367. Martinsburgh. (Extinct).

Juris Lodge, No. 417. Port Leyden, and afterwards near Lyons Falls, in Greig. Meetings Saturdays.

A few "Daughters of Rebekah" were admitted at the Juris Lodge, in 1853 or 1854, but no others are, it is believed, reported.

Sons of Temperance.—Eleven lodges of this order have existed in this county, all of which are extinct. They were formed between 1844 and 1850, the first at Copenhagen, and the last at Lowville, viz:

Copenhagen Lodge No. 45; Constableville No. 46; Collinsville No. 63; Port Leyden No. 64; Cedar Grove (Deer river) No. 65; West Martinsburgh No. 170; New Bremen No. 206; Houseville No. 217; Dayspring (Martinsburgh) No. 218; Turin No. 219, and Lowville No. 267. Eight of these reported Jan. 1852, a total of 228 contributing members.

Daughters of Temperance.—A society of 12 members of this order, named "Hope of the Fallen Union," was organized in Martinsburgh Jan. 9, 1851, by Mrs. J. A. Granger of Champion. It was of ephemeral duration.

Good Templars.—This order was instituted at Martinsburgh in June and at Deer river in July 1854.

CHAPTER VIII.

RELIGIOUS BODIES.

Methodist Episcopal.—The churches of this county are included in the Black River conference, which was formed in 1835.[1] This region was embraced in the N. Y. conference till 1809, in that of Genesee from 1809 to 1829, and in that of Oneida from 1829 to 1835. The county formed a part of Albany district till 1808, of Cayuga district from 1808 to 1812, of Oneida district from 1812 to 1820, and of Black River district from 1820 to 1839. The Herkimer and Gouverneur districts divided the county from 1839 to 1844, since which theAdams district has embraced nearly its entire area.

The presiding elders of the Black River district were Rinaldo M. Everts, 1821–2; Dan. Barnes, 1823–5; Goodwin Stoddard, 1826; Nathaniel Salisbury, 1827–30; Josiah Keyes, 1831–2; John Dempster,[2] 1833, and Gardner Baker 1836–9. In the Herkimer district it was Geo. Gary[3] in 1836–9, and Aaron Adams in 1840–1. In Gouverneur district, W. S. Bowdish, 1839; Lewis Whitcomb in 1841; and N. Salisbury in 1842–3. In Adams district in has been L. Whitcomb in 1844; N. Salisbury in 1845–6; Isaac Stone[4] in 1847; Geo. C. Woodruff in 1848–9; Geo. Gary in 1850–1; A. J. Phelps in 1852; Gardner Baker in 1853–9.

The Black River circuit formed in 1804, embraced the whole of the northern part of the state west and north of the great forest. Turin circuit was formed in 1812, but in 2 years was discontinued. Lowville and Martinsburgh together formed a circuit from 1832 to 1840, when the latter was separated. Watson Mission was formed in 1834, and in about ten years it became a circuit. New Bremen became a mission in 1849, and Copenhagen a circuit in 1840. The Black river circuit was changed to the Turin circuit in 1844. New Boston became a mission in 1851.

While the Black River circuit embraced the whole county, its ministers were Griffin, Sweet, and Asa Cummins in 1804; G. Sweet and Seymour Ensign in 1805; Mathew Van Duzan and William Vredenburgh in 1806; Datus Ensign in 1807; M. Van Duzan and Luther Bishop in 1808; L. Bishop and Wm. Jewett in 1809; Joseph Willis and Chandley Lambert[1] in 1810; Wm. Snow and Truman Gillett in 1811; Joseph Kinkead in 1812; Isaac Puffer and Goodwin Stoddard in 1813; C. Lambert in 1814; Ira Fairbank and

---

[1] This conference was incorporated by special act, April 17, 1841, with power to hold real estate not exceeding $20,000, and an income not over $10,000 annually.

[2] *Mr. Dempster* went as a missionary in Buenos Ayres. He is now at the Garrett Biblical institute, Evanston, Ill.

[3] *Mr. Gary* was born in Middlefield, N. Y., Dec. 8, 1793, and admitted to trial as a preacher, while but fifteen years of age. Having been employed many years in New England and central New York, he was in 1844 appointed to take charge of Oregon mission, where he remained four years. He died at Camden, N. Y., March 25, 1855, having labored 46 years, of which 23 were as a presiding elder, 6 as a missionary, and 16 on circuits or stations.

[4] Mr. S. was born in Hoosick, N. Y., March 28, 1797, and died in Onondaga county, Sept. 10, 1850, having served in the ministry nearly thirty years.

[1] *Chandley Lambert* was born in Alford, Mass., March 27, 1781, and at the age of twenty-seven entered the Methodist ministry, in which he labored zealously about twenty years. He subsequently settled in Lowville where he died, March 16, 1845.

James Hazen in 1815; I. Fairbank and G. Stoddard in 1816; J. Willis in 1817; Andrew Prindle and Abraham Lippet in 1818; A. Prindle and Henry Peck in 1819; Nathaniel Reeder and J. Willis in 1820; Benjamin Dighton in 1821; C. Lambert in 1822; Truman Dixon, Squire Chase[2] and Elijah King (sup.) in 1823; Benj. G. Paddock and N. Salisbury in 1824; B. G. Paddock and S. Chase in 1825; I. Puffer and John Ercanbrack in 1826; I. Puffer and I. Stone in 1827; John H. Wallace and I. Stone in 1828; Calvin Hawley in 1829; Josiah Keyes and L. Whitcomb in 1830, and Anson Fuller in 1831–2.

The Black River conference was held in the grove south of Turin village, July 31, 1839, and at Lowville July 17, 1846.

The Missionary society of the B. R. Q. M. Conf. was founded Dec. 29, 1827 and a constitution adopted May 3, 1828.

Presbyterian.—The Watertown Presbytery includes this county. It was formed in 1830, from the St. Lawrence Presb. which was organized from that of Oneida in 1816, and held its first session in Martinsburgh in the fall of that year. The Revs. Jas. Murdock, Isaac Clinton, Samuel F. Snowden, Jeduthan Higby, jr., and David Banks (of Watertown), were original members of this body. The principal facts concerning the union and withdrawal of churches, are noted under the towns where they severally occur.

Congregational.—The Black River association was formed at Lowville, Sept. 1, 1807, by delegates from churches at Leyden, West Leyden, Turin, Lowville, Denmark, and six towns in Jefferson county.

The Free Communion Baptists, were first organized in this county in 1813, by persons who had belonged to the Baptist church, but were led to differ upon doctrinal points, probably through the influence of persons from Russia, Herkimer county. The B. R. yearly meeting, adopted its constitution in Sept., 1830, and embraced the region between East Canada creek and the Genesee. In the spring of 1844, this sect was merged in the Free Will Baptists, and their

---

[2] Mr. Chase was born in Scipio, N. Y., Feb. 15, 1803, was licensed to preach in June 1822, and was soon after received on trial in the Genesee conference. He preached at various places in this and Oneida conference, and in 1831 was appointed presiding elder of Potsdam district. In 1836 he was sent by his own request on a mission to Liberia where he remained about two years, when he returned with greatly impaired health. In 1841, while at Lowville, the opportunity for returning to the African mission offered, and he again sailed to Liberia where he remained till March 1843. He died at Syracuse while attending conference, July 26, 1843, and was buried at Houseville. He married Julia, daughter of Eli Rogers of Martinsburgh.

number in Lewis county, has become very small. They are embraced in the St. Lawrence yearly, and the Jefferson quarterly meetings. Small societies exist in Diana, Harrisburgh, West Turin and Watson.

Baptists.—The Black River Baptist association, was formed in 1808, at which time there existed a church at Denmark of 29 members under the Rev. Peleg Card, and another at Turin of 65 members under the Rev. Stephen Parsons. The association then also included Jefferson and parts of St. Lawrence and Oswego counties numbering in all 9 churches, 371 members, and 5 ministers. The B. R. missionary soc. was formed in 1817, and up to 1844, had received $7,837.

Roman Catholics.—This county is embraced in the Diocese of Albany, and contains nine churches, of which two are unfinished. They are distributed as follows: Crogan 1, Diana 1, Harrisburgh 1, New Bremen 2, Pinckney 1, West Turin 3.

Universalists.—The B. R. association was formed June, 1823, and includes this county, Jefferson and Oswego. The only churches erected within our limits are at Denmark and Talcottville.

FRIENDS.—There is but one society of this sect in the co. (Lowville), which belongs to the Le Ray Monthly meeting.

Revivals of religion have occurred in the winter of 1803–4, at Turin (among the Baptists), in 1818, 1822, 1831, 1832, 1842–3, and 1857. In that of 1832 the Rev. Jacob Knapp held meetings at the Line church, at Lowville and at Turin. The Rev. Jedediah Burchard in the same year held meetings at Stow square, Denmark and Leyden Hill. That of 1857, was characterized by the absence of excitement, and by its apparently spontaneous origin.

CHAPTER IX.

THE NEWSPAPER PRESS.

The Black River Gazette, the first newspaper printed north of the Mohawk valley within the state, was begun at Martinsburgh, March 10th, 1807, by James B. Robbins, and continued a year. It was Republican in politics, and chiefly under the patronage of Gen. Martin. The press was removed to Watertown and used in printing the first paper in

Truly Yours
Wm. G. Easton

Jefferson county. While at Martinsburgh, this paper was 19 by 21 inches in size, with four columns to the page, and the type was of the old style with the long s. Ephraim Luce was post rider.

The Lewis County Sentinel was begun at Martinsburgh, Oct. 12, 1824, by Charles Nichols, and published one year, at $2.00 by post or $1.75 if taken at the office. The size was 19 by 22 inches, four columns to the page. Neutral in politics.

The Martinsburgh Sentinel and Lewis County Advertiser was first issued Oct. 13, 1829, by James Ketchum Averill. Terms $2.00 to village and mail subscribers, $1.75 if taken at the office and $1.50 in clubs of ten or more. If not paid till the end of the year, $2.50. It was a small sheet, with five columns to the page, and ended in Feb., 1830. Democratic in politics. Mr. Averill has since been long connected with the press in the north-eastern part of the state.

The Lewis County Gazette was begun in Lowville in the spring of 1821, by Lewis G. Hoffman, and was continued nearly two years, when its publisher removed to Black Rock. He now resides in Waterford, Saratoga co. This paper was 18 by 24 inches, with four columns to the page, and was issued weekly at $2.50 per annum. In politics it was Bucktail.

The Black River Gazette was begun by Wm. L. Easton[1] at Lowville, Oct. 19, 1825, and published until Dec. 1, 1830, by him, when Joseph M. Farr became publisher and continued it until 1833. It began of the same size as the Lewis Co. Sentinel, upon the same press that had been used by that paper, but the second year was enlarged by one column to the page, and in the second volume till No. 33, H. L. and W. L. Easton were associated. It was issued at $2.00 per annum, and professed to be impartial and independent in politics. The nominations of both parties were kept standing in its columns previous to elections, and it was open to discussion upon any subject of public interest until 1832, when it adopted the anti-masonic nominations and advocated the election of William Wirt to the presidency. Mr. Easton became a joint publisher again Oct. 10, 1832, and continued such till the end.

---

1 *William L. Easton* was born in Berkshire county, Mass., in 1806, came to this county in 1825, and has since mostly resided at Lowville. He was one of the first directors of the Bank of Lowville, which office he held nearly twenty years, and was for some time its cashier and president. He was surrogate of Lewis county about four years.

The Lewis Democrat was begun by Le Grand Byington March, 25, 1834, and was published one year. It supported the whig party, advocated Seward's claims as candidate for governor. Size and terms the same as that of the B. R. Gazette, the press and type of which were employed upon this paper. Its editor has since figured in the Ohio legislature, and now resides at Iowa City.

The Lewis County Republican was begun at Martinsburgh by James Wheeler May 18, 1830, as the organ of the Democratic party in the county—the type and press being the same that had been used by Mr. Averill. On the 12th of September, 1836, it was transferred to Daniel S. Bailey, who continued to publish it until united with the Northern Journal, Jan. 1, 1860. It was issued from a wooden Ramage press until Mr. Bailey procured a new iron press, and in Jan., 1853, a steam power press was procured. In the spring of 1845 it was removed to Lowville, and a few years after returned to Martinsburgh. During the campaign of 1848 it supported the Hunker portion of the Democratic party, in 1852 it supported Pierce, and in 1854 it became Republican. Being thus brought upon the same political platform with the Northern Journal, the proprietor of the latter purchased Mr. Bailey's interest, and Jan. 4, the first number of the Journal and Republican was issued.

Few country newspapers have been conducted with more discretion and ability than this, during the long period it was in the hands of Mr. Bailey. We are indebted to the early files of this paper for many valuable facts in these pages.

The Lewis County Democrat, the first and only paper printed at Turin, was begun by Horace R. Lahe, Sept. 22, 1846, with new type and press bought for its use, partly by the aid of a local subscription, but chiefly by Clement Whitaker, Homer Collins and Jonathan C. Collins, who advanced money with the agreement that Lahe should purchase at the end of a year. This was accordingly done.

It supported the Radical or Barnburning branch of the Democratic party, and in the campaign of 1848 was strongly Free Soil in politics. Terms $1.50. In Jan., 1850, it was removed to Martinsburgh, where a few numbers only were published, and soon after to Boonville where its press and material have since been in use.

The Lewis County Banner was begun at Lowville Sept. 8, 1856, as the organ of the Democratic party and advocate of Buchanan for the presidency. It was conducted the first year by N. B. Sylvester, subsequently by E. A. Teall and Almont Barnes, and since Sept. 1, 1858, by Henry Allgœver. It is the only Democratic paper in the county.

The Northern Journal, was commenced at Lowville, by Ambrose W. Clark from Otsego co., Feb. 22, 1838, at $2 per annum, and of nearly its present size. At the end of the eighth vol. 1846, Edwin R. Colston[1] became its publisher, and in Nov., 1847, the paper appeared under the name of of C. W. Haven as editor. Jason C. Easton, became owner March 9, 1848, and in Oct. 1848, William Oland Bourne of New York followed as publisher, until 1850. After appearing a few months under the names of Wm. X. Ninde, printer, and V. R. Martin, editor, Mr. Easton resumed the paper and in the spring of 1853, became associated with Homer C. Hunt, under the firm of Easton & Hunt, and continued to the close of vol. 16. Cordial Storrs, jr., became proprietor December 28, 1853, and having conducted the paper two years was followed Jan. 2, 1856, by Geo. W. Fowler. On the 27th of Oct., 1858, Henry A. Phillips, became publisher and has since continued. This paper was established as the organ of the Whig party in the county, and in 1854, it became Republican. It has uniformly supported the nominees of this party, except in 1858, when it substituted the name of Mr. Lyon for congress as an independent candidate, in opposition to the nominee of the Republican party. Late in 1859, Mr. Phillips purchased the Lewis County Republican, and Jan. 4, 1860, the two were first issued under the title of

The Journal and Republican, at Lowville, Mr. Bailey remaining for a time associate editor. The typographical execution of the new paper is neat, and its articles are well selected. It is the only organ of the Republican party in the county.

The Dollar Weekly Northern Blade, was begun at Constableville, August, 1854, by Fairchild and Bealls. It was changed from small folio to quarto at the end of the first year, and Fairchild became sole publisher in July, 1855. The third volume became folio. In February, 1856, Galusha P. Eames became publisher, and in September of that year, J. S. Kibbe's name appeared as editor. While in Eames's possession the paper was enlarged to 24 by 30 inches. On the 23d of April, 1857, Wm. R. Merrill and Edwin R. Cook became publishers and changed its name to

---

[1] Mr. Colston died in Brooklyn, Oct. 11, 1857, aged 33 years.

The News Register, and in the spring of 1858, removed the office to Carthage and began the publication of the Carthage Standard.

The Hawk Eye, a juvenile four page quarto sheet supposed to have been printed at Lowville, appeared at Constableville a few weeks in the fall of 1855. To oppose this

The Young America was printed at the Blade office a few weeks. It was somewhat larger, but scarcely more respectable than its pigmy opponent.

CHAPTER X.

OFFICIAL AND PROFESSIONAL LISTS.

CONGRESSMEN.—Until 1808, this county formed with Herkimer, Oneida, Jefferson and St. Lawrence, the 15th District; from 1808 to 1812, with Herkimer, Jefferson and St. Lawrence, the 10th; from 1812 to 1822, with Jefferson and St. Lawrence, the 18th; from 1822 to 1832, with Jefferson, Oswego and St. Lawrence (double district), the 20th; from 1832 to 1842, with Herkimer, the 16th; from 1842 to 1851, with St. Lawrence, the 18th; and since 1851, with Jefferson, the 23d. With one exception, the representatives from this county, have resided in Lowville.

18th Congress, 1823–5. Ela Collins.
26th-27th Con., 1839-41. Andrew W. Doig.
22d Congress, 1831–3. Chas. Dayan.
30th Congress, 1847–9. Wm. Collins.
33d Congress, 1853–5. Caleb Lyon, of Lyonsdale.

STATE SENATORS.—This county formed a part of the Western District until 1815, when it was included in the Eastern. From 1822 to 1846 it formed a part of the 5th, and since 1846, of the 21st District. It now elects with Jefferson county. The senators from Lewis county have been:

1809–12. Walter Martin, Martinsb'g.
1819–22. Levi Adams, Martinsb'g.
1827–28. Charles Dayan,[1] Lowville.
1834–37. Francis Seger, Greig.
1843–46. Carlos P. Scovil, Martinsburgh.
1847. Nelson J. Beach, Watson.
1851. Caleb Lyon of Lyonsdale,[2] Greig.
1852–53. Ashley Davenport, Denmark.
1858–59. Jos. A. Willard, Lowville.

---

1 Elected in place of George Brayton of Oneida county, resigned.

2 Elected March 27, 1851, in place of Alanson Skinner of Jefferson county, resigned.

ASSEMBLYMEN.—Lewis county was united with Jefferson and St. Lawrence as one assembly district, until 1808, since which it has been entitled to one member alone. Its members in the assembly have been:

1808. Lewis Graves, Denmark.
1809. Judah Barnes, Turin.
1810. Lewis Graves, Denmark.
1811. Nathaniel Merriam, Leyden.
1812. William Darrow, Lowville.
1813. Levi Collins, West Turin.
1814. Chillus Doty, Martinsburgh.
1815. Ela Collins, Lowville.
1816–7. Chillus Doty, Martinsburgh.
1818. Levi Hart, Turin.
1819. Levi Robbins, Denmark.
1820. Nathaniel Merriam, Leyden.
1821. Stephen Hart, Turin.
1822. Chester Buck, Lowville.
1823. Abner W. Spencer, Denmark.
1824. Caleb Lyon, Greig.
1825. Amos Buck, Jr., Denmark.
1826. Amos Miller, Leyden.
1827. John W. Martin, Martinsb'rg.
1828–9. Geo. D. Ruggles, Lowville.
1830. Joseph O. Mott, Turin.
1831. Harrison Blodget, Denmark.
1832. Andrew W. Doig, Lowville.
1833. Eli Rogers, Jr., Turin.
1834. Geo. D. Ruggles, Lowville.
1835–6. Charles Dayan, Lowville.
1837. Geo. D. Ruggles, Lowville.
1838. William Dominick, Greig.
1839. Sanford Coe, Leyden.
1840. Chester Buck, Lowville.
1841. Eliphalet Sears, Leyden.
1842. Carlos P. Scovil, Martinsburgh.
1843. Amos Buck, Denmark.
1844. Alburn Foster, Martinsburgh.
1845. Dean S. Howard, Greig.
1846. Nelson J. Beach, Watson.
1847. Thomas Baker, Leyden.
1848. David D. Reamer, Diana.
1849. Diodate Pease, Martinsburgh.
1850. John Newkirk, Pinckney.
1851. Caleb Lyon[1] of Lyonsdale, Greig.
1851. Dean S. Howard, Greig.
1852. John Benedict, Lowville.
1853. Seymour Green, Osceola.
1854. Jonathan C. Collins, W. Turin.
1855. Aaron Parsons, Leyden.
1856. David Algur, Leyden.
1857. Lucian Clark, Denmark.
1858. Homer Collins, West Turin.
1859. Lyman R. Lyon, Greig.
1860. Richardson T. Hough, Lewis.

FIRST JUDGES of the county court, appointed until 1847.

Daniel Kelley, March 29, 1806.
Jonathan Collins, June 1, 1809.
Silas Stow, June 27, 1815.
Edward Bancroft, Jan. 24, 1823.
John W. Martin,[2] March 16, 1833.
Francis Seger,[3] April 9, 1843.
Edward A. Brown, Nov., 1855.
Henry E. Turner, Nov., 1859.

SHERIFFS, with the date of appointment or election.

Chillus Doty, April 3, 1805.
Ehud Stephens, June 9, 1808.
John Ives, Feb. 28, 1810.
Chillus Doty, March 2, 1811.
Silas Stow, March 2, 1814.
Levi Adams, March 15, 1815.
Sylvester Miller, June 15, 1818.
Ehud Stephens, June 6, 1820.
Ira Stephens, Jan. 10, 1821.
Sylvester Miller, Feb. 12, 1821.
Ira Stephens, Nov., 1822.
Chester Ray, Nov., 1858.
David Miller, Nov., 1825.
Hezekiah Scovil, Nov., 1828.
Ashley Davenport, Nov., 1831.
John Whittlesey, Nov., 1834.
Elias Gallup, Nov., 1837.
Alvin Farr, Nov., 1840.
Elihu Parsons, Nov., 1843.
George Shepard, Nov., 1846.
Aaron Parsons, jr., Nov., 1849.
Peter Kirley, Nov., 1852.
Gilbert E. Woolworth, Nov., 1855,

---

1 Lyon resigned April 26, 1851, and Howard was elected to fill the vacancy for the extra session.

2 Judge Martin in an address to the grand jury upon his retiring from the bench in April, 1843, remarked that during an official term of ten years he had not been required to sentence one prisoner to state prison. There was not at that time a single distillery in the county.

3 Elected at the first judicial election, June 1847.

COUNTY CLERKS. Appointed before 1822, and since elected.

Richard Coxe, April 3, 1805.
Edward Bancroft, March 12, 1816.
John Safford, June 6, 1820.
Edward Bancroft, Feb. 13, 1821.
Martin Hart, Nov., 1822.
Andrew W. Doig, Nov., 1825.
Carlos P. Scovil, Nov., 1831.
Charles Orvis, Nov., 1840.
Julius A. White, Nov., 1843.
Lucian Clark, Nov., 1846.
Harrison Barnes,[1] Nov., 1849.
Sidney Sylvester, Nov., 1855.
Walter B. Foster, Nov., 1858.

SURROGATES previous to 1846, when this office was united with that of county judge.

Isaac W. Bostwick, April 3, 1805.
Chillus Doty, March 15, 1815.
Barnabas Yale, June 6, 1820.
Chillus Doty, Feb. 13, 1821.
Sylvester Miller, March 28, 1823.
Andrew W. Doig, Feb. 28, 1835.
William L. Easton, Feb. 7, 1840.
Daniel S. Bailey, Feb. 7, 1844.

COUNTY TREASURERS, appointed by the board of supervisors until 1846, since which time they have been elected triennially. 1805, Oct. 25, Daniel Kelley; 1808, Oct. 6, Ela Collins; 1809, D. Kelley; 1814, James H. Leonard; 1823, Baron S. Doty; 1824, John W. Martin; 1840, Enoch Thompson; 1845, Charles L. Martin; 1846, Lyman R. Lyon; 1847, Ela N. Merriam; 1852, Moses M. Smith; 1855, Diodate Pease.

THE LEWIS COUNTY BAR.—In the absence of a connected official record of the names of those who have been admitted to the bar of this county, the following list is offered as embracing nearly all of the legal profession who have resided, or who now live in the county. Those known to be deceased are marked with a star. More than a third of the remainder had removed from the county. The residence given is that while engaged professionally here. Many dates are blank from our inability to refer to the record as this goes to press.

Adams, Charles D.	Lowville,	Jan. 1852.
Barnes, Alanson H.	Martinsburgh.	
*Barnes, Harrison	"	
Bennett, David M.	"	
*Bostwick, Isaac W.	Lowville,	Dec. 10, 1805.
Brown, Edward A.	"	
Brown, George L.	Martinsburgh.	
Carpenter, Hiram	Lowville,	1834.
*Collins, Ela	"	May 6, 1807.
Collins, William	"	
*Conklin, Thomas L.	Martinsburgh.	
Davenport, Leonard C.,	Lowville,	July 7, 1851.
Davis, Perry	Copenhagen.	
Dayan, Charles	Lowville,	1819.
Doty, Baron S.	Martinsburgh.	

[1] Mr. Barnes died at Martinsburgh, June 29, 1859, aged 37 years.

Hawes, Albert	Copenhagen.	
Hazen, S. D.	"	
Henry, Edmund	Lowville.	
Keene, R. E.	Copenhagen,	1854.
Kilham, Leonard C.	Martinsburgh.	
Knox, Ziba	Lowville,	Aug. 18, 1826.
Lahe, John	Constableville.	
*Low, Cornelius	Lowville.	
*Martin, Vivaldi R.	"	1846.
Mereness, Abram I.	Martinsburgh,	1859.
Merrill, Elaida S.	Copenhagen,	May, 1846.
Merrill, Nathaniel	"	July, 1855.
*Miller, Morris S.	Lowville,	Dec. 10, 1805.
*Mott, Joseph O.	Turin.	
Muscott, J. M.	"	
*Page, Henry,	"	
*Parish, Russell	Lowville,	May 6, 1817.
Pawling, John	Copenhagen.	
*Rathbun, Solomon	Martinsburgh,	May 6, 1807.
Scovil, Carlos P.	"	
Seger, Francis	Greig,	1826.
*Shaler, William D.	Turin.	
Shaw, R. K.	Copenhagen,	April, 1855.
Stephens, Cornelius E.	Lowville,	Oct. 1, 1855
Stephens, W. Hudson,	"	July 7, 1851.
Sylvester, Nathaniel B.	"	April 5, 1852.
*Talcott, Samuel A.	"	Sept. 21, 1813.
Turner, Henry E.	"	
Wilson, Alba S.	Deer River,	1857.
*Yale, Barnabas	Martinsburgh,	Dec. 20, 1808.

Medical Profession.—A county medical society was early formed, under the act of 1806, and was represented at the state society in 1808, by Jonathan Bush, and in 1810 by John Safford. The loss of its records by fire, Oct. 15, 1849, has thrown oblivion over the proceedings of this body. Its seal had for its device an open lancet, and the letters L. C. M. S. in script, entwined. The statute, requiring a copy of the credentials of physicians, to be filed in the clerk's office, has enabled us to prepare the following list. It does not embrace every regularly qualified physician who has resided in the county, as some of the earlier ones, filed their papers in Oneida county, and quite a number of the more recent may have neglected this duty, or the papers may have been mislaid or accidentally overlooked. This list will therefore be regarded as positive only so far as it goes.

Adams, Ira, June 17, 1817.
Adams, Seth, May 21, 1826.
Allen, Ebenezer, Nov. 24, 1842.
Allen, Samuel, Feb. 21, 1806.
Avery, Stephen W., July 2, 18[illegible]1.
Bagg, Henry, Aug. 26, 1846.
Bartholomew, Erasmus D., May 31, 1825.
Bass, Samuel, Sept. 15, 1812.
Bates, William, June 26, 1832.
Bischoff, Frederick, April 30, 1856.
Bliss, John S., Sept. 6, 1843.
Bradish, James S., March 19, 1855.
Buckley, Lyman, Feb. 26, 1841.
Budd, Charles D., June 20, 1849.
Budd, David, Jan. 3, 1832.
Dewey, Walter, Jan. 1, 1807.
Dickinson, Noah, Sept. 11, 1807.

Foot, Anson, Feb. 25, 1806.
French, Elkanah, Sept. 8, 1833.
Gage, Alden, jr., Aug. 14, 1813.
Hanon, Dennis B., Jan. 16, 1844.
Hastings, Charles P., March 21, 1842.
Hawn, Abraham, Jan. 6, 1832.
Huntingdon, Ralph, Jan. 29, 1808.
Jerome, Levi R., March 12, 1844.
Kellogg, Joseph, April 3, 1843.
Miller, David, March 19, 1818.
Miller, Sylvester, Feb. 12, 1816.
Orvis, Charles, Oct. 1, 1836.
Peden, James T., Jan. 26, 1844.
Perry, David, Aug. 12, 1806.
Shaw, Otis, Oct. 25, 1833.
Stevens, S. Rodney, July 10, 1829.
Stone, A. C., July 6, 1842,
Sturtevant, James M., July 19, 1832.
Sweet, Jonathan, July 11, 1805.
Taylor, Francis L., Aug. 1, 1832.
Thompson, William, July 18, 1832.
Wait, Samuel C., April 10, 1833.
Wellman, Manly, July 19, 1805.
Whiting, John, Dec. 15, 1826.
Wood, Charles, May 3, 1836.
Woodman, Joseph, May 3, 1830.

CHAPTER XI.

MISCELLANEOUS NOTICES.

PERSONAL STATISTICS.—The accompanying table presents the total population of each town as reported in the official censuses. It will be borne in mind that the decrease is in some cases only *apparent*, and due to the division of towns.

The number of electors under the former system of property qualification was as follows:

	Freeholders worth over $250.	Freeholders worth $50 to $250.	Renting tenements worth over $5 per annum.	Total.
1807,	574	72	450	1096
1814,	614	71	499	1184
1821,	740	34	617	1391

POLITICAL STATISTICS.—The vote upon governor at the several elections in this county has been as follows:

1807.—*Morgan Lewis*, 419 ; *D. D. Tompkins*, 411.

1810.—*D. D. Tompkins*, 533 ; *J. Platt*, 302. The former had majorities in every town except Denmark and Harrisburgh.

1813.—*D. D. Tompkins*, 313 ; *S. Van Rensselaer*, 229. The former had majorities except in Denmark, Martinsburgh and Turin.

1816.—*D. D. Tompkins*, 326 ; *Rufus King*, 228. Mr. King had a majority only in Denmark.

1817.—*DeWitt Clinton*, 381 ; *Peter B. Porter*, ——

1820.—*DeWitt Clinton*, 334 ; *D. D. Tompkins*, 314. The former had majorities except in Harrisburgh, Lowville and Pinckney.

	Population of Towns in Lewis County at Various Periods.										No. of voters by Towns at Various Periods.			
	1800	1814	1820	1825	1830	1835	1840	1845	1850	1855	1825	1835	1845	1855
Croghan,	....	....	....	....	....	....	....	1014	1135	1531	....	....	131	208
Denmark,	....	1495	1745	1989	2370	2522	2388	2551	2824	2381	380	527	612	584
Diana,	....	....	....	....	309	449	883	793	970	1177	....	83	153	231
Greig,	....	....	....	....	662	538	592	880	1074	1203	....	96	171	289
Harrisburgh,	....	399	520	722	712	803	850	986	1367	1240	125	158	220	295
Highmarket,	....	....	....	....	....	....	....	....	....	1125	....	....	....	208
Lewis,	....	....	....	....	....	....	....	....	....	1157	....	....	....	165
Leyden,	622	871	1203	1156	1502	1687	2438	1941	2253	1856	259	370	427	432
Lowville,	300	1604	1943	2107	2334	2097	2047	2167	2377	2144	388	443	521	495
Martinsburgh,	....	997	1497	1950	2382	2288	2272	2408	2677	2489	358	470	548	539
Montague,	....	....	....	....	....	....	....	....	....	571	....	....	....	112
New Bremen,	....	....	....	....	....	....	....	....	1510	1647	....	....	....	258
Osceola,	....	....	....	....	....	....	....	213	412	513	....	....	43	109
Pinckney,	....	404	507	664	763	796	907	996	1208	1039	106	158	223	262
Turin,	440	1078	1812	2388	1661	1907	1704	1882	1826	1748	504	385	425	416
Watson,	....	....	....	693	909	1163	1707	2763	1138	930	128	183	309	208
West Turin,	....	....	....	....	1635	1843	2042	1624	3793	2478	....	289	504	473
Total	1362	6848	9227	11669	15239	16093	17830	20218	24564	25229	2248	3161	4287	5284

In 1810 the population was not reported by towns. The total of the county was 6433.

1822.—*Joseph C. Yates*, 776; *Solomon Southwick*, 1, in Martinsburgh. The vote on Lieut. Governor was 467 for Root, and 300 for Huntington.

1824.—*S. Young*, 678; *DeWitt Clinton*, 502. Clinton's only majority was in Denmark.

1826.—*W. B. Rochester*, 768; *DeWitt Clinton*, 726. The towns of Denmark, Harrisburgh, Turin and Watson gave majorities for Clinton.

1828.—*M. Van Buren*, 964; *S. Thompson*, 778; *S. Southwick*, 66. Van Buren had majorities in Greig, Leyden, Lowville, Martinsburgh, Pinckney, Turin and Watson, and Thompson in all the other towns.

1830.—*E. T. Throop*, 1031; *F. Granger*, 618; *E. Root*, 14. Throop had majorities in Diana, Greig, Leyden, Lowville, Pinckney, Turin, Watson and West Turin, and Granger in the other towns.

1832.—*W. L. Marcy*, 1450; *F. Granger*, 836. Marcy had majorities in all the towns except Denmark, Harrisburgh and Lowville.

1834.—*W. L. Marcy*, 1230; *W. H. Seward*, 852. The majorities were the same as in 1832.

1836.—*W. L. Marcy*, 1101; *J. Buel*, 400. Marcy had majorities in every town except Lowville.

1838.—*W. L. Marcy*, 1308; *W. H. Seward*, 1156. Marcy had majorities in Greig, Leyden, Martinsburgh, Pinckney, Turin, Watson & West Turin, and Seward in other towns.

1840.—*W. L. Marcy*, 1786; *W. H. Seward*, 1690; *G. Smith*, 40. Marcy had majorities in Diana, Greig, Leyden, Pinckney, Watson and West Turin, and Seward in the other towns.

1842.—*W. C. Bouck*, 1716; *L. Bradish*, 1519; *A. Stewart*, 64. Bouck had majorities in Croghan, Diana, Greig, Harrisburgh, Lowville, Martinsburgh and Turin, and Bradish in the other towns.

1844.—*S. Wright*, 2080; *M. Fillmore*, 1649; *A. Stewart*, 153. Wright had majorities in Croghan, Greig, Leyden, Osceola, Pinckney, Turin, Watson and West Turin, and Fillmore in the other towns.

1846.—*J. Young*, 1828; *S. Wright*, 1172; *H. Bradley*, 166. Young had majorities in every town except Croghan, Diana, Osceola, Pinckney and Watson, which went for Wright.

1848.—*H. Fish*, 1286; *J. A. Dix*, 1250; *R. H. Walworth*, 804; *W. Goodell*, 10. Fish had majorities in Denmark, Diana, Harrisburgh, Lowville, Martinsburgh, Pinckney and Turin; Dix in Croghan, Leyden, New Bremen, Osceola, Watson and West Turin, and Walworth in Greig.

1850.—*H. Seymour*, 2004; *W. Hunt*, 1618; *W. L. Chaplin*, 5. Seymour had majorities in every town except Denmark, Harrisburgh, Lowville and Martinsburgh, which went for Hunt.

1852.—*H. Seymour*, 2549; *W. Hunt*, 1787; *M. Tompkins*, 268. Seymour had majorities in Diana, Greig, Leyden, Martinsburgh, Montague, New Bremen, Osceola, Pinckney, Turin, Watson and West Turin; Hunt in Denmark, Harrisburgh and Lowville, and Tompkins in Croghan.

1854.—*H. Seymour*, 1583; *M. H. Clark*, 1449; *D. Ullmann*, 138; *G. C. Bronson*, 131. Clark had majorities in Denmark, Greig, Harrisburgh, Lowville, Martinsburgh, Montague, Osceola and Turin, and Seymour in the other towns.

1856.—*J. A. King*, 2949; *A. J. Parker*, 1173; *E. Brooks*, 431. King had majorities in every town except High Market and Lewis, which went for Parker.

1858.—*E. A. Morgan*, 2557; *A. J. Parker*, 1861; *G. Smith*, 126; *L. Burrows*, 38. Morgan had majorities in every town except Croghan, High Market, Lewis, Montague, New Bremen, Osceola, Pinckney and West Turin, which went for Parker.

Constitutional Votes.—In April 1821, the county voted for convention, 958; and against convention, 94. In 1822, the county voted 550 *for*, and 138 *against* adopting the Constitution.

In 1845, the vote for a convention was 1277, and against one, 738. The vote on the amended constitution, was 1828 *for*, and 370 against it. Upon granting equal suffrage to colored persons, the vote was, for 879, and against, 1,189.

State Loans.—This county received a share of the $400,000 loan of 1808, in proportion to number of its electors. Of the $5,355,694.28 U. S. deposit fund received by this State in 1837, $103,501.02 came to this county. The capital reported Dec. 6, 1859, was $32,977.80. The present commissioners are Orrin Woolworth of Turin and Leonard C. Kilham of Martinsburgh.

Aid to the Greeks.—On the 20th of Feb., 1827, a meeting was held in Lowville village to adopt measures for aiding the Greeks then struggling for independence and reported as famishing and destitute. This expression of sympathy was but a part of a general feeling which at that time prevailed through the country. The circular of the Albany executive committee was read, and a series of resolutions adopted, in which the people "once first in science, freedom, arts and arms" were declared entitled to aid as a Christian country struggling against Tartar tyranny. The clergy were invited to call attention to the subject from the pulpit, and town officers were urged to solicit donations on town meeting day. A central committee composed of Philo Rockwell and Edward Bancroft of Martinsburgh, and Isaac W. Bostwick, David Perry and James H. Leonard of Lowville, was appointed, and the following persons were requested to solicit gifts in clothing, grain or money, to be transmitted to the state committee at Albany, viz.: Dr. Sylvester Miller, *chairman*, Orrin Wilbur, *secretary*, Joseph A. Northrup, Stephen Leonard, Eli Collins, Palmer Townsend, Isaiah Bailey, Moses Waters, Truman Stephens, Wm. Shull, Constant Bosworth, John Stephens, Wm. Dingman, Chester Buck, Geo. D. Ruggles, Daniel T. Buck, Lemuel Wood, Benjamin Davenport, James Henry, Solomon King, jr., Thomas Townsend, Benjamin Hillman, Eleazer Hill, Jacob Dimick, Melancton W. Welles, and Jared House. A spirited address was prepared and circulated, and in the first week $120 were raised. The ship *Chancellor*, which sailed from New York in the spring with supplies, arrived safely and proved timely and serviceable to these people. These efforts continued to the spring of 1828, when a contribution of $170 in cash and clothing was sent from Lowville, and formed a part of the outfit of the brig *Herald*, which sailed about the close of May. A general county meeting was held at the court house in Martinsburgh in April, 1828, for the promotion of this object, and town committees were appointed.

California Companies.—While the citizens of Lewis have thus proved themselves susceptible to the appeals of oppressed humanity in classic Greece, not a few must confess that the golden fame of California lost none of its essentials in traveling across from the other side of our continent. Under this impulse were formed *The Lewis County Mining Association* and the *Lewis County Mining Co.* The former organized at Turin, Feb. 10, 1849, consisted of fourteen members who were joined by others, but disbanded in a few days, and only a few went to California. The latter, formed at Lowville a few days after, was to have expired April 1, 1851. Capital limited to 300 shares of $50, and affairs under seven directors, chosen annually. The persons going to dig gold, were to have expenses paid, except clothing, and were entitled to half the proceeds, the balance being divided among the stockholders. The diggers were to act under a superintendent, and the articles of agreement required them to be honest, temperate, sabbath-keeping and industrious. If sick, they were to be nursed, and if they died they were to be decently buried, if circumstances permitted. The constitution and by-laws, as published in the Northern Journal, February 27, 1849, never went into effect, chiefly from the impossibility of finding any men willing to go on the terms proposed, and the utter inability of the company to raise money for sending them. Notwithstanding an allusion to the 1st day of April, there is no doubt but that the enterprise began and ended in good faith. Perhaps fifty men from this county went to California for gold, nearly all of whom returned wiser but poorer.

THE NATIONAL SEMI-CENTENNIAL CELEBRATION was held at Lowville, July 4, 1826, and presented a feature of peculiar interest from the number of revolutionary veterans assembled from all parts of the county to honor it with their presence. Fifty-five of these were present at the dinner, and their names, present and former residence and age were presented as follows:

Names.	Residence.	Former Residence.	Ages.
Levi Adams,	Martinsburgh,	Granby, Ct.,	63.
Charles Allen,	do	Windsor, Ct.,	64.
Joseph Anderson,	Denmark,	Cummington, Vt.,	71.
Jonathan Austin,	Harrisburgh,	Charleston, R. I.,	71.
Jonathan Ball,	Lowville,	Southborough, Mass.,	75.
Jesse Benjamin,	Martinsburgh,	Preston, Ct.,	68.
Luther Bingham,	Turin,	Canterbury, Ct.,	67.
Taylor Chapman,	Lowville,	Windsor, Ct.,	63.
Leonard Chambers,	Denmark,	Dublin, Ire.,	78.
Samuel Clark,	do	Newton, Mass.,	71.
Isaac Clinton,	Lowville,	Milford, Ct.,	68.
Josiah Dewey,	Leyden,	Lebanon	68.
Benjamin Dowd,	Turin,	Middleton, Ct.,	64.
Giles Easton,	Martinsburgh,	East Hartford, Ct.,	64.
Thomas Farr,	do	Chesterfield, N. H.,	67.
Samuel Garnsey,	Lowville,	Dummerston, Vt.,	64.
Timothy Gorden,	Martinsburgh,	Freehold, N. J.,	70.
Samuel Gowdy,	do	Enfield, Ct.,	66.
Elijah Granger,	do	Southwick, Mass.,	64.
Peter Hathery,	Turin,	Minden, N. Y.,	59.
John Ives,	do	Meriden, Ct.,	65.
Solomon King,	Lowville,	Amenia, N. Y,,	70.
William Kisner,	Harrisburgh,	Canajoharie, N. Y.,	66.
Nathaniel Lane,	Lowville,	Peekskill, N. Y.,	58.
Ezekiel Lyman,	Turin,	Canterbury, Ct.,	66.
Zelak Mead,	Harrisburgh,	Salem, N. Y.,	75.
William Millor,	Martinsburgh,	Middletown, N. Y.,	67.
Ithamer Morgan,	Turin,	West Springfield, Mass.,	64.
Charles Morse,	Lowville,	Plainfield, Ct.,	63.
Jeremiah Mott,	Martinsburgh,	Elizabethtown, N. J.,	63.

L*

Ichabod Murray, Lowville,....New Milford, Ct.,......70.
Jacob Nash, Denmark,........Braintree, Mass.,......90.
Henry Mumford, Martinsburgh,.Boston, Mass.,........86.
Silas Perkins, do .Windham, Ct.,........62.
Isaac Perry, Lowville,........Fredericksburgh, N. Y., 66.
Salmon Root, Martinsburgh,...Farmington, Ct.,.......63.
Peter Ryal, Denmark,........ Fishkill, N. Y.,........67.
Elijah Skeels, Martinsburgh,...Kent, Ct.,............73.
Levi Smith, Leyden,..........Haddam, Ct.,..........73.
John Shull, Lowville,.........Palatine, N. Y.,.......81.
Hendrick Schaffer, Lowville,..Manheim, N. Y.,.......66.
Abiather Spaulding, Denmark,.Dover, N. Y.,.........69.
James Stevens, Lowville,.....Glastonbury, Ct.,......69.
Nicholas Streeter, Mart'sburgh, Stone Arabia, N. Y.,...74.
Joseph Talmadge, do East Hampton, N. Y.,..71.
Edward Thompson, Lowville,..Granby, Ct.,..........66.
Jesse Thrall, do ..Windsor, Ct.,.........72.
Daniel Topping, Turin,........Southampton, N. Y.,...84.
Willard Warriner, Mart'sburgh,Wilbraham, Mass.,.....70.
Joseph Van Ingen, Denmark,..Schenectady, N. Y.,....63.
Jeremiah Wilcox, Mart'sburgh, Middletown, Ct.,.......81.
Josiah Woolworth, Leyden,...Ellington.............73.
Levi Woolworth, Turin,.......Suffield, Ct.,..........69.
Samuel Weyman, Martinsburgh,Brethren, Mass.,.......67.
Mathias Wormwood, Lowville,.Johnstown, N. Y.,.....75.

Gen. Ruggles acted as marshal of the day, and the following military companies participated in the celebration, viz: Artillery from Turin, Capt. Homer Collins; Light Infantry from Martinsburgh, Capt. Conkey; Rifles from Lowville, Capt. Dodge; and Rifles from Martinsburgh, Capt. Coates. The Union band of Lowville Academy under Capt. G. De Feriet, discoursed patriotic music and the Rev. Isaac Clinton delivered an oration at the Methodist church.

The census of 1840, returned the names of thirty-eight revolutionary pensioners, of whom fourteen were widows. Their names and ages were as follows:

Denmark, Elizabeth Graves, 77; John S. Clark, 78; Louisa Munger, 79; Hannah Mores, 88; Elias Sage, 83; Joseph Van Ingen; Peter Royal, 80.

Greig, John Slaughter, 86.

Harrisburgh, Elias Jones, 81; William Risner, 81; Garret Marcellus, 80.

Lowville, John Buck, 76; Elisha Buck; William Chadwick, 79; Arthur Gordon, 80.

Leyden, Lydia Dewey, 79; Elizabeth Cone, 76; Ada Miller, 86; Lewis Smith, 87; William Topping, 75; Hezekiah Johnson, 79.

Martinsburgh, Ruth Adams; Jesse Benjamin, 81; Anna

Easton, 69; Lydia Green, 80; Edward Johnson, 81; Salmon Root, 77; Peter Vandriessen, 75; Bartholomew Williams, 76.

Pinckney, Catharine Forbes, 84.

Turin, Benjamin Dowd, 79; Giles Foster, 83.

Watson, Sarah Puffer, 75; Jacob Shutz, 78; Elizabeth Webb, 81; Lewis Day, 73; Sarah Farr, 73.

West Turin, Jonathan Collins, 84; Simeon Strickland, 54.

THE MILITIA of Lewis, Jefferson and St. Lawrence co's. were formed into the 26th Brigade, April 11, 1805, and Walter Martin was appointed *brigadier general*. The 46th regiment, formed on the same date, had for its officers, Jonathan Collins *lieut. col.*, Leonard Sage *pay master*, Wm. Holladay *qr. master*, and Wm. Darrow *surgeon*. The following were appointed captains: Jonathan Edwards, Morris S. Miller, Solomon Buck, Jabez Wright, Oliver Bush, Ephraim Luce, Enos Scott, and Richard Coxe. Upon the appointment of Collins to the office of judge, Richard Coxe succeeded as *lt. col. com.*, Feb. 11, 1811, and this officer held this rank when war was declared.

The 101st regiment was formed June 15, 1808, comprising the towns of Lowville, Denmark, Harrisburgh, and Pinckney, its first officers being Luke Winchell, *lt. col. com.*, Solomon Buck *1st major*, Zeboam Carter, *2d major*, Wm. Card *adjutant*, Andrew Mills *qr. master*, and Wm. Darrow *surgeon*. Its first captains were John Bush, Nathan Cook, David Cobb, Wm. Clark, Robert Clafton, Jesse Wilcox and Ezra King. Zeboam Carter was colonel of this regiment when war was declared and these two regiments comprised the whole county through that period.

The first troop of horse was formed in this county in 1809, having Levi Collins *capt.*, Abner Clapp *1st lieut.*, Adoniran Foot *2d lieut.*, Johnson Talcott *cornet*, and Leonard House, Levi Hart and David Waters, *sergeants*.[1]

The troubles with England occasioned an act of congress passed March 30, 1808, detaching 100,000 men from the militia and placing them under the orders of the general government. Of these 14,389 were drawn from this state and 350 from Martin's brigade. None of the militia of this region were called out under this act. On the 10th of April, 1812, in anticipation of a war, the president was authorized to require the several states to organize, arm

[1] The first roll comprised besides the above, Warren Church, Oliver Allis, Comfort Parsons, James Henry, John Waters, Elisha and Richard Arthur, Elijah Halladay, James Coates, Selah Hills, Joshua Loomis, Joseph Bradford, James Miller, Ithamer Ward, Aaron Parks, Johnson Foster, Benj. Baker, Gurdon Lord, Winthrop Allen, Levi Hunt, Eber Hubbard and John Clobridge.

and equip their proportions of 100,000 men to be officered from the militia then existing, or others at the option of the states and to receive the same pay, rations and emoluments as in the regular army when in actual service. The whole or a part of this draft might be called out as occasion required, and the levies were to be drawn for a term of six months. Under this authority, 13,500 men were detached in this state, and 230 from the 26th brigade. A company was drafted for three months, under Captain Lyman Deming of Denmark, in the regiment of Col. Christopher P. Bellinger of German Flats. They served at Sackets Harbor from May 12 to August 21, 1812, when they were discharged.

War was declared June 12, while these men were in service, and upon the receipt of the news the governor by general orders, dated June 23, authorized Gen. Brown to call upon the militia of Lewis, Jefferson and St. Lawrence counties, and equip them at the state arsenals at Watertown and Russell. Under this authority one company of 72 men besides officers was called into service from this county for a term of six months, under Capt. Nathan Cook of Lowville, and placed under Col. Thomas B. Benedict of DeKalb. This company drew their arms at Watertown, escorted two heavy loads of arms to the arsenal at Russell, and repaired to Ogdensburgh where they remained in the presence of the enemy through the season, and assisted in repelling the attack in October.[1] Rowland Nimocks of Turin, was lieut., and Ebenezer Newton of Pinckney, ensign of this company. Major Oliver Bush was on duty in this draft.

During the winter following some arms and ammunition were deposited in Martinsburgh in the care of Gen. Martin, and 200 muskets and some ammunition in Turin, Leyden and Lowville upon the bond of Richard Coxe, Daniel Kelley, James H. Leonard, Jesse Wilcox, Levi Hart and Levi Collins.[2] An alarm for the safety of Sackets Harbor, occasioned by the arrival of Sir George Prevost in Kingston, and a threatened attack by crossing on the ice, led Gen. Dearborn to call out the militia *en masse* in this and other counties on the 1st of March, 1813, and they remained at the harbor and at Brownville till the 20th[3] under Brig. Gen. Oliver

[1] Capt. Cook was arrested by order of Gen. Brown upon a charge of cowardice on the occasion of this attack, but was honorably acquitted, and the affair did him no injury where the facts were known. He was afterwards colonel of the regiment in which he belonged.

[2] Governor Tompkins's message of April 1, 1813.

[3] Col. Coxe's (46th) regiment consisted of companies under captains Truman Stephens and Adam Conkey of Martinsburgh, Winthrop Shepard and Hezekiah Scovil of Turin, Ethemer Wetmore and John Felshaw of Leyden,

Collins of Oneida county. The fear of an attack ceased with the melting of the ice, and a project for an aggressive movement was postponed until the fleet could coöperate. A third draft for three months was made in Sept., 1813, consisting of 60 men under Capt. Winthrop Shepard of Turin, and a company under Capt. Wm. Root of Denmark. They served under Gen. Collins in the regiment of Col. Geo. H. Nellis from Sept. 14 to Nov. 4, 1813, at Sackets Harbor and Brownville, during the costly preparations for the miserable failure of Wilkinson in his boasted descent upon Montreal.[1] An inspection return dated Sept., 1813, showed that the 26th brigade contained in the 46th and 101st regiments (Coxe's and Carter's), seven companies each, and a total of 301 and 367 rank and file.

A call *en masse* was made, and the militia of the county served in one regiment, under Col. Carter, from July 30 to August 22, 1814, at Sackets Harbor.[2] Gen. Martin was on duty upon this occasion. The last call *en masse* was made October 7, 1814, and the militia of Lewis county were comprised in four consolidated companies under Col. Carter.[3] They served at Sackets Harbor till November 11, 1814. Two companies of cavalry under Capt. Sanford Safford, Abner Clapp and Calvin McKnight, served at Brownville in Maj. Levi Collins's regiment, and a company of Silver Grays under Capt. Jonathan Collins, volunteered for the service and were on duty from October 28, to November 9, 1814, in Lieut. Col. Calvin Britain's regiment.[4]

The above comprises the military service of the citizens

---

and Luke Winchell of Lowville. Col. Carter's (101st) regiment included the companies of captains Moses Waters, Joel Murray and Cyrus Trowbridge of Lowville, Israel Kellogg and Francis Saunders of Denmark, and Capt. Hart Humphrey of Harrisburgh. Winchell's company consisted of "Silver Greys" or exempts, Bradford Arthur served as lieutenant.

1 This draft included Montgomery, Madison, Otsego, Herkimer, Oneida, Onondaga, Jefferson and Lewis counties. In the general orders of Oct. 4, the general rendezvous was ordered to be at Martinsburgh, Lowville or Champion as Gen. Collins might direct. The 26th brigade (Martin's) was directed to furnish 2 captains, 4 lieutenants, 4 ensigns, 10 sergeants, 12 corporals, 2 drummers and 180 privates. While encamped near the harbor the snow fell a foot deep, and the weather was severe.

2 Captains Waters, Root, Conkey, Tallmadge, Kellogg, Knapp, Trowbridge, Murray, Scovil, Shepard, Wetmore and Felshaw, served with their companies at this call.

3 Under Captains Kellogg, Root, Tallmadge and Waters. The general orders making this call were dated Oct. 3, and state that Sackets Harbor is in immediate danger of invasion. Oneida, Herkimer and Lewis counties were comprised in the call, the whole to be under the command of Gen. Collins.

4 This company of exempts numbered 56 men, officers and privates. A few citizens of Pinckney joined a company of exempts in Lorraine, under Capt. Joseph Wilcox.

of Lewis county during the war.[1] The settlements were frequently alarmed by rumors of Indian invasions from Canada. The route through the county became a thoroughfare of armies, and every resource of the valley was called into use to supply the troops passing through, or the garrisons on the frontier. The first body of regulars that passed was Forsyth's rifle company.[2] Armies under Gens. Dearborn, Izard,[3] Covington and Dodge,[4] besides many small parties of regulars, marines, militia and sailors, trains of artillery and arms under escort, went through at various times.

In the winter of 1813–4, some ten or fifteen teamsters were hired from the north part of this county, and many more from Jefferson, to remove flour from Sackets Harbor to French Mills, and from thence to Plattsburgh. They had returned as far as Chateaugay, where 32 teamsters had stopped at an inn for the night, and were carousing to wear away the tedious hours, as sleep in such a crowd was out of the question. Their gayety was suddenly arrested by the entrance of a British officer, who informed them that the house was surrounded by his men, and that they were all prisoners. Their sleighs were loaded with plunder and they set out for Cornwall, where, after four days' detention, they were paid and dismissed.

Notes upon the Seasons, 1799.—The summer pleasant, and cooled by frequent showers. A slight frost occurred early in September, which was not followed by hard frost till Dec. Heavy rains occurred in Sept. and Oct., followed by a mild and pleasant Autumn. The winter following was open, with snow of moderate depth.

1800.—Snows disappeared on the last of March; the crops good and the autumn more pleasant than the former. The winter of 1801–2 was memorable as warm and open. Many families, intending to remove from New England by the first sleighing, were detained till Feb. 24, when a deep snow fell but soon wasted.

1802.—Plowing in March. Warm and wet in the early part of the season, giving a great amount of vegetable growth, but towards harvest the wheat fields were struck with rust, destroying the crop.

---

[1] The author is indebted to Leonard C. Davenport of Lowville, for many facts concerning drafts and calls upon the militia.

[2] Shadrack Snell of Martinsburgh, a lad, ran away, joined this company, was taken prisoner on the lines, and died in Dartmoor prison.

[3] Izard's army passed in September, 1812.

[4] Gen. D. was from Johnstown, and married Washington Irving's sister. His brigade of about 1000 men was quartered a few days at the old Academy.

1803.—Long memorable as the *dry summer.* The streams were, it is said, lower than ever since known. This region of country suffered from the drouth much less than portions of Jefferson co.

1807.—A snow storm from the north east, set in on the 31st of March, and continued till April 5. It fell on a level five feet deep, did not drift, and went off almost as soon as it came, producing a flood which has never since been equalled upon Black river. The grist mill at Martinsburgh was swept off on this occasion. The season which followed was good for crops.

1806 to 1812.—A series of cold summers, although in 1806 the corn crop in Lowville was excellent.

1811.—Spring rye sowed in Leyden March 21.

1813.—Oct. 12, snow two feet deep in Denmark. In the winter following the snow fell deep and was much drifted.

1815.—Crops good, wheat and potatoes excellent, corn light.

1816.—Long memorable as the *cold season.* The spring was mild and a few days of April oppressively warm. This was followed by cold, and frost occurred in every month of the year. On Pinckney it snowed and drifted like winter. June 6th, 7th, 8th, the snow lay ancle deep in the fields and many newly shorn sheep perished. In Denmark the snow lay an inch deep on the 9th of June, and ice formed a quarter of an inch thick, corn and garden vegetables generally were killed, but grass was an average crop, and in Lowville the wheat was not cut off. A frost on the 26th of August, killed down what remained of the corn. The autumn was mild, and the winter late. On the 26th of December, there was no snow, but the ground was frozen.

1817.—The potatoe crop was exceedingly fine, in one instance 700 bushels to the acre. Other crops were excellent.

1820.—May 25, snow an inch deep in Denmark.

1824.—May 14, snow four inches deep in Denmark. On the 26th the ground was frozen hard, and on the 28th of October, snow lay a foot and a half deep. The winter following was open, and there was not two weeks of sleighing. The snow was gone March 1st.

1828.—Hot sunshine and copious showers produced a sickly season. Root crops were excellent, but winter wheat blasted and yielded more straw than grain.

1829.—An unusually bountiful year, wheat, rye, corn and almost every fruit of the earth good. Apples yielded abundantly, but there were no plums. December was like

April, warm and spring like. Six weeks before there had been snow enough for sleighing.

1830.—A more abundant yield than on any previous year. Barn room was every where insufficient, and most grains (especially wheat) superior. Corn was not as good as usual, owing to spring frosts. Rains frequent in harvest. Apples and plums plenty. A terrific hail storm crossed Leyden June 14. The track was half a mile wide and from four to five long, and the storm was preceded 15 to 20 minutes by roaring of thunder.

1832.—Drouth very severe.

1833.—A rainy season and heavy freshets.

1834.—May 14, snow three feet deep in drifts in Denmark, and on the 18th nearly as great, plum and cherry trees in blossom were broken down with snow, and many trees were killed by frost.

1835.—A remarkable yield of wheat, averaging in some fields 35 to 40 bushels to the acre.

1841.—May 6, great freshet, and much damage done at and below Carthage.

1849.—Memorable for drouth and running fires in the woods east of the river.

1853.—Summer dry and grasshoppers abundant. About the middle of September rains revived vegetation, and in some places fruit trees put forth blossoms in the fall.

1856.—Sept. 15, destructive hail storm crossed Turin attended with wind and rain. About 3000 panes of glass broken.

1857.—May. Flood from melting snows.

EPIDEMICS.—A fever of a typhoid type appeared in the county in the winter of 1812–13 in common with a large district of country in the northern and eastern states, and in Canada. It was especially prevalent in March and April, and was more fatal to men of strong constitutions than to those naturally feeble. It was attended with great pain in the stomach and chest, burning fever, and in the last moments with delirium.

A malignant erysipelas prevailed extensively throughout the county in the spring of 1843 and in 1845, proving especially fatal to parturient women. The slightest wound or abrasion would sometimes become the seat of extensive ulceration, and sloughing, and the loss of parts thus occasioned was extremely slow in replacing. Other less marked periods of mortality have occurred, but only as portions of wide spread epidemics, and few sections of the union present fewer instances of sickness from local causes than this. Intermittent and other fevers from miasma, are altogether unknown, unless contracted in other places.

TORNADOES.—Of these, several have swept over the county since its settlement, and traces of others, as shown by fallen timber and young trees, indicate that these fearful tempests had traversed this region before its settlement. The first and greatest one ever witnessed in the county, occurred on Sunday evening, June 3, 1810, and forms an epoch in the memories of early settlers. It passed nearly a due east course from West Martinsburgh across the river near the Watson bridge, and far beyond into the wilderness, leaving a track of broken and prostrate trees over a space a mile and a quarter wide and of unknown length. It was attended by torrents of rain and vivid and incessant lightning. Its approach was announced by a fearful roaring in the woods, and the crash of falling timber was lost in terrific peals of thunder. The affrighted inhabitants fled to their cellars or sought in the open air an asylum from the dangers which their own dwellings threatened. The clouds which had been gathering in dense black masses, having poured an immense volume of water along the track of the storm, cleared up as soon as it had passed, and the remainder of the evening was beautifully serene and quiet. Although many buildings were unroofed or prostrated, it is wonderful to relate that no lives were lost.

In 1823, a tornado passed over the unsettled country near the S. W. corner of the county, leaving a track two miles long and half a mile wide, on which no trees were left standing. This occurred about a mile south of the deep valley of Salmon river, and nearly parallel with it, in the present town of Osceola.

A tornado from the north west passed over Harrisburgh, Sept. 9, 1845, tearing down trees over a track in some places forty or fifty rods wide. It struck the saw-mill of Jacob Windecker and the house of Richard Livingston in Lowville, where it prostrated a building attached, and did other damage to buildings but destroyed no lives. Eleven days later, the great northern tornado swept the forest from Antwerp to lake Champlain, mostly through an uninhabited region and likewise without the loss of human life.

At half past five o'clock on the afternoon of July 5, 1850, a tornado cloud was seen, like an immense cloud of smoke, rapidly whirling and advancing down the hill about a mile south of Turin village. It passed eastward to the river, demolishing two or three barns, unroofing several houses, and prostrating everything that lay in its track. It is reported that plank were torn up from the road, grass twisted out by the roots, and solid objects on the ground removed. No lives were lost.

EARTHQUAKES have been felt several times since the settlement of the county, but seldom sufficient to create a sensible motion of the earth. They were indicated by a deep rolling noise like distant thunder, or like wagons driven over frozen ground. Such an instance occurred in the county late in the evening of Jan. 22, 1832, and in Martinsburgh April 8, 1836. On the first of March 1838, a slight shock was felt at Lowville, at nine o'clock in the evening, and another in December 1839. At half past two o'clock on the morning of March 12, 1853, an earthquake was felt throughout the county, windows, stoves and crockery were rattled, in Lowville one chimney was thrown down, and even the bells in the stone church and academy were rung by the movement. The effect was more sensible in brick and stone, than in framed houses, and some persons awakened by the noise and frightened by the motion, ran into the open air, lest they should be buried in their own houses. The phenomenon was attended by a distant deep rumbling sound, gradually approaching and then dying away in the opposite direction. As it approached it was interrupted by a series of explosions like bursts of thunder, and the noise is described as peculiarly grand, appalling and unearthly. It continued from one to three minutes, and was heavy in Turin, Lowville, Copenhagen and Adams, and light in Watertown.

NOTES ON NATURAL HISTORY.—*Beaver* were known in the more remote sections of the forest in this county until after settlement. Their dams, and the meadows formed by decay of timber thus flowed, were common on the high plateau region west of the valley, and rarely on the limestone terraces. It is probable that a few scattered beaver still live in the east woods.

Moose have been often killed east of the river where they are still found. Elk's horns prove the former existence in our county of this animal, now wholly extinct in the state.

Wolves once common and still found in the east woods. Of these there are two varieties, the black and the common. The former are large, powerful and fierce. The county bounties for their destruction have been $10 till 1819, except 1815, and on various years since. A special act, April 18, 1838, allowed the addition of $10 for wolves and $5 for their whelps. State premiums of $347.50 were awarded in

1816; $180 in 1817; $282.50 in 1818; $440 in 1819; $500 in 1820; $720 in 1821; $40 in 1822; $72.50 in 1823, and $52.50 in 1824. In the whole state during these years it was $88,714.15, chiefly in Franklin county.

Panthers have seldom been found west of the river, and bounties have usually been the same as for wolves.

Squirrel hunts, were formerly held. Large parties would meet, appoint two captains, choose sides, and on a given day devote themselves wholly to the sport. The heads were counted in the evening, and the vanquished party paid the supper and sometimes the powder and shot. The unit of reckoning was usually a red squirrel. In one of these contests, a black squirrel was counted 2, a partridge 2, a woodchuck 4, a fox 6, a deer 8, a wolf 12, and a bear 12. The last two were usually rated much higher.

White swans.—A flock was seen on the river March, 1826. One of them when shot was found 7 feet 10 inches from tip to tip of wings, and weighing 17 pounds.

Pigeons, have in some years appeared in great numbers, especially in the spring of 1829, 1849 and 1858, when they nested in the beech woods of Montague, and West Turin.

Fish.—In Fish creek salmon formerly abounded. No perch were found in Black river or its tributaries until about 1843, when B. Smith and A. Higby, jr., put about 30 specimens into Brantingham lake. They have greatly multiplied, are now common. Trout, dace, suckers, bullheads and eels, form the other principal native fishes of our streams and lakes.

Topography and Geology.—Lewis co. lies mostly in the valley of the Black river,[1] which flows centrally through it from south to north. The river is broken by frequent cascades and rapids, until it reaches the High falls where it plunges down a steep, broken ledge of gneiss rock, to the still water which affords a navigable channel to Carthage, 42½ miles below. This is the lowest part of the county and is 714 feet above tide level. The amount of water passing at Carthage at the lowest stages has been

---

[1] The Indian name of this river, as given by L. H. Morgan of Rochester, in his *League of the Iroquois*, is Kä-hu-ah-go As given by the St. Regis Indians to the author in 1852, it is Ni-ka-hi-on-ha-ko-wa, and by Squier, in his *Aboriginal Monuments of New York*, Ka-mar-go. The authority first cited gives the name of Deer river, as Gä-ne-gä-to-da; Beaver river, Ne-hä-sä-ne; Otter creek, Dä-ween-net; Moose river, Te-ca-hun-di-an-do; Great Fish creek, Ta-ga-söke; Salmon river, Gä-hen-wa-ga; Sandy creek, To-kä-dä-o-ga-he; and Indian river, O-je-quack. The St. Regis name Indian river, O-tsi-qua-ke, "where the black ash grows with knots for making clubs."

computed at 30,000 cubic feet per minute. The principal tributaries of Black river on the east, are Beaver river, Crystal, Independence, Otter and Fish creeks, and Moose river, which issue from lakes or swamps mostly, and have their waters highly discolored by organic or mineral matter in solution. On the west, the river receives Deer river. Stony, Sulphur-spring, Lowville, Martin's, Whetstone, House's, Bear and Mill creeks, Sugar river and a few other streams. Such of these as rise in swamps on the western plateau region are also highly discolored, but the smaller ones, fed by springs from the slates and limestones, are very clear. Along the river, but little above its level, are extensive swamps in Martinsburgh, Lowville, and Denmark, on the west side, some of which are capable of being brought into use. They were mostly covered with ash and alders, but the lower one of these was in 1854, burnt off, and is now covered with wild grass and reeds capable of being mowed. The soil of this vlaie, or natural meadow, is a deep black muck underlaid by clay. Along the river-bank is a ridge of hard land formed by its overflow, and west of it, a drift ridge of sand covered with hemlock timber. Still west of this, is a long narrow cedar swamp, extending several miles. It is higher than the meadow near the river and has furnished a large amount of bog iron ore for the Carthage furnace.[1] A *cedar lot* has by many been regarded as an essential appendage of a farm.

The river flows over limestone a short distance from Oneida county, when its bed comes upon gneiss rock, the primitive formation extending from about half a mile west of the river throughout the whole eastern part of the county, excepting a portion of Diana. This rock when it appears at the surface, rises into rounded ridges, mostly naked, or with soil only in the crevices and hollows. It is largely composed of feldspar and quartz, with particles of hornblende, magnetic iron ore, and more rarely of garnets. It is everywhere irregularly stratified and highly inclined. The general surface rises gradually from the river eastward, until it reaches an elevation of from 1,500 to 2,000 feet above the river on the eastern border. This rock covers a comparatively small part of the surface, the intervals being

---

[1] This ore never occurs in swamps liable to overflow from the river. It has been found largely in Watson, New Bremen and Denmark, occurring as a loam, or in solid masses, sometimes replacing the particles of roots, leaves and wood, but preserving their form. It is said to have been mostly exhausted, but if allowed to remain without drainage, would be again deposited. Limited quantities of this ore have been found in Diana.

a light sandy soil of drift, with occasional intervals of alluvial deposit, sometimes appearing to have been formerly lakes. The disintegration of this rock affords the iron sand so common along the streams, and upon the shores of lakes in this region. A vein of magnetic iron ore has been opened in the north part of Greig, but not worked to any extent, In Diana, white crystaline limestone occurs, presenting a great variety of interesting minerals, and many instructive points for the study of geology. The region is highly metamorphic, and presents marked indications of former igneous agencies.

The minerals of Diana and vicinity, are *Apatite* in small green crystals; *Calcite* in great variety, including satin spar, and a coarse crystaline limestone of sky blue tint; *Hornblende; Mica* of the varieties known as Phlogopite; *Pyroxene*, white and black in crystals, and in grains known as coccolite; *Quartz* in crystals, and of the forms known as ribbon agate chalcedony; *Rensselaerite; Scapolite* in rounded pearly gray crystals; *Serpentine*, opaque and greenish; *Sphene* of the variety known as Ledererite; *Sulphurets of copper and of iron; Tremolite; Wollastonite* or tabular spar, and *Zircon* in square prisms, sometimes a third of an inch on a side, and with terminal prisms. Mining for *silver* was attempted by Enoch Cleveland many years since, and a small blast furnace was put up which produced a few hundred pounds of very hard metal apparently iron. The reputed ore is a fine grained greenish black rock which occurs abundantly, and appears to consist of chlorite and specular iron ore in variable proportions.

The primitive region of this county still comprises large areas of unsettled lands, and presents the same wild forest scenery of lakes, dark winding streams, tangled swamps and sombre pine and hemlock forests, as when first explored by surveyors and hunters. The whole of Diana, and about half of Croghan are drained by the Indian and Oswegatchie rivers. A small part of Diana is underlaid by calciferous sandstone, which usually occurs level and covered by a thin but fertile soil. Detached capping masses of Potsdam sandstone also occur in this town, but the most remarkable locality of this rock in the county, is due east of Martinsburgh village, where a stratum is found resting directly upon the gneiss, in the bed of Martin's creek. Its thickness does not exceed three feet, and its surface exposure is slight. It is directly covered by limestones and is composed of masses of pebbles and sand cemented as if by heavy pressure.

Parallel with the river, and on an average of about a mile west, rises an irregular series of terraces, consisting of birdseye, Black river and Trenton limestones. The first of these may be quarried in rectangular blocks, and is highly valuable for building and for lime. A portion of it furnishes hydraulic lime, which has been made to some extent in Lowville and Martinsburgh. It does not form a surface rock of much extent and occurs chiefly on the edge of the lower terrace, and in the beds of streams. It is covered by the Black river limestone which forms the surface rock between the first and second terrace, is not adapted to building, contains masses of flint, and is so soluble that every exposed angle has been rounded and every seam widened by the action of rains and running water. Streams usually sink into crevices and flow under it, often forming caverns of limited extent, especially in Leyden. The Trenton limestone forms the highest and broadest terrace of the series, rising from 300 to 600 feet above the river, and spreading out into the level fertile region which every traveler through the county has admired. These limestones seldom appear at the surface except at the edge of the terraces and in the water courses, and every stream flowing across them has more or less of a smooth rocky bed, and a picturesque cascade where it tumbles down to the next lower level. Deer and Sugar rivers and Martin's creek have worn deep yawning chasms into the rock, and present cascades of singular wildness and beauty well worthy of a visit by the pleasure-seeking tourist.

The western tributaries of Black river have usually no valleys, except the immediate channel they have worn. Drift agencies have given the appearance of several oblique valleys coming down from the northwest across the limestone terraces, which usually have a drift deposit on their northern side, while on the south the rock is exposed and often furrowed in the direction of these oblique valleys. Deer river might almost as well have turned northward at Copenhagen into Sandy creek, as to have taken its present course.

In Martinsburgh and Lowville, veins of calcite with the sulphurets of zinc, lead and iron have been found. In the former, carbonate of lead, and in the latter fluor spar occurred. These mineral veins are of scientific interest, from the evidence they afford of electrical deposit. They were formed in what appeared to be natural fissures of the rock, and the sulphuret of zinc was attached to each wall, upon which was a layer of lead ore and lastly of pyrites, the latter often covering the crystals of calcite or appearing with cavities left by their solution. The lead was sometimes crystalized and imbedded in spar, or grouped with clusters of that mineral in masses of much beauty.

A range of high lands, known as *Tug Hill*,[1] runs through the county parallel with the river, and from three to seven miles from it. It rests upon the limestone and consists of Utica slate and Hudson river shales, rising by a rounded slope to an elevation of from 500 to 1000 feet above the flats below, and spreading out in a level or slightly broken region, into Oneida, Oswego and Jefferson counties. Innumerable beaver meadows occur along the sluggish streams rising from extensive swamps in this region, and the waters from this plateau flow from it into the Mohawk and Black rivers and lake Ontario. The largest streams flowing from this region are Fish creek and Salmon river, each of which have valleys of considerable extent, and receive numerous tributaries. Deer river also gathers the waters of a wide district. The large streams flowing down have uniformly worn deep channels, the larger of them several miles in length, and in Martinsburgh presenting some of the wildest scenery in the state.[2] Every spring torrent has its ravine, and the limestone flats below, are so covered with slate

---

[1] Said to have been named by Isaac Perry and —— Buell, on their first journey into the county, upon reaching the top of the hill on the old road west of Turin village.

[2] The more interesting of these is *Whetstone gulf*. The chasm extending about three miles up, is bordered by precipitous banks 200 to 300 feet in height. The first two miles are mostly occupied by a heavy growth of timber, but the last mile presents but little of this, except what overhangs the banks, or finds root on the steep, crumbling slate rock. The stream is here quite irregular in its course, presenting sharp angles and sudden turns, which afford, at every step, new points of interest, and a constant succession of magnificent views. The walls approach nearer as we ascend the stream, until they may be both reached by the outstretched arms, and the torrent is compressed into a deep, narrow chasm, which forbids farther progress without difficulty and danger. A rough wagon road has been made about two miles up the gulf, and in low water parties can cross the stream everywhere without difficulty.

About two miles west of Martinsburgh village, on Martin's creek, occurs another gorge worn in the slate hills, of much the same character. From a vast triangular pyramid of slate rock formed by the junction of two gulfs, it has acquired the name of *Chimney point*. To the left of this, as seen from the banks above, a stream of moderate size falls in a beautiful cascade about sixty feet, breaking into a sheet of foam upon the rough bed, down which it glides. A few rods below it unites with the longer and larger branch, whose ravine extends half a mile further up. Upon following the latter we arrive at a cascade, where the stream falling from a narrow chasm into a pool, forbids further progress. The strata of slate, elsewhere nearly or quite level, are here highly inclined, but the disturbance in the stratification only extends a few rods. Chimney point has the advantage of presenting its finest view from the banks, but such as prefer to descend, will find themselves amply rewarded by the pleasing variety of scenery which the locality presents. This

gravel, that the line of junction of the two rocks can nowhere be seen in the county. Leyden Hill is a detached mass of this slate formation, cut off by a valley from the main portion. The road from Constableville to Rome, rises about 1000 feet above the latter place and runs many miles over this range of highlands, which comprises the whole of Lewis, Osceola, High Market, Montague and Pinckney, and parts of Leyden, West Turin, Turin, Martinsburgh, Harrisburgh and Denmark. The black oxyde of manganese occurs in swamps in Martinsburgh on the top of Tug hill, and weak sulphur springs known in the early settlement as *deer licks*, are common but unimportant.[1] The limestones and slates in this county abound in characteristic fossils of great scientific interest. About half a mile below the foot of Tug hill, on the line of junction between the slate and limestone, there occurs a strip of clay averaging perhaps forty rods in width, which may be traced from one end of the county to the other. In the state of nature this was a line of ash or cedar swamp, and when cleared and drained it affords a strong meadow or grass land, but it can not well be plowed. The slates allow the rains to percolate down through their

---

ravine is surrounded by cultivated fields, but is still as wild a solitude as when first found by the surveyors.

A thrilling incident occurred at Chimney point, in the spring of 1834, which, were it not well authenticated would scarcely appear credible. It is, however, too well known and attested to admit of a doubt, and must be placed on the list of wonderful escapes. Chillus D. Peebles, who lived adjacent, was clearing the land, and rolling the logs off into the gulf, when by an unexpected motion of a log he was thrown off the precipice. He fell about one hundred and fifty feet, and struck on the steep slope formed by the gravel crumbled from the cliffs above, from whence he bounded and rolled to the bottom, about a hundred feet further. The accident was seen by a man not far off, who hastened to descend by the usual path, expecting to find the unfortunate man dashed to atoms or mangled and dying on the crags below. To his infinite surprise he met Peebles, who had got up and started to return, which he did without aid, and in less time than the person who came to assist him. Upon reaching the top he was delirious, but after a few days he returned to his labor as usual.

[1] One of these occurs near the head of Whetstone gulf, and another 1 mile S. W. of Houseville on House's creek. One sulphur spring of some interest occurs in the limestone on the land of S. B. Dewey, on lot 14 in the N. W. part of Lowville, which from the earliest settlement has enjoyed a local reputation for its medicinal properties. It issues from the foot of a low terrace of Trenton limestone, within a few feet of the upper strata of that rock, and its sulphurous taste and odor is apparently due to sulphuret of iron disseminated in the rock. It occurs on the west side of a small mill stream a few rods below Gladwin's grist mill, and the spot is shaded by a thin growth of trees. The spring is curbed about three feet deep and the water is clear. Now and then a few bubbles of inflammable gas rise from the bottom, and at some periods the discharge of gas is said to be sufficiently active to give the spring the appearance of boiling. The water may be easily drank and flows off at the rate of about six quarts in a minute.

seams until the water reaching the limestone finds its way to the surface in this line of springs. West of the strip, slate may be found anywhere, by digging through the soil and drift. East of it, it can be found nowhere, except in broken gravel washed down by streams.

Drift deposits occur promiscuously over every part of the county, usually in rounded ridges. The largest of these are south-east of Denmark village, where the deposit is miles in extent and of great depth. By the term *drift*, we wish to include all earthly matter or detached rocky masses lying upon the undisturbed rock, excepting soil derived from the disintegration of the rock underneath, and the alluvium or soil washed down and deposited by water, or formed by organic growth. The soil of the drift is variable, being in some places light and sandy, while at others it is hard loom or clay. In the Primary region, especially in Diana, there are found in many places, flat intervales and marshes which appear to have been formerly lakes that have been filled in by the encroachment of vegetable growth and by the soil washed down from the ridges adjacent. Peat has been observed in some of these marshes, and marl deposited in the bottom of the lakes. Boulders of gneiss and other primary or igneous rock, are found promiscuously resting upon all the formations of the county, or imbedded in the soil. In many cases clusters of these masses are found together, favoring by their appearance the theory that they had been transported by fields of floating ice, at a period when this region was covered by the ocean.

The scenery of the county, excepting the ravines and cascades above described, presents nothing majestic, and may be regarded as beautiful rather than grand. From the western side of the river, the eastern slope appears rising by insensible degrees until lost in the blue level range of the forests of Herkimer county, with here and there a point slightly elevated above the general surface, indicating the position of the higher mountain peaks of Hamilton county. The highest primary ranges in Lewis county, occur in its south eastern corner, in the town of Greig. On an autumnal morning, or after a summer shower, patches of white mist resting upon the surface, indicate the position and extent of the forest lakes, and at times a curtain of fog hanging over the river, may shut out the view entirely. As viewed from the brow of the slate ranges, the panorama of the valley and of the distant horizon is exceedingly beautiful, and sunrise as seen from these hills on a clear morning, will amply repay the labor of an early walk to their summit. The beaver meadows of the western plateau region, are usually bordered by a thrifty growth of balsam fir trees,whose dense conical masses of dark evergreen, give a characteristic aspect to the scenery of these open meadows in the bosom of the forests. No prospect can be conceived more cheerless than the swamps which extend for miles along the head waters of Fish creek, and other streams, which have their sources in these highlands. They are mostly without trees or shrubs, excepting here and there a slender tamarack, festooned with gray hanging moss. Where the soil is of sufficient stability to support them, a growth of alder shrubs may be traced along the margin of the channels, but in many places the surface may be shaken to the distance of many feet, and a pole may be thrust to an almost indefinite depth.

Viewed from the eastern side, the limestone terraces and slate hills on the west, are seen to great advantage, and the successive steps by which the surface rises, are distinctly observable. The cultivation of sixty years has quite changed the natural surface of the landscape, and a patch of reserved woodland here and there alone remains. Viewed from a distant eastern point, the horizon towards the north drops down as the hills are of less elevation towards the lake, and the terraces become much broader. At the period when lake Ontario flowed up to the lake ridges, now nearly four hundred feet above its surface, the north eastern portion of the county might have been submerged, as traces of these ridges are found in Wilna, near the borders of this county.

INDEX.

Academies, 129, 135, 162, 188, 215.
Adams, Levi, 175; Dr. Seth, 155; Wm. Root, 166.
Aldrich, Jonathan, house of burned, 80; Peter W., 128.
Alford, Asahel, murdered, 224.
Allen, Dr. Samuel, 82, 88.
Alpina, 73, 96, 100.
Alsop, Thomas, 30, 248.
Angerstein, John Julius, title of, 33.
Antwerp Company's lands, 25, 70, 71.
Arson, trial for, 153.
Arthur, Richard, notice of fam. of, 175.
Ashley, Otis, jr., shot, 182.
Assemblymen, chron. list of, 289.
Astor, John Jacob, owner of lands, 31.
Balloon, from Oswego, 226.
Bancroft, Edward, notice of, 180.
Bank of Lowville, 157; Lewis county, 186; of the People, 160; Valley, 160.
Bannister, Rev. Henry, 166.
Baptist Association, 284.
Bar, list of the Lewis county, 290.
Barnes's Corners, Pinckney, 206.
Barnes, Judah, 211.
Barney, Eliam E., 165.
Bands of Instrumental Music, 157, 214.
Beach, John, 218; Nelson, Jr., 218.
Bears, encounter with, 117, 128.
Beaver Falls, Croghan, 196.
Beaver Lands, tract known as, 53.
Beavers, notice of, 306; dams of, 198.
Belfort, Croghan, 78.
Belletre's expedition, 21.
Benton, Z. H., 100.
Bent's Settlement, Croghan, 78.
Birdseye maple, statistics of, 119.
Black river, erroneous location of, 20, 25, 34; elevation of, 307; Indian name of, 307; canal, 263; company, 262; tract, 24, 25, 26, 27.
Blake, Patrick, 56, 58, 59, 62, 76.
Blodget, Jesse, family of, 84.
Boards of Health, cholera, 88, 155.
Bog iron ore, where found, 223, 308.
Bonaparte, Joseph, 71, 72, 77, 94, 95, 96, 98; lake, 96, 97.
Booge, Rev. Aaron, J., 189.
Boon, Gerret, 121.
Boshart, Garret, 143.
Bossuot, Jean Baptiste, 77.
Bostwick, Isaac W., 84, 113, 149, 178.
Boylston, Thos., 25; tract, 25, 27, 28.
Brantingham, Thomas H., 32; tract, 25, 31.
Brass band, Turin, 214.
Breese, Arthur, land agent, 32.
Bridges, 89, 103, 119, 135, 196, 226.
Brodhead, Charles C., surveys of, 52, 125, 139.
Brown, Charles; academy of, 91.
Brown, Gen. Jacob, 2, 6, 56; John, 33.
Brown's Tract, 25, 33, 111.
Brunel, Mark I., 50, 51, 52.
Buck, Chester, 134.
Budd, Dr. David, 246, 291.
Burr, Aaron, lands owned by, 22, 34.
Burnand Eugine, Swiss proprietor, 99.
Bush, Zaccheus and family, 211.
California, so called in Harrisburgh, 114; companies, 296.
Canaan, Timothy, child of, burnt, 185.
Canal statistics, 260; surveys, 259; description of, 266.
Card, Peleg, 86.
Cardinal lines of Castorland, 52.
Carret, James, agent, 77.
Castorland, 25, 34 to 70, 104.
Castorville, 56, 57, 80.
Cattle, sale of; anecdote, 213.
Cavanaugh, Michael; respite of, 131.
Caverns in Black river limestone, 130, 310.
Cedar timber, 308, 312.
Celebrations, semi-centennial, academic, 166; 50th, of 4th of July, 297.
Census returns, 292, 293.
Chassanis, operations of, 34 to 70.
Charter of Lowville academy, 163.
Chimney Point, gulf in Martinsb'g, 311.
Clapp, Ezra, 212, 213, 235.
Clark, Rev. Charles, 169.
Clay strip, through the county, 312.
Clerk's Office, Martinsburgh, 17.
Climbing, extraordinary, 89.
Clinton, Rev. Isaac, 164; 261;

Coin (so called), of Company of New York, 44.
Collins, Ela, and family, 152; Jonathan and family, 230.
Collinsville, West Turin, 246.
Colquhoun, Patrick, 24, 31, 32, 33, 124.
Columbian society, Turin, 215.
Commissioners for locating county seat 13; Bank, 157, 186.
Company of New York, 35, 39, 195.
Conferences, M. E., statistics of, 281.
Congressmen, list of, 288.
Conklin, Thomas L., 184.
Consequa, a Chinaman, lands of, 117.
Constable, James, 29, 198, 241; extracts from the diary of, 3, 177, 178, 199, 234, 237; John, 242; William, 22, 23, 24, 26, 28, 29, 30, 31, 34, 39, 124, 238; William, jr., 238, 239.
Constable's Four Towns, 25, 28, 240.
Constableville, West Turin, 245.
Constitution, votes on, 295; of the company of New York, 40.
Contract system in land titles, 29, 236.
Convention at Denmark, 3, 123.
Cooper, James, murder of, Leyden, 131.
Copenhagen, origin of name of, 86.
Cornelia, township of, 25, 171.
Costar, John G., titles of, 117.
County, act erecting, 8; changes in, 11, 95; seat, efforts to secure 1, 2, 13; buildings, 14, 160; clerks, 290; courts, 14, 162.
Coxe, Richard, 17, 56, 76, 123, 231.
Court House, Martinsburgh, 16; Lowville, 160.
Crary, Joseph, surveyor, 83, 113.
Cratzenberg, Wm., indicted for murder, 88.
Crofoot, Elisha, and family, 231.
Croghan, town of, 74.
Cronk's Corners, Pickney, 206.
Darrow, Dr. William, 143.
Daughters of Temperance, 281.
Davis, George, notice of, 30, 243.
Davenport families, Lowville, 148.
Dayan, Charles, 153, 195, 262, 264.
Dayanville, New Bremen, 195.
Dean, Faxton, drowned in Martin's Mill, 181.
Deeds to first settlers of Lowville, 144.
Deer, 129, 213; licks, 312; river, 90.
Denmark, town of, 81.
Deponceau, Peter S., agent of Bonaparte, 71, 72.
Deserters from Kingston returned, 233.
Desjardins, Simon, 46, 50, 51, 53, 62.
Devouassoux, J. T., French settler, 75.
Dewey, Dr. Royal Dwight, 208; Walter, 208.
DeWolf's purchase; Antwerp co., 70.
DeZotelle, Louis, sup'sed death of, 77.
Diana, town of, and how named, 94.
Division of Oneida co, 1 to 8, 209.
Doig, Andrew W., 154.
Doty, Chillus, 175, 178.
Drafts from militia, 299.
Drift deposits, 309; defined, 313.
Drowning, narrow escape from, 145, 247.
Dustin's Track, first road in co., 251.
Eager, Fortunatus, 145.
Earthquakes, notices of, 306.
Easton, William L., 158, 270, 285.
Edwards, Ogden, on the character of W. Constable, 242.
Elk, notice of, now extinct, 306.
Emigration, European, 78, 119, 237.
Epidemics, notices of, 237, 304.
European settlements, 78, 119, 237.
Executors of W. Constable's estate, 29.
Expeditions through the valley, 21.
Favarger, Charles, agent, 100.
Fay, Cyrus M., teacher, 165.
Ferries on Black river, 103, 225.
Fire Company, Lowville village, 156.
Fires, 80, 88; deaths by, 80, 185, 247; in woods, 78, 225, 247.
Fish, 117, 307; creek reservation, 23.
Floods, 89, 128, 181.
Flora, township of West Turin, Highmarket and Lewis, 25, 114, 116, 228, 236.
Forged credentials of Gerry, 91.
Foreigners, vote for removal of from Turin, 210.
Forest scenery, east of river, 309.
Fort Johnson, the model of Martin's house, 179.
Forty Thieves, so called, 185.
Foster, Giles, and family, 211.
Fourth of July, semi-centennial celebration, 297.
French, Abel, agent, 83, 84, 90, 204.
French company; see "Company of New York;" revolution, favored emigration, 35; road, 54, 57; settlement, 54, 55, 80, 196.
Freudenrich, Frederick, titles of, 100.
Friends, society of, 284.
Geology of the county, sketch of, 307.
German settlements, 78, 119.
Gerry, W. H., clerical imposter, 91.
Glensdale, Martinsburgh, 186.
Goff, Deuel, notice of, 208.
Good Templars, secret order of, 281.
Graves, Lewis, 81.
Greig, town of, 101; John, 33, 101.
Greeks, aid to the, 295.
Green, David I., titles of, 30; Seymour, agent, 202, 203.
Greenleaf, James, 32, 33.
Hall, Samuel, local agent, 233.
Hamilton, Alexander, 29, 113.
Hammond, Theodore S., titles of, 73.
Handel, township of Pinckney, 24, 112, 203.
Harrisburgh, town of, 112.
Harrison, Richard, 26, 82, 113.
Harris, Foskit, 98.
Harrisville, Diana, 98.
Hart, Levi, 208; Stephen, 211.
Health committee, Lowville, 155.
Hemlock timber, prejudice against, 28.

Hemp, culture of noticed, 88.
Henderson, William, titles of, 26, 204.
Herreshoff, Charles, suicide of, 111.
Higby, Amos, 211; Amos jr., 215.
High falls, Black river, 246, 307; Deer river, 89; incidents at, 89, 90.
High Market, town of, 114.
Hoffman, Josiah Ogden, titles of, 26, 83.
Hough, Dr. Horatio Gates, 178; Richardson T., 117, 119.
House, Eleazer, and family of, 212.
Houseville, Turin, 214.
Hovey, Aaron, death of, Lowville, 146.
Hybla, township of Osceola, 25, 197.
Illingworth, Samuel, 195.
Indians, 146; names of streams, 307; titles, 21, 23.
Inman, William, 31, 32, 124.
Inman's Triangle, 25, 28, 31, 121.
Instinct, remarkable case of, 142.
Irish settlers, 115, 237.
Iron, manufacture of, 97, 98, 100, 111.
Ives, Maj. John, and family, 216, 228.
Jail, 16, 17; liberties, 14; St. Lawrence prisoners, 17.
Jay, William, titles in Lewis, 117.
Jetton, of Company of New York, 44.
Johnson, Edward, 211.
Jones, John, title of, 31.
Joulin, Pierre, agent and exile, 56, 57, 59, 62, 64, 107.
Judges, list of, first county, 289.
Judson, David C., titles of, 73, 101.
Kelley, Daniel, notice of, 144.
Kelsey, Eber, 128.
Kerr, James, title of, 32, 33.
Kiabia, so called in High Market, 115.
Kilham, Thos., notice of fam. of, 211.
Kimball, Rev. David, 190; Rev. Reuel, 132.
King's Falls, on Deer river, 90.
Knox, Ziba, notice of, 154.
La Farge, John, titles of, 72, 73, 96, 99.
Lambot sisters, French proprietors, 76.
Land titles, history of, 20.
Lead ore, notices of, 183, 310.
Leonard, James H., and family, 151; Stephen, 151.
Le Ray, James D., 56, 57, 64, 66, 67, 68, 70, 71, 72, 75, 77; Vincent, 54, 79.
Lery's expedition in the French war, 21.
Lewis county bank, notices of, 186.
Lewis, Morgan, namesake of county, 11; town of, 116.
Leyden, town of, 121; Hill, 131, 312.
Libraries, 91, 129, 161, 188, 206, 214, 225.
Livingston, Brockholst, titles of, 32. 33; Philip, 33.
Lord, Asa, notice of, 126.
Lost in the woods, 118, 184.
Lottery for state roads, 252, 253.
Lowd, Dr. John, 85.
Louisburgh, now Sterlingburgh, 97.
Low, Cornelius, 187; Nicholas, 26, 27, 76, 135; notes from land books of, 143.
Lowville, town of, 133; village of, 150, 156.
Lucretia, township of, Turin, West Turin and Martinsburgh, 24, 115, 210.
Lumber manufacture, 110, 119, 130.
Lyon, Caleb, 33, 111; Caleb of Lyonsdale, 96; Lyman R., 33, 34, 96.
Lyonsdale, Greig, 111.
Lyons Falls, West Turin, 246.
McAdamized road proposed, 256.
McCarthy, Lawrence, executed, 224.
McCollister, John, notice of, 176.
Macomb's purchase, 21; great tracts of, 23, 24.
McDowell, Robert, surveyor, 138.
McVicker, Edward, titles of, 29; Jas., titles of, 30; John, ex'r., &c., 9, 31.
Mail routes, notice of, 258.
Mantua, township of Denmark, 24, 81.
Martin, Gen. Walter, 172; Vivaldi R., 154.
Martinsburgh, town of, 171; village of, 186.
Mayhew, David P., Principal, 166.
Medical Profession, imp'ft. list of, 291.
Memorial of R. Tillier, 57; reply to, 65.
Merriam, Ela, 258, 259; Nathaniel, 122.
Methodist Episcopal Conferences, 284.
Militia organization, drafts, &c., 299; "riot," 86.
Mill, first in county, 229 239; in Lowville, 146; swept off, 181.
Miller, Rev. James, 231; Morris S., 84, 148; Col. Seth, 245; Dr. Sylvester, 155.
Mineral localities, 155, 309, 310.
Montague, town of, 193.
Monterey, Croghan, former P. O., 78.
Moore, Capt. John, shot, 182.
Moose, notice of, 306.
Morris, Gouverneur, 55, 56, 57, 59, 62, 63, 65, 70, 76; Robert, 32.
Munger's Mills, Denmark, 85.
Murders, notices of, 87, 131.
Murdock, Rev. James, 190.
Myer's Mills, Denmark, 90.
Natural History, notes on, 306.
Naumburg, P. O. in Croghan, 80.
New Boston, Pinckney, 206.
New Bremen, town of, 194.
Newspaper Press, notices of, 284.
New Survey, in town of Lewis, 116, 123.
Northrup, Joseph A., 154.
Norton, Rev. Elijah, 189.
Number Three Road, 147.
Oars, manufacture of, 119.
Oboussier, Jacob, 55, 195.
Ogden, Samuel, titles of, 32, 33; Thos. L., 82.
Oneida co., plans for division of, 1 to 8, 209.
Osceola, town of, 197.
Oswegatchie road, 252.
Oyster keg hoops, manufacture of, 120.
Paddock, Loveland, title of, 73, 101.
Pahud, Joseph, agent, 101.

Panthers, notices of, 224, 307.
Paper mill, Martinsburgh, 181.
Parish, Russell, 153.
Parsons, Eld. Stephen, and family, 93, 230; Zerah, 125.
Patent, for academic building, 165.
Pauperism, statistics of, 17.
Peebles, J., 177; Chillus D., fall of, 312.
Perry, Dr. David, 154; Capt. Isaac, 148.
Personal Statistics, tables of, 292.
Petition for erection of Lewis co., 6.
Pharoux, Peter, 46, 50, 51, 52, 53, 62, 68, 105.
Phillippe, Louis, travels in America, 51, 241; La Farge, his agent, 73.
Phœnix bank, New York, 30.
Pickand, Rev. James D., 168.
Pierrepont, Hezekiah B., 29, 31, 117, 199, 243.
Pigeons, notices of, 307.
Pike, Gen. Z. M., sword of, 166.
Pinckney, town of, 203.
Pitcher, Reuben, and family, 176.
Plank roads, statistics of, 98, 256.
Political statistics, Gov's elect'n, 292.
Pomona, township of, 25, 210, 228.
Poor House, notice of, 135.
Porcia, township of Martinsb'g, 25, 171.
Port Leyden, village in Leyden, 129.
Post, Wm. and Gerardus, titles of, 73.
Potash manufacture, notices of, 80, 129, 145, 151, 177.
Prussian Settlement, Croghan, 80.
Puffer, Rev. Isaac, 223, 226; Isaac G. killed, 224.
Railroads, notices of, 89.
Rathbone, John, titles of, 31.
Rags, poetical advertisement for, 182.
Receipt, form used by French co., 36.
Religious societies, 80, 91, 101, 111, 114, 120, 132, 167, 189, 194, 196, 207, 215, 226, 247, 281.
Reamer, David D., 98.
Remonstrance ag'st erection of co., 7.
Revolutionary reminiscence, Lowville, 138; soldiers, 297.
Roads, 27, 34, 54, 57, 118, 123, 135, 147, 198, 209, 228, 237, 250.
Rock Island, near Port Leyden, 130.
Rockwell, Philo, 178.
Rogers, Jonathan, 141; Rev. Joshua M., 248.
Rohr's Mills, New Bremen, 80.
Roman Catholics, notice of, 284.
Rope manufactory, Copenhagen, 88.
Roseburgh, Mrs., captivity of, 138.
Rurabella, t'nship of Osceola, 25, 197.
Safford, Dr. John, 178.
Saint Michel, Louis de., 75, 76, 77.
St. Regis mining co., 100.
Salmon, Rev. Martin, 217; (fish) formerly in Fish creek, 233, 307.
Salt, first load to Lowville, 147.
Sauthier's map, errors of, 20, 25.
Sawyer, Rev. Leicester Ambrose, 190.
Scenery, general notice of, 313.
Schools, 91, 114, 122, 129, 161, 179, 214, 238.
Scrantom, Abraham, and Hamlet, 236.
Seal, first county, 1, 14; of Company of New York, 40; Bank of Lowville, 157; Lowville academy, 162.
Seasons, notes upon, 302.
Seger, Francis, 33, 263, 264.
Senators, state, list of, 288.
Shaler, Nathaniel, 27, 29, 228.
Shaler's roads in Turin, 256.
Shaw, Sam., wounded by Myers, 224.
Shepard, families of, 211.
Sheriffs, county, list of, 200.
Silver Grays, companies of, 87, 301.
Silver mine, so called, Lowville, 155.
Sistersfield, tract named, Croghan, 76.
Sligo, name proposed, 115.
Smith, William S., titles of, 24, 25, 34.
Snows, deep, 205, 303.
Soil, of drift formation, 313.
Sons of Temperance, 281.
Spafford's Landing, Lowville, 142.
Speculations in lands, noticed, 26, 27.
Squirrel hunts, usages at, 307.
State loans, amount to this county, 295; roads, 250, 252.
Staves manufactory of, 89, 130.
Steam saw mills, 89.
Stephens, Ehud, and family, 139.
Stewart, P. Somerville, 78.
Sterlingbush, Diana, 98.
Storrs, Lemuel, 116, 125.
Storrsburgh, a proposed name, 123.
Stow, Joshua, 116, 125; Silas, 139.
Stow's Square, 137, 147.
Streams of Castorland, old and modern names, 53; tributary to Black river, 308.
Stump mortar, first mill in Turin, 214.
Suchard, Louis, purchaser, 99, 100.
Sugar River falls, described, 130.
Sulkouski, prince, 101.
Sulphur Springs, 138, 312.
Surrogates, list of county, 290.
Surveys, 28, 29, 32, 33, 34, 51, 52, 54, 83, 113, 115, 116, 123, 138, 195, 198, 201, 240; interrupted, 249.
Survilliers, Count de, see "Bonaparte Joseph."
Swansmill company, title of, 69.
Swans, white flock of, seen, 307.
Swiss company, 56, 59, 73.
Talcott, Samuel A., 152; families, in Leyden, 127.
Talcottville, Leyden, 131.
Tanneries, 78, 80, 99, 130, 196.
Tassart, A., title of, 75.
Taylor, Stephen W., principal, 164.
Tiffany bridge, Mart'sgh, Greig, 104.
Tillier, Rodolphe, 53 to 68, 75, 195.
Toll bridge, incorporated, 226.
Topography of the county, 307.
Topping, William, first settler, 125.
Tornadoes, notices of, 202, 305.
Totten and Crossfield's purchase, 20.
Towns, alphabetical list of, 74.

Town Hall, Lowville, 135, 161; meeting stolen in Watson, 221.
Treaties, Indian, 21, 23.
Treasurers, list of county, 290.
Tug Hill described, 311.
Turin, town of, 207; village of, 214.
Turnpikes, notices of, 209, 254.
Underhill, Richard W., titles of, 32.
Universalist association, 284.
Valley Bank, Lowville, 160.
Valuation of towns in 1809, 16.
Varick, Abraham, rope manu'fr, 88.
Voters, number in Leyden, 127.
Votes at each election of Governor, 292; on constitution, 295.
Voyage, first down Black river, 140.
Waggoner, Henry, death of, 87.
Walker, Thomas, agent, 32.
War, militia drafts in, 297.
Ward, James T., agent and proprietor, 32; Samuel, 24, 25, 31, 33, 39.
Washington, funeral address, 128.
Water power, 89, 108, 130.
Waters, Mary Ann, death of, 183; Moses, 147.
Watson, town of, 218.
Watson, James T., proprietor, 219; tract of, 25, 34.
Well, remarkable, Greig, 111.
Welles, Melancton W., ag't, 145, 223.
Wentworth, Erastus, principal, 166.
West Leyden, P. O. in Lewis, 117.
West Martinsburgh P. O., 186.
West Turin, town of, 227.
Whetstone gulf, description of, 311.
Whittlesey, Samuel, anecdote of, 182.
Wilcox, families, Lowville, 148.
Wilder, Luke, notice of, 155.
Wilkinson, John, notice of, 211.
Willard, Gen. Jos. A., notice of, 156.
Williamson, Capt. Charles, 31, 32, 62, 102.
Wolves, notices of, 213, 224, 306.
Woolworth families, Turin, 211.
Wright, Benjamin, 28, 29, 32, 83, 113, 115, 116, 138, 178, 198, 204; families in Denmark, 84, 85.
Xenophon, township of Lewis, 25, 116.
Yale, Barnabas, notice of, 180; Rev. Calvin, 190.
Yeomans, David P., principal, 166.
Zinc ore, found, 310.

www.ingramcontent.com/pod-product-compliance
Lightning Source LLC
LaVergne TN
LVHW010138110826
845151LV00002B/377

* 9 7 8 1 4 2 5 5 3 9 0 3 0 *